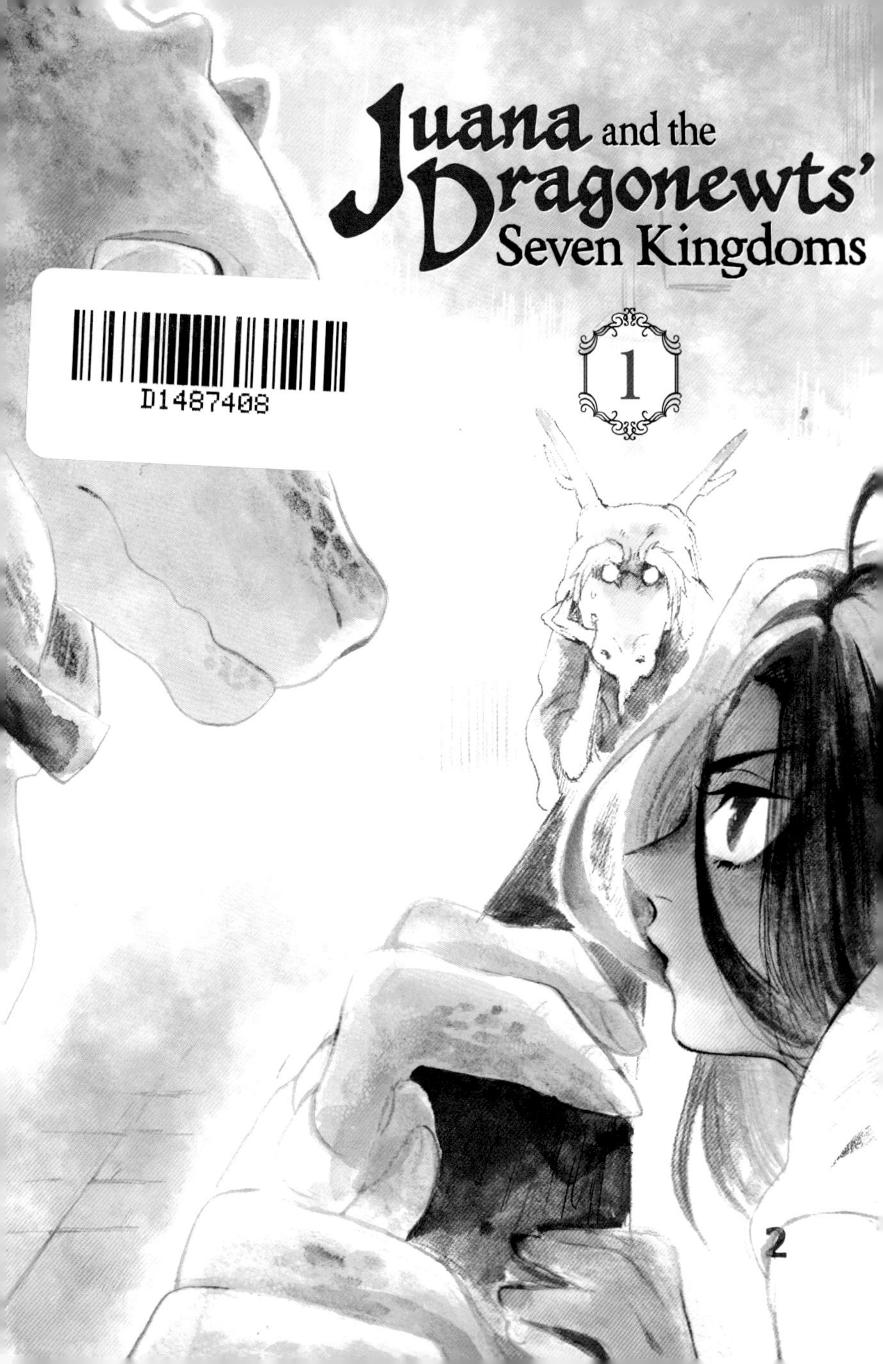
Juana and the Dragonewts' Seven Kingdoms
1
2

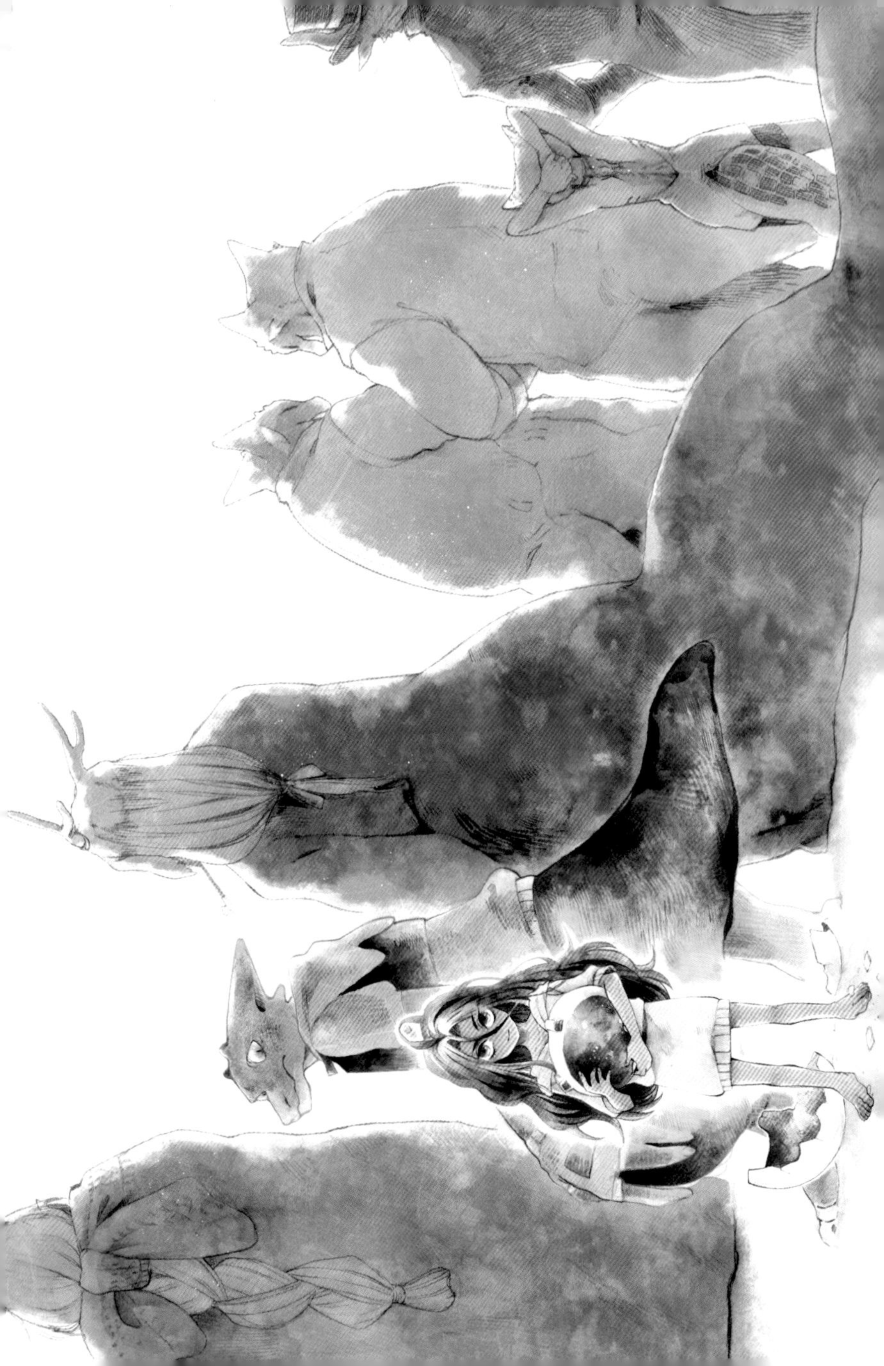

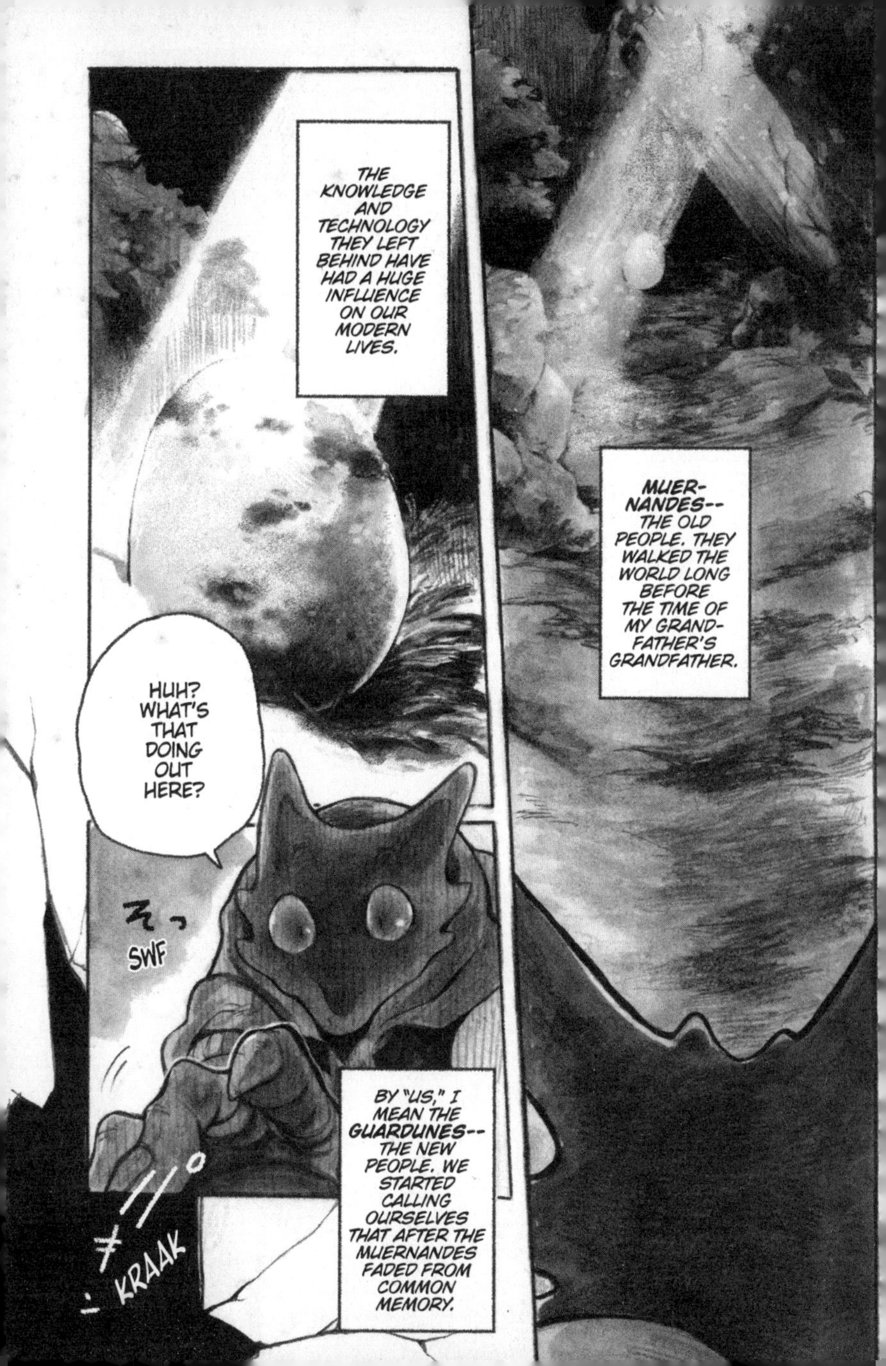

MUERNANDES-- THE OLD PEOPLE. THEY WALKED THE WORLD LONG BEFORE THE TIME OF MY GRANDFATHER'S GRANDFATHER.
THE KNOWLEDGE AND TECHNOLOGY THEY LEFT BEHIND HAVE HAD A HUGE INFLUENCE ON OUR MODERN LIVES.
HUH? WHAT'S THAT DOING OUT HERE?
SWF
BY "US," I MEAN THE GUARDUNES-- THE NEW PEOPLE. WE STARTED CALLING OURSELVES THAT AFTER THE MUERNANDES FADED FROM COMMON MEMORY.
KRAAK

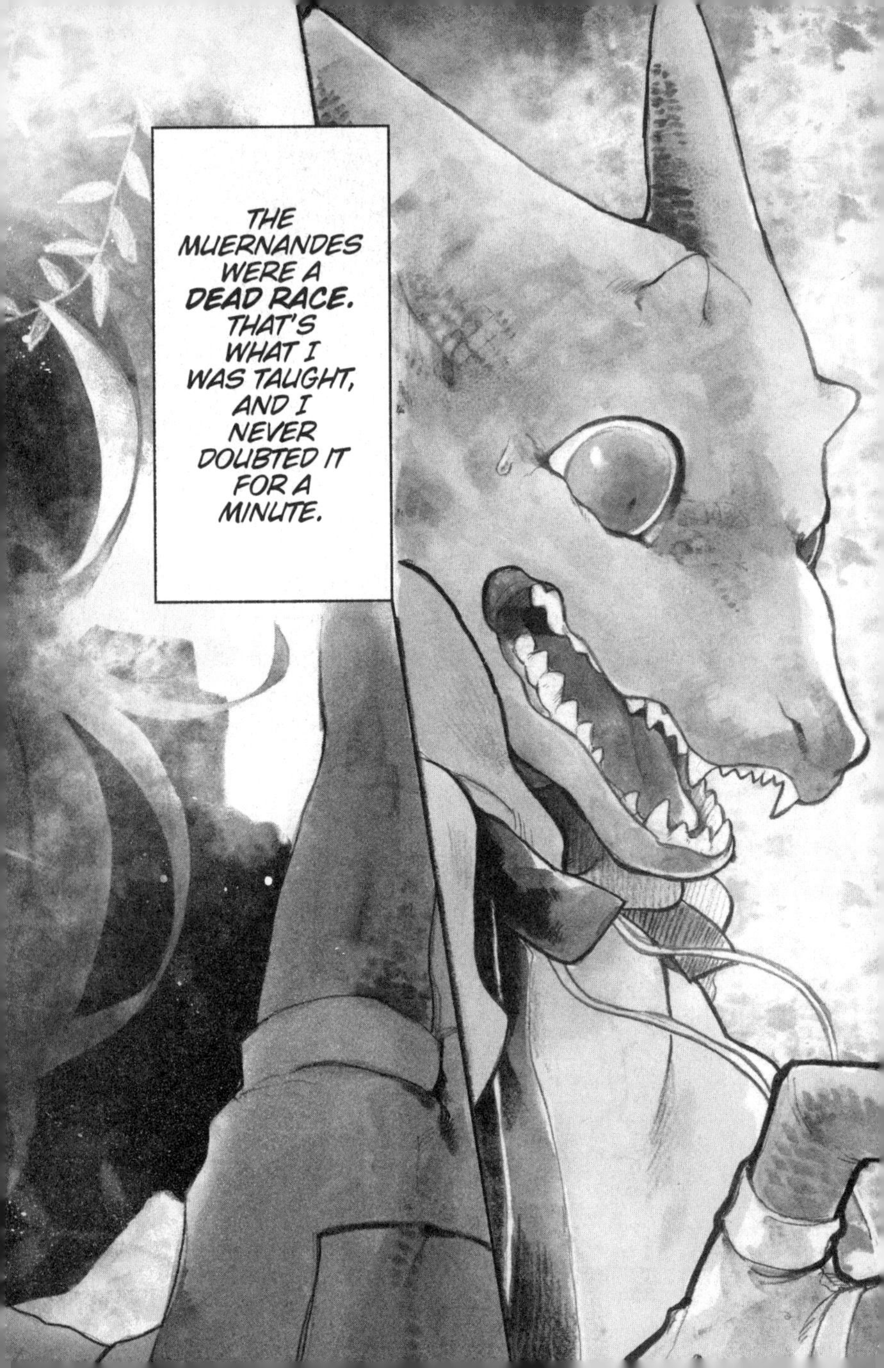
THE MUERNANDES WERE A DEAD RACE. THAT'S WHAT I WAS TAUGHT, AND I NEVER DOUBTED IT FOR A MINUTE.

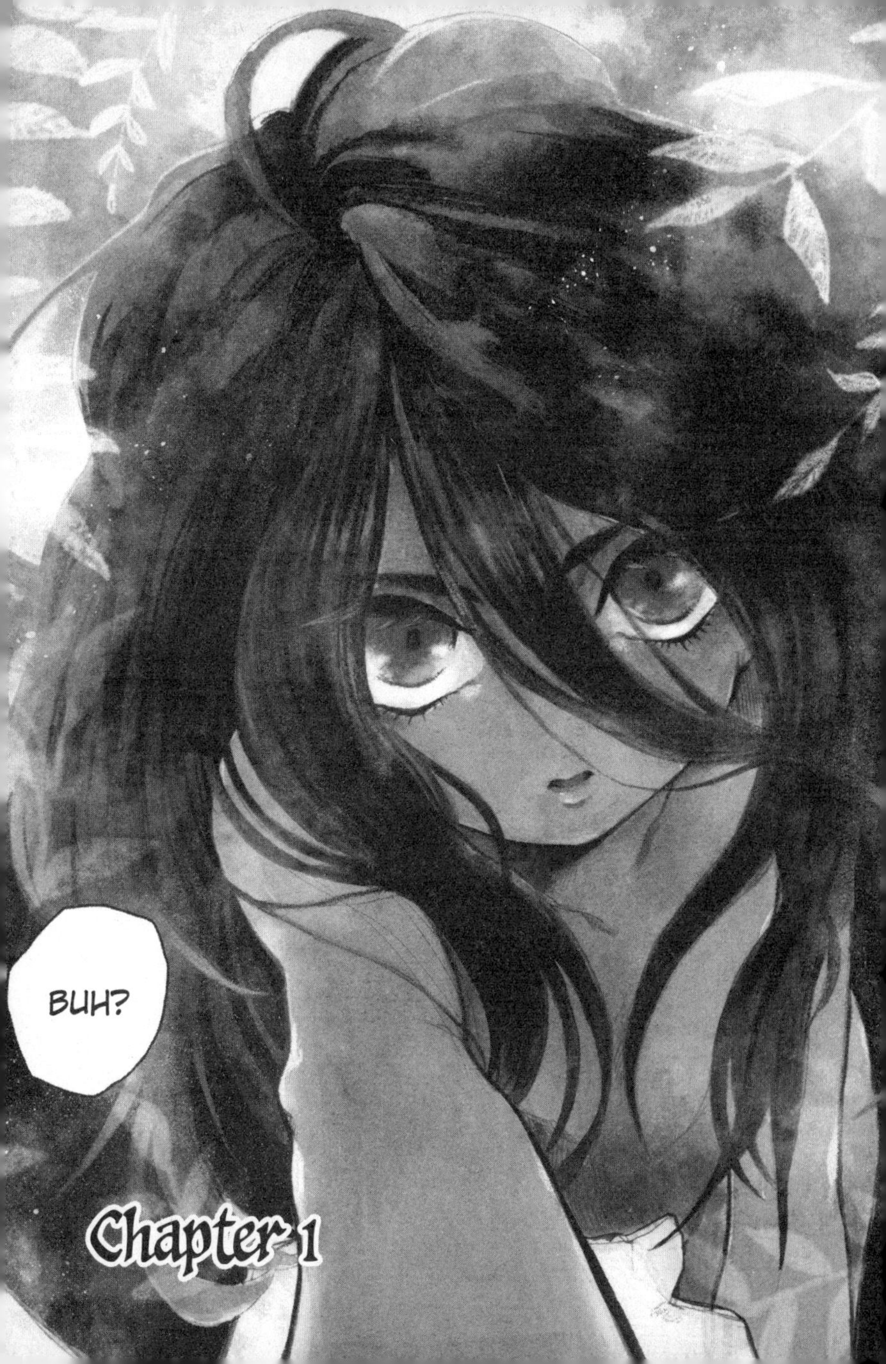
BUH?
Chapter 1

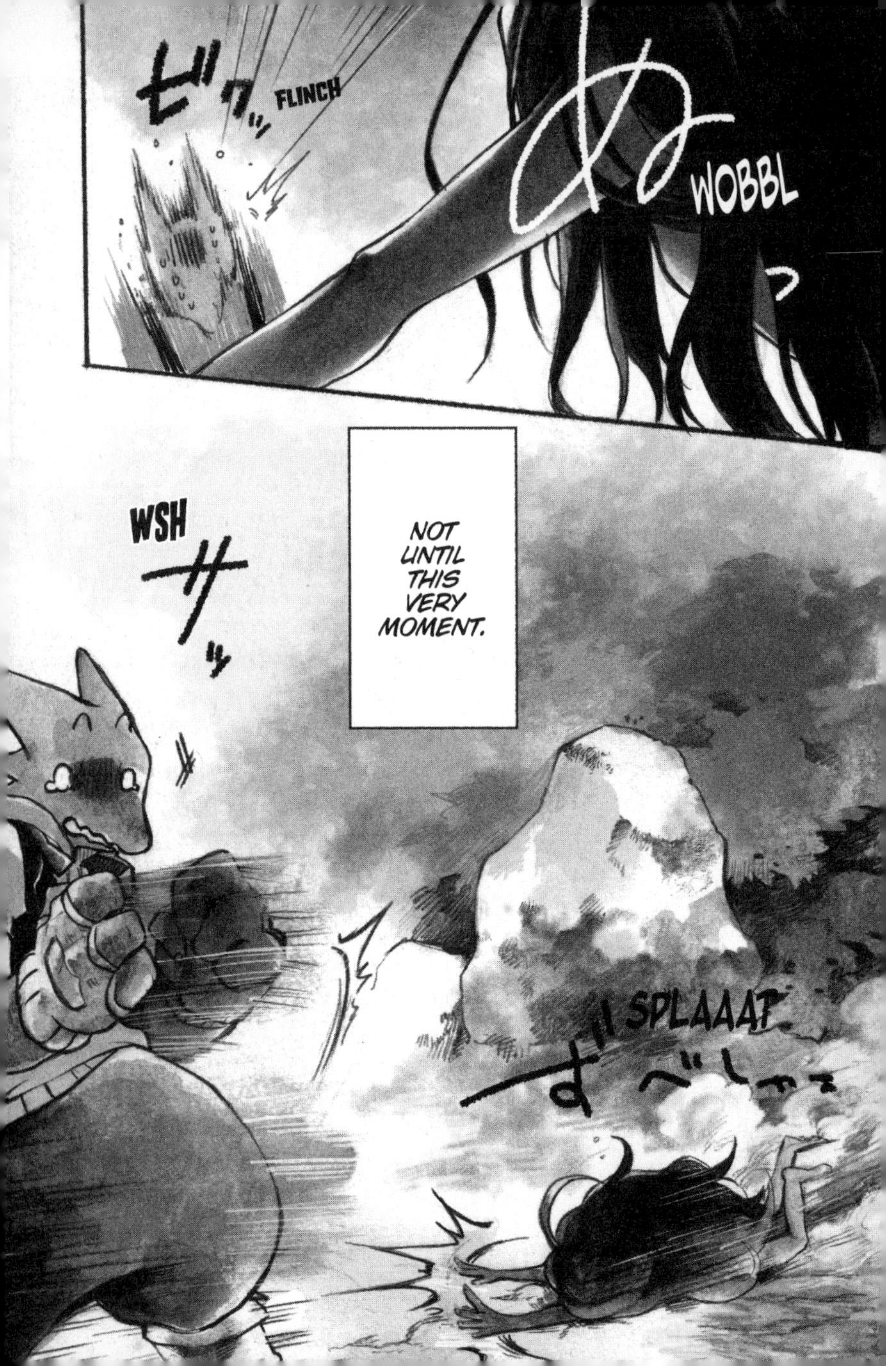
WOBBL
FLINCH
NOT UNTIL THIS VERY MOMENT.
WSH
SPLAAAT

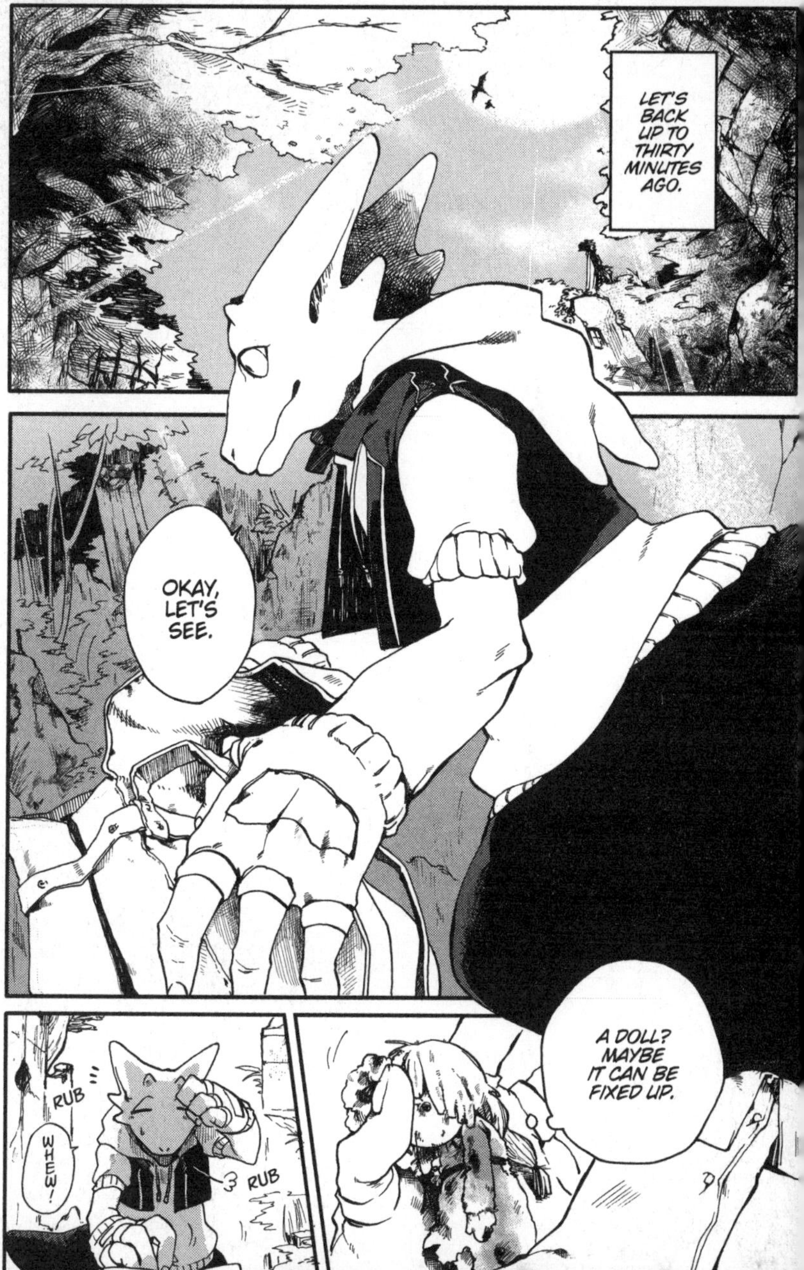
LET'S BACK UP TO THIRTY MINUTES AGO.
OKAY, LET'S SEE.
A DOLL? MAYBE IT CAN BE FIXED UP.
RUB
WHEW!
RUB

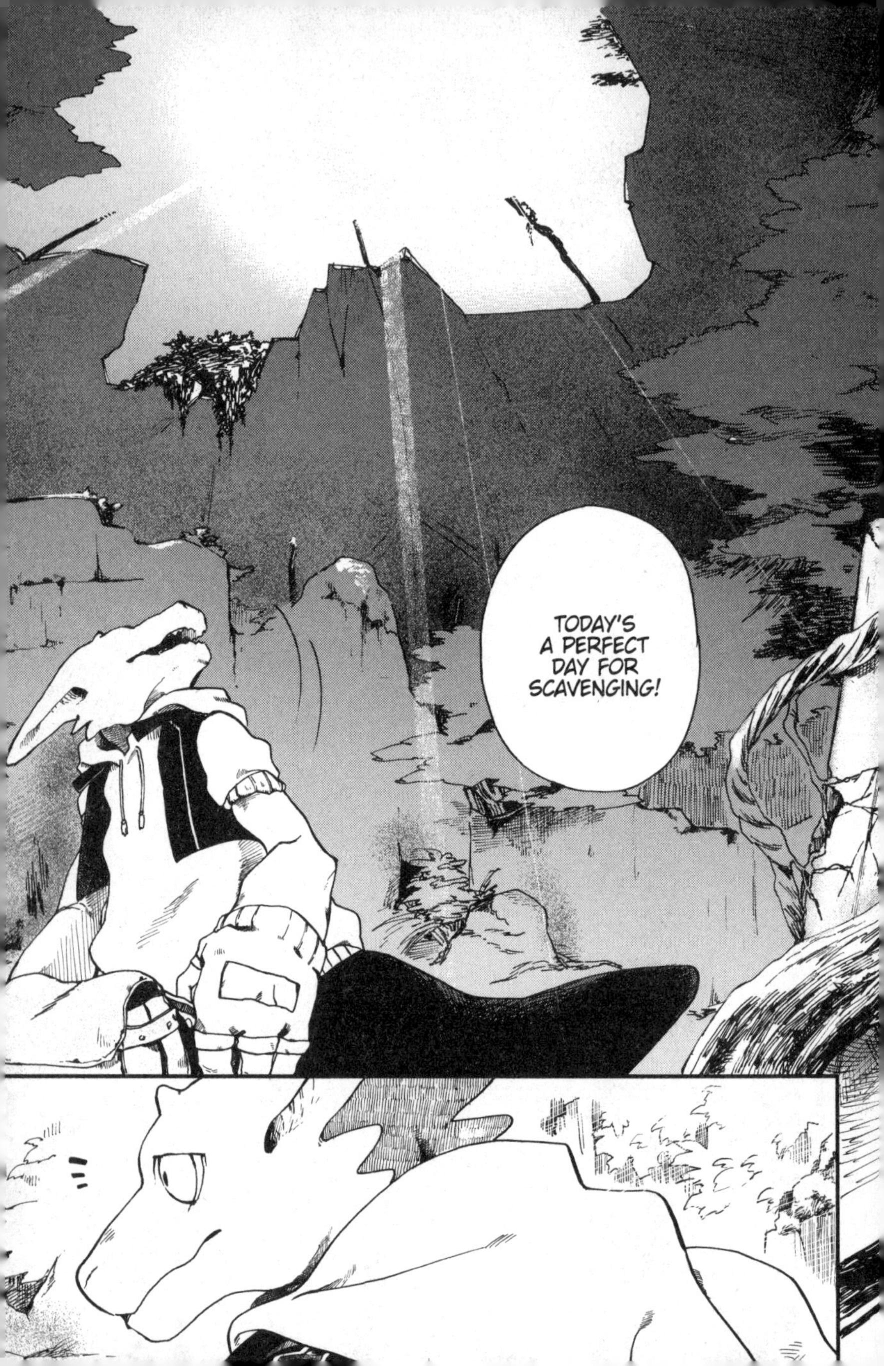
TODAY'S A PERFECT DAY FOR SCAVENGING!

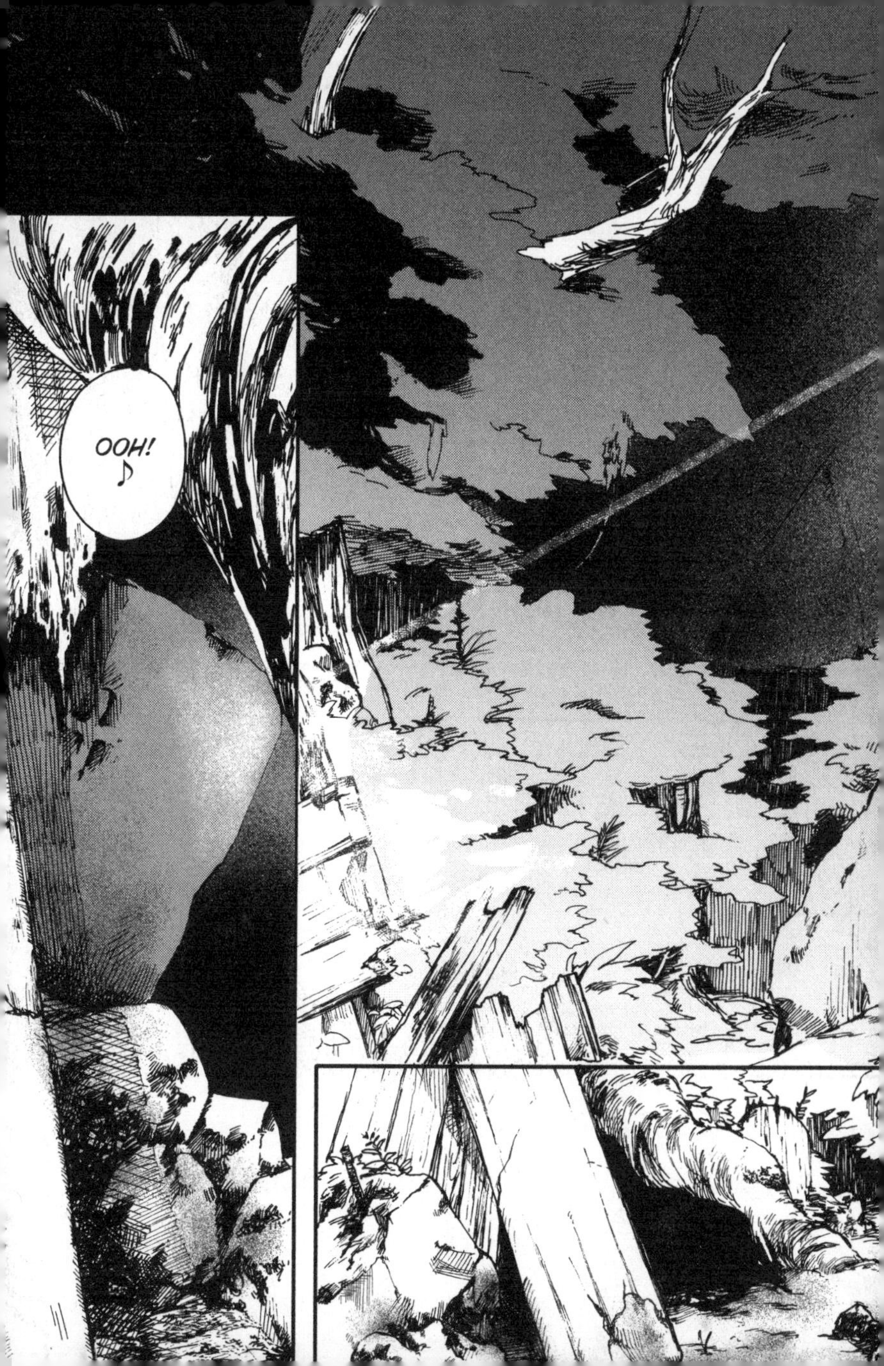
OOH! ♪

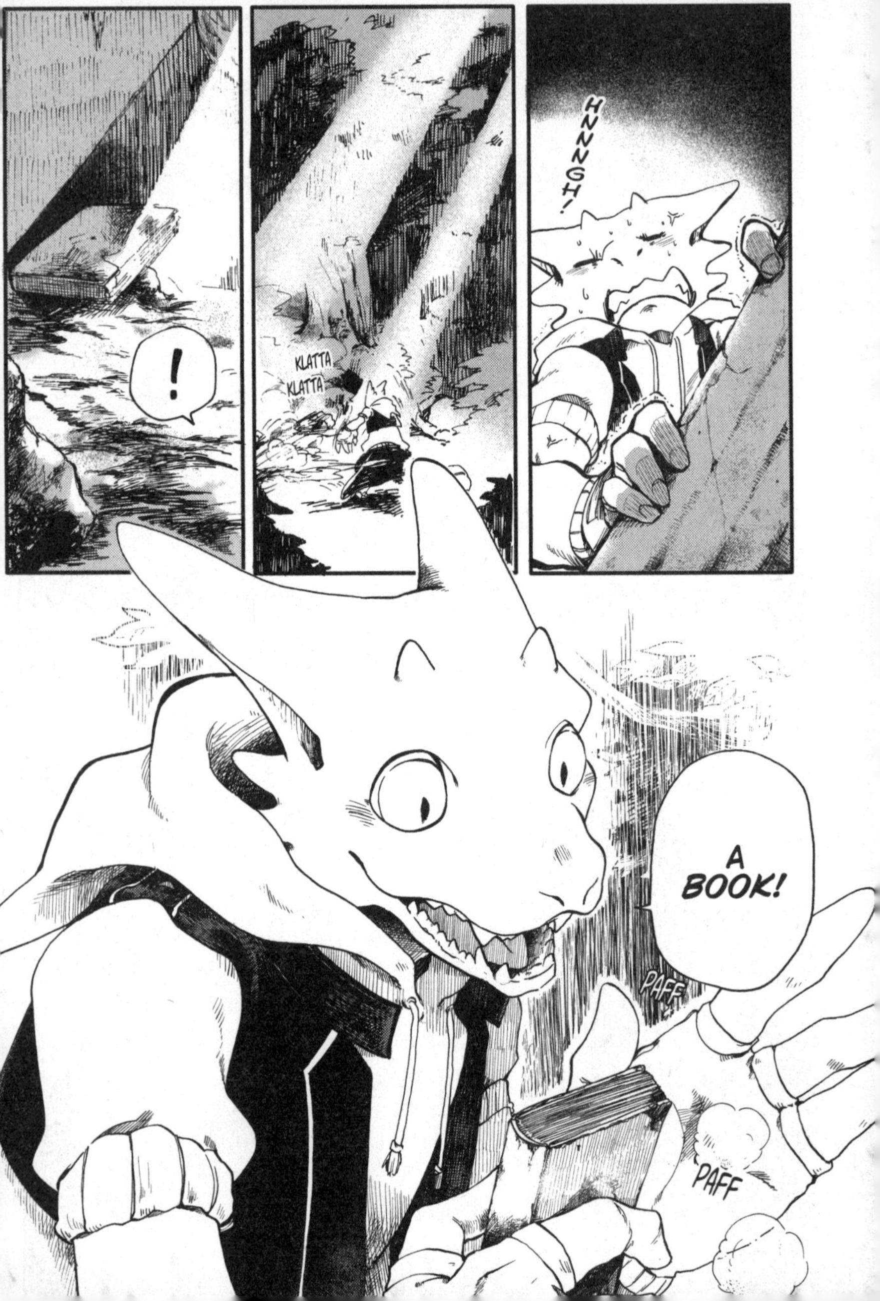
HNNNGH!
KLATTA
KLATTA
!
A BOOK!
PAFF
PAFF

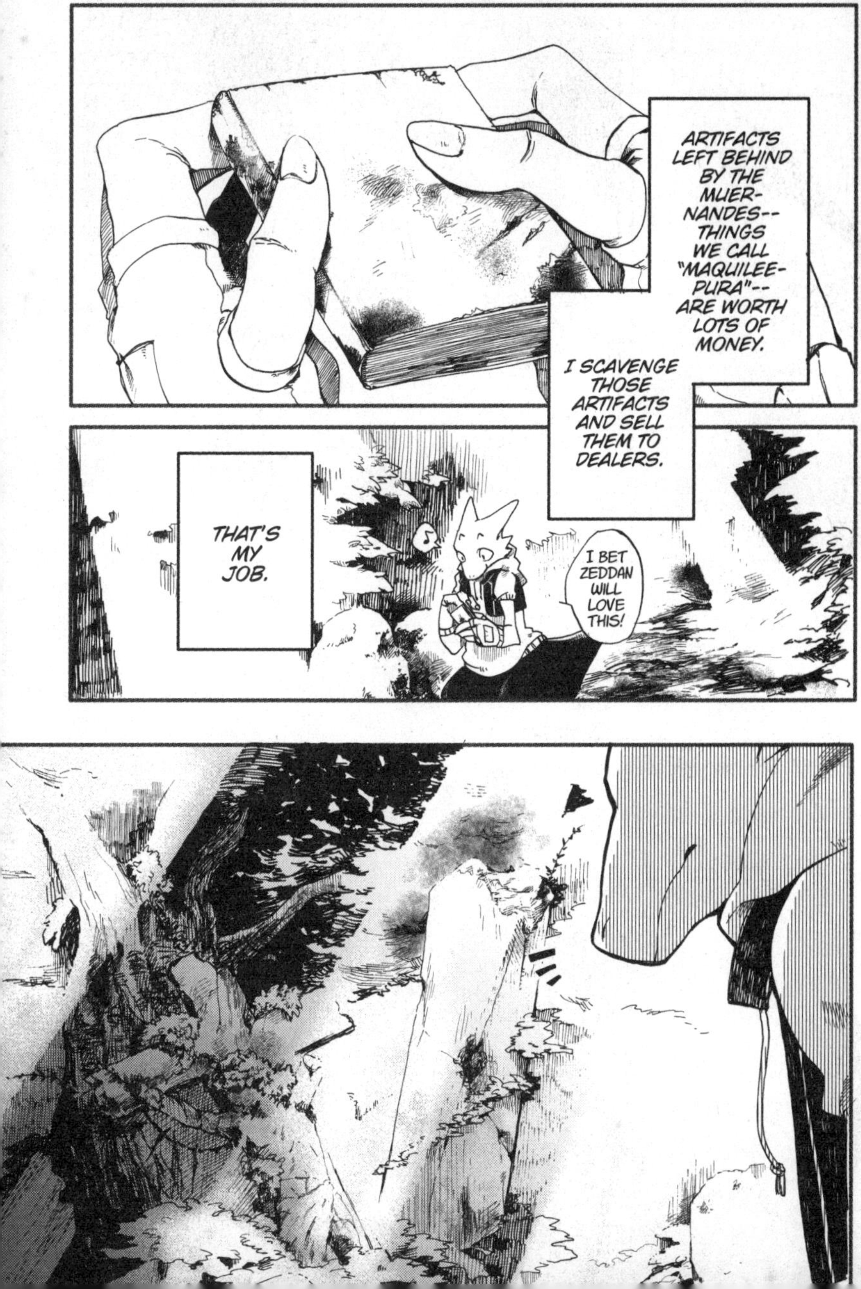
ARTIFACTS LEFT BEHIND BY THE MUER-NANDES--THINGS WE CALL "MAQUILEE-PURA"--ARE WORTH LOTS OF MONEY.
I SCAVENGE THOSE ARTIFACTS AND SELL THEM TO DEALERS.
THAT'S MY JOB.
I BET ZEDDAN WILL LOVE THIS!

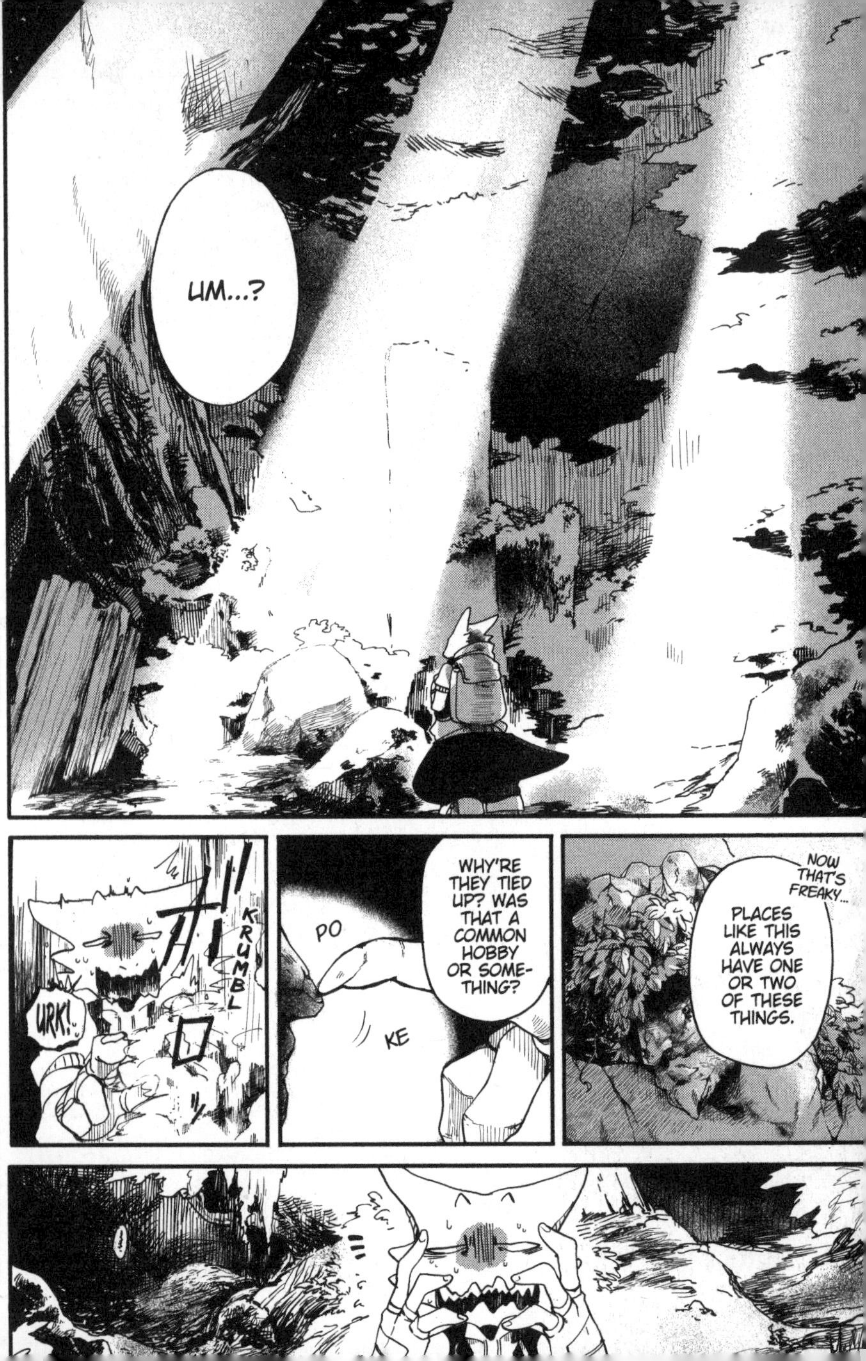
UM...?
NOW THAT'S FREAKY...
PLACES LIKE THIS ALWAYS HAVE ONE OR TWO OF THESE THINGS.
WHY'RE THEY TIED UP? WAS THAT A COMMON HOBBY OR SOME-THING?
PO
KE
KRUMBL
URK!

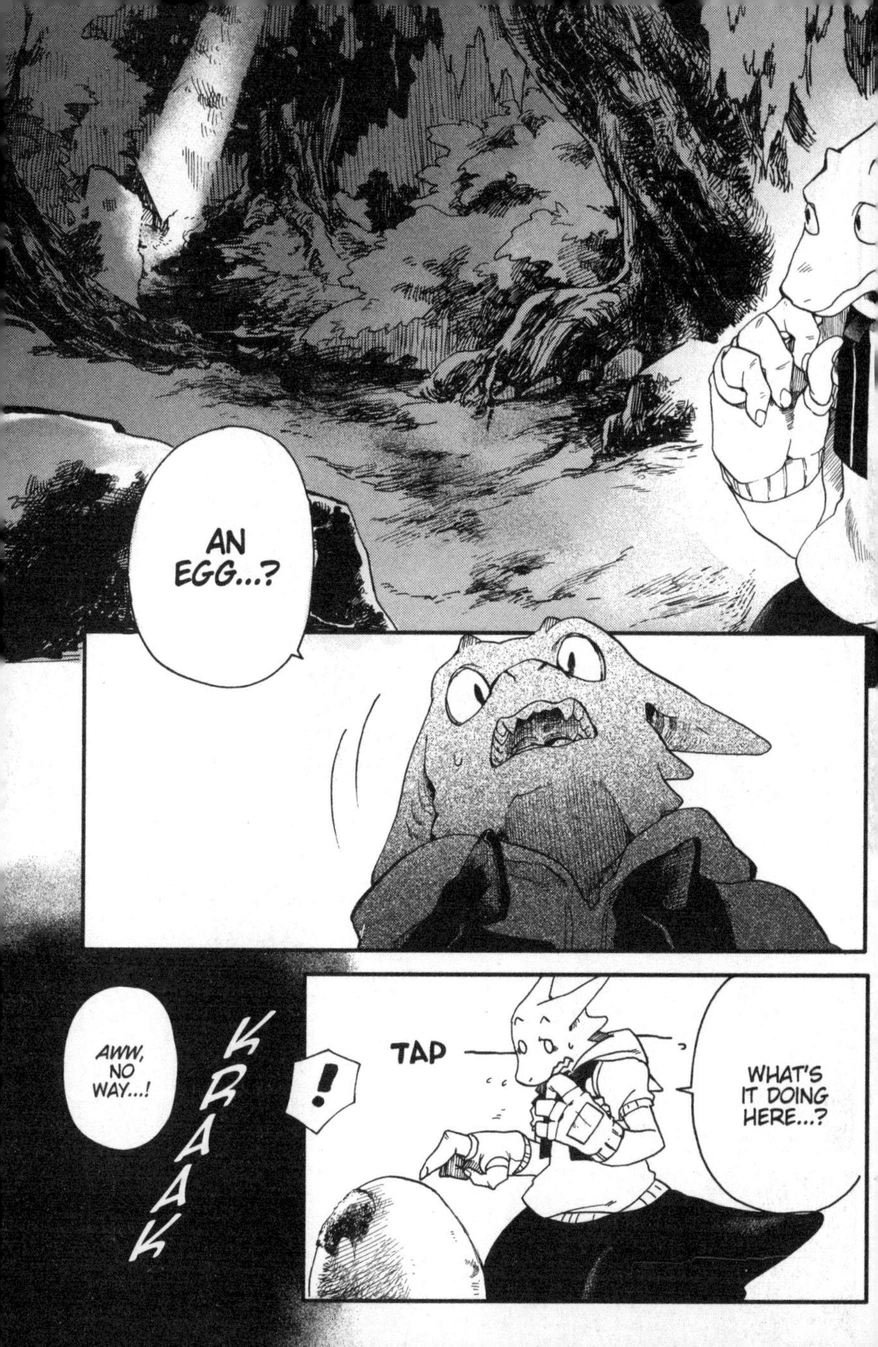
AN EGG...?
WHAT'S IT DOING HERE...?
TAP
!
KRAAK
AWW, NO WAY...!

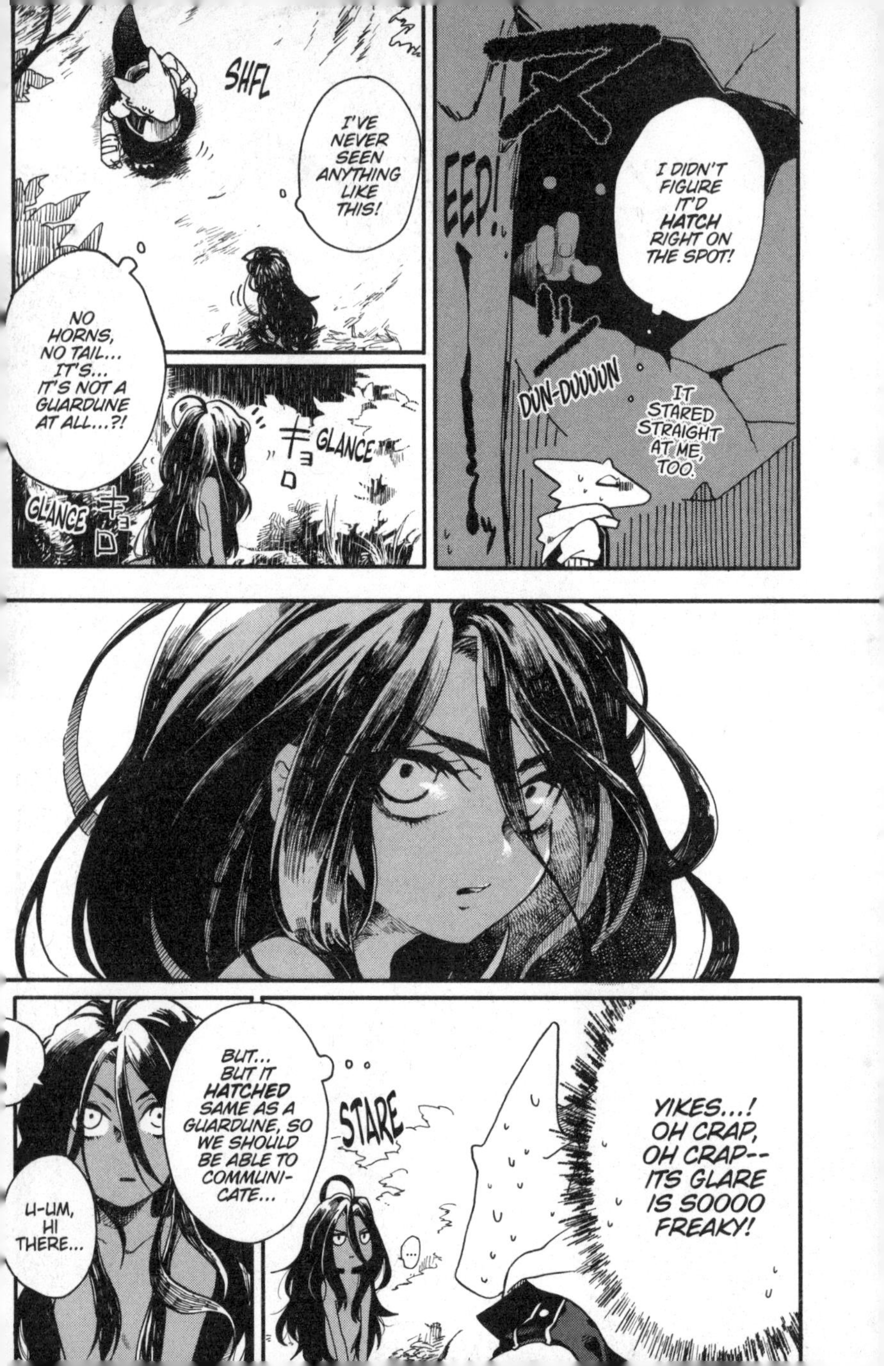
I DIDN'T FIGURE IT'D **HATCH** RIGHT ON THE SPOT!
EEP!
DUN-DUUUUN
IT STARED STRAIGHT AT ME, TOO.
I'VE NEVER SEEN ANYTHING LIKE THIS!
SHFL
NO HORNS, NO TAIL... IT'S... IT'S NOT A GUARDUNE AT ALL...?!
ギョロ
GLANCE
ギョロ
GLANCE
YIKES...! OH CRAP, OH CRAP-- ITS GLARE IS SOOOO FREAKY!
BUT... BUT IT **HATCHED** SAME AS A GUARDUNE, SO WE SHOULD BE ABLE TO COMMUNI-CATE...
STARE
...
U-UM, HI THERE...

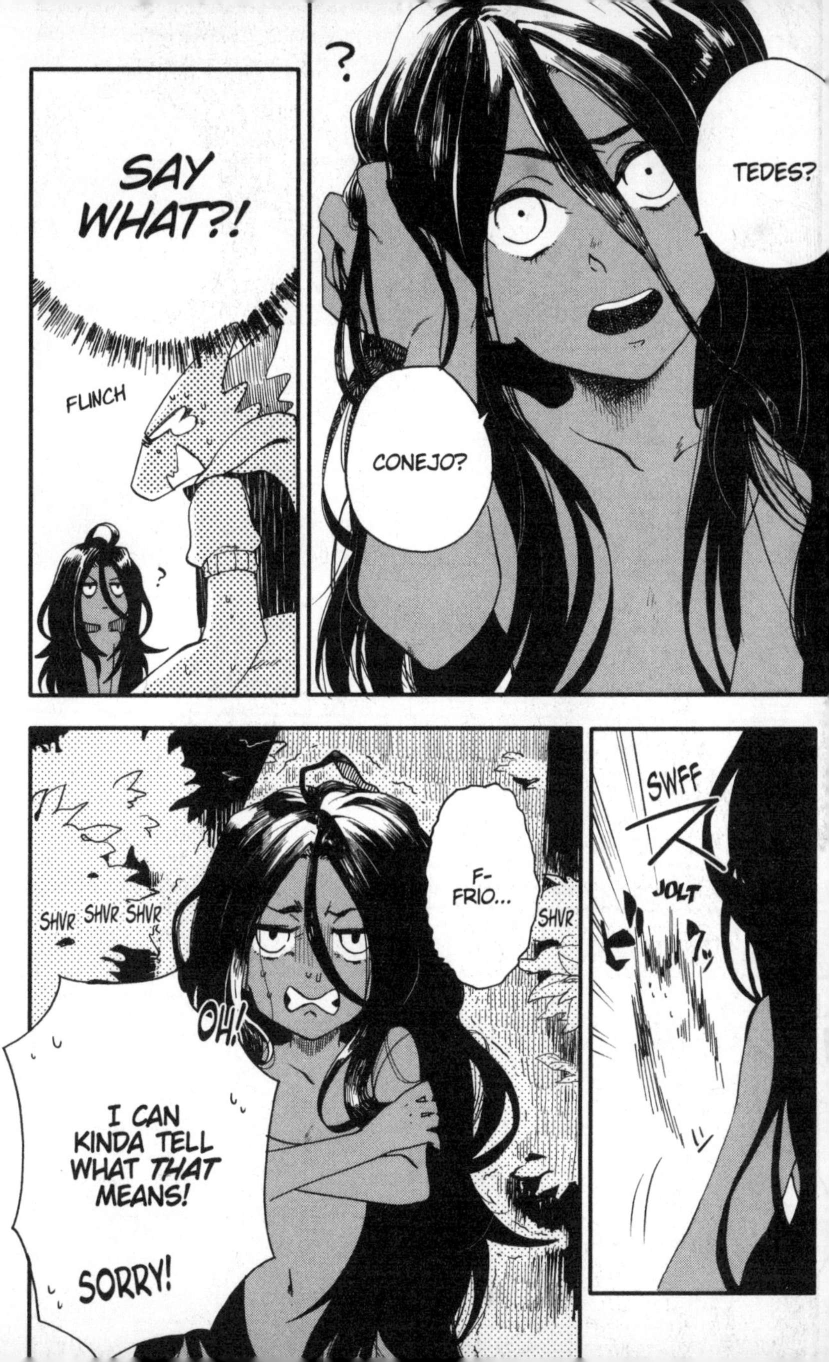
TEDES?
?
CONEJO?
SAY WHAT?!
FLINCH
?
SWFF
JOLT
F-FRIO...
SHVR
SHVR SHVR SHVR
OH!
I CAN KINDA TELL WHAT *THAT* MEANS!
SORRY!

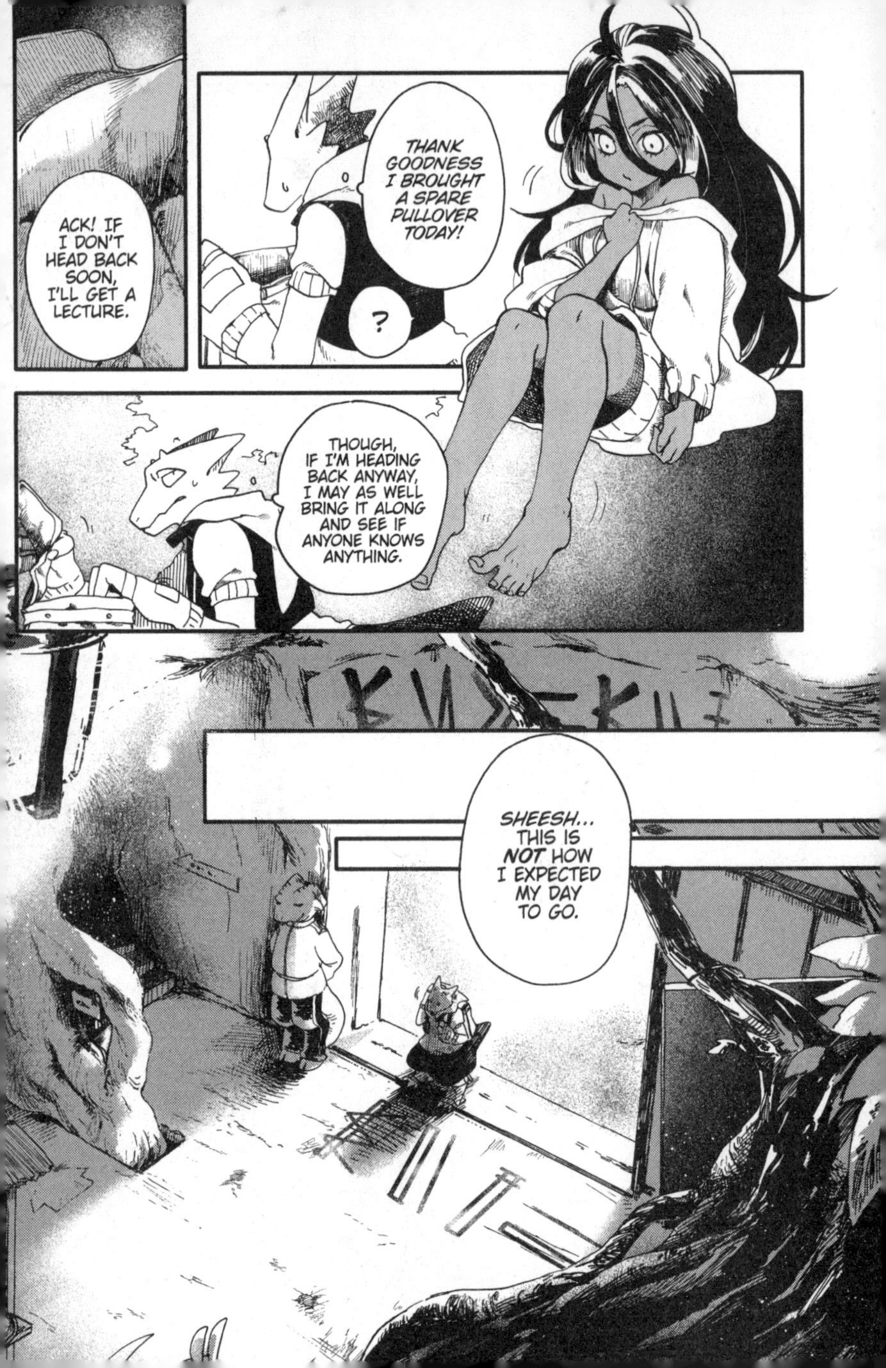
THANK GOODNESS I BROUGHT A SPARE PULLOVER TODAY!
?
ACK! IF I DON'T HEAD BACK SOON, I'LL GET A LECTURE.
THOUGH, IF I'M HEADING BACK ANYWAY, I MAY AS WELL BRING IT ALONG AND SEE IF ANYONE KNOWS ANYTHING.
SHEESH... THIS IS NOT HOW I EXPECTED MY DAY TO GO.

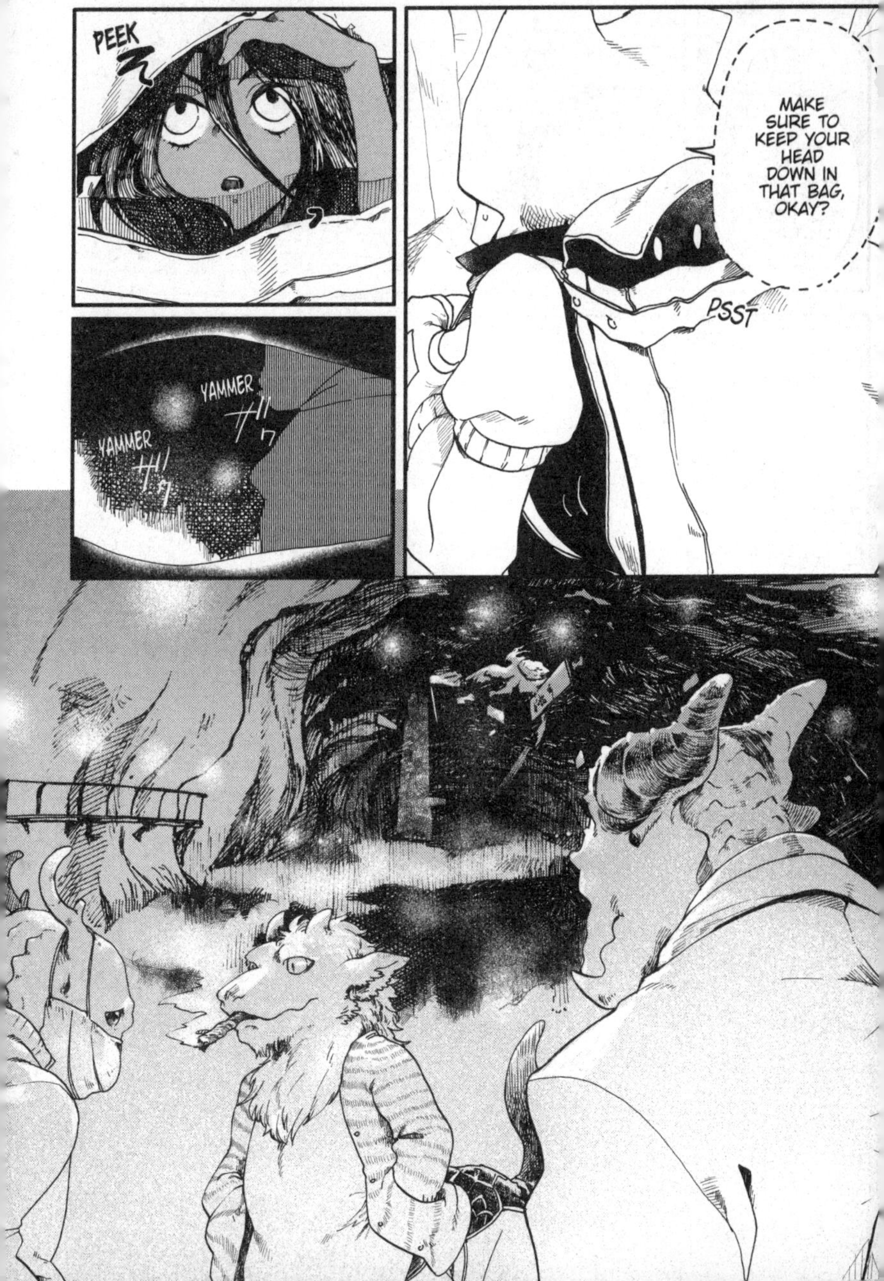
MAKE SURE TO KEEP YOUR HEAD DOWN IN THAT BAG, OKAY?
PSST
PEEK
YAMMER
YAMMER

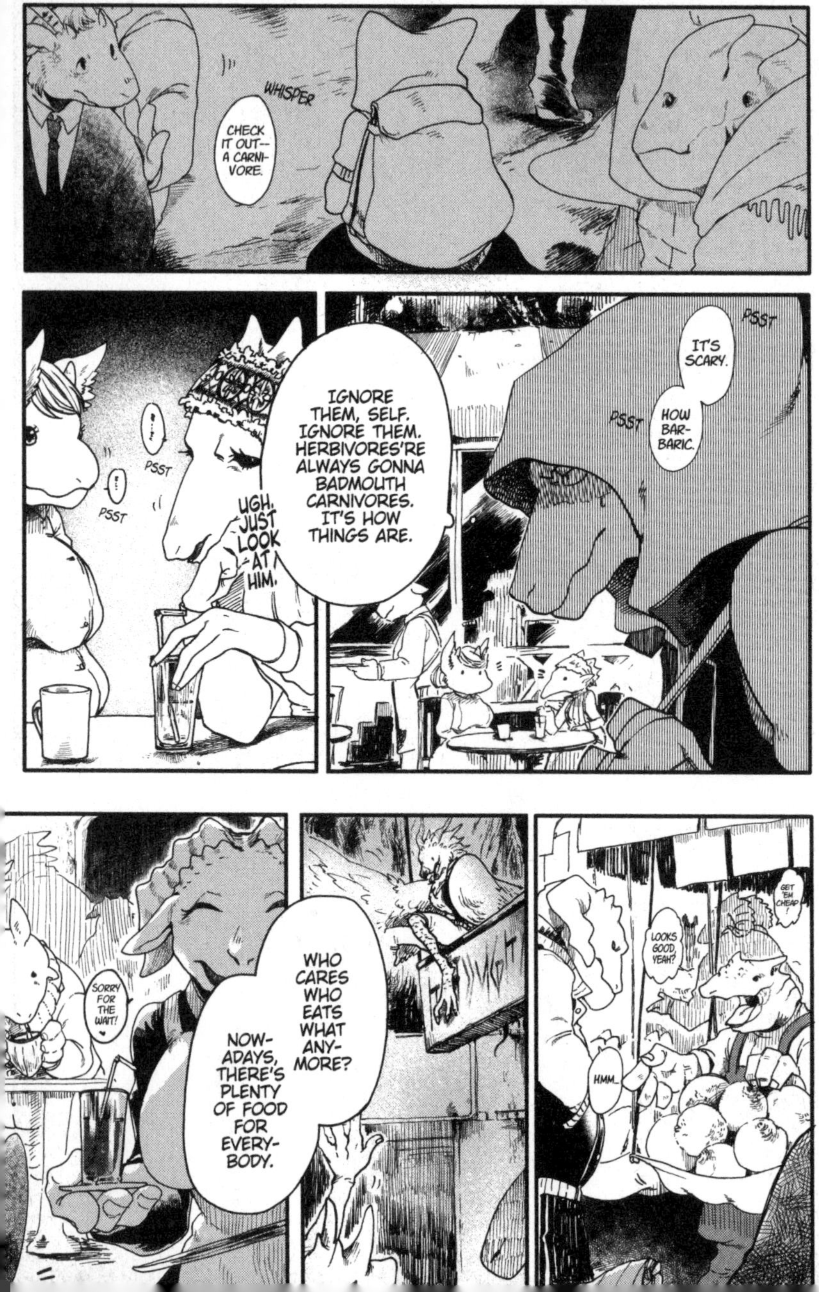
WHISPER
CHECK IT OUT-- A CARNIVORE.
PSST
IT'S SCARY.
PSST
HOW BAR-BARIC.
IGNORE THEM, SELF. IGNORE THEM. HERBIVORES'RE ALWAYS GONNA BADMOUTH CARNIVORES. IT'S HOW THINGS ARE.
UGH. JUST LOOK AT HIM.
PSST
PSST
GET 'EM CHEAP!
LOOKS GOOD, YEAH?
HMM...
WHO CARES WHO EATS WHAT ANYMORE?
NOW-ADAYS, THERE'S PLENTY OF FOOD FOR EVERY-BODY.
SORRY FOR THE WAIT!

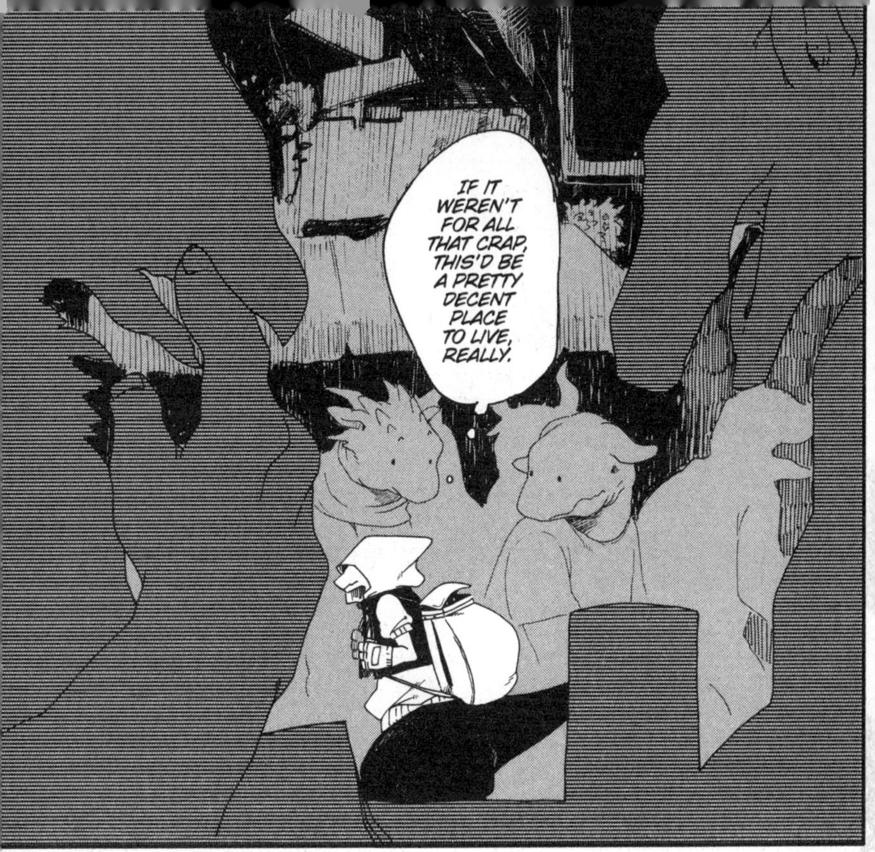
IF IT WEREN'T FOR ALL THAT CRAP, THIS'D BE A PRETTY DECENT PLACE TO LIVE, REALLY.

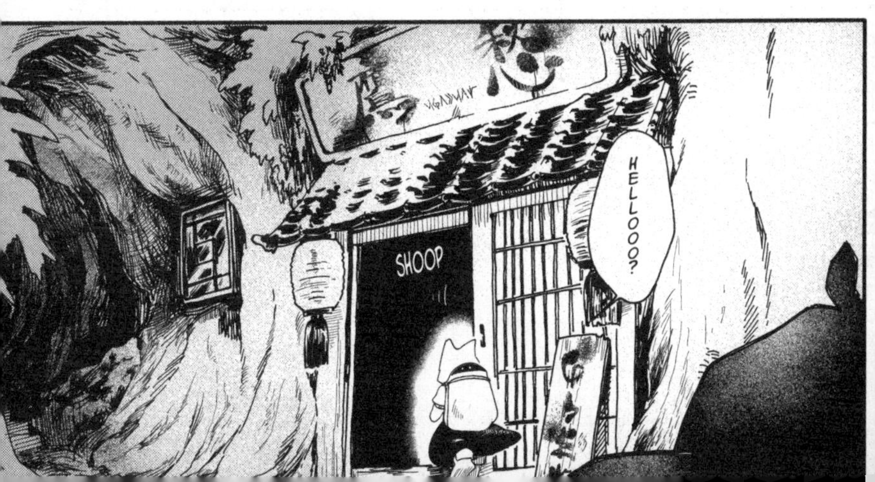
HELLOOOO?
SHOOP

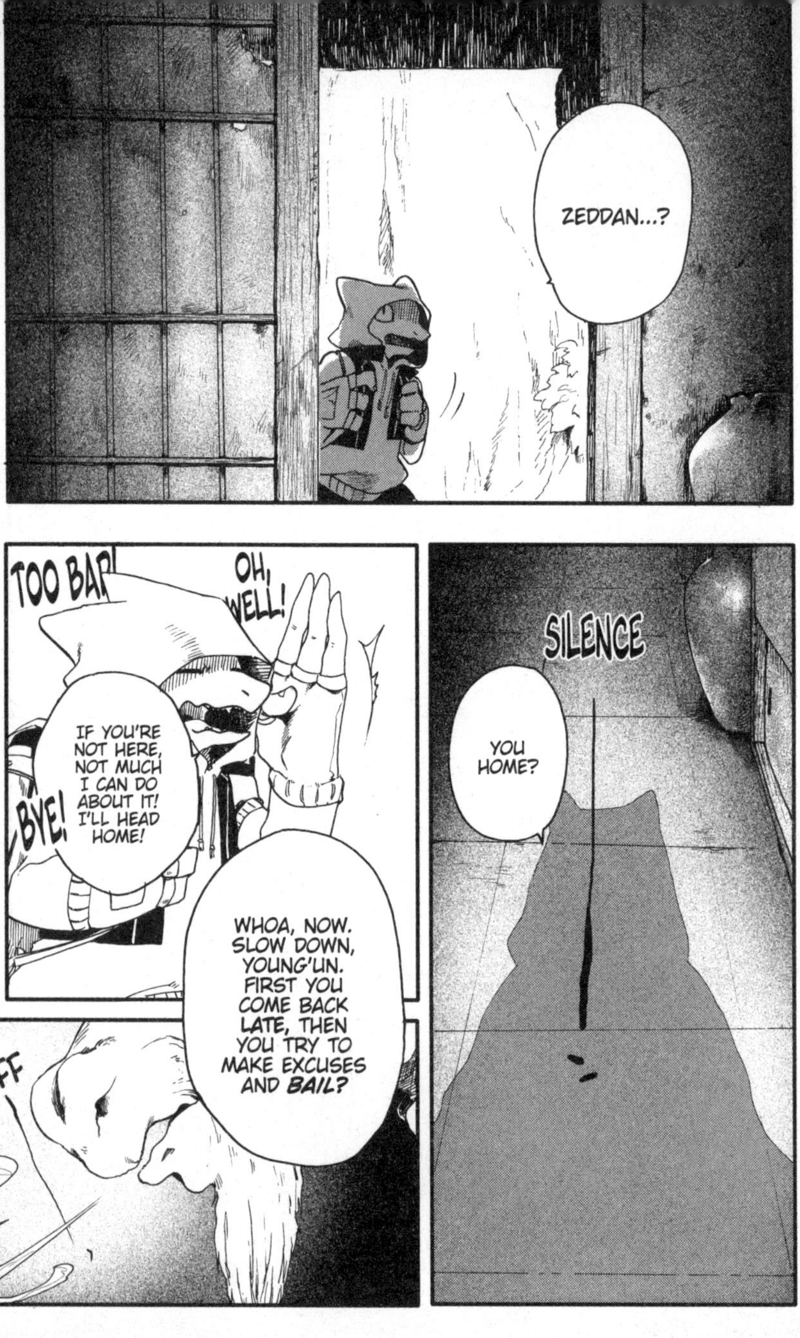
ZEDDAN...?
SILENCE
YOU HOME?
OH, WELL!
TOO BA
IF YOU'RE NOT HERE, NOT MUCH I CAN DO ABOUT IT! I'LL HEAD HOME!
BYE!
WHOA, NOW. SLOW DOWN, YOUNG'UN. FIRST YOU COME BACK LATE, THEN YOU TRY TO MAKE EXCUSES AND *BAIL?*
FF

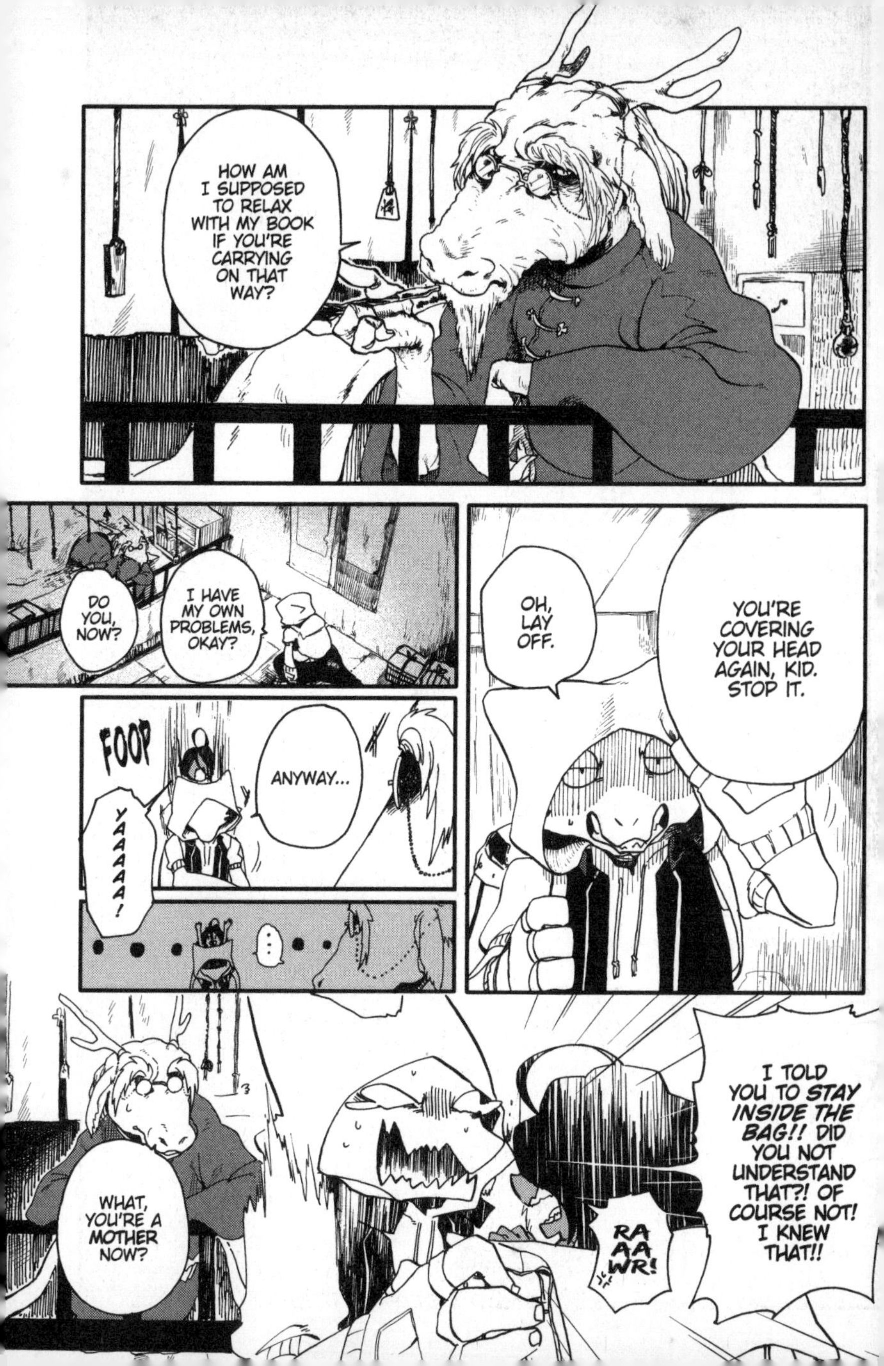

HOW AM I SUPPOSED TO RELAX WITH MY BOOK IF YOU'RE CARRYING ON THAT WAY?
YOU'RE COVERING YOUR HEAD AGAIN, KID. STOP IT.
OH, LAY OFF.
I HAVE MY OWN PROBLEMS, OKAY?
DO YOU, NOW?
ANYWAY...
FOOP
YAAAAAA!
...
I TOLD YOU TO *STAY INSIDE THE BAG!!* DID YOU NOT UNDERSTAND THAT?! OF COURSE NOT! I KNEW THAT!!
RAAAWR!
WHAT, YOU'RE A MOTHER NOW?

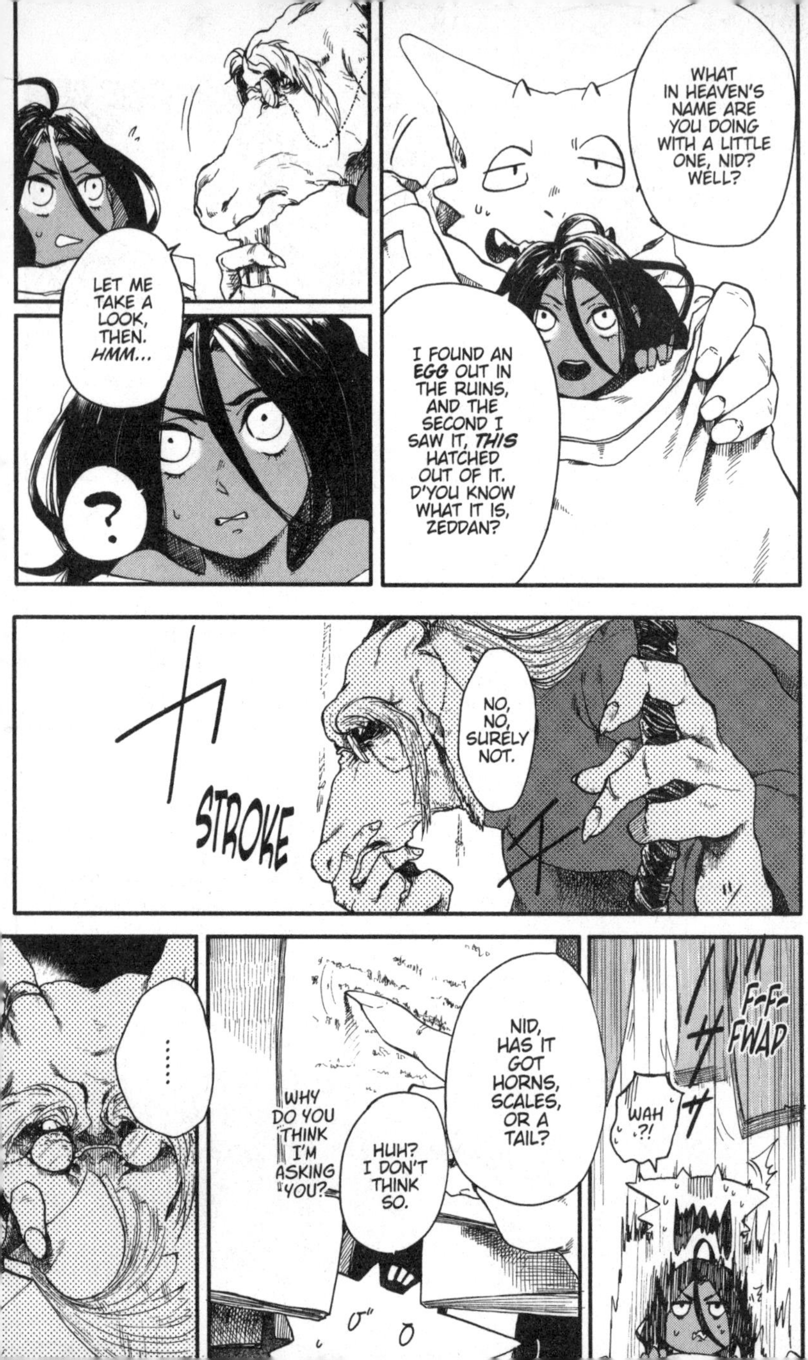
WHAT IN HEAVEN'S NAME ARE YOU DOING WITH A LITTLE ONE, NID? WELL?
I FOUND AN EGG OUT IN THE RUINS, AND THE SECOND I SAW IT, THIS HATCHED OUT OF IT. D'YOU KNOW WHAT IT IS, ZEDDAN?
LET ME TAKE A LOOK, THEN. HMM...
?
NO, NO, SURELY NOT.
STROKE
F-F-FWAP
WAH?!
NID, HAS IT GOT HORNS, SCALES, OR A TAIL?
HUH? I DON'T THINK SO.
WHY DO YOU THINK I'M ASKING YOU?
......

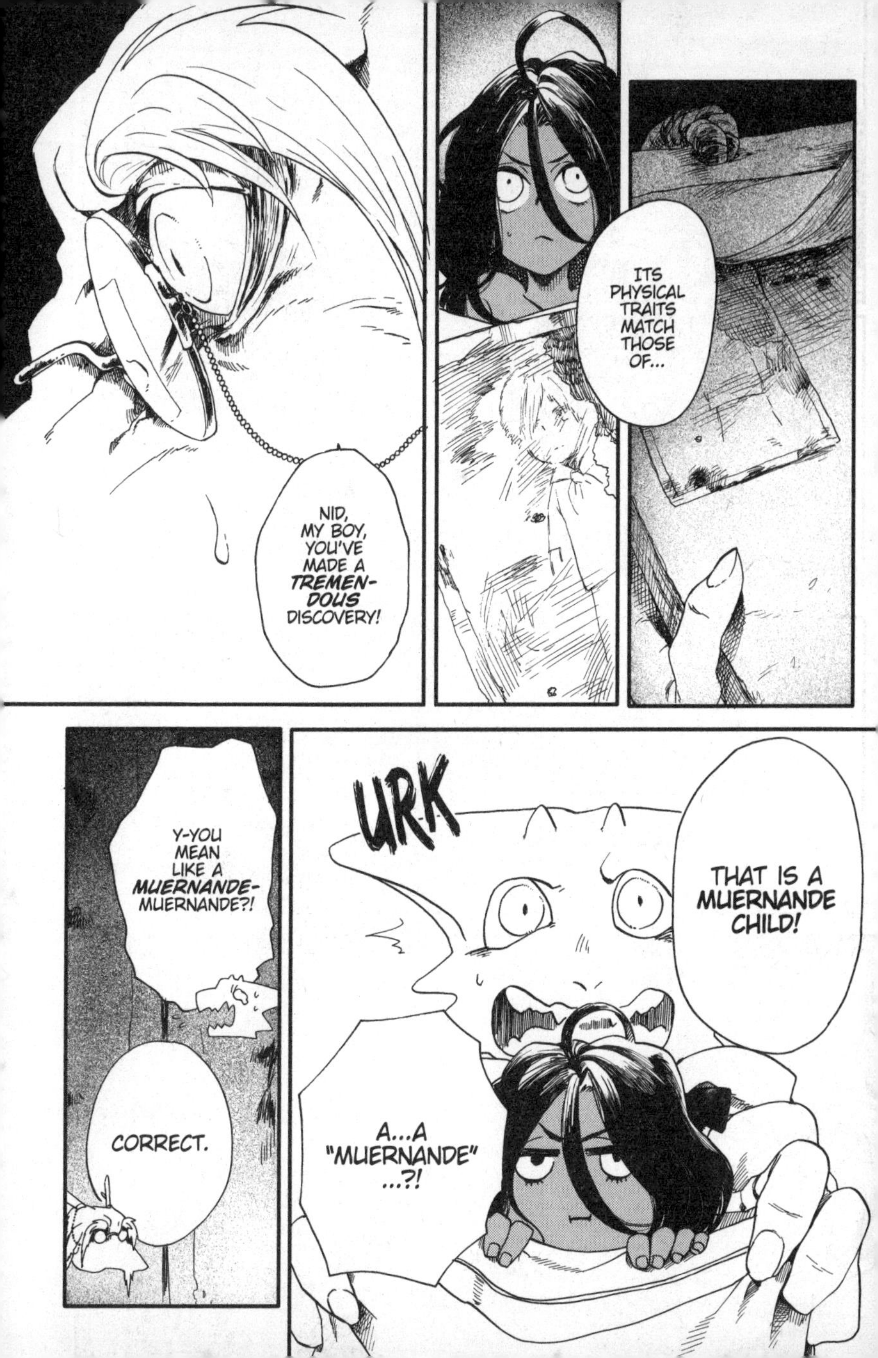
ITS PHYSICAL TRAITS MATCH THOSE OF...
NID, MY BOY, YOU'VE MADE A TREMENDOUS DISCOVERY!
THAT IS A MUERNANDE CHILD!
URK
A...A "MUERNANDE" ...?!
Y-YOU MEAN LIKE A MUERNANDE-MUERNANDE?!
CORRECT.

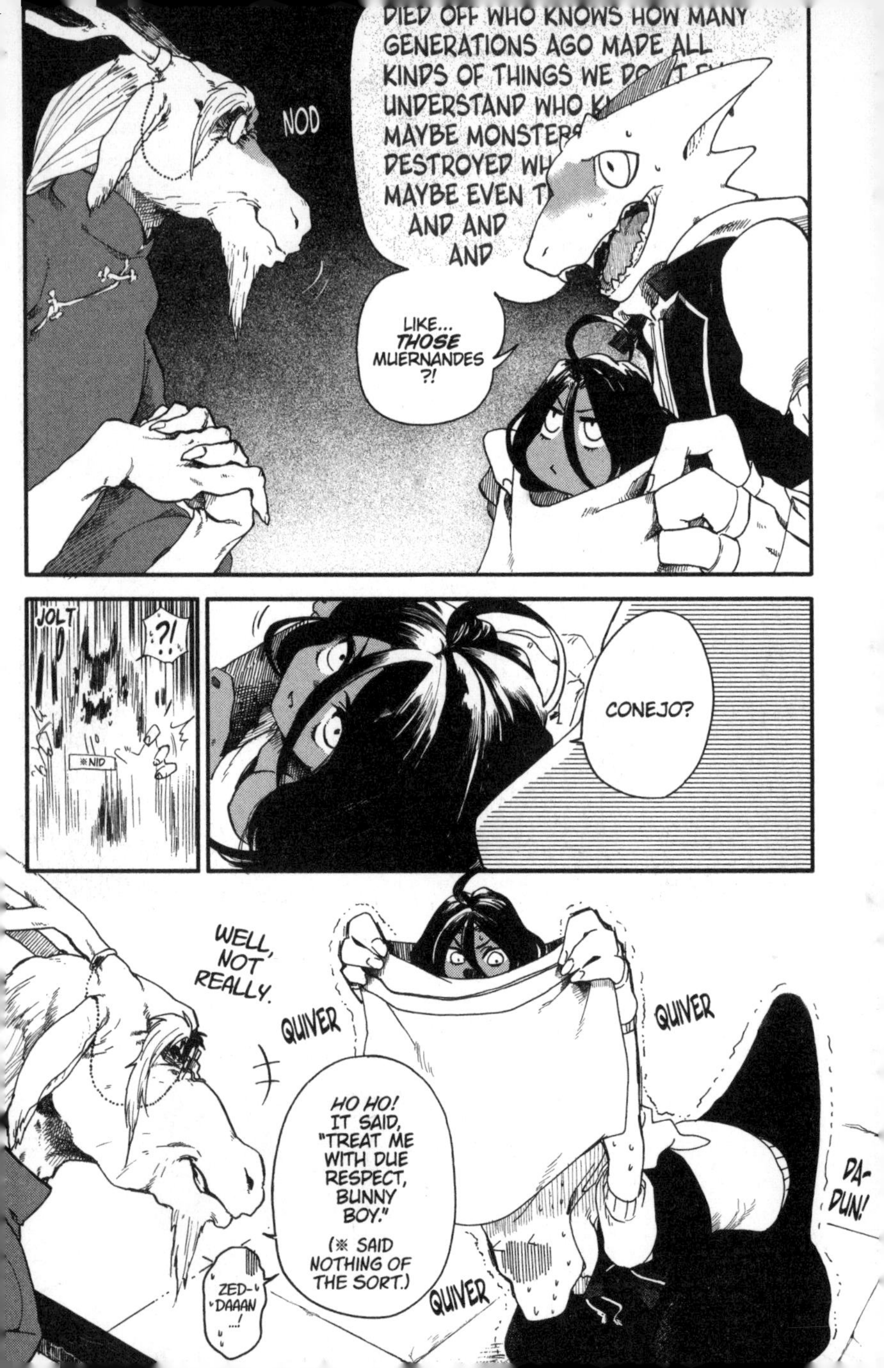
DIED OFF WHO KNOWS HOW MANY GENERATIONS AGO MADE ALL KINDS OF THINGS WE DO UNDERSTAND WHO K MAYBE MONSTER DESTROYED WH MAYBE EVEN T AND AND AND
NOD
LIKE... ***THOSE*** MUERNANDES ?!
CONEJO?
JOLT
?!
※NID
QUIVER
WELL, NOT REALLY.
QUIVER
HO HO! IT SAID, "TREAT ME WITH DUE RESPECT, BUNNY BOY." (※ SAID NOTHING OF THE SORT.)
DA-DUN!
QUIVER
ZED-DAAAN ...!

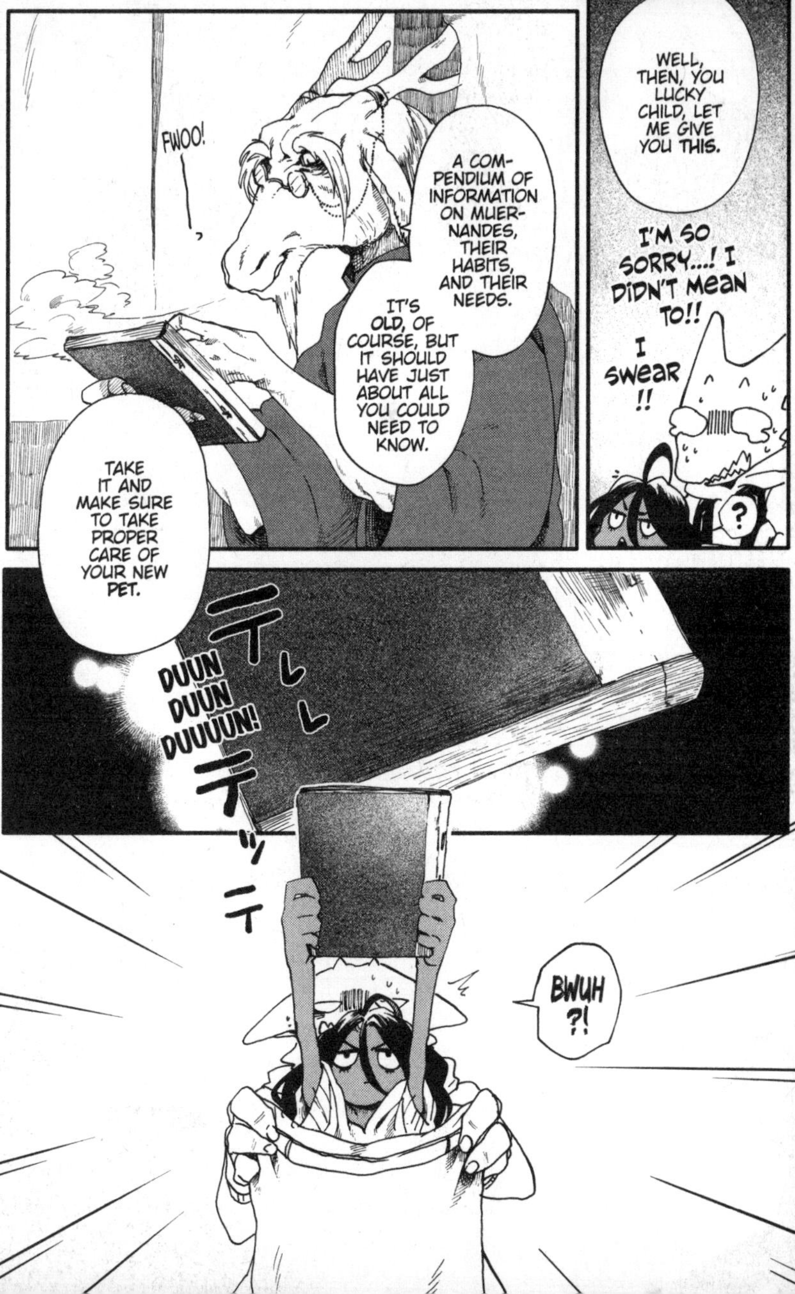
WELL, THEN, YOU LUCKY CHILD, LET ME GIVE YOU THIS.
I'M SO SORRY...! I DIDN'T MEAN TO!!
I SWEAR!!
?
FWOO!
A COM-PENDIUM OF INFORMATION ON MUER-NANDES, THEIR HABITS, AND THEIR NEEDS.
IT'S OLD, OF COURSE, BUT IT SHOULD HAVE JUST ABOUT ALL YOU COULD NEED TO KNOW.
TAKE IT AND MAKE SURE TO TAKE PROPER CARE OF YOUR NEW PET.
DUUN DUUN DUUUUN!
BWUH?!

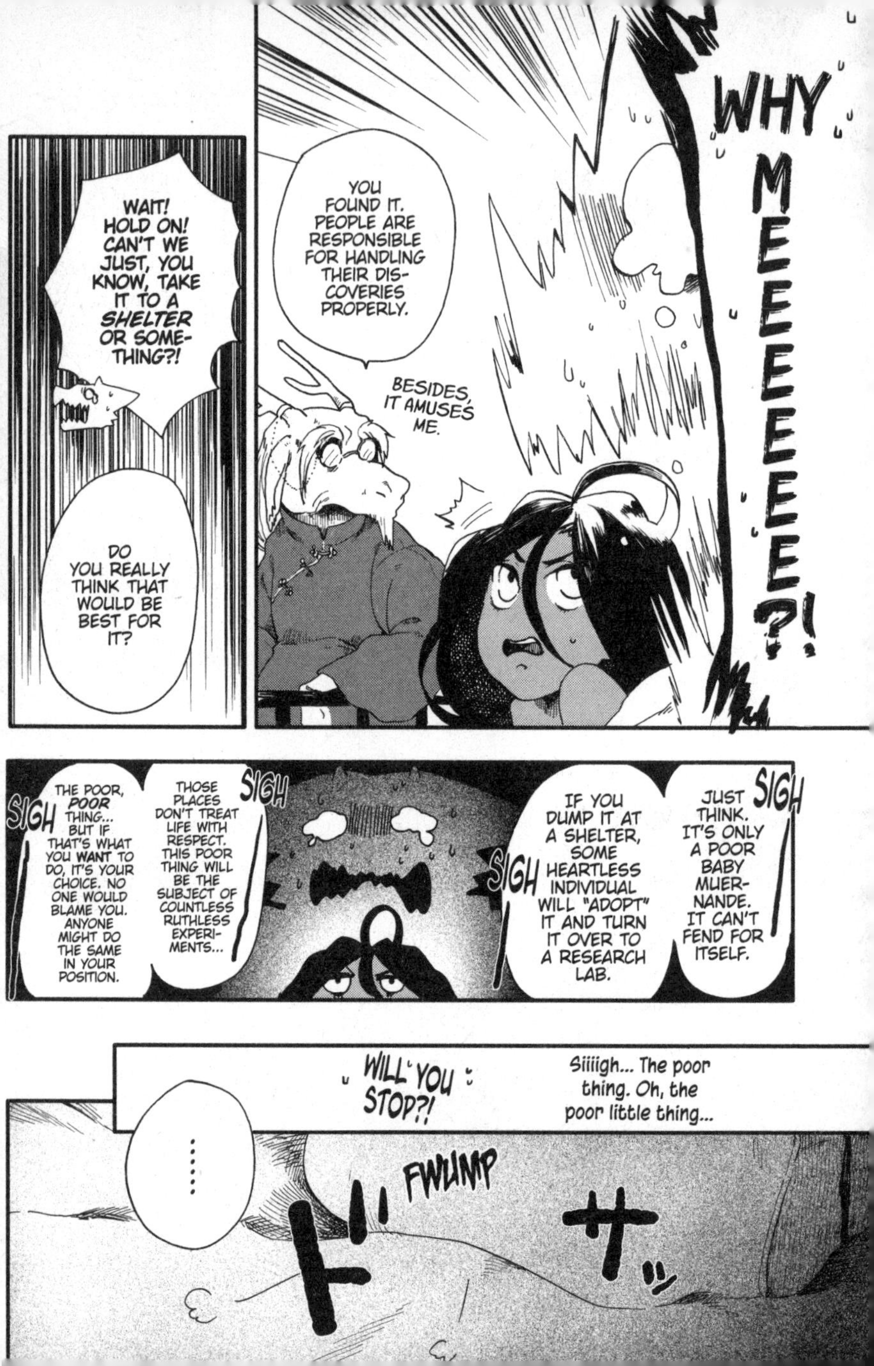
WHY MEEEEEEEE?!
YOU FOUND IT. PEOPLE ARE RESPONSIBLE FOR HANDLING THEIR DIS-COVERIES PROPERLY.
BESIDES, IT AMUSES ME.
WAIT! HOLD ON! CAN'T WE JUST, YOU KNOW, TAKE IT TO A SHELTER OR SOME-THING?!
DO YOU REALLY THINK THAT WOULD BE BEST FOR IT?
SIGH
JUST THINK. IT'S ONLY A POOR BABY MUER-NANDE. IT CAN'T FEND FOR ITSELF.
IF YOU DUMP IT AT A SHELTER, SOME HEARTLESS INDIVIDUAL WILL "ADOPT" IT AND TURN IT OVER TO A RESEARCH LAB.
SIGH
SIGH
THOSE PLACES DON'T TREAT LIFE WITH RESPECT. THIS POOR THING WILL BE THE SUBJECT OF COUNTLESS RUTHLESS EXPERI-MENTS...
SIGH
THE POOR, POOR THING... BUT IF THAT'S WHAT YOU WANT TO DO, IT'S YOUR CHOICE. NO ONE WOULD BLAME YOU. ANYONE MIGHT DO THE SAME IN YOUR POSITION.
Siiiigh... The poor thing. Oh, the poor little thing...
WILL YOU STOP?!
......
FWUMP

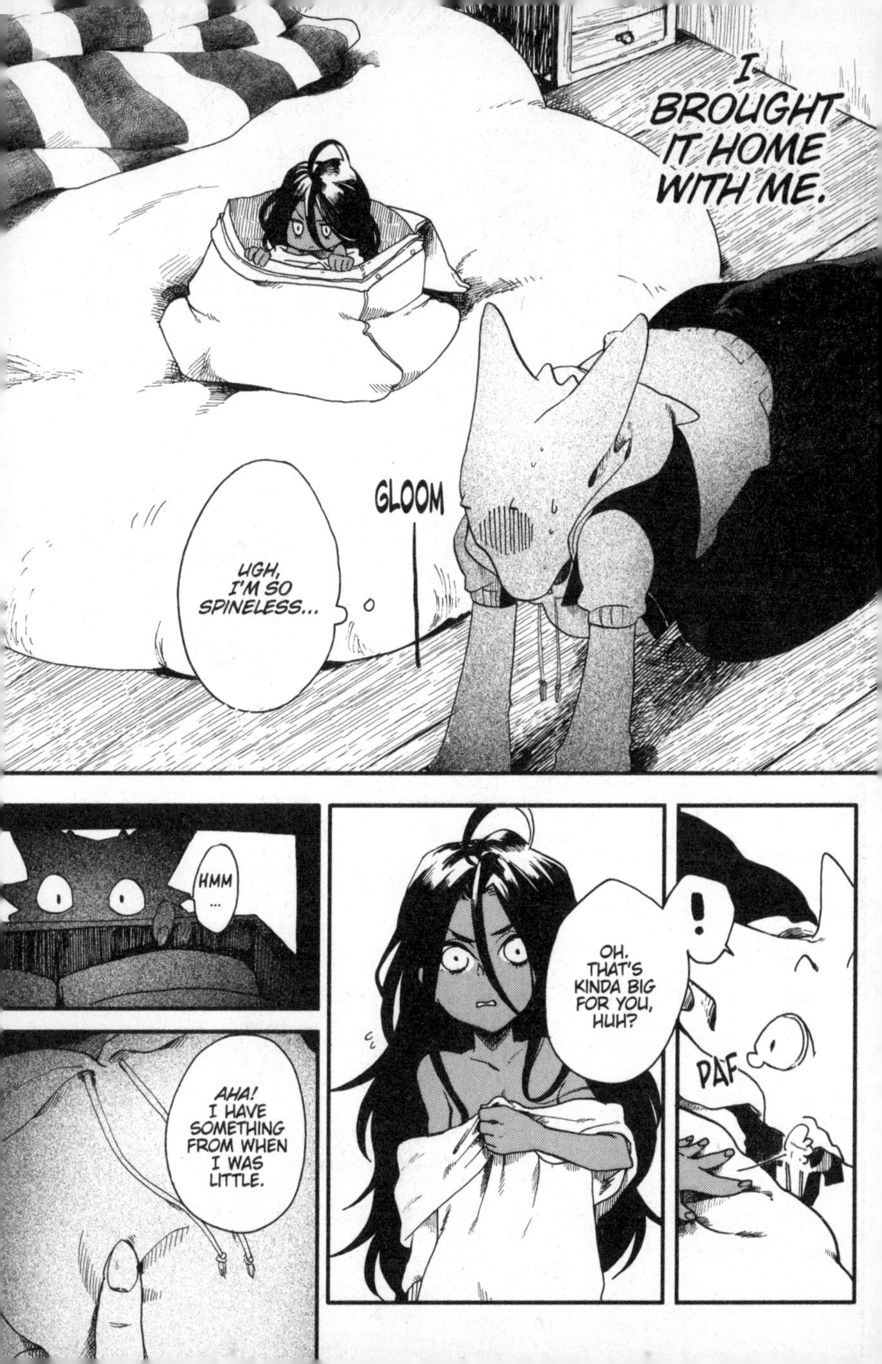
I BROUGHT IT HOME WITH ME.
GLOOM
UGH, I'M SO SPINELESS...
!
OH. THAT'S KINDA BIG FOR YOU, HUH?
PAF
HMM ...
AHA! I HAVE SOMETHING FROM WHEN I WAS LITTLE.

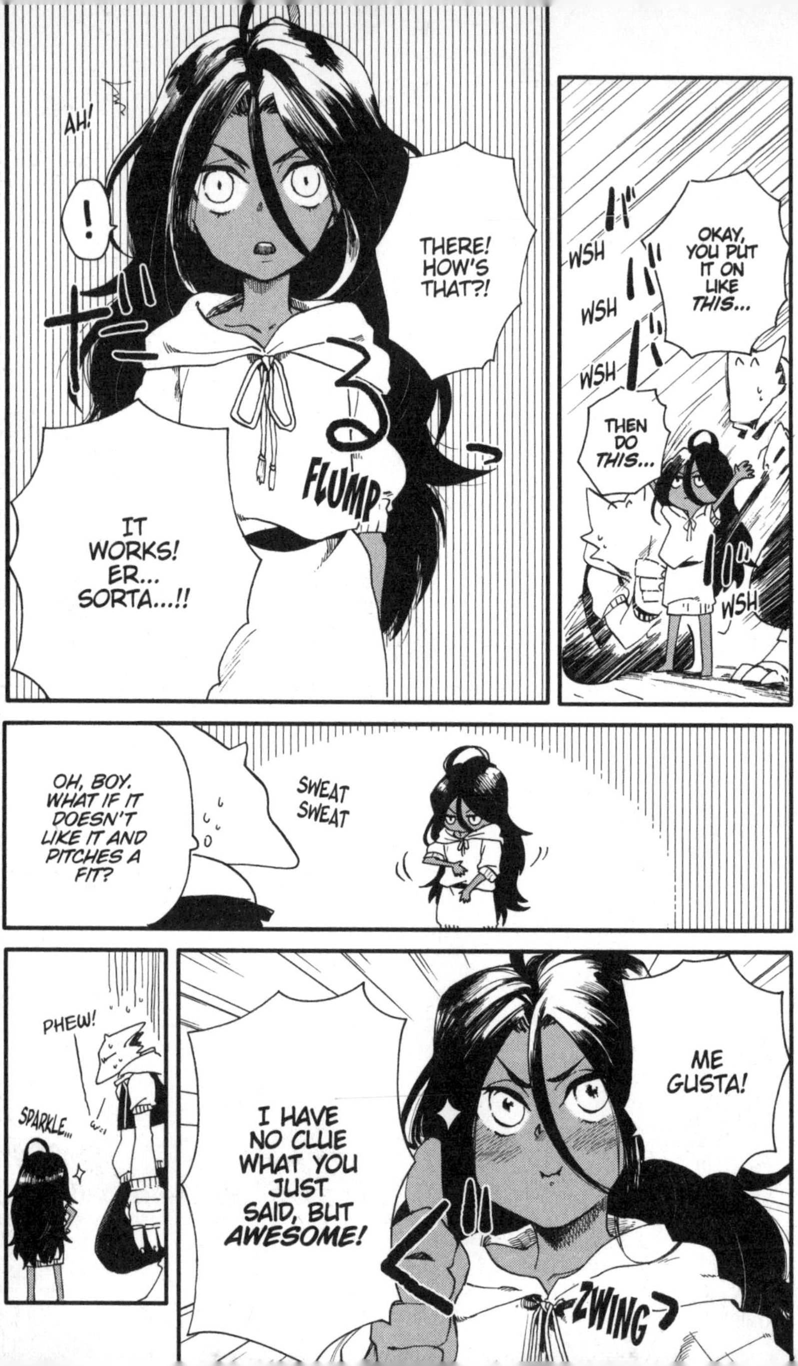
OKAY, YOU PUT IT ON LIKE THIS...
WSH
WSH
WSH
THEN DO THIS...
WSH
THERE! HOW'S THAT?!
AH!
!
FLUMP
IT WORKS! ER... SORTA...!!
SWEAT SWEAT
OH, BOY. WHAT IF IT DOESN'T LIKE IT AND PITCHES A FIT?
ME GUSTA!
I HAVE NO CLUE WHAT YOU JUST SAID, BUT AWESOME!
ZWING
PHEW!
SPARKLE...

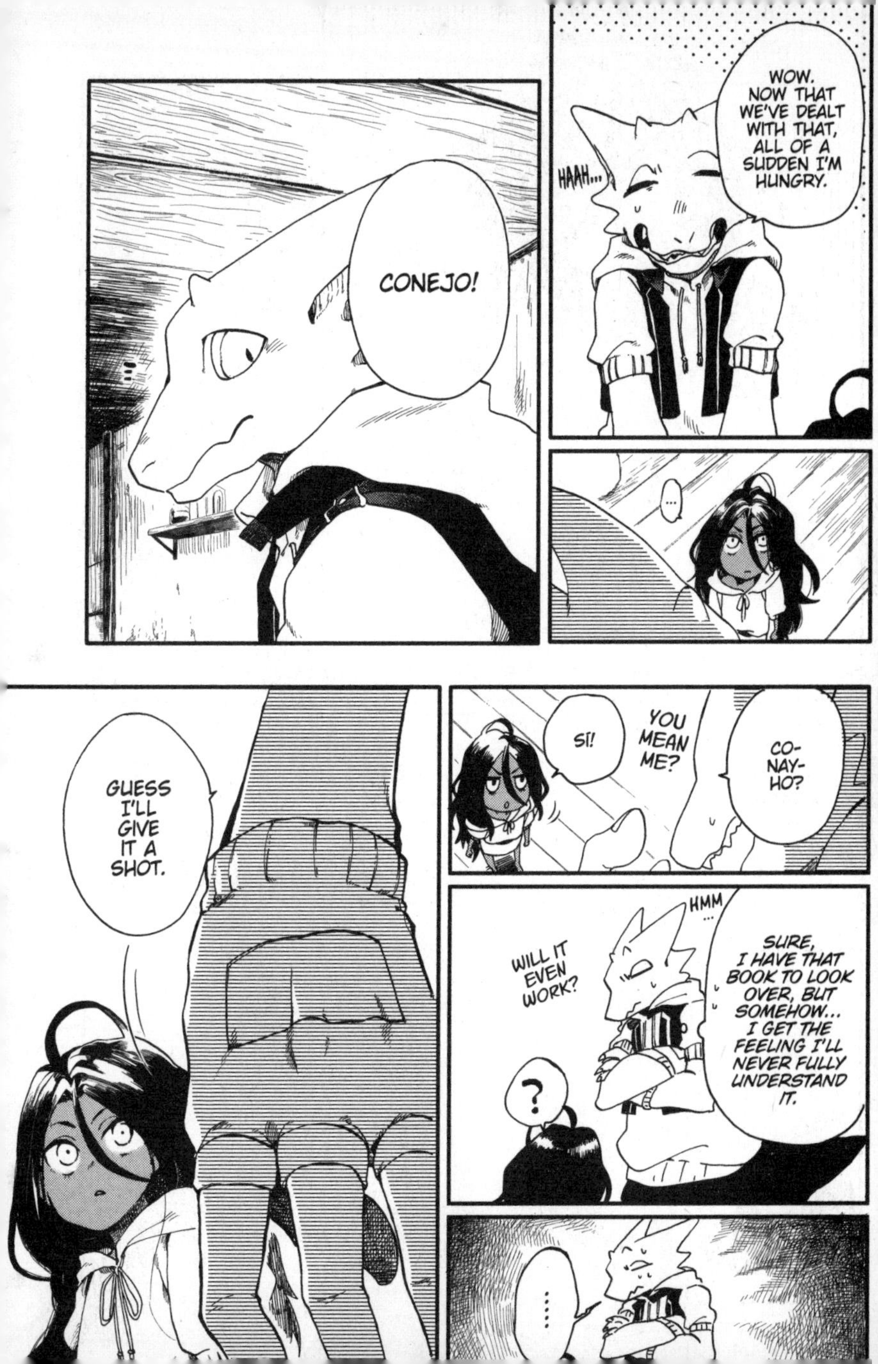
WOW. NOW THAT WE'VE DEALT WITH THAT, ALL OF A SUDDEN I'M HUNGRY.
HAAH...
...
CONEJO!
CO-NAY-HO?
YOU MEAN ME?
SÍ!
HMM...
SURE, I HAVE THAT BOOK TO LOOK OVER, BUT SOMEHOW... I GET THE FEELING I'LL NEVER FULLY UNDERSTAND IT.
WILL IT EVEN WORK?
?
.....
GUESS I'LL GIVE IT A SHOT.

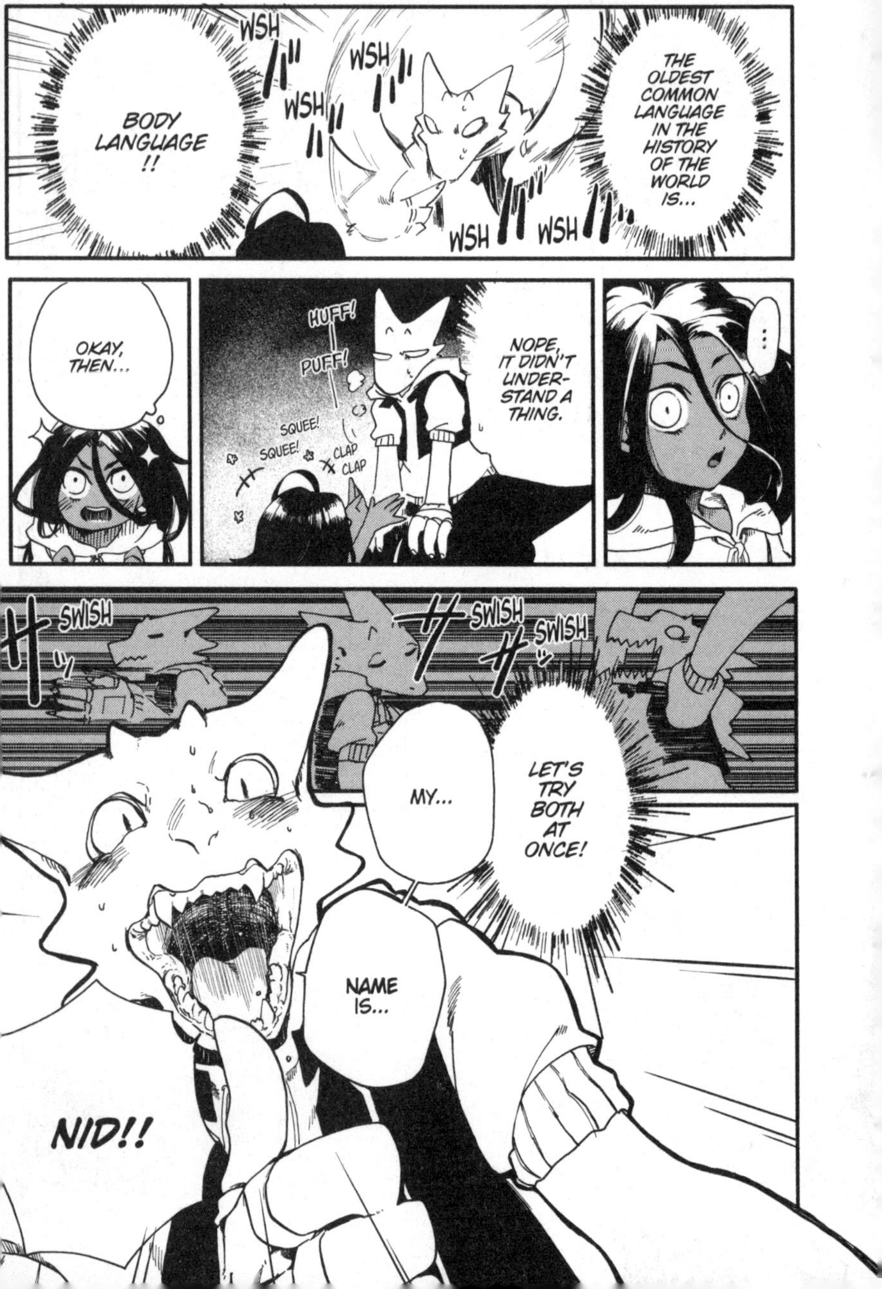
THE OLDEST COMMON LANGUAGE IN THE HISTORY OF THE WORLD IS...
WSH WSH
WSH
WSH
WSH
BODY LANGUAGE!!
...
NOPE, IT DIDN'T UNDERSTAND A THING.
HUFF! PUFF!
SQUEE! SQUEE!
CLAP CLAP
OKAY, THEN...
SWISH
SWISH
SWISH
LET'S TRY BOTH AT ONCE!
MY...
NAME IS...
NID!!

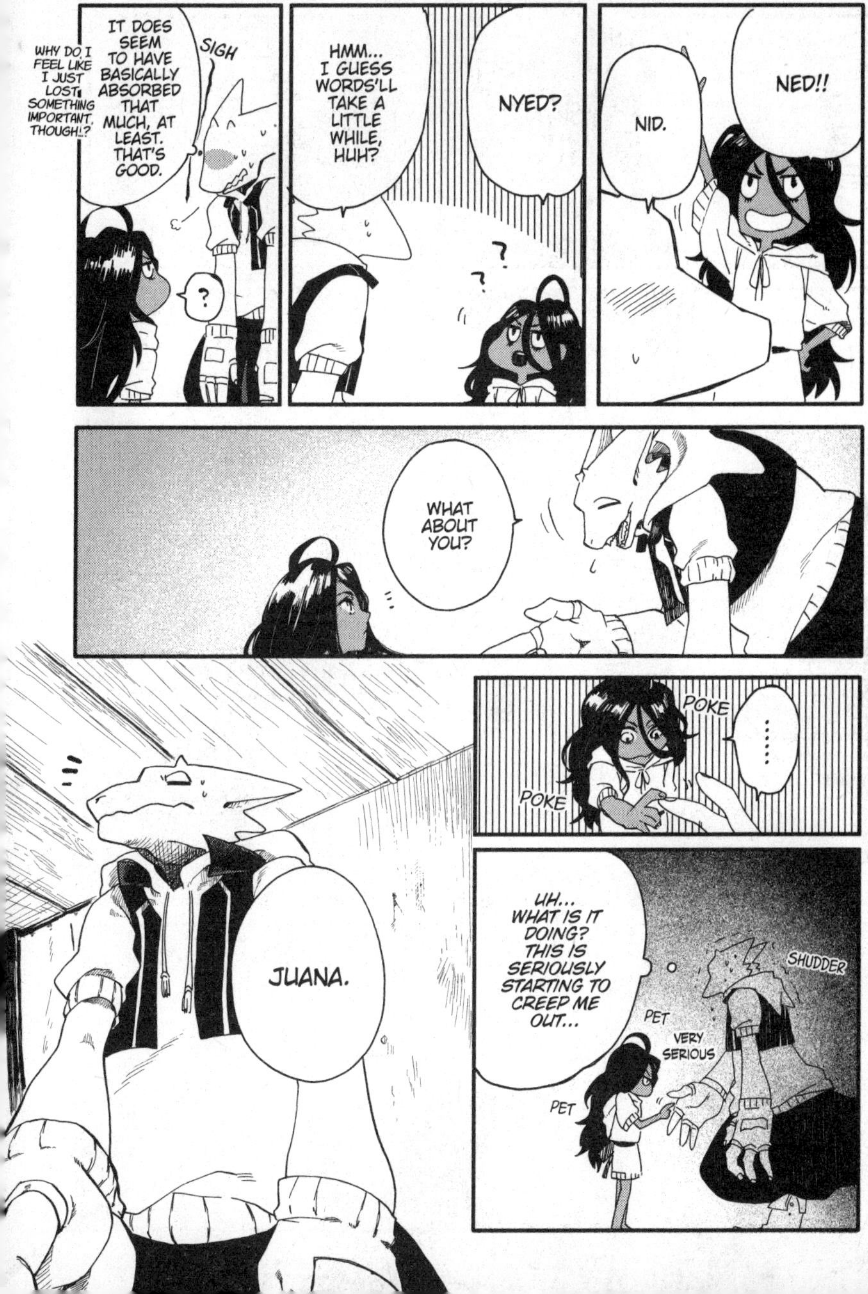

NED!!
NID.
NYED?
HMM... I GUESS WORDS'LL TAKE A LITTLE WHILE, HUH?
?
?
SIGH
IT DOES SEEM TO HAVE BASICALLY ABSORBED THAT MUCH, AT LEAST. THAT'S GOOD.
WHY DO I FEEL LIKE I JUST LOST SOMETHING IMPORTANT, THOUGH!!?
?
WHAT ABOUT YOU?
......
POKE
POKE
SHUDDER
UH... WHAT IS IT DOING? THIS IS SERIOUSLY STARTING TO CREEP ME OUT...
PET
VERY SERIOUS
PET
JUANA.

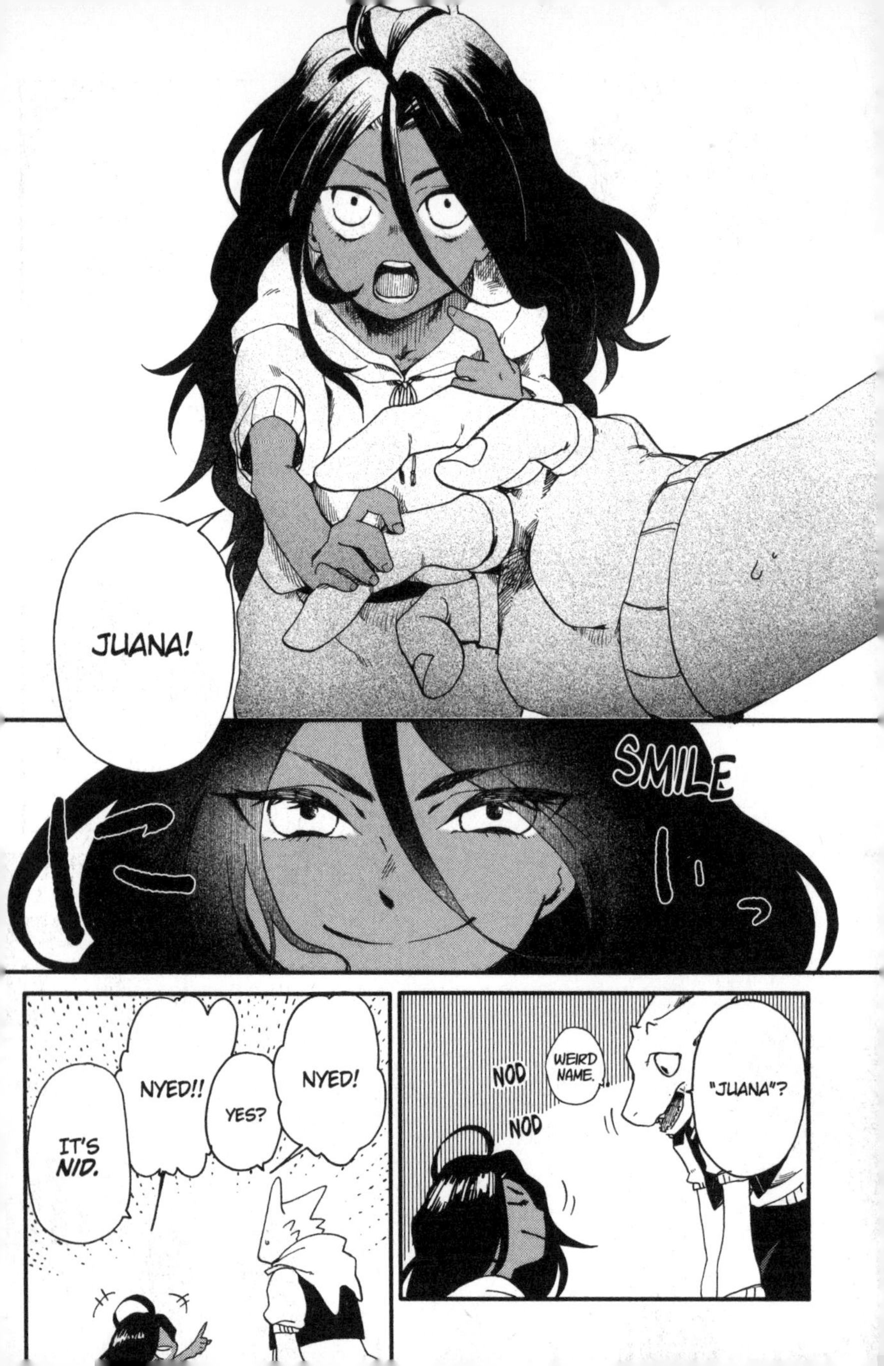
JUANA!
SMILE
"JUANA"?
NOD
NOD
WEIRD NAME.
NYED!
YES?
NYED!!
IT'S NID.

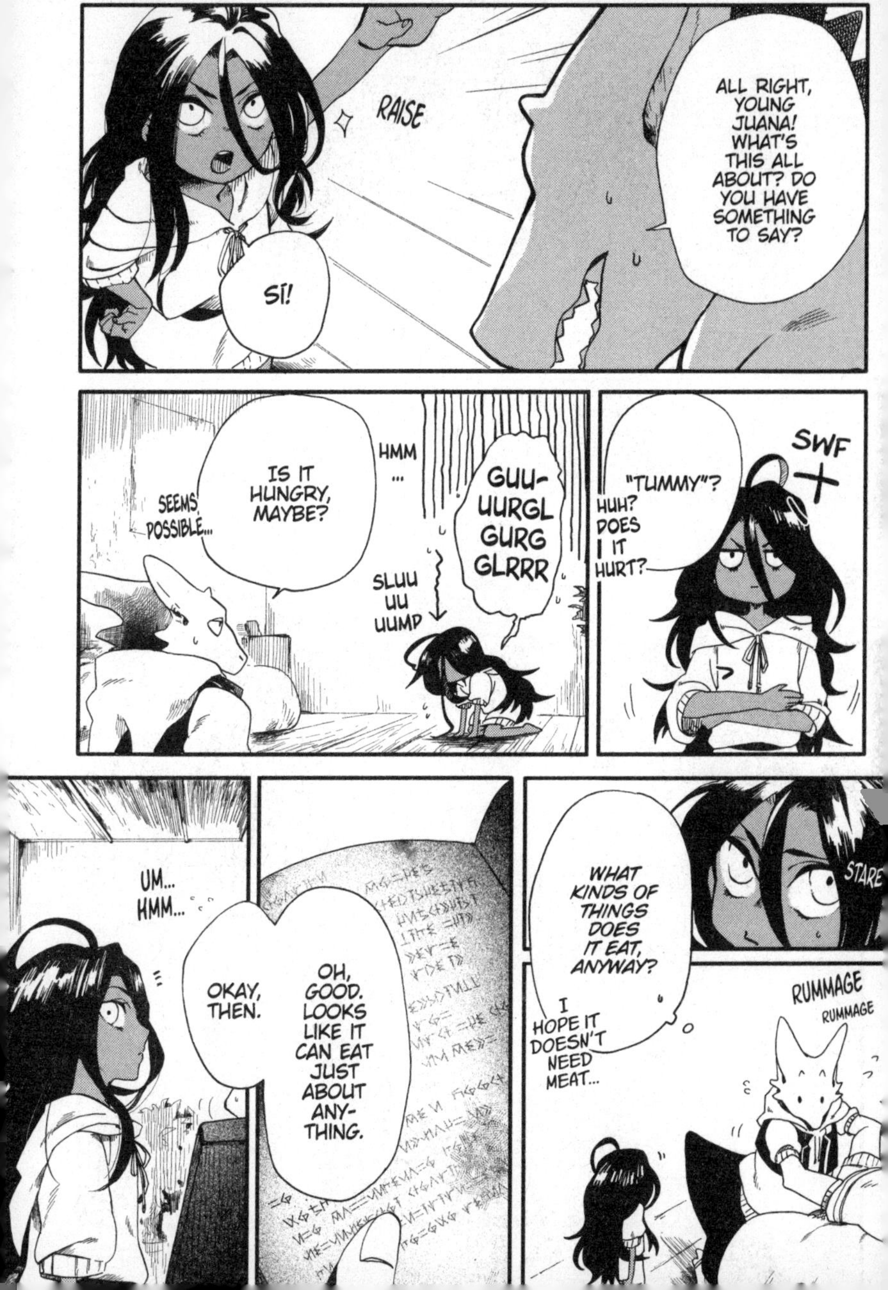
ALL RIGHT, YOUNG JUANA! WHAT'S THIS ALL ABOUT? DO YOU HAVE SOMETHING TO SAY?
RAISE
SÍ!
SWF
"TUMMY"?
HUH? DOES IT HURT?
HMM ...
GUU-UURGL GURG GLRRR
SLUU UU UUMP
IS IT HUNGRY, MAYBE?
SEEMS POSSIBLE...
STARE
WHAT KINDS OF THINGS DOES IT EAT, ANYWAY?
RUMMAGE
RUMMAGE
I HOPE IT DOESN'T NEED MEAT...
OH, GOOD. LOOKS LIKE IT CAN EAT JUST ABOUT ANY-THING.
OKAY, THEN.
UM... HMM...

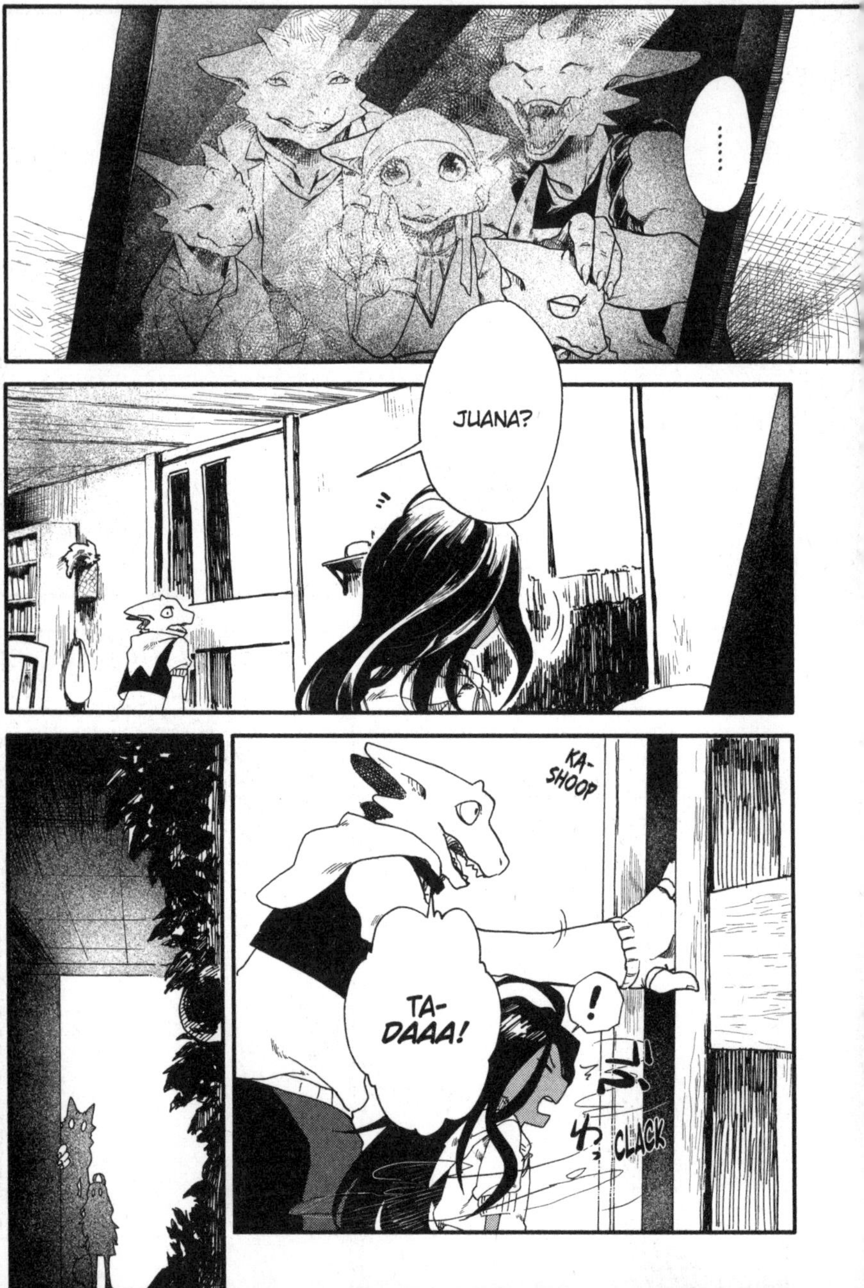
......
JUANA?
KA-SHOOP
TA-DAAA!
!
CLACK

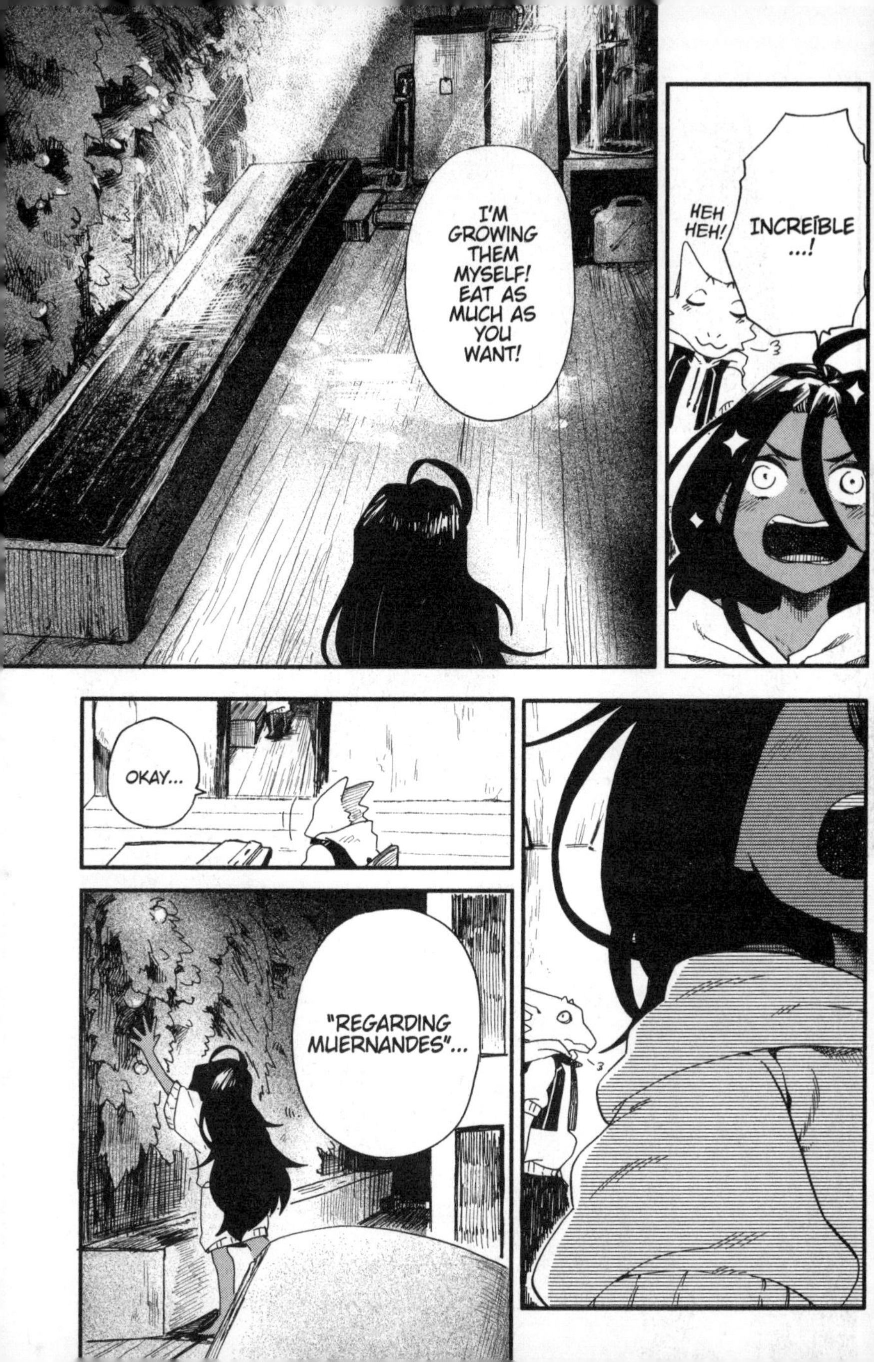
INCREÍBLE ...!
HEH HEH!
I'M GROWING THEM MYSELF! EAT AS MUCH AS YOU WANT!
OKAY...
"REGARDING MUERNANDES"...

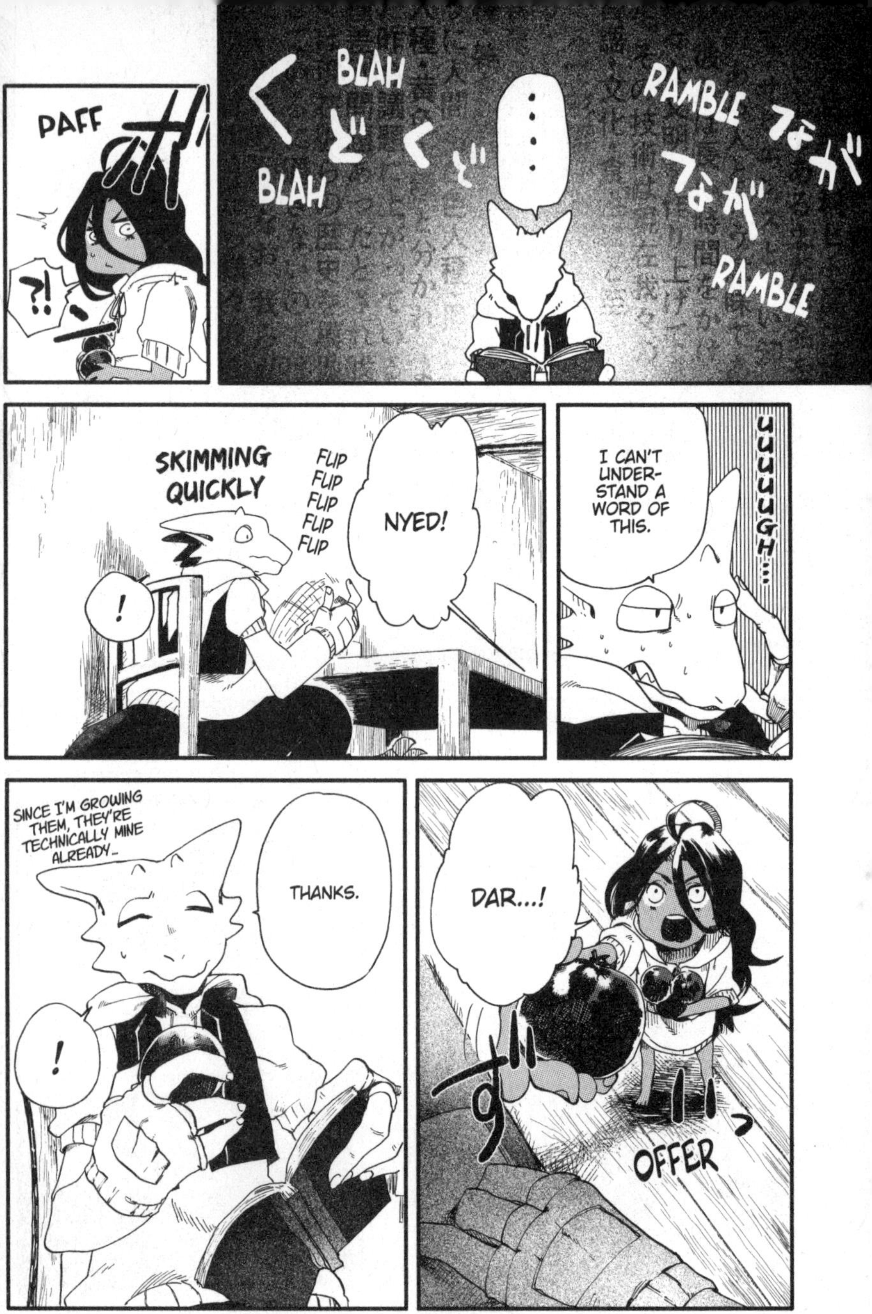
…
RAMBLE ながなが RAMBLE
くどくど
BLAH BLAH
PAFF
?!
UUUUUGH…
I CAN'T UNDER-STAND A WORD OF THIS.
NYED!
FLIP FLIP FLIP FLIP FLIP
SKIMMING QUICKLY
!
DAR…!
OFFER
THANKS.
SINCE I'M GROWING THEM, THEY'RE TECHNICALLY MINE ALREADY…
!

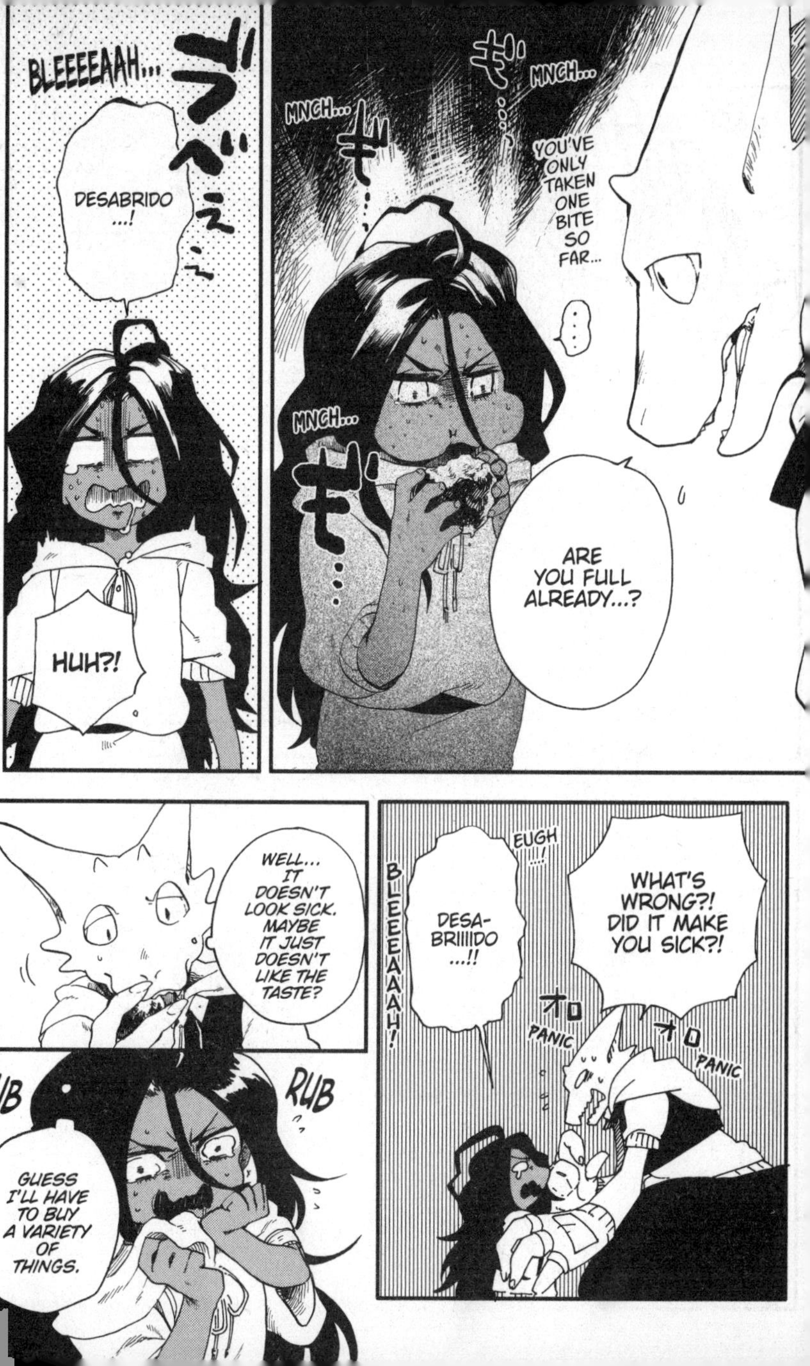
ぎ…
MNCH...
YOU'VE ONLY TAKEN ONE BITE SO FAR...
...
MNCH...
ぎ…
MNCH...
ぎ…
ARE YOU FULL ALREADY...?
BLEEEEAAH...
DESABRIDO ...!
HUH?!
WHAT'S WRONG?! DID IT MAKE YOU SICK?!
EUGH ...!
DESA-BRIIIIDO ...!!
BLEEEEAAAH!
PANIC
PANIC
WELL... IT DOESN'T LOOK SICK. MAYBE IT JUST DOESN'T LIKE THE TASTE?
RUB
RUB
GUESS I'LL HAVE TO BUY A VARIETY OF THINGS.

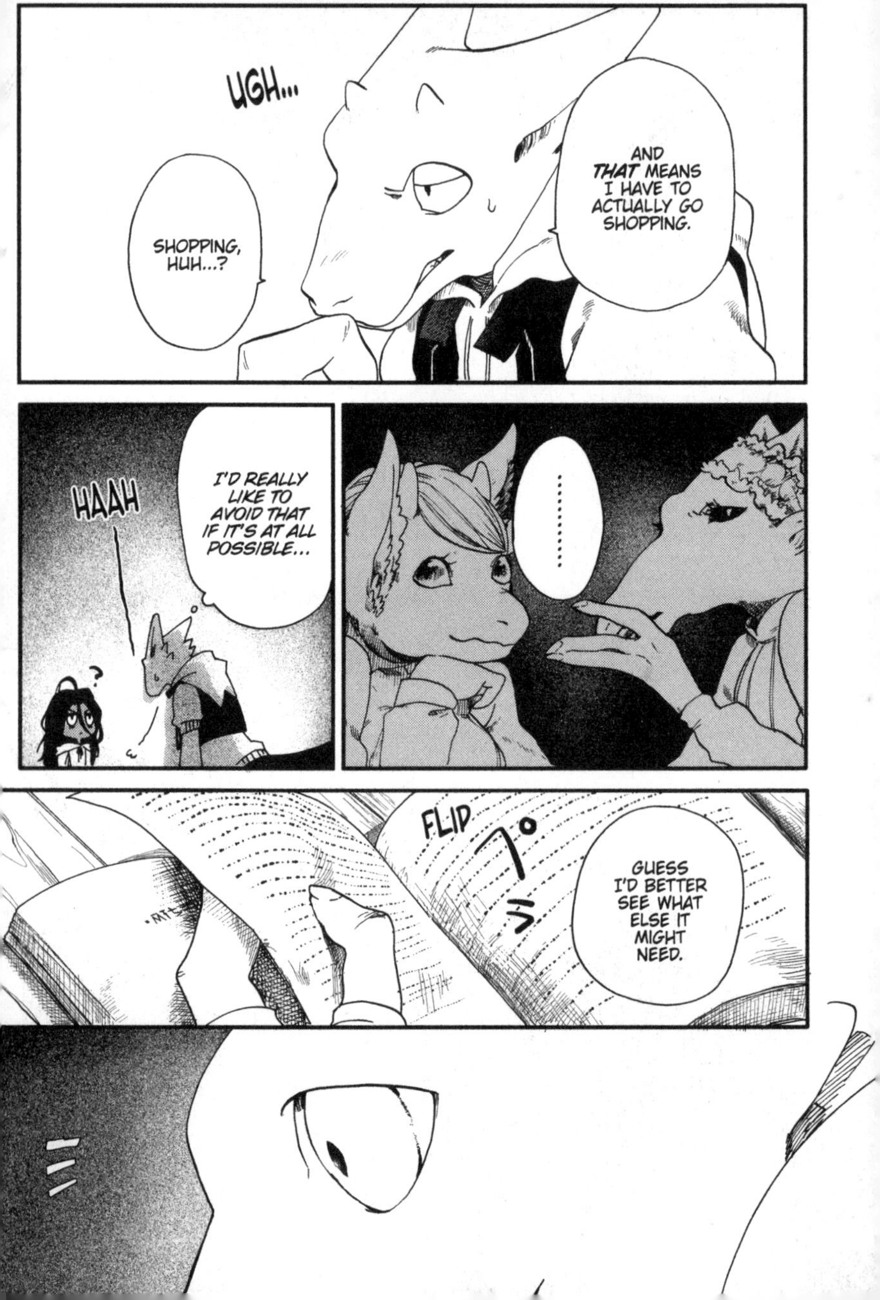
AND THAT MEANS I HAVE TO ACTUALLY GO SHOPPING.
UGH...
SHOPPING, HUH...?
......
I'D REALLY LIKE TO AVOID THAT IF IT'S AT ALL POSSIBLE...
HAAH
GUESS I'D BETTER SEE WHAT ELSE IT MIGHT NEED.
FLIP

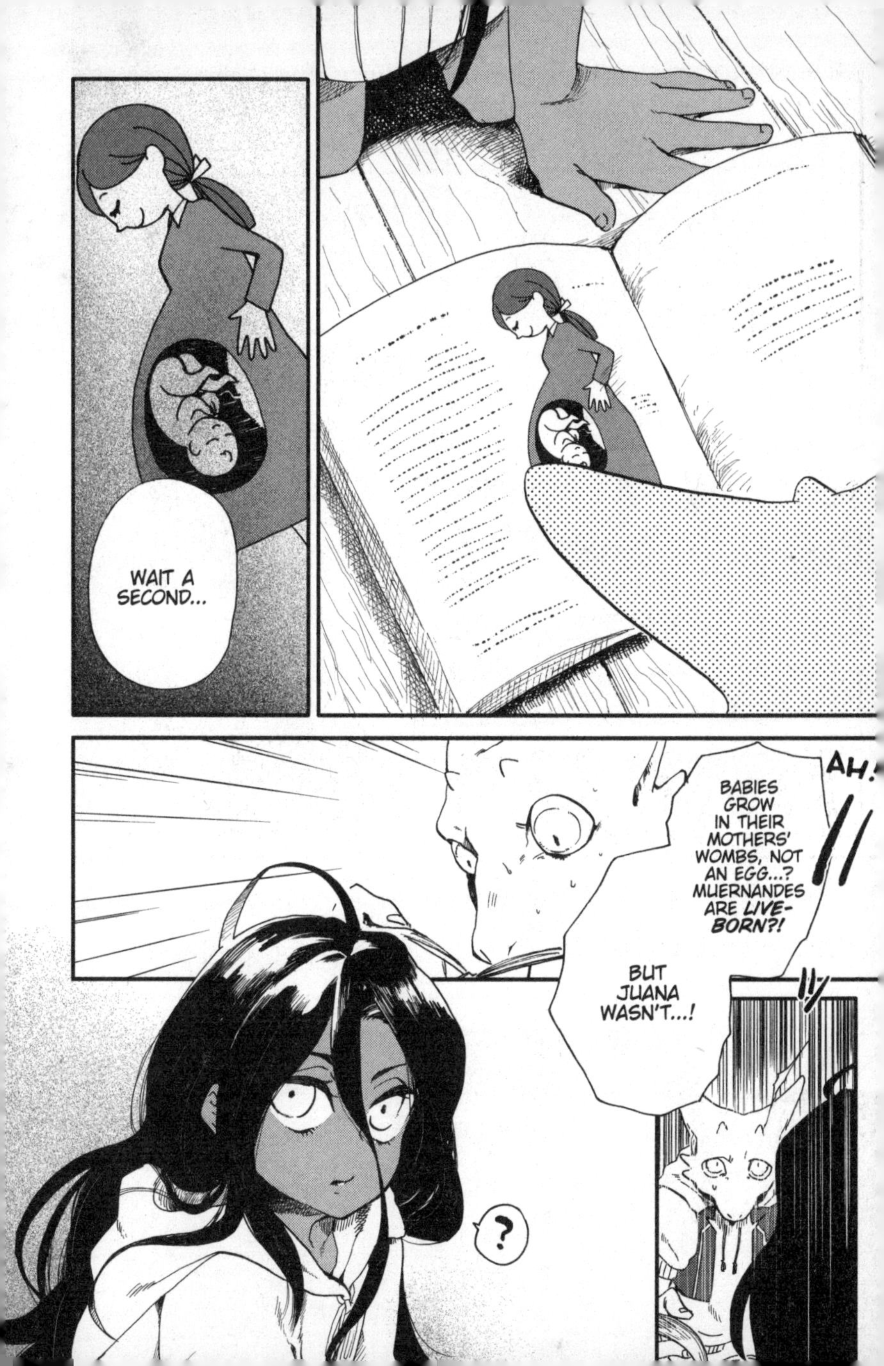
WAIT A SECOND...
AH!
BABIES GROW IN THEIR MOTHERS' WOMBS, NOT AN EGG...? MUERNANDES ARE *LIVE-BORN*?!
BUT JUANA WASN'T...!
?

KRAK

KRIIK

KRIK

I COULD'VE SWORN...

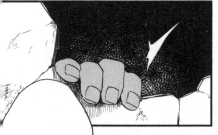

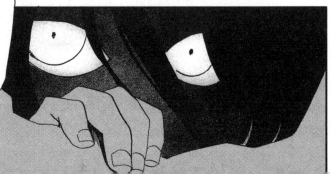

THAT I SAW IT *HATCH* ...!

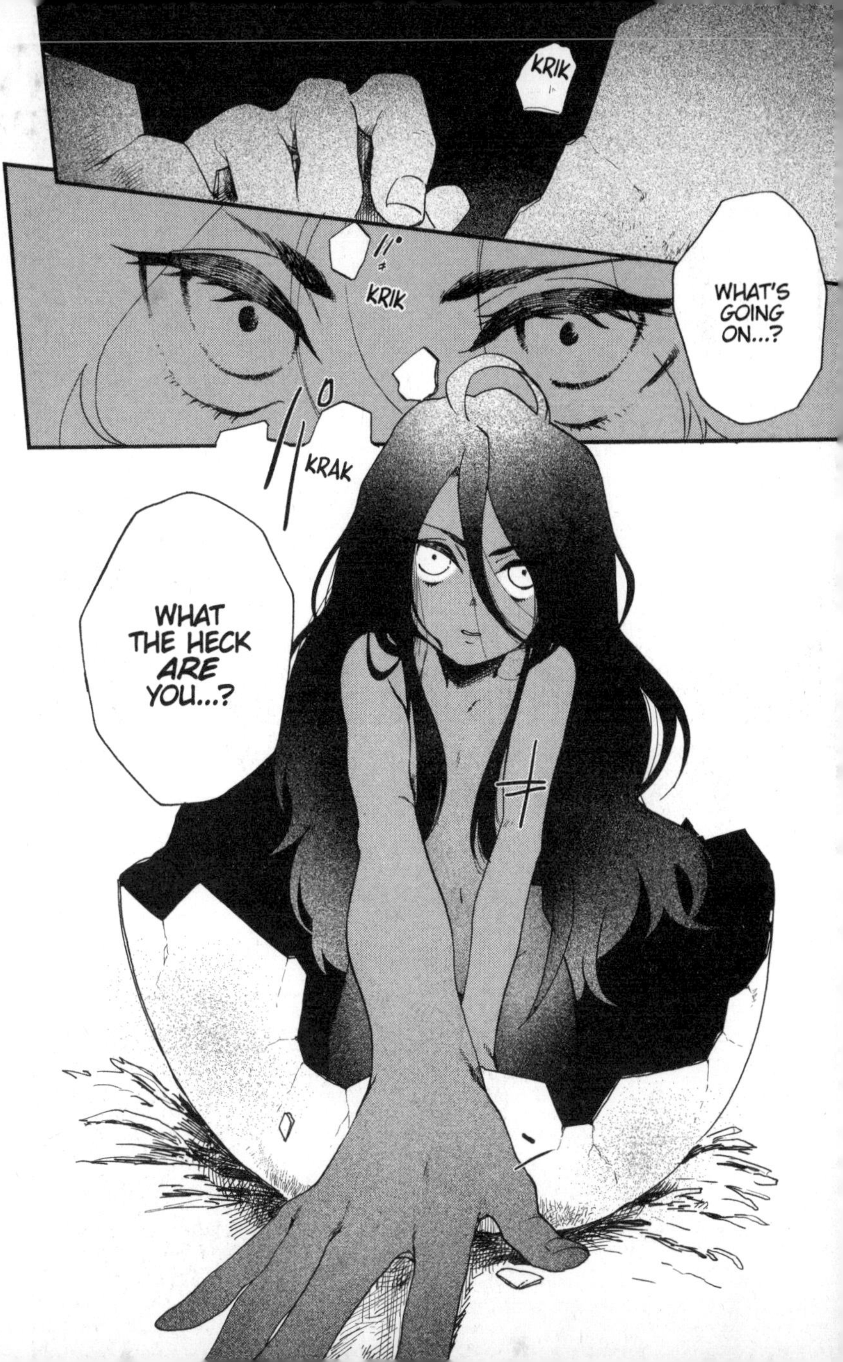
KRIK
WHAT'S GOING ON...?
KRIK
KRAK
WHAT THE HECK ARE YOU...?

Juana and the Dragonewts' Seven Kingdoms

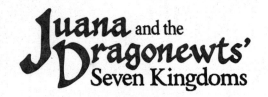

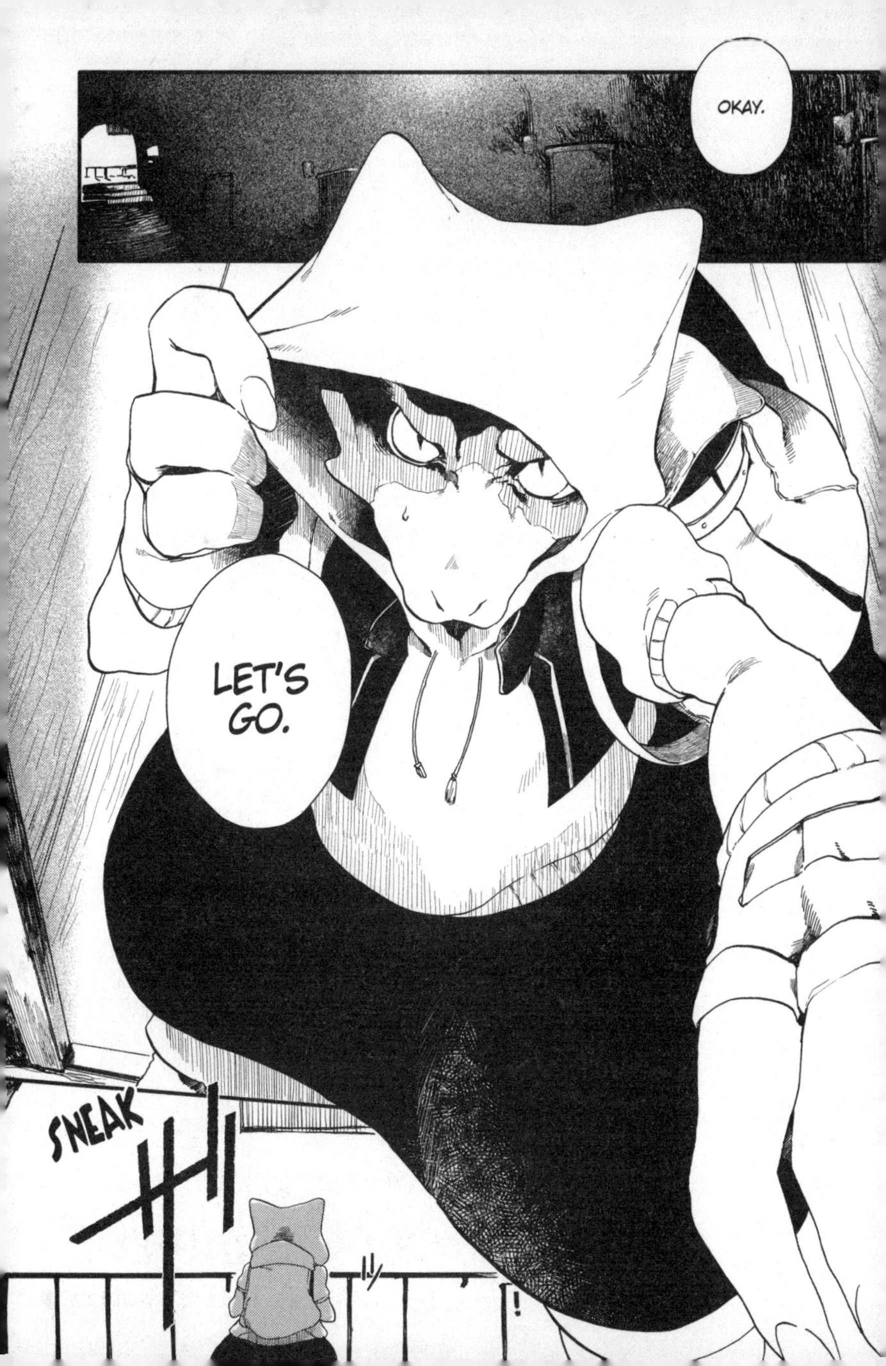
OKAY.
LET'S GO.
SNEAK
!!
!

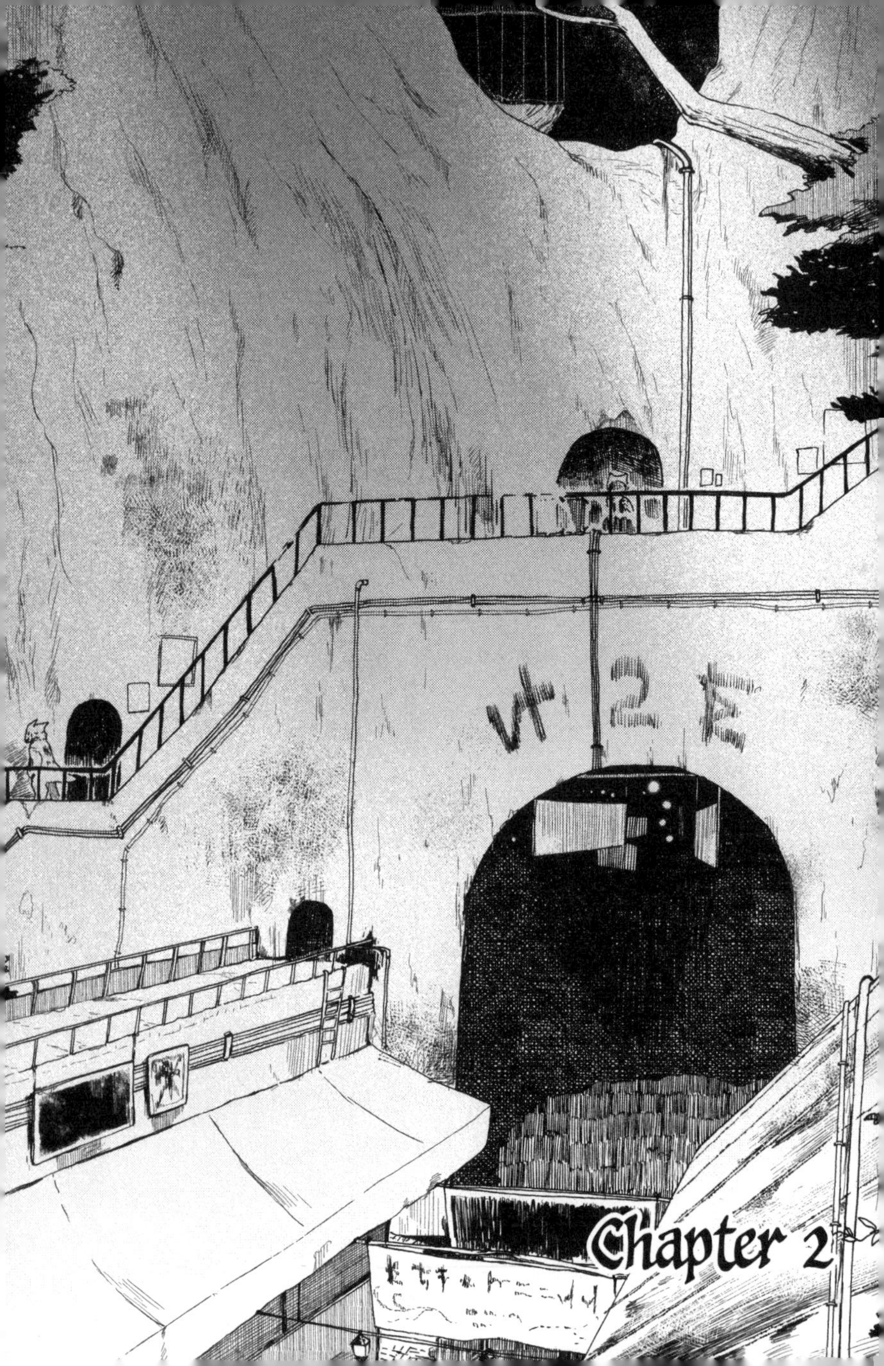
Chapter 2

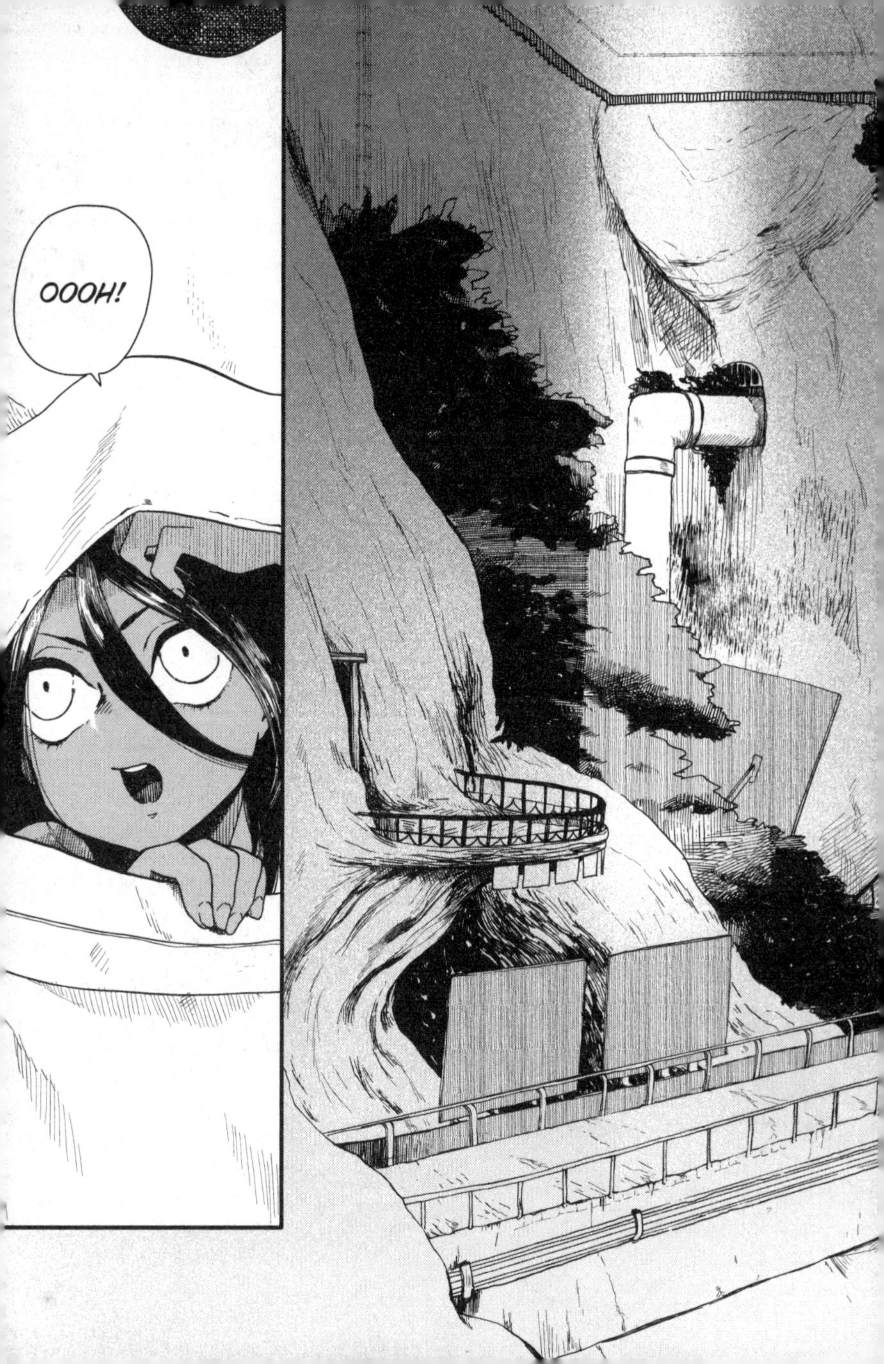
OOOH!

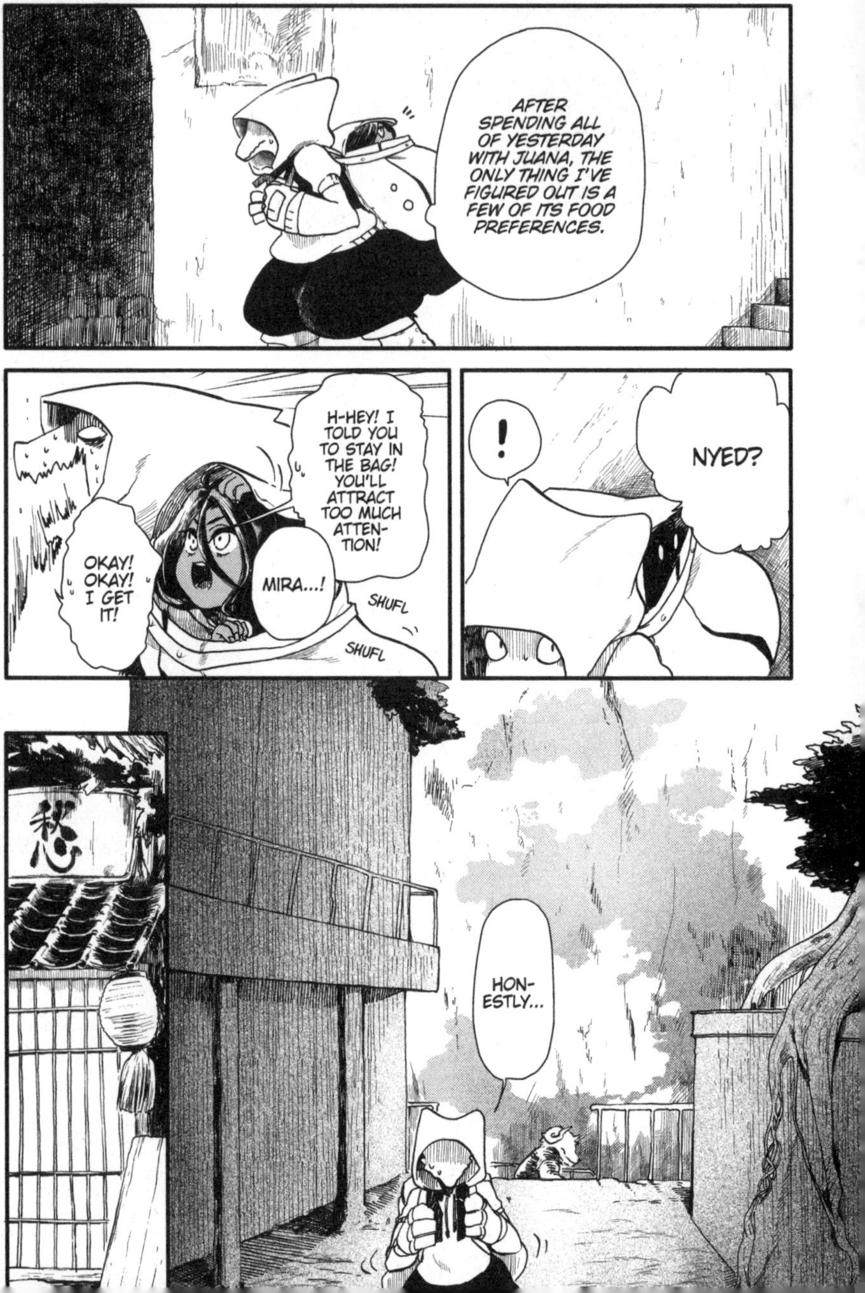
AFTER SPENDING ALL OF YESTERDAY WITH JUANA, THE ONLY THING I'VE FIGURED OUT IS A FEW OF ITS FOOD PREFERENCES.
NYED?
!
H-HEY! I TOLD YOU TO STAY IN THE BAG! YOU'LL ATTRACT TOO MUCH ATTEN-TION!
MIRA...!
SHUFL
SHUFL
OKAY! OKAY! I GET IT!
HON-ESTLY...

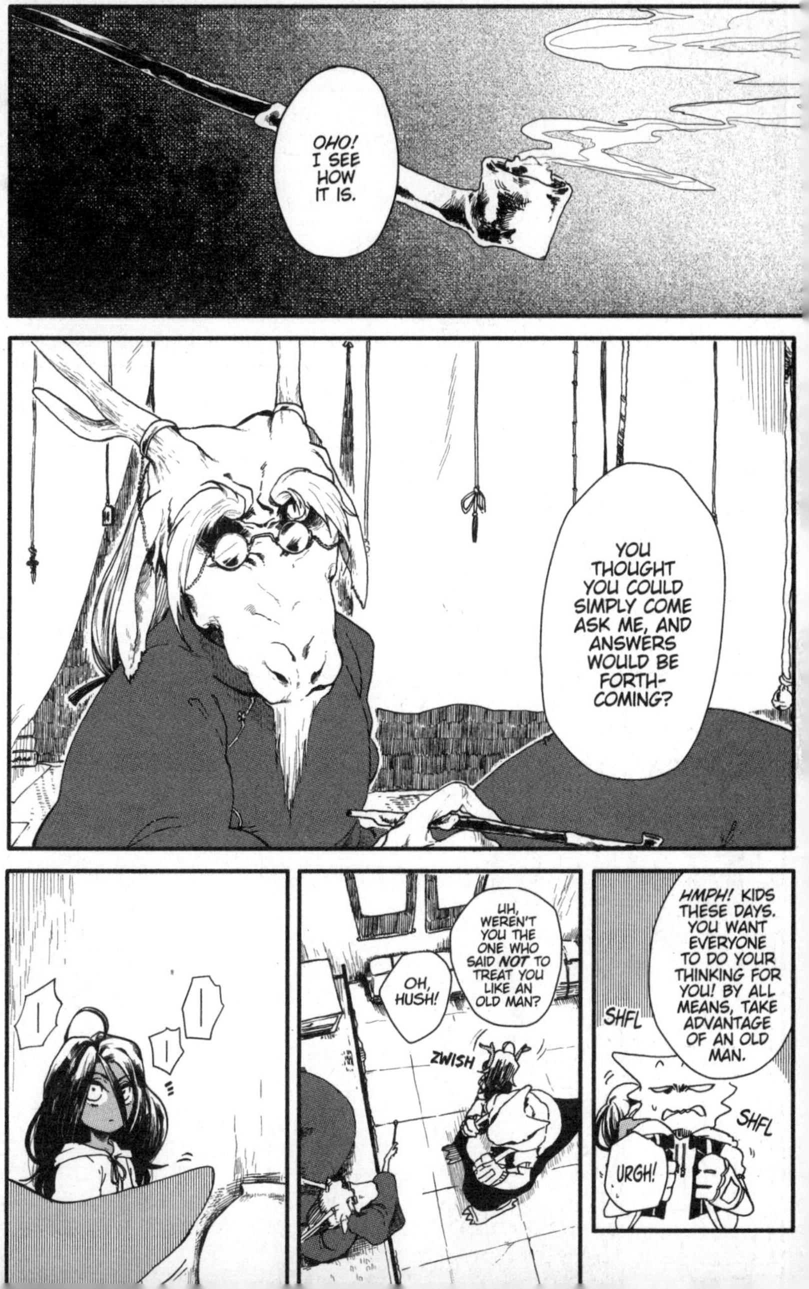
OHO! I SEE HOW IT IS.
YOU THOUGHT YOU COULD SIMPLY COME ASK ME, AND ANSWERS WOULD BE FORTH-COMING?
HMPH! KIDS THESE DAYS. YOU WANT EVERYONE TO DO YOUR THINKING FOR YOU! BY ALL MEANS, TAKE ADVANTAGE OF AN OLD MAN.
SHFL
SHFL
URGH!
UH, WEREN'T YOU THE ONE WHO SAID NOT TO TREAT YOU LIKE AN OLD MAN?
OH, HUSH!
ZWISH

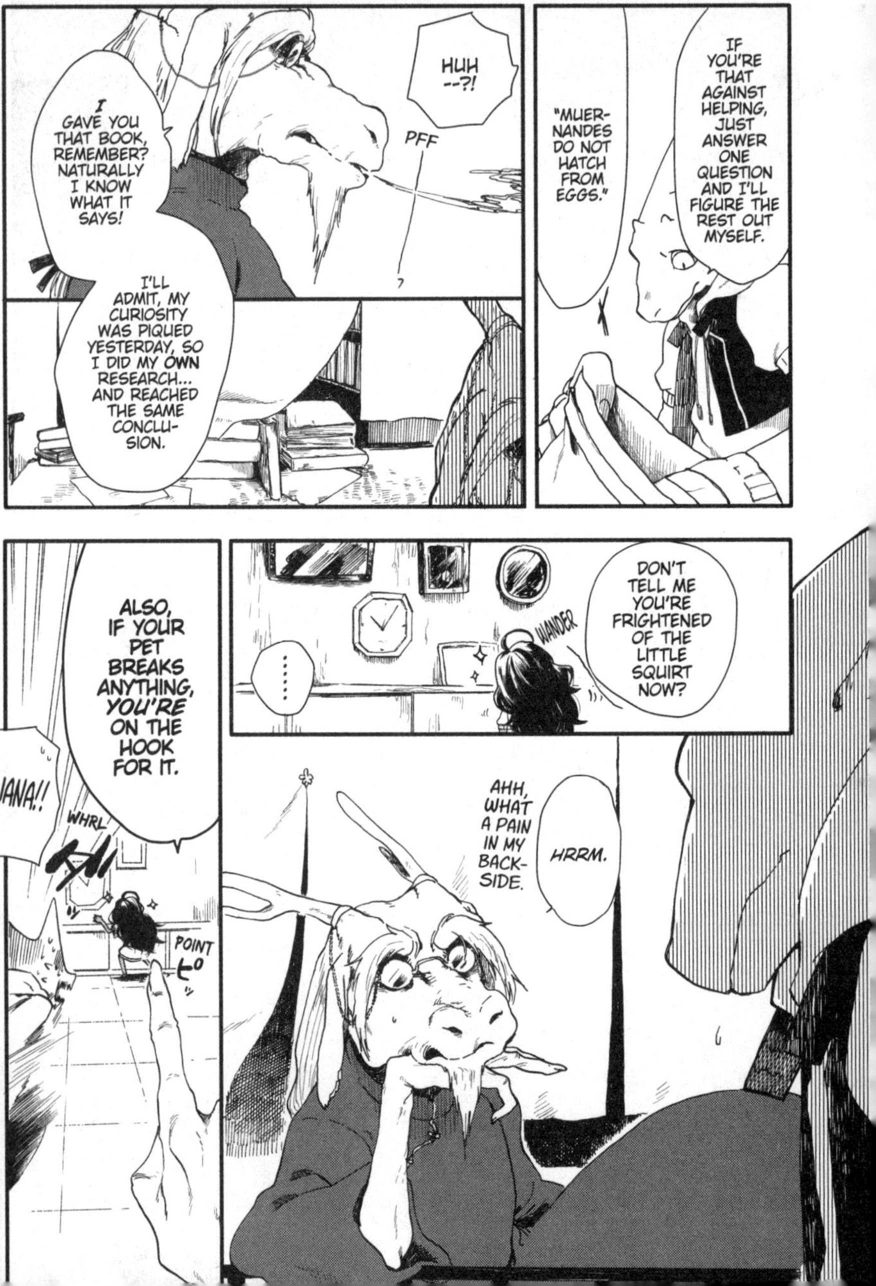
IF YOU'RE THAT AGAINST HELPING, JUST ANSWER ONE QUESTION AND I'LL FIGURE THE REST OUT MYSELF.
"MUER-NANDES DO NOT HATCH FROM EGGS."
HUH --?!
PFF
I GAVE YOU THAT BOOK, REMEMBER? NATURALLY I KNOW WHAT IT SAYS!
I'LL ADMIT, MY CURIOSITY WAS PIQUED YESTERDAY, SO I DID MY OWN RESEARCH... AND REACHED THE SAME CONCLU-SION.
DON'T TELL ME YOU'RE FRIGHTENED OF THE LITTLE SQUIRT NOW?
WANDER
......
AHH, WHAT A PAIN IN MY BACK-SIDE.
HRRM.
ALSO, IF YOUR PET BREAKS ANYTHING, YOU'RE ON THE HOOK FOR IT.
JANA!!
WHRL
POINT

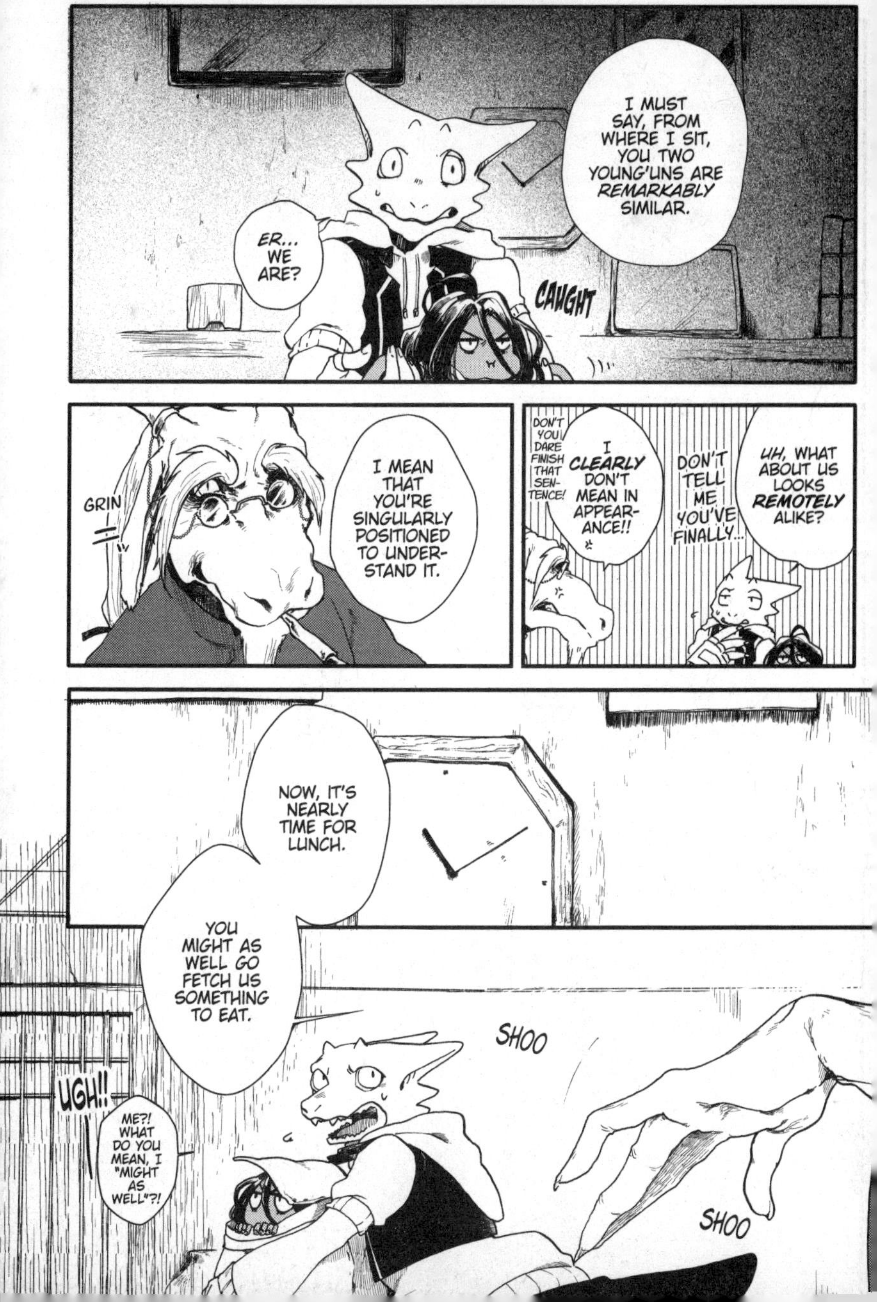
I MUST SAY, FROM WHERE I SIT, YOU TWO YOUNG'UNS ARE *REMARKABLY* SIMILAR.
ER... WE ARE?
CAUGHT
UH, WHAT ABOUT US LOOKS *REMOTELY* ALIKE?
DON'T TELL ME YOU'VE FINALLY...
I *CLEARLY* DON'T MEAN IN APPEARANCE!!
DON'T YOU DARE FINISH THAT SENTENCE!
I MEAN THAT YOU'RE SINGULARLY POSITIONED TO UNDERSTAND IT.
GRIN
NOW, IT'S NEARLY TIME FOR LUNCH.
YOU MIGHT AS WELL GO FETCH US SOMETHING TO EAT.
SHOO
UGH!!
ME?! WHAT DO YOU MEAN, I "MIGHT AS WELL"?!
SHOO

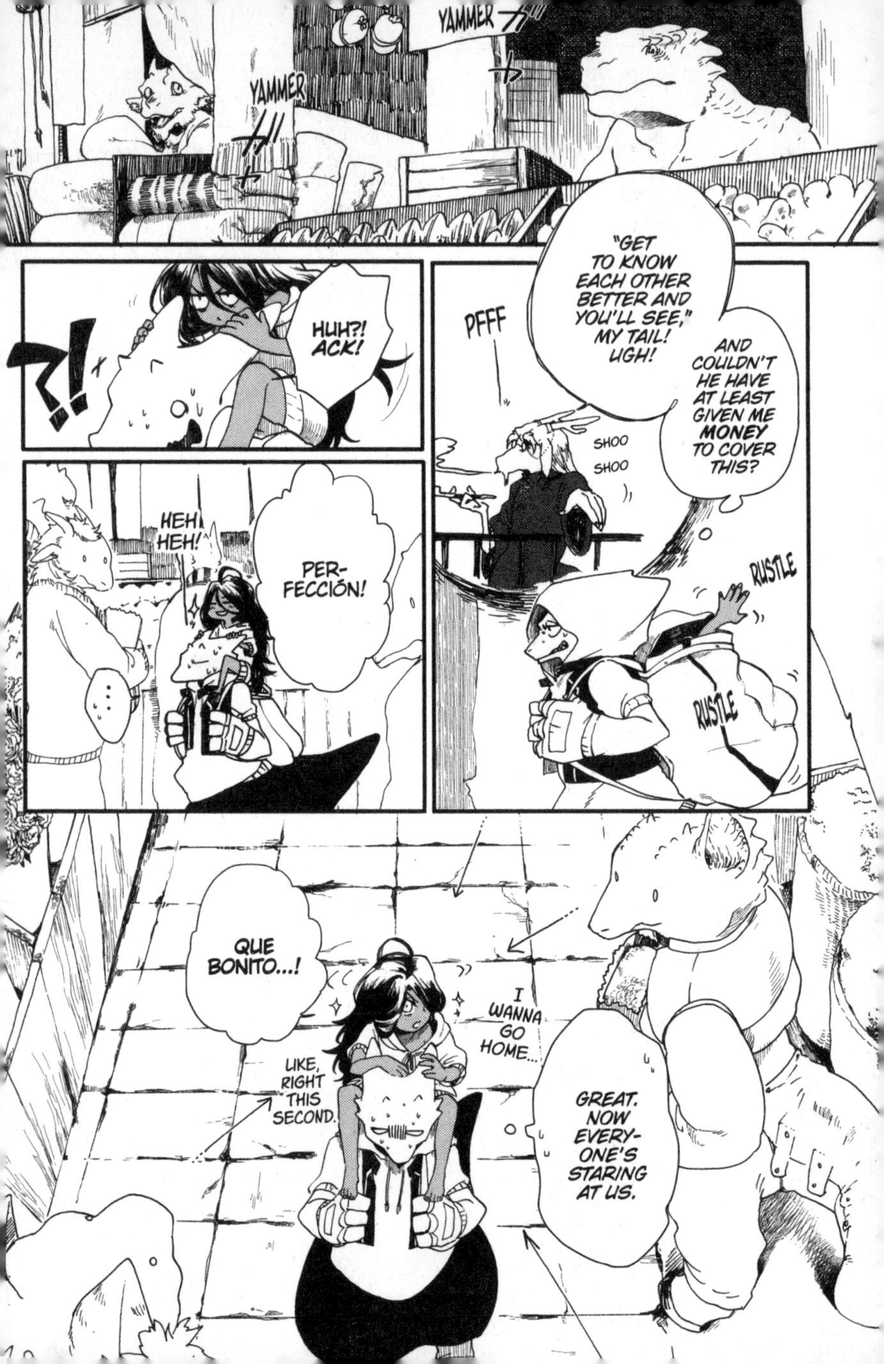
YAMMER
YAMMER
"GET TO KNOW EACH OTHER BETTER AND YOU'LL SEE," MY TAIL! UGH!
AND COULDN'T HE HAVE AT LEAST GIVEN ME MONEY TO COVER THIS?
PFFF
SHOO SHOO
RUSTLE
RUSTLE
HUH?! ACK!
?!!
PER-FECCIÓN!
HEH HEH!
GREAT. NOW EVERY-ONE'S STARING AT US.
I WANNA GO HOME...
LIKE, RIGHT THIS SECOND.
QUE BONITO...!

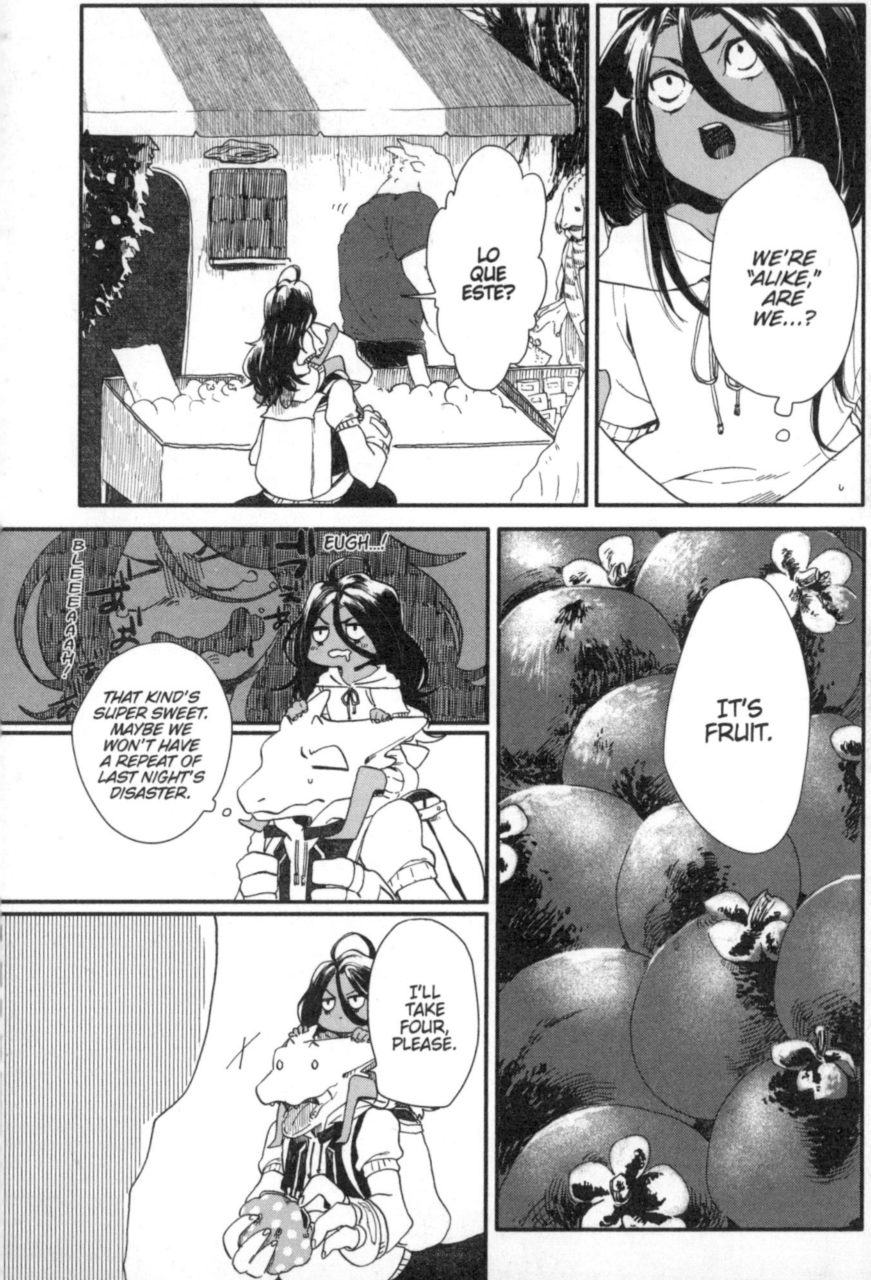
WE'RE "ALIKE," ARE WE...?
LO QUE ESTE?
IT'S FRUIT.
EUGH...!
BLEEEAAAAH!
THAT KIND'S SUPER SWEET. MAYBE WE WON'T HAVE A REPEAT OF LAST NIGHT'S DISASTER.
I'LL TAKE FOUR, PLEASE.

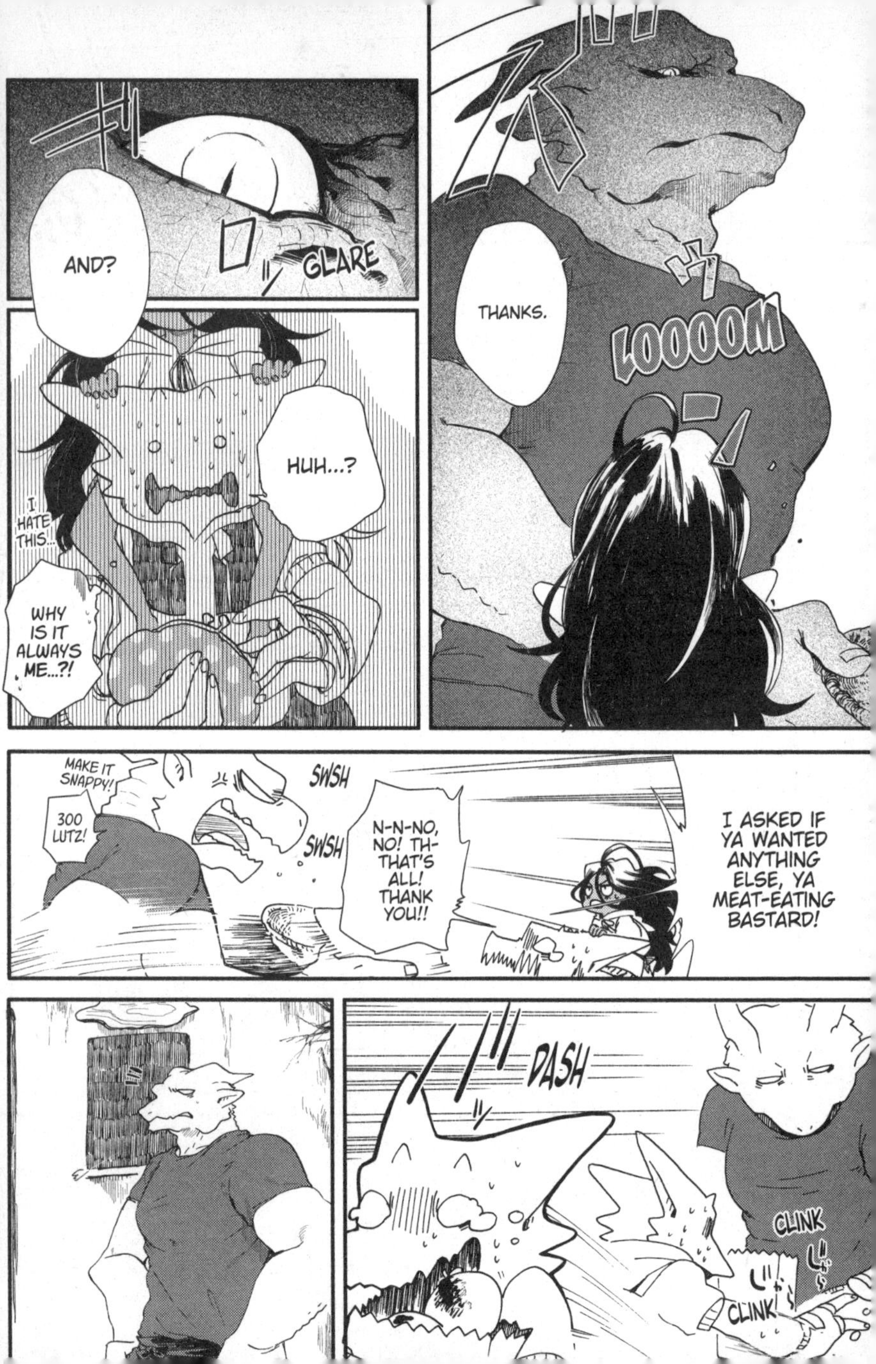
THANKS.
LOOOOM
AND?
GLARE
HUH...?
I HATE THIS...
WHY IS IT ALWAYS ME...?!
I ASKED IF YA WANTED ANYTHING ELSE, YA MEAT-EATING BASTARD!
N-N-NO, NO! TH-THAT'S ALL! THANK YOU!!
SWSH
SWSH
MAKE IT SNAPPY!
300 LUTZ!
DASH
CLINK
CLINK

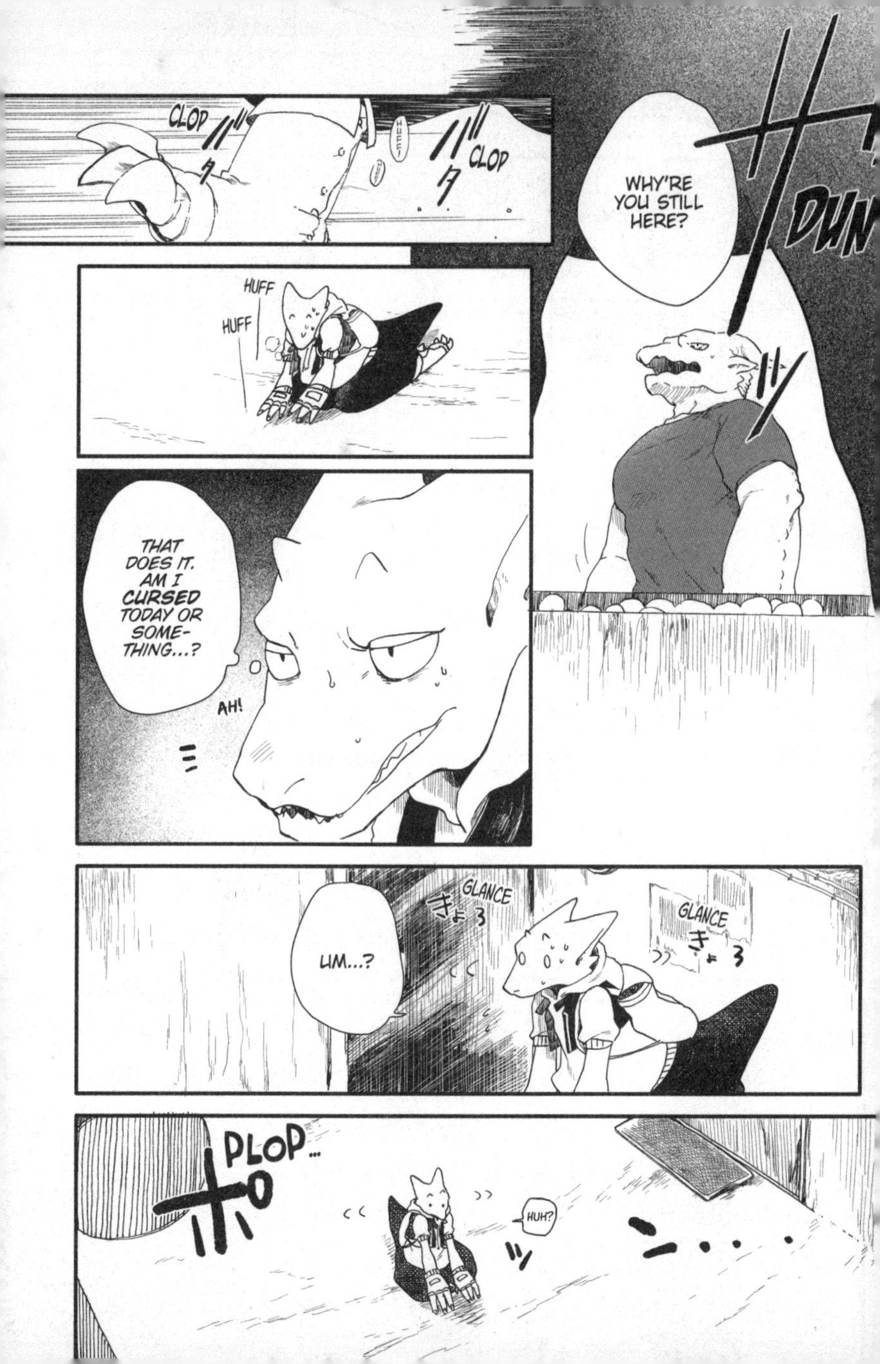
DUN
WHY'RE YOU STILL HERE?
CLOP
HUFF
CLOP
HUFF
HUFF
THAT DOES IT. AM I CURSED TODAY OR SOME-THING...?
AH!
GLANCE
UM...?
GLANCE
HUH?
PLOP...

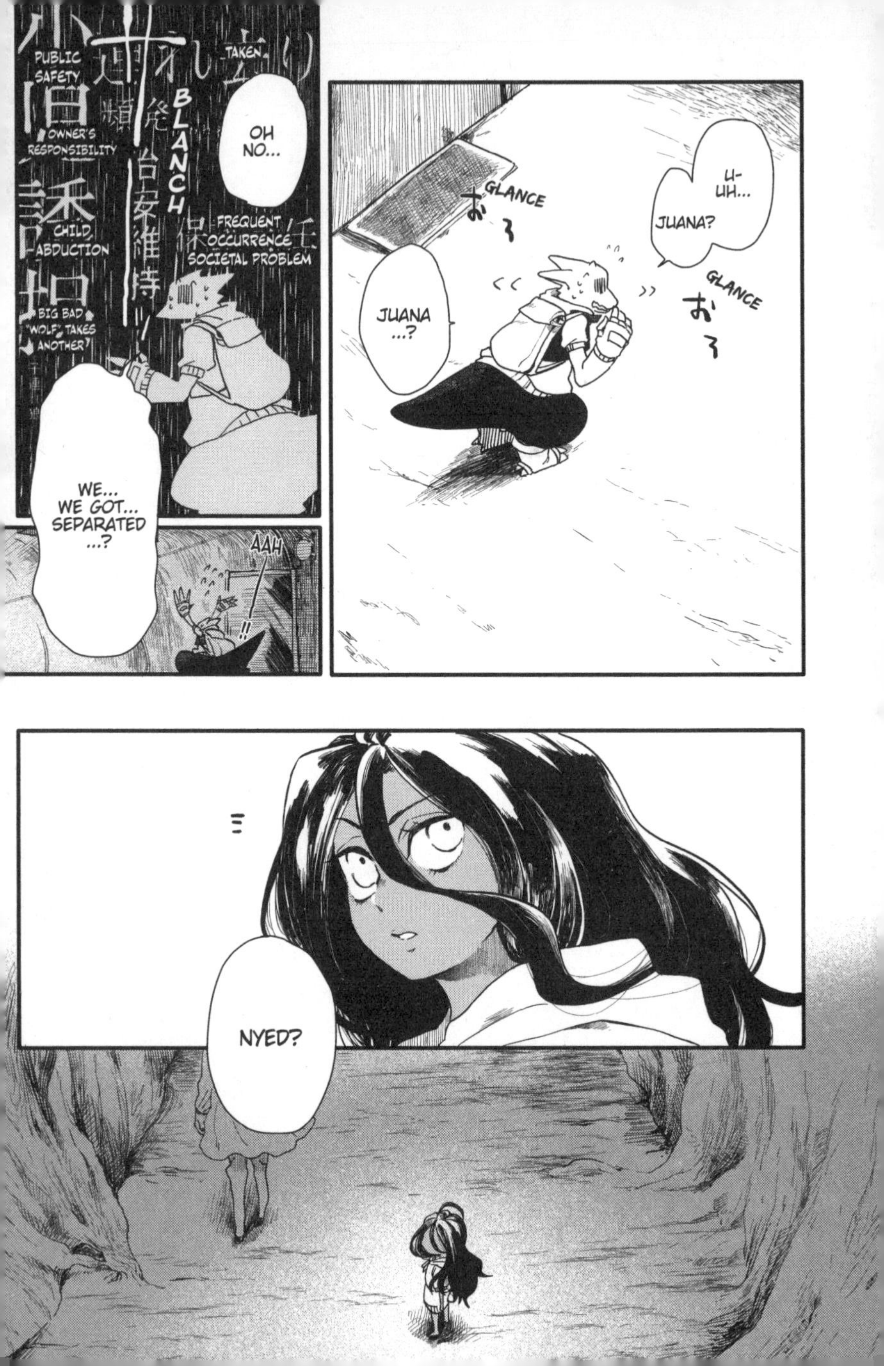
U-UH... JUANA?
GLANCE
GLANCE
JUANA ...?
TAKEN
OH NO...
BLANCH
FREQUENT OCCURRENCE
SOCIETAL PROBLEM
PUBLIC SAFETY
OWNER'S RESPONSIBILITY
CHILD ABDUCTION
BIG BAD "WOLF" TAKES ANOTHER?
WE... WE GOT... SEPARATED ...?
AAH!!
NYED?

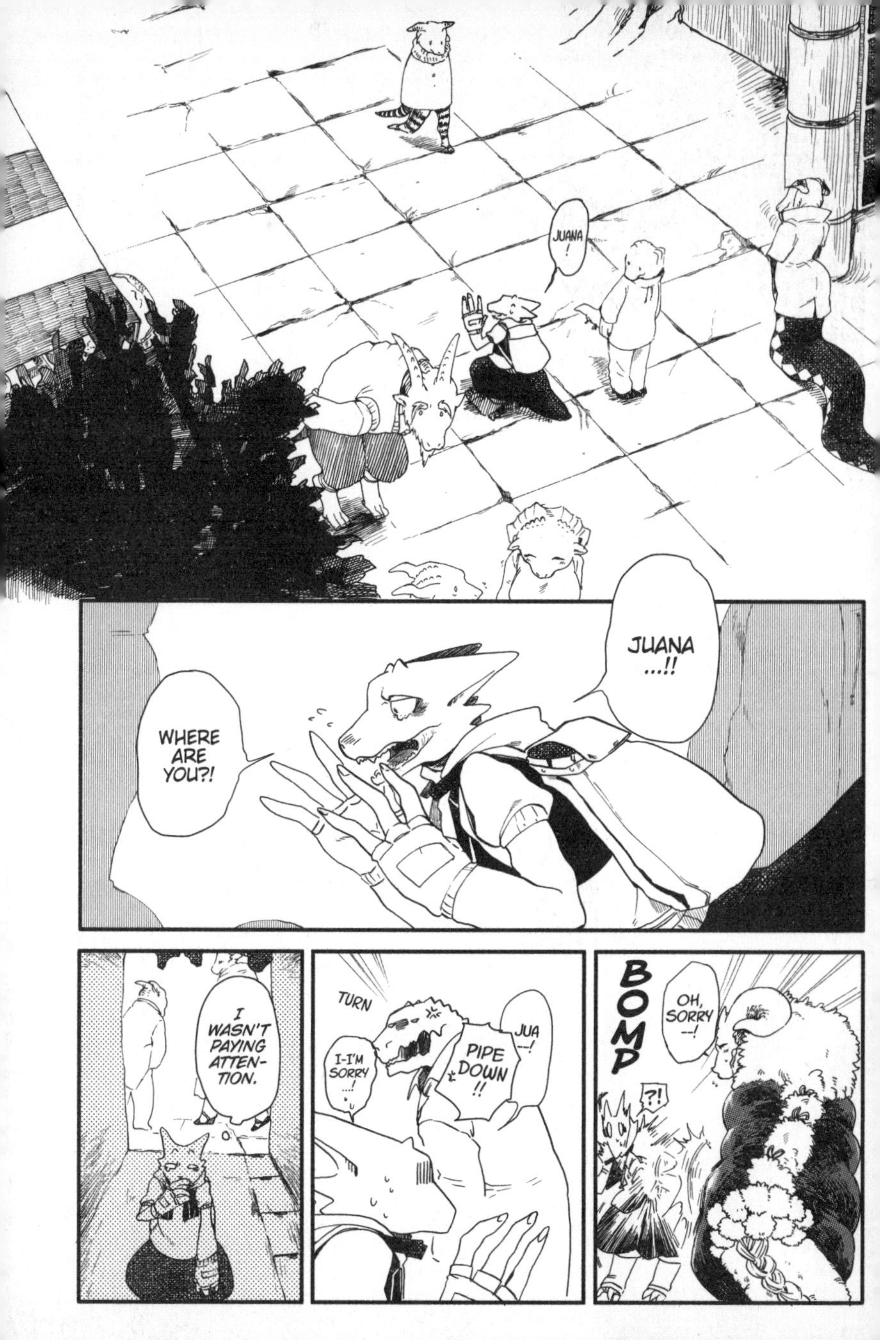
JUANA!
JUANA...!!
WHERE ARE YOU?!
BOMP
OH, SORRY—!
?!
JUA—!
PIPE DOWN!!
TURN
I-I'M SORRY...!
I WASN'T PAYING ATTENTION.

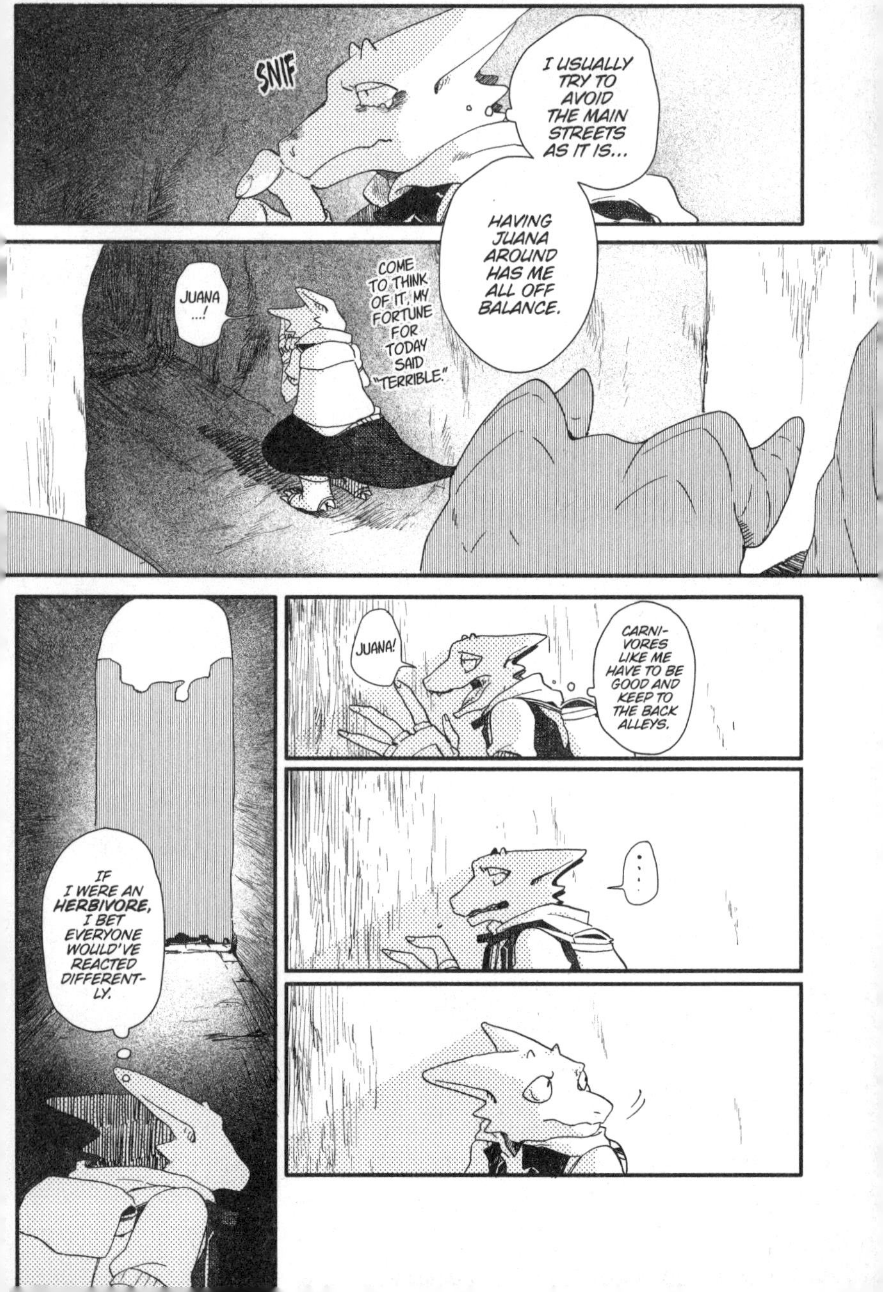
I USUALLY TRY TO AVOID THE MAIN STREETS AS IT IS...
SNIF
HAVING JUANA AROUND HAS ME ALL OFF BALANCE.
COME TO THINK OF IT, MY FORTUNE FOR TODAY SAID "TERRIBLE."
JUANA...!
CARNI-VORES LIKE ME HAVE TO BE GOOD AND KEEP TO THE BACK ALLEYS.
JUANA!
...
IF I WERE AN HERBIVORE, I BET EVERYONE WOULD'VE REACTED DIFFERENT-LY.

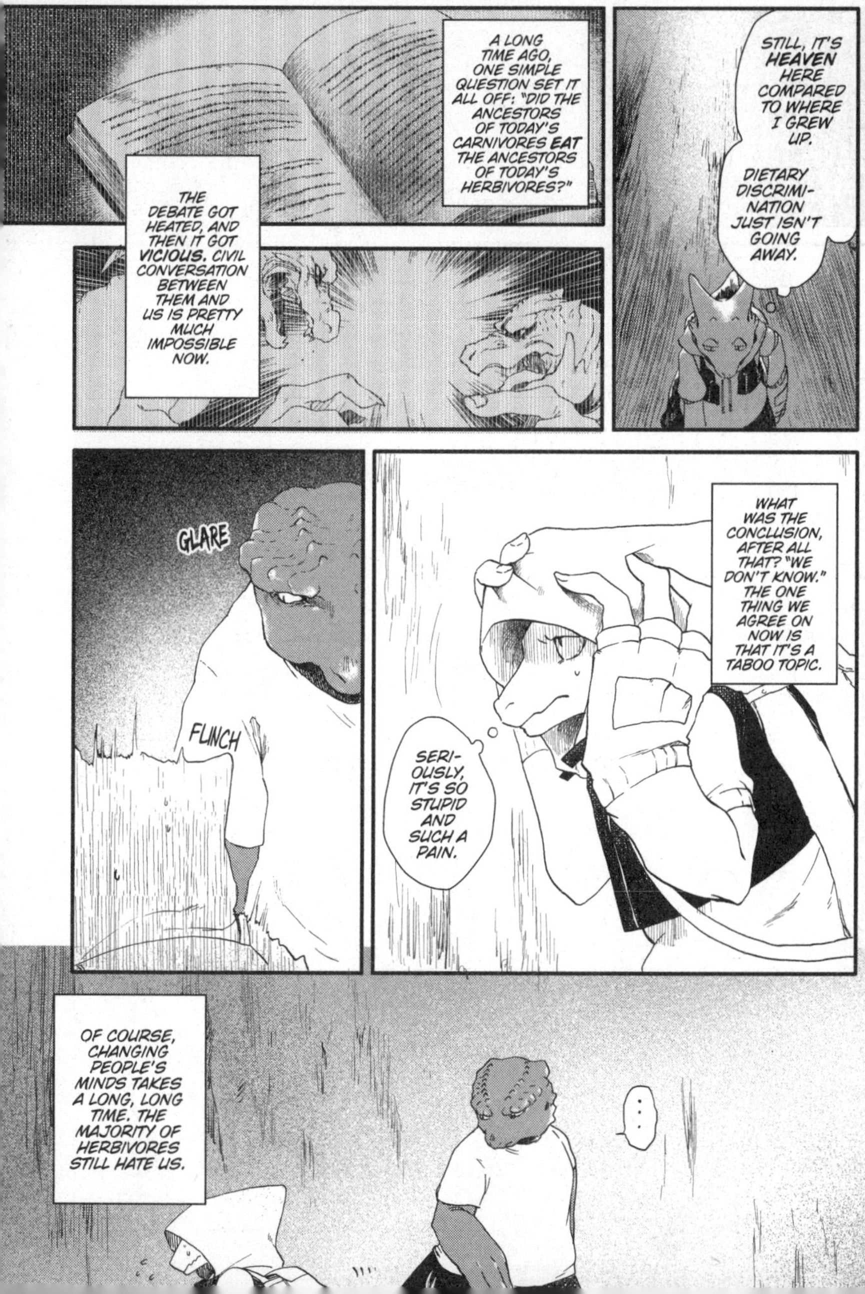
STILL, IT'S HEAVEN HERE COMPARED TO WHERE I GREW UP.
DIETARY DISCRIMI-NATION JUST ISN'T GOING AWAY.
A LONG TIME AGO, ONE SIMPLE QUESTION SET IT ALL OFF: "DID THE ANCESTORS OF TODAY'S CARNIVORES EAT THE ANCESTORS OF TODAY'S HERBIVORES?"
THE DEBATE GOT HEATED, AND THEN IT GOT VICIOUS. CIVIL CONVERSATION BETWEEN THEM AND US IS PRETTY MUCH IMPOSSIBLE NOW.
WHAT WAS THE CONCLUSION, AFTER ALL THAT? "WE DON'T KNOW." THE ONE THING WE AGREE ON NOW IS THAT IT'S A TABOO TOPIC.
SERI-OUSLY, IT'S SO STUPID AND SUCH A PAIN.
GLARE
FLINCH
OF COURSE, CHANGING PEOPLE'S MINDS TAKES A LONG, LONG TIME. THE MAJORITY OF HERBIVORES STILL HATE US.
...

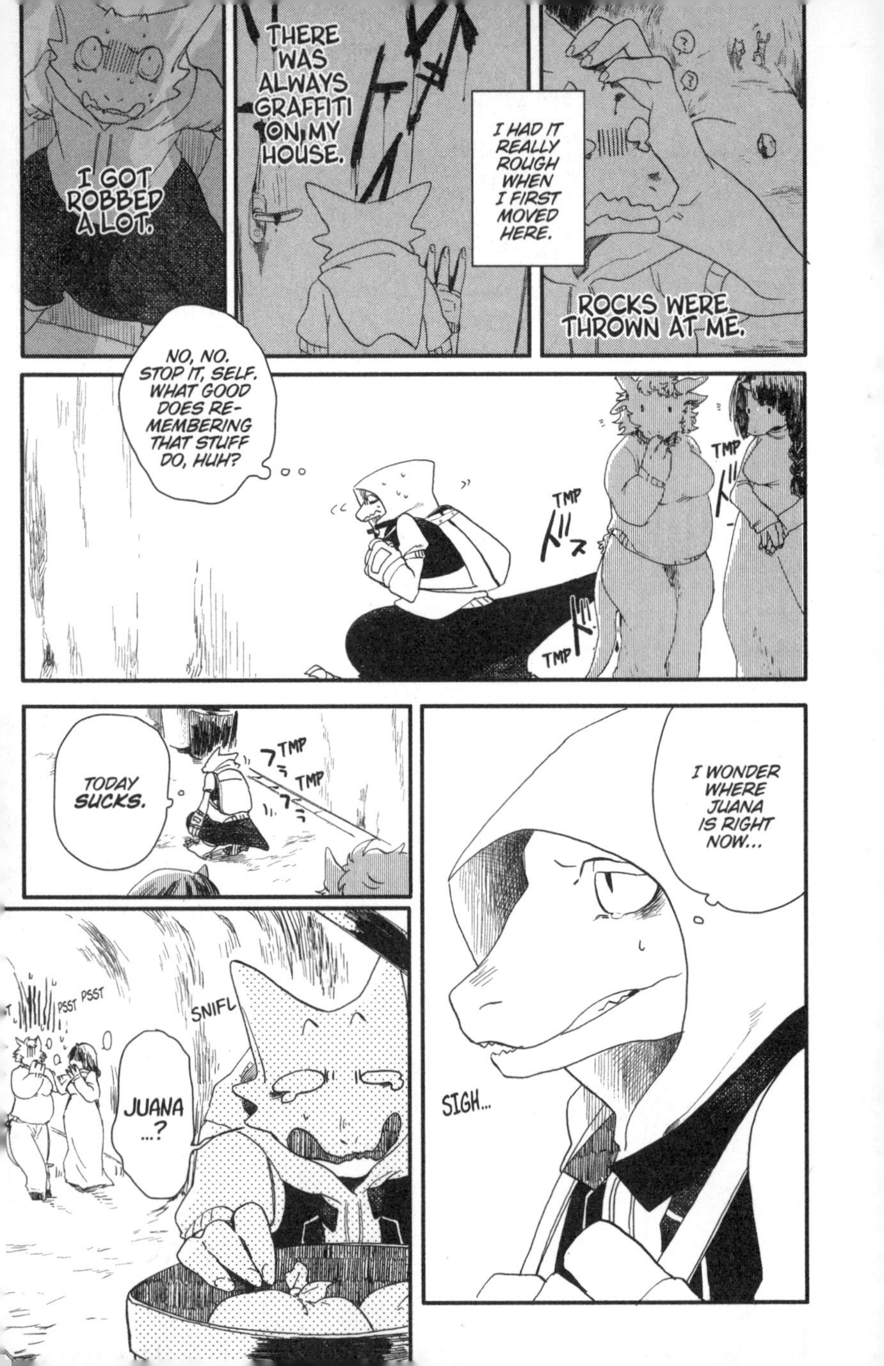
I HAD IT REALLY ROUGH WHEN I FIRST MOVED HERE.
ROCKS WERE THROWN AT ME.
THERE WAS ALWAYS GRAFFITI ON MY HOUSE.
I GOT ROBBED A LOT.
NO, NO. STOP IT, SELF. WHAT GOOD DOES RE-MEMBERING THAT STUFF DO, HUH?
TMP
TMP
TMP
I WONDER WHERE JUANA IS RIGHT NOW...
SIGH...
TODAY SUCKS.
TMP
TMP
SNIFL
PSSST PSST
JUANA ...?

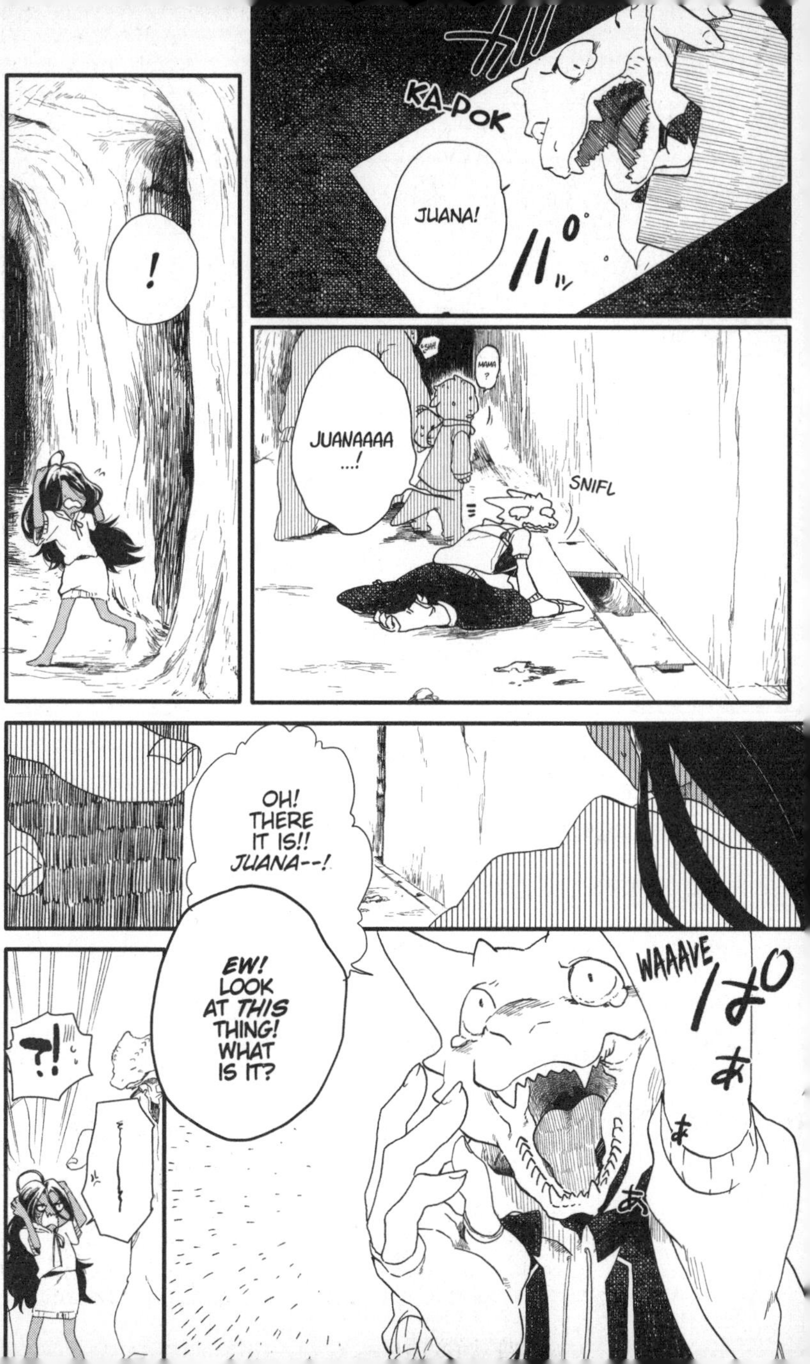
KA-POK
JUANA!
SHH!
MAMA ?
JUANAAAA ...!
SNIFL
!
OH! THERE IT IS!! JUANA--!
WAAAVE
EW! LOOK AT THIS THING! WHAT IS IT?
?!

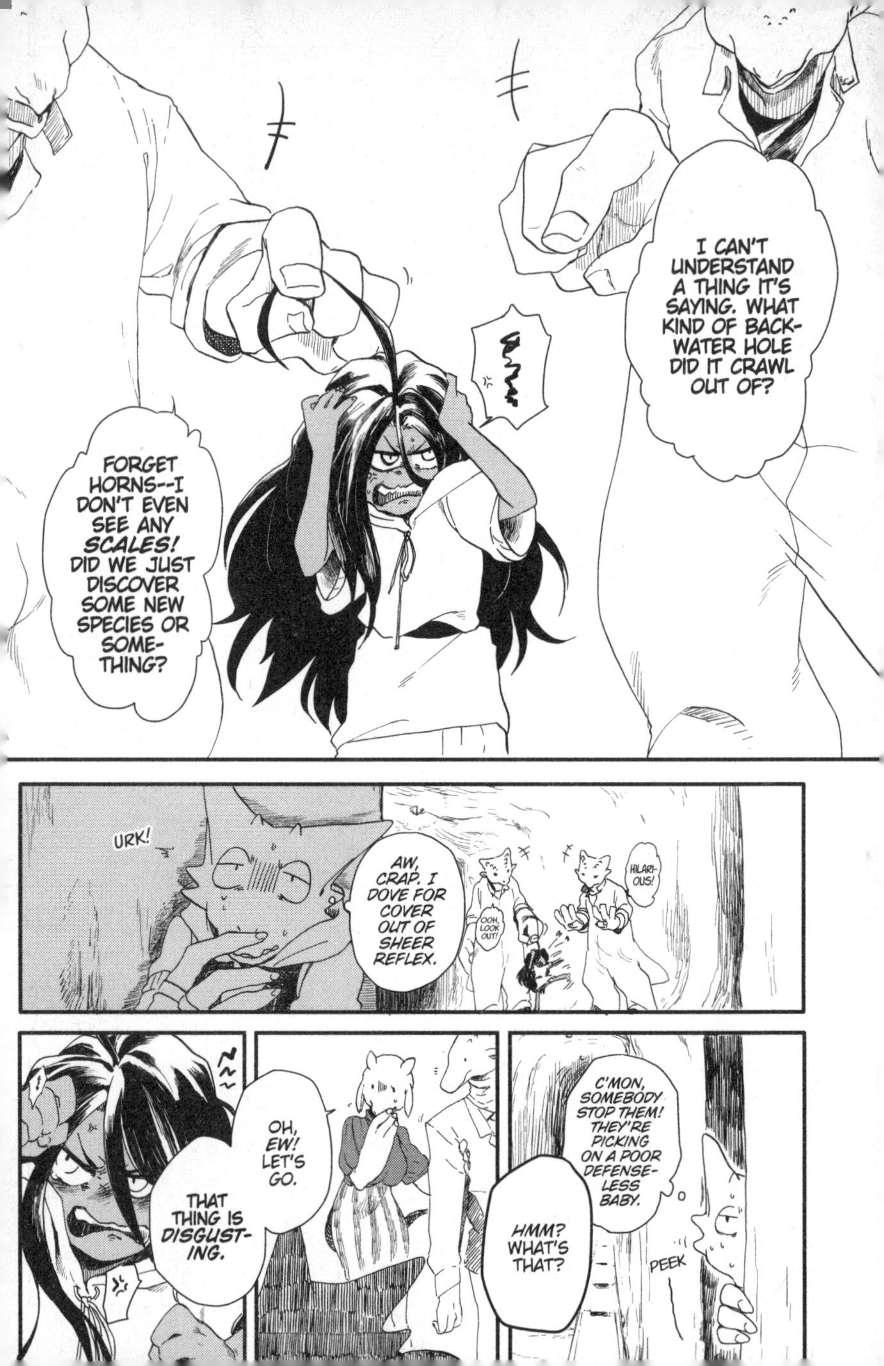
I CAN'T UNDERSTAND A THING IT'S SAYING. WHAT KIND OF BACK-WATER HOLE DID IT CRAWL OUT OF?
FORGET HORNS--I DON'T EVEN SEE ANY SCALES! DID WE JUST DISCOVER SOME NEW SPECIES OR SOME-THING?
HILARI-OUS!
OOH, LOOK OUT!
AW, CRAP. I DOVE FOR COVER OUT OF SHEER REFLEX.
URK!
C'MON, SOMEBODY STOP THEM! THEY'RE PICKING ON A POOR DEFENSE-LESS BABY.
PEEK
HMM? WHAT'S THAT?
OH, EW! LET'S GO.
THAT THING IS DISGUST-ING.

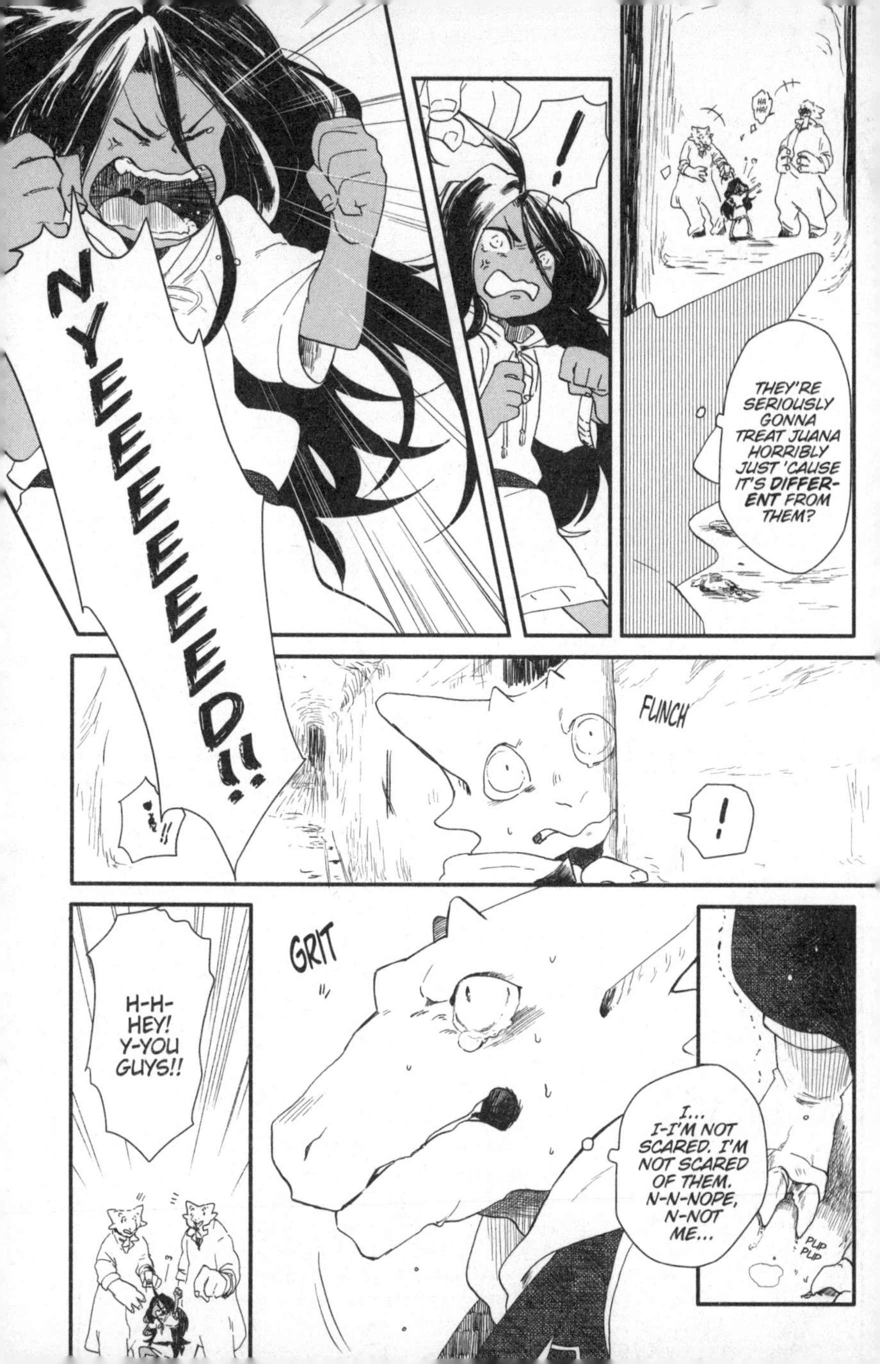
HA HA!
THEY'RE SERIOUSLY GONNA TREAT JUANA HORRIBLY JUST 'CAUSE IT'S **DIFFERENT** FROM THEM?
!
NYEEEEEED!!
FLINCH
!
!!
I... I-I'M NOT SCARED. I'M NOT SCARED OF THEM. N-N-NOPE, N-NOT ME...
PLIP PLIP
GRIT
H-H-HEY! Y-YOU GUYS!!

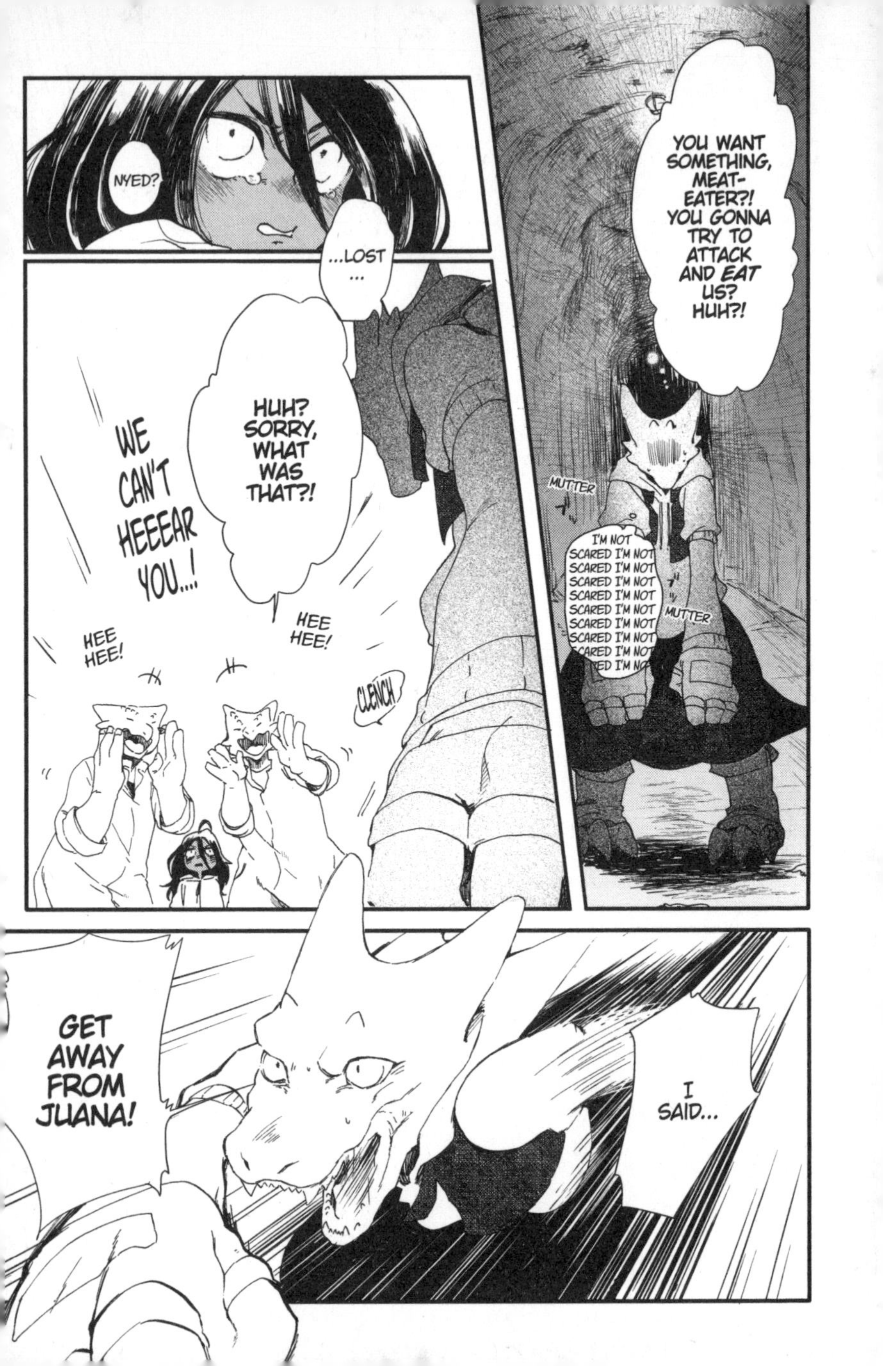
YOU WANT SOMETHING, MEAT-EATER?! YOU GONNA TRY TO ATTACK AND EAT US? HUH?!
MUTTER
I'M NOT SCARED I'M NOT SCARED I'M NOT SCARED I'M NOT SCARED I'M NOT SCARED I'M NOT SCARED I'M NOT SCARED I'M NOT CARED I'M NOT ED I'M NO
MUTTER
NYED?
...LOST ...
HUH? SORRY, WHAT WAS THAT?!
WE CAN'T HEEEAR YOU...!
HEE HEE!
HEE HEE!
CLENCH
I SAID...
GET AWAY FROM JUANA!

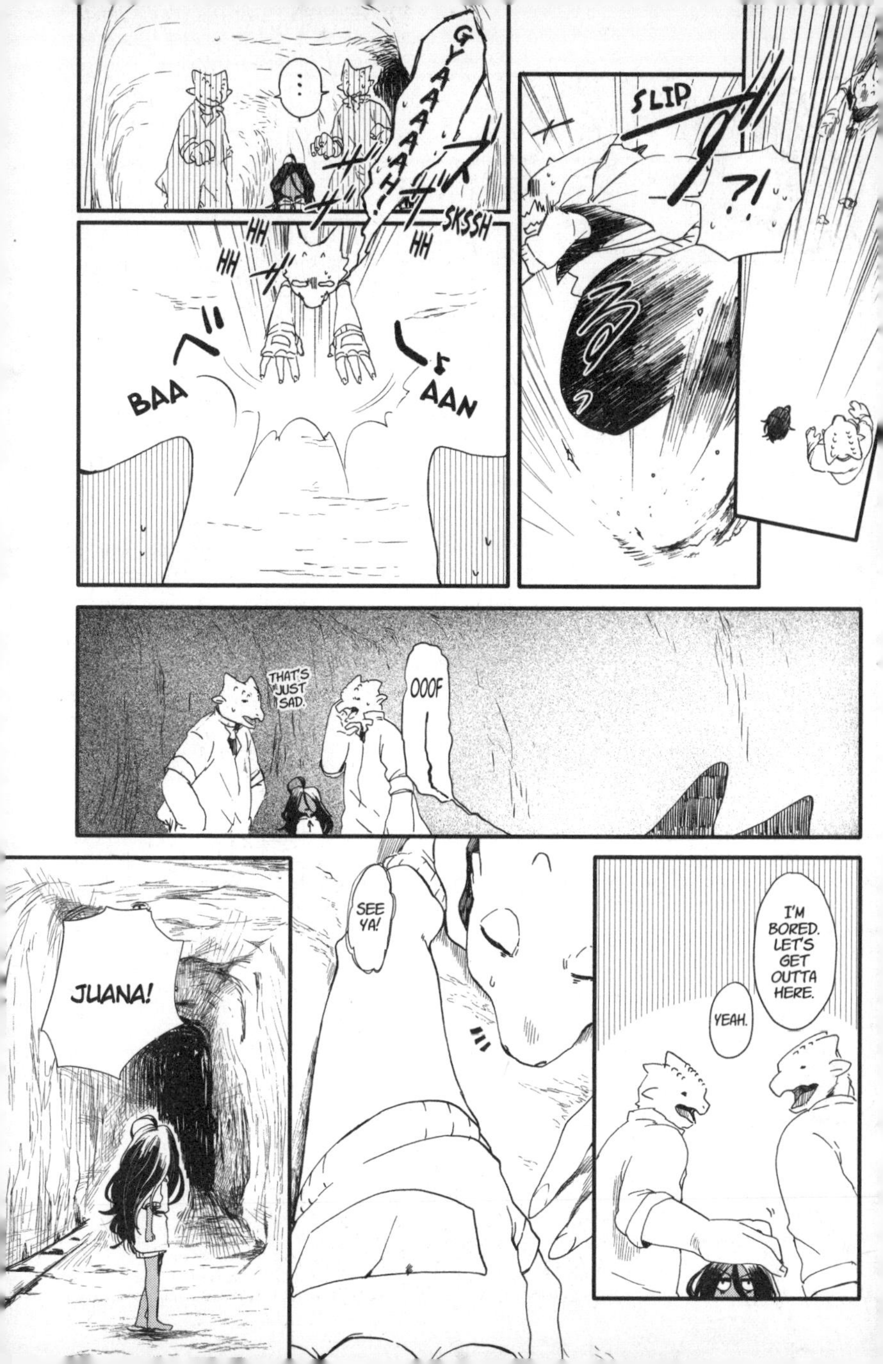
SLIP
?!
...
GYAAAAAH!
HH
HH
HH
SKSSH
BAA
AAN
OOOF
THAT'S JUST SAD.
I'M BORED. LET'S GET OUTTA HERE.
YEAH.
SEE YA!
JUANA!

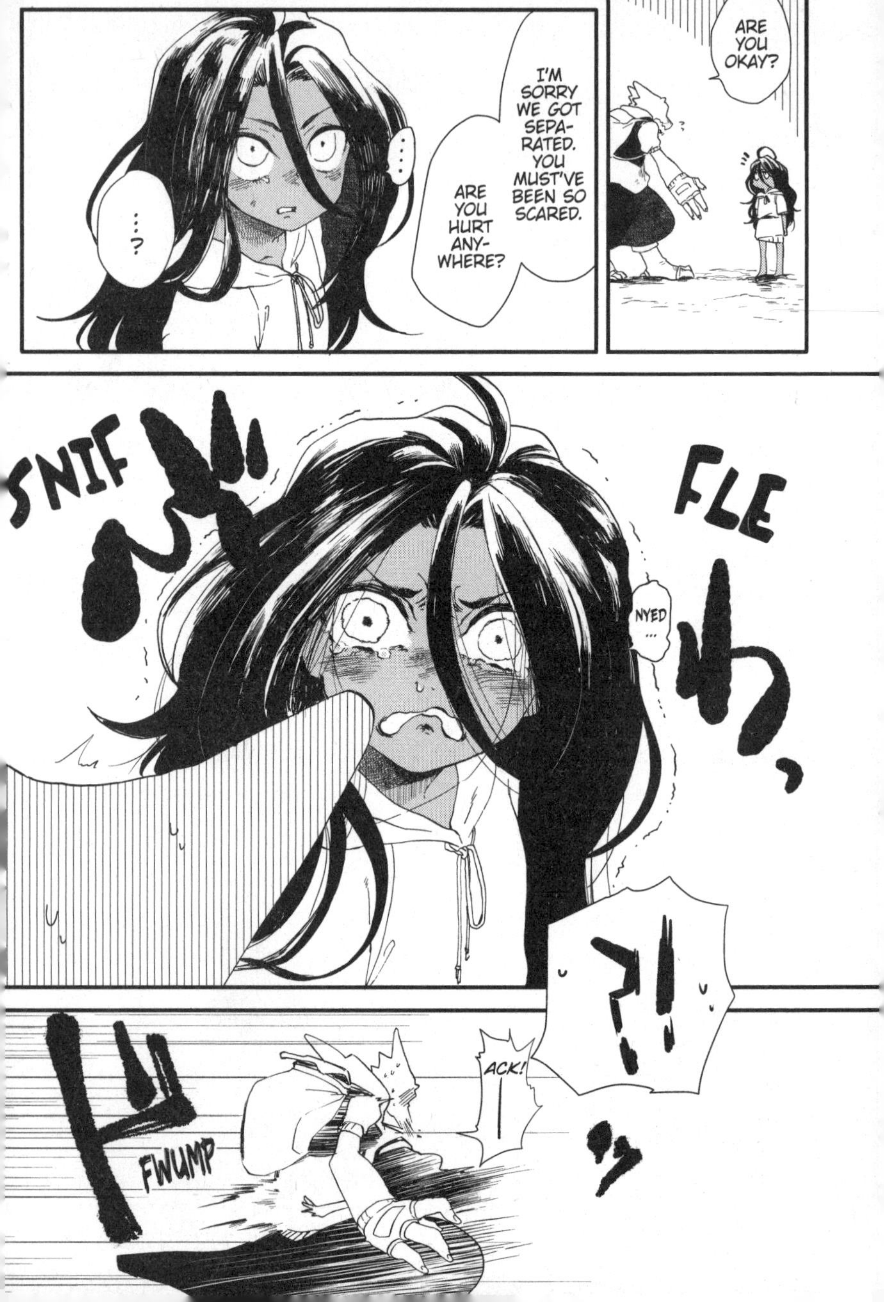
ARE YOU OKAY?
I'M SORRY WE GOT SEPA-RATED. YOU MUST'VE BEEN SO SCARED.
ARE YOU HURT ANY-WHERE?
...
...?
FLE
NYED ...
SNIF
ACK!
FWUMP

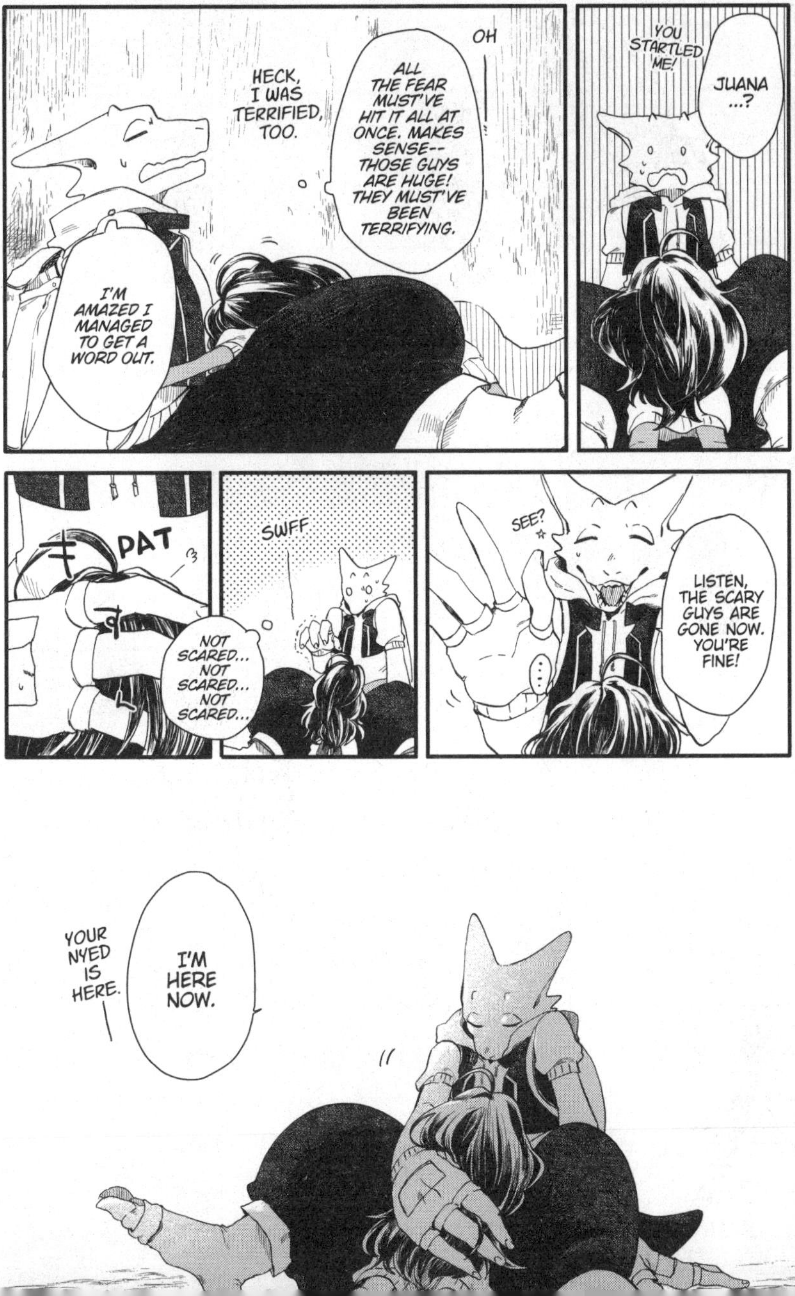
JUANA ...?
YOU STARTLED ME!
OH
ALL THE FEAR MUST'VE HIT IT ALL AT ONCE. MAKES SENSE-- THOSE GUYS ARE HUGE! THEY MUST'VE BEEN TERRIFYING.
HECK, I WAS TERRIFIED, TOO.
I'M AMAZED I MANAGED TO GET A WORD OUT.
SEE?
LISTEN, THE SCARY GUYS ARE GONE NOW. YOU'RE FINE!
SWFF
NOT SCARED... NOT SCARED... NOT SCARED...
PAT
I'M HERE NOW.
YOUR NYED IS HERE.

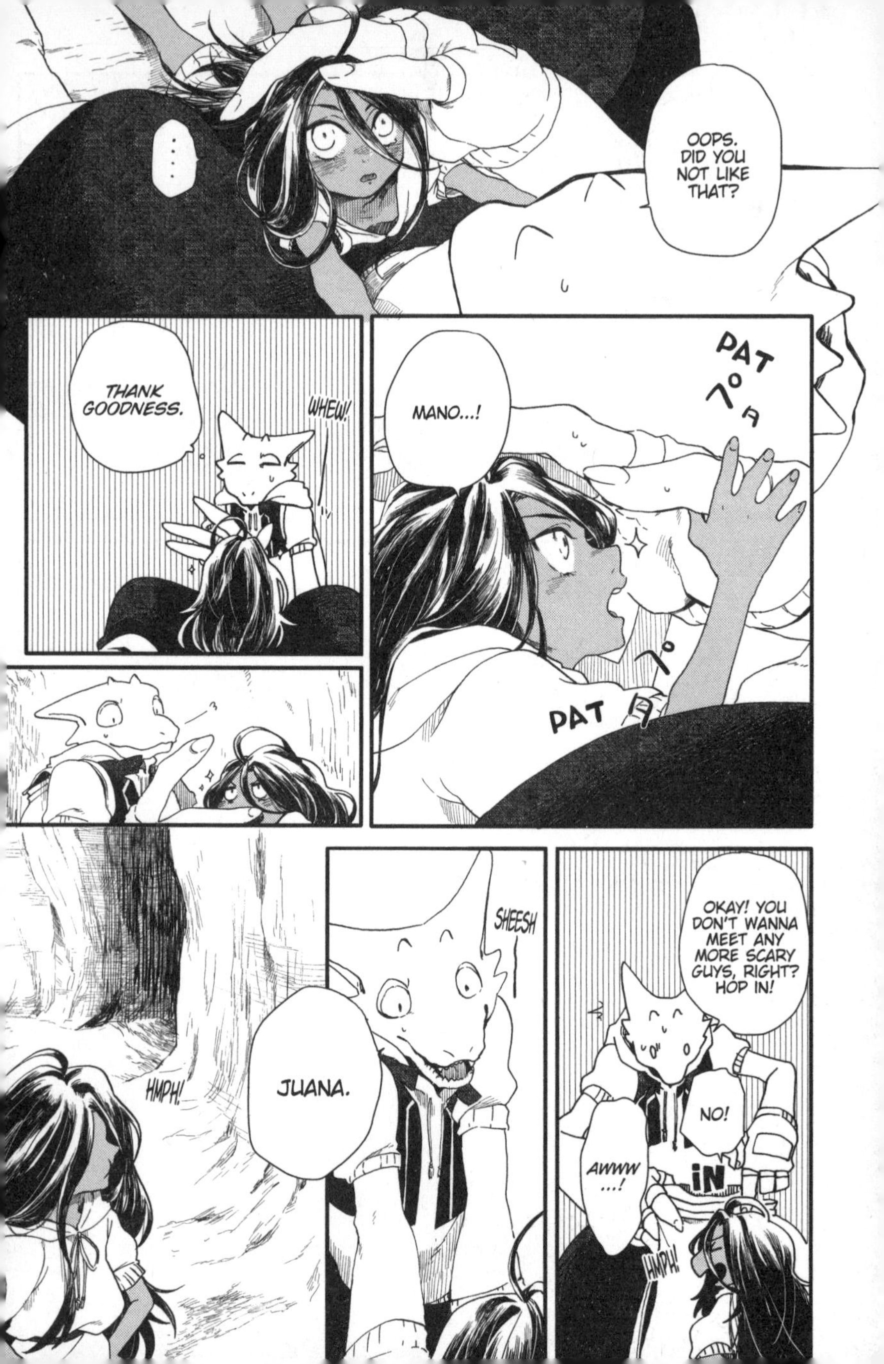
OOPS. DID YOU NOT LIKE THAT?
...
PAT
MANO...!
PAT
THANK GOODNESS.
WHEW!
OKAY! YOU DON'T WANNA MEET ANY MORE SCARY GUYS, RIGHT? HOP IN!
NO!
IN
AWWW ...!
HMPH!
SHEESH
JUANA.
HMPH!

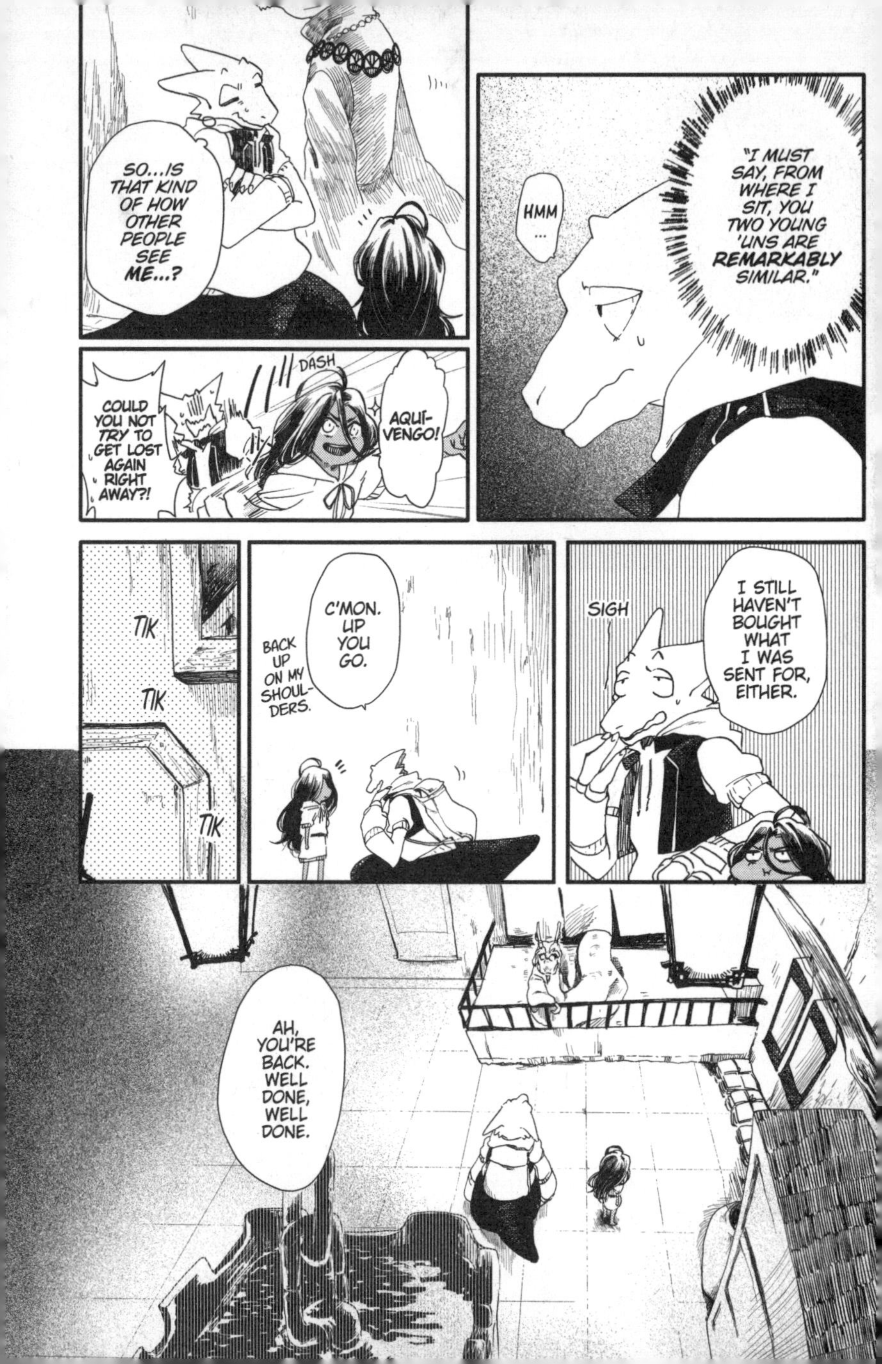

"I MUST SAY, FROM WHERE I SIT, YOU TWO YOUNG 'UNS ARE **REMARKABLY** SIMILAR."
HMM ...
SO...IS THAT KIND OF HOW OTHER PEOPLE SEE **ME**...?
DASH
AQUI-VENGO!
COULD YOU NOT *TRY* TO GET LOST AGAIN RIGHT AWAY?!
I STILL HAVEN'T BOUGHT WHAT I WAS SENT FOR, EITHER.
SIGH
C'MON. UP YOU GO.
BACK UP ON MY SHOUL-DERS.
TIK
TIK
TIK
AH, YOU'RE BACK. WELL DONE, WELL DONE.

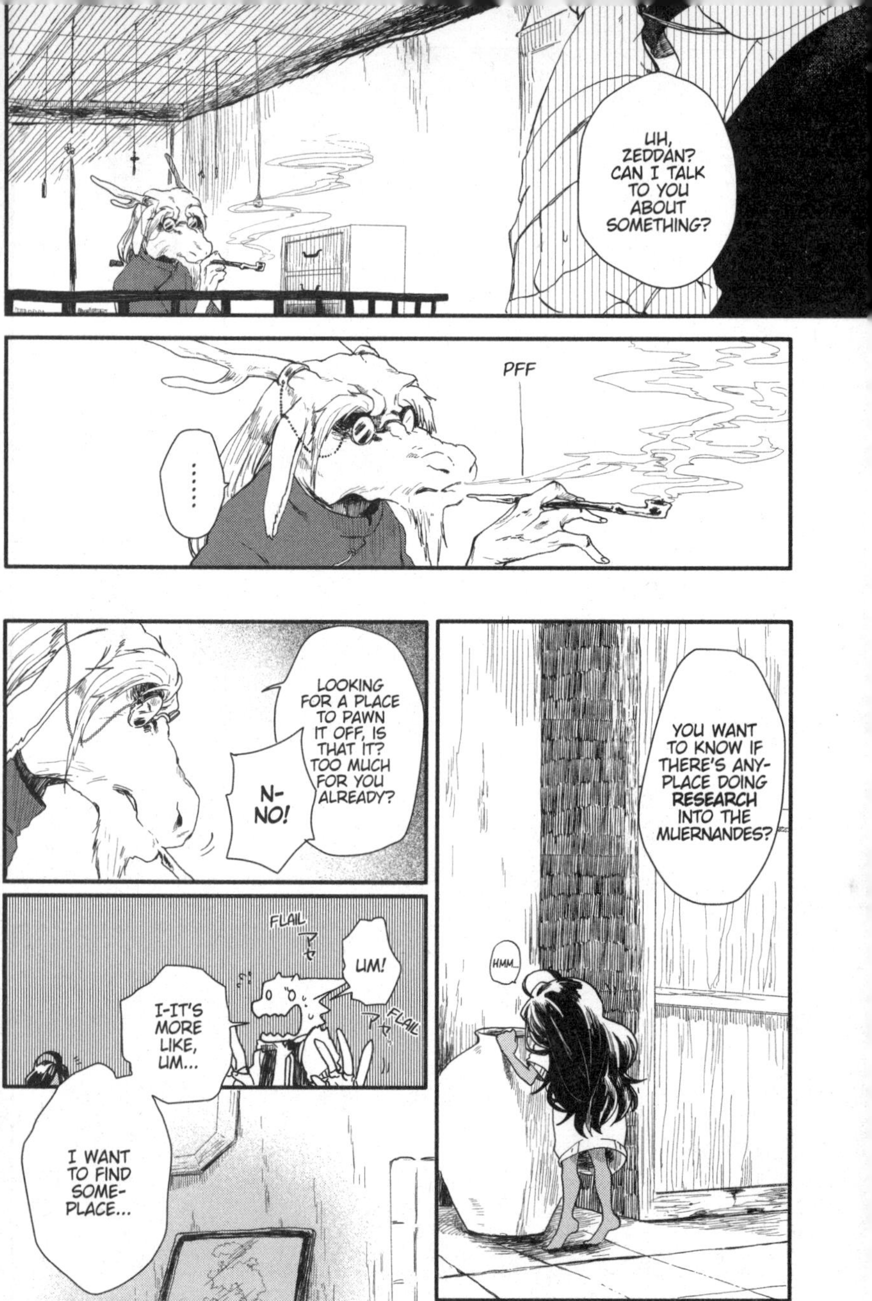
UH, ZEDDAN? CAN I TALK TO YOU ABOUT SOMETHING?
PFF
......
YOU WANT TO KNOW IF THERE'S ANY-PLACE DOING **RESEARCH** INTO THE MUERNANDES?
HMM...
LOOKING FOR A PLACE TO PAWN IT OFF, IS THAT IT? TOO MUCH FOR YOU ALREADY?
N-NO!
FLAIL
UM!
FLAIL
I-IT'S MORE LIKE, UM...
I WANT TO FIND SOME-PLACE...

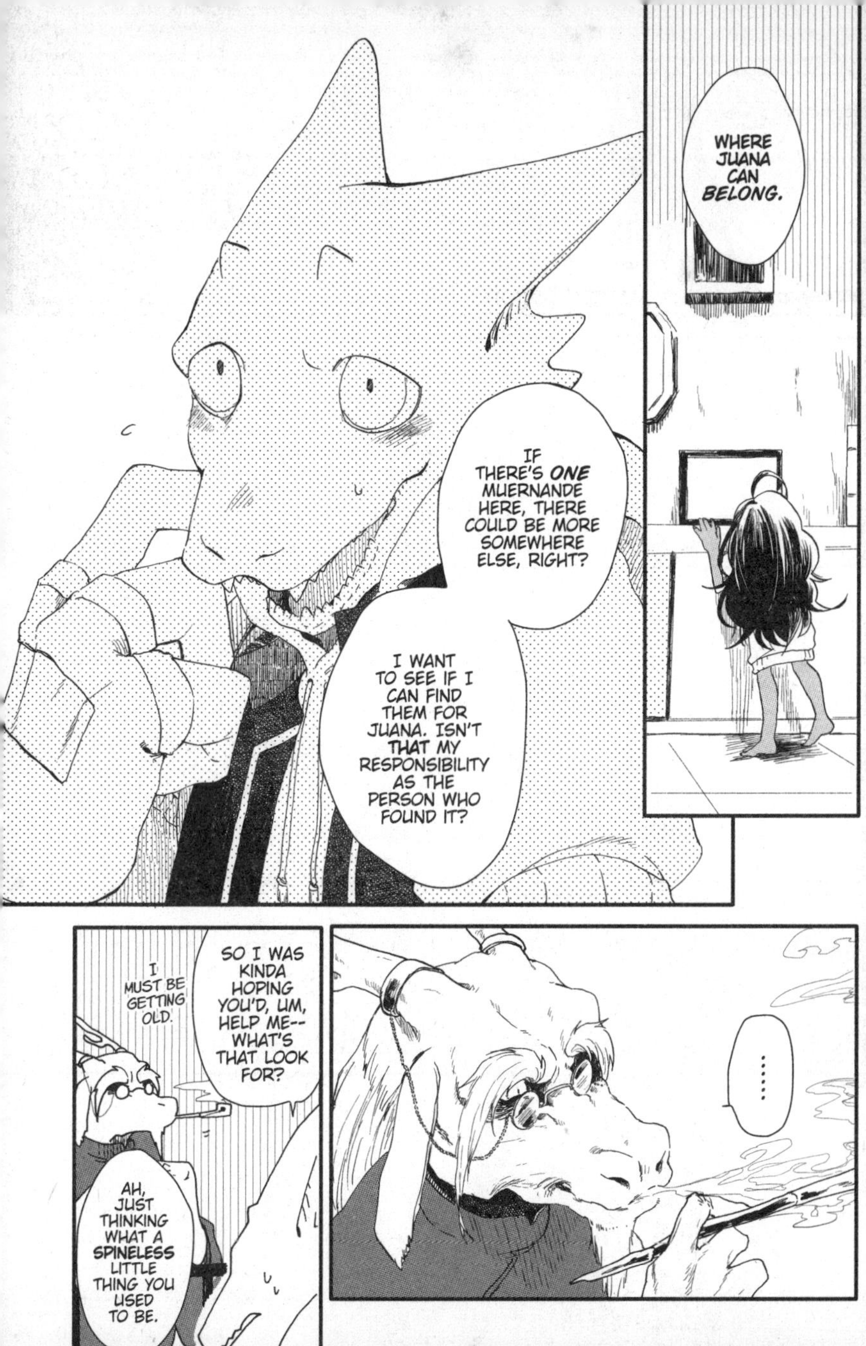
WHERE JUANA CAN BELONG.
IF THERE'S ONE MUERNANDE HERE, THERE COULD BE MORE SOMEWHERE ELSE, RIGHT?
I WANT TO SEE IF I CAN FIND THEM FOR JUANA. ISN'T THAT MY RESPONSIBILITY AS THE PERSON WHO FOUND IT?
......
SO I WAS KINDA HOPING YOU'D, UM, HELP ME-- WHAT'S THAT LOOK FOR?
I MUST BE GETTING OLD.
AH, JUST THINKING WHAT A SPINELESS LITTLE THING YOU USED TO BE.

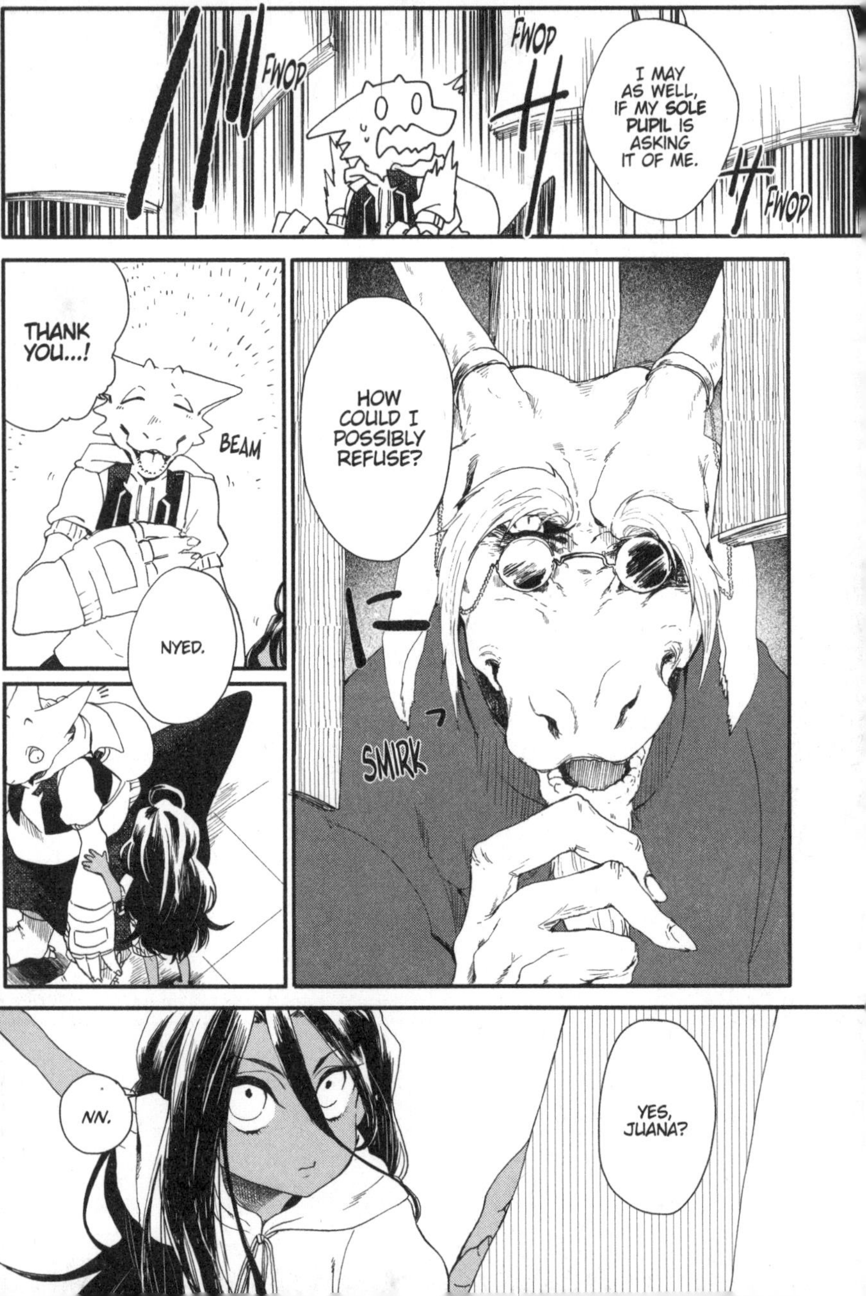
I MAY AS WELL, IF MY SOLE PUPIL IS ASKING IT OF ME.
FWOP
FWOP
FWOP
HOW COULD I POSSIBLY REFUSE?
SMIRK
THANK YOU...!
BEAM
NYED.
YES, JUANA?
NN.

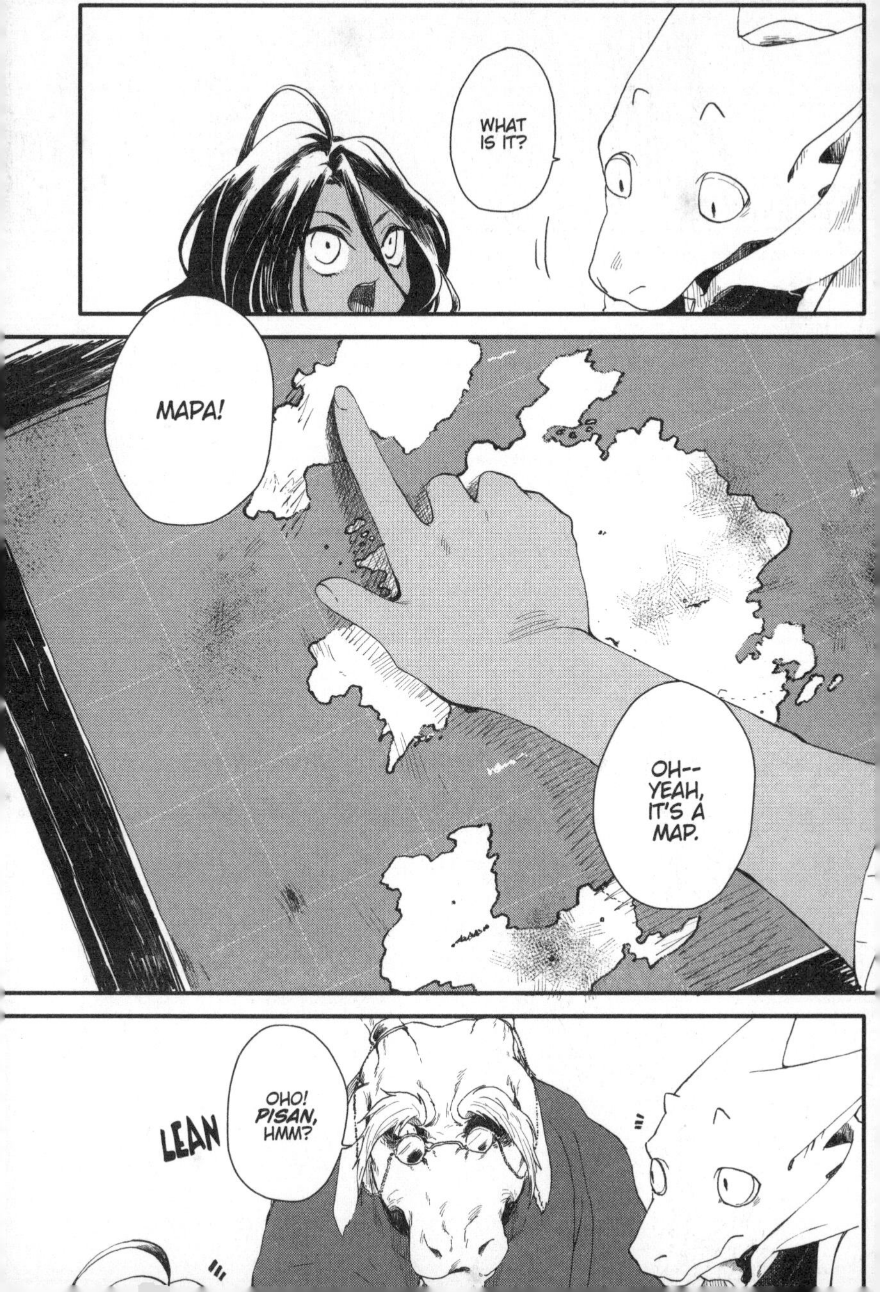
WHAT IS IT?
MAPA!
OH-- YEAH, IT'S A MAP.
LEAN
OHO! *PISAN*, HMM?

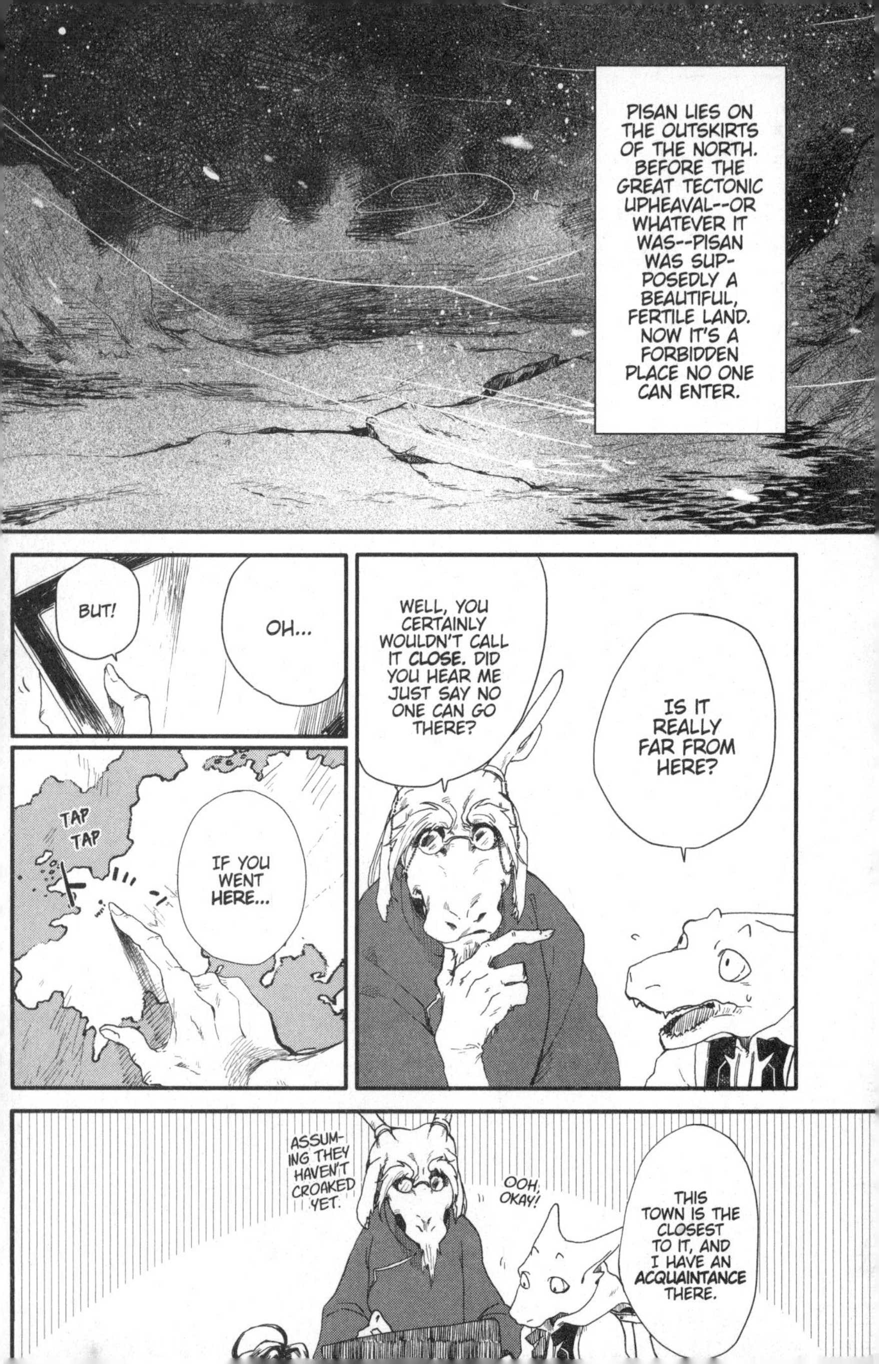
PISAN LIES ON THE OUTSKIRTS OF THE NORTH. BEFORE THE GREAT TECTONIC UPHEAVAL--OR WHATEVER IT WAS--PISAN WAS SUPPOSEDLY A BEAUTIFUL, FERTILE LAND. NOW IT'S A FORBIDDEN PLACE NO ONE CAN ENTER.
IS IT REALLY FAR FROM HERE?
WELL, YOU CERTAINLY WOULDN'T CALL IT **CLOSE**. DID YOU HEAR ME JUST SAY NO ONE CAN GO THERE?
OH...
BUT!
IF YOU WENT HERE...
TAP TAP
THIS TOWN IS THE CLOSEST TO IT, AND I HAVE AN **ACQUAINTANCE** THERE.
OOH, OKAY!
ASSUMING THEY HAVEN'T CROAKED YET.

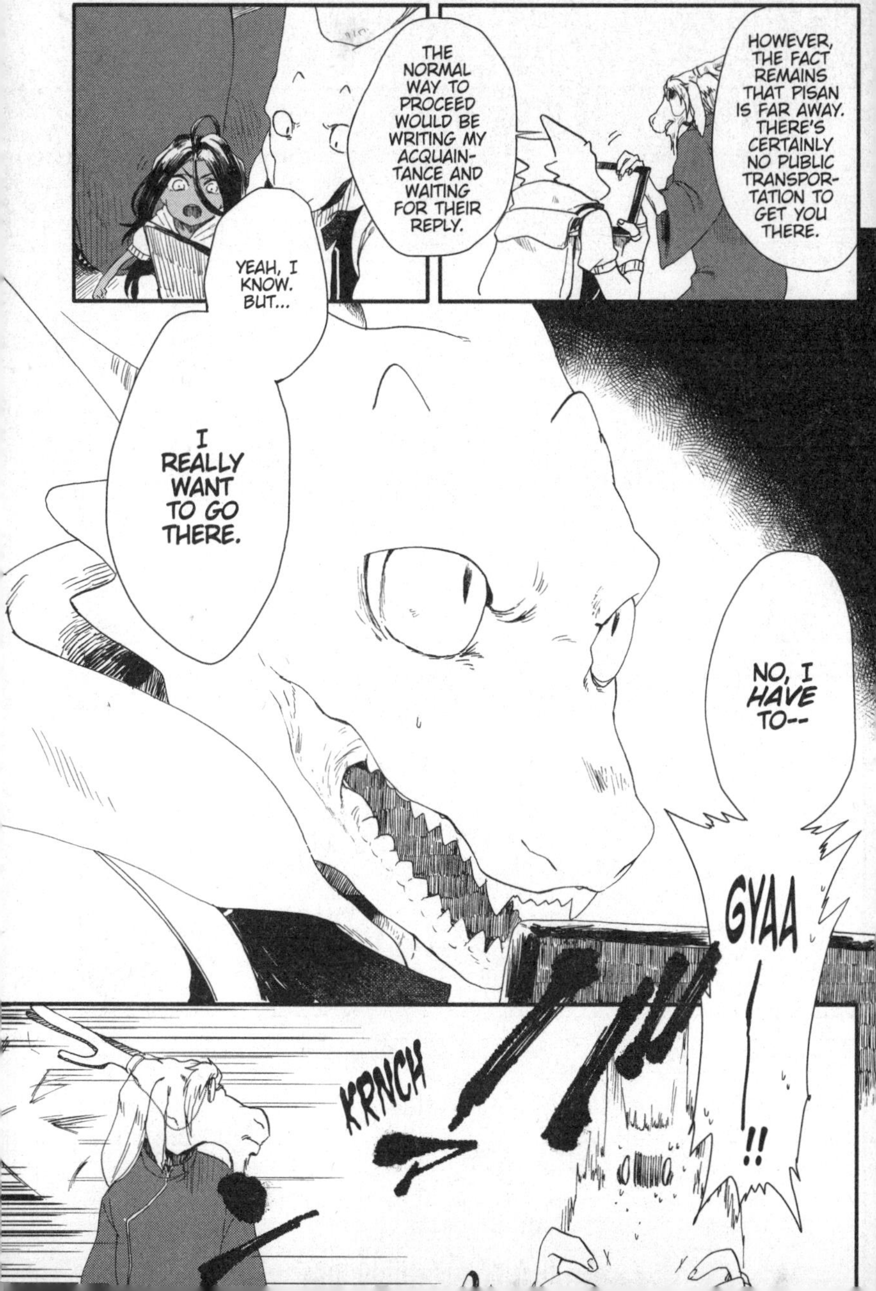
HOWEVER, THE FACT REMAINS THAT PISAN IS FAR AWAY. THERE'S CERTAINLY NO PUBLIC TRANSPORTATION TO GET YOU THERE.
THE NORMAL WAY TO PROCEED WOULD BE WRITING MY ACQUAINTANCE AND WAITING FOR THEIR REPLY.
YEAH, I KNOW. BUT...
I REALLY WANT TO GO THERE.
NO, I *HAVE* TO--
GYAA!!!
KRNCH

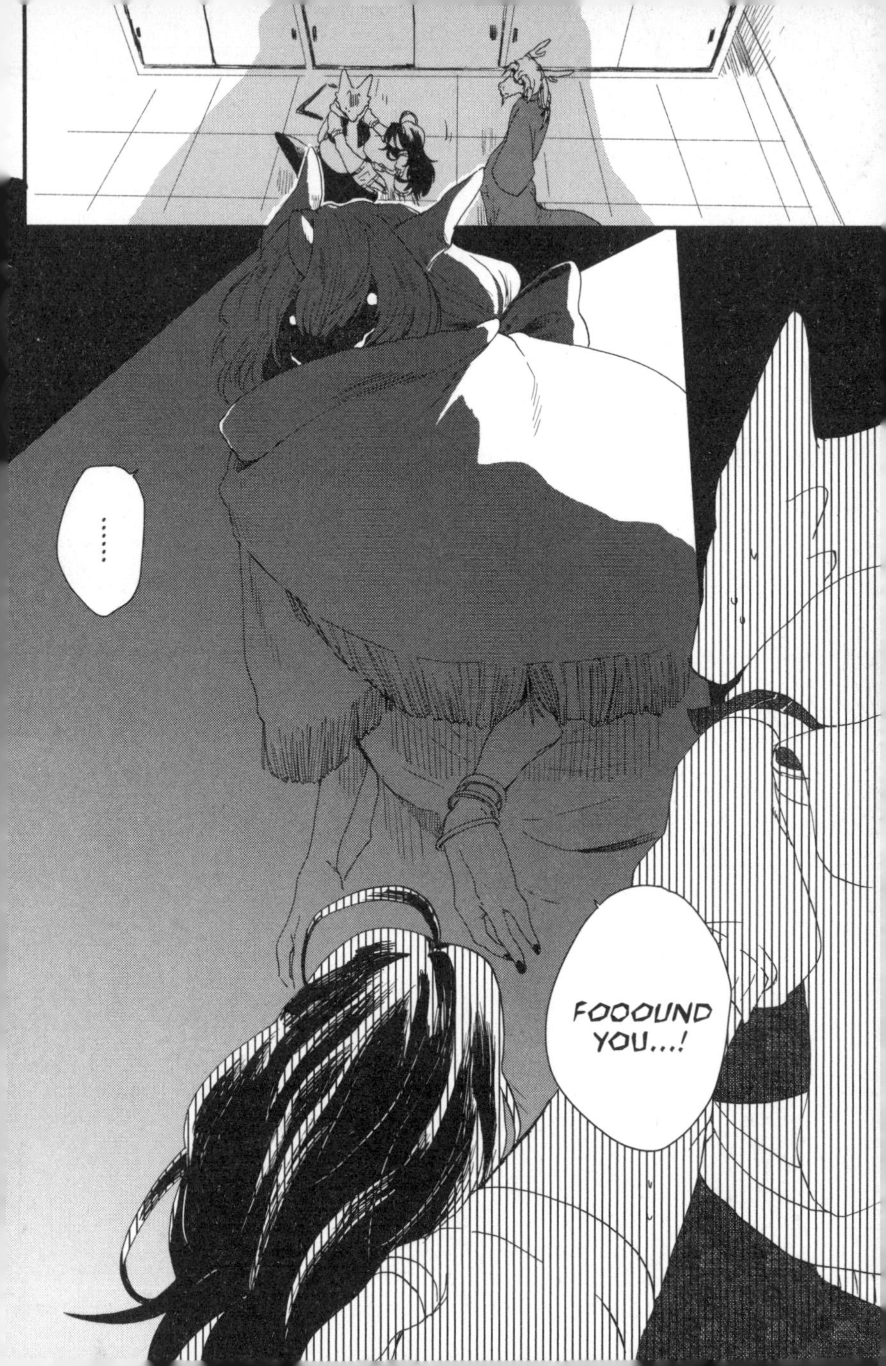
......
FOOOUND YOU...!

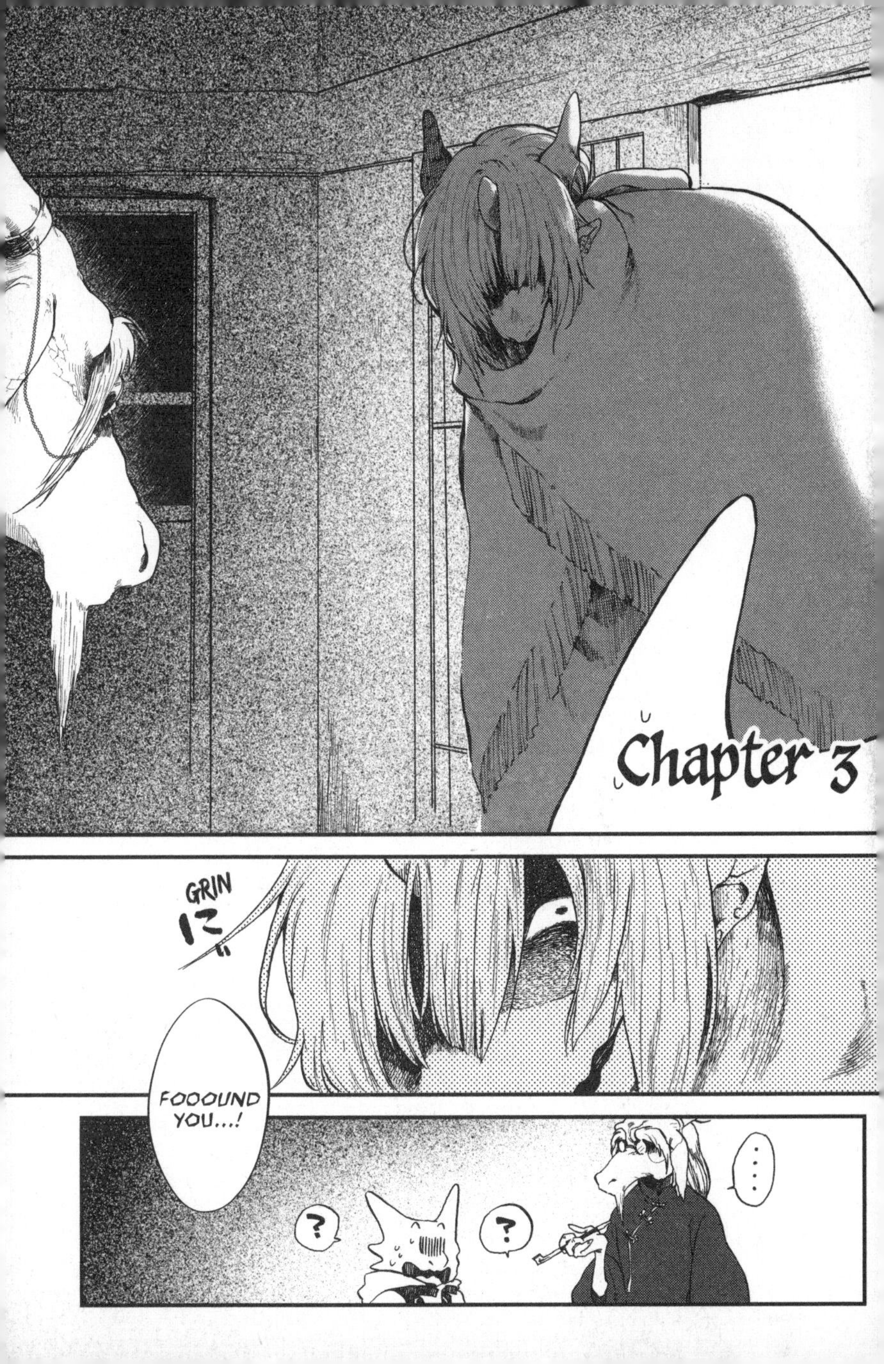
Chapter 3
GRIN
に
FOOOUND YOU...!
....
?
?

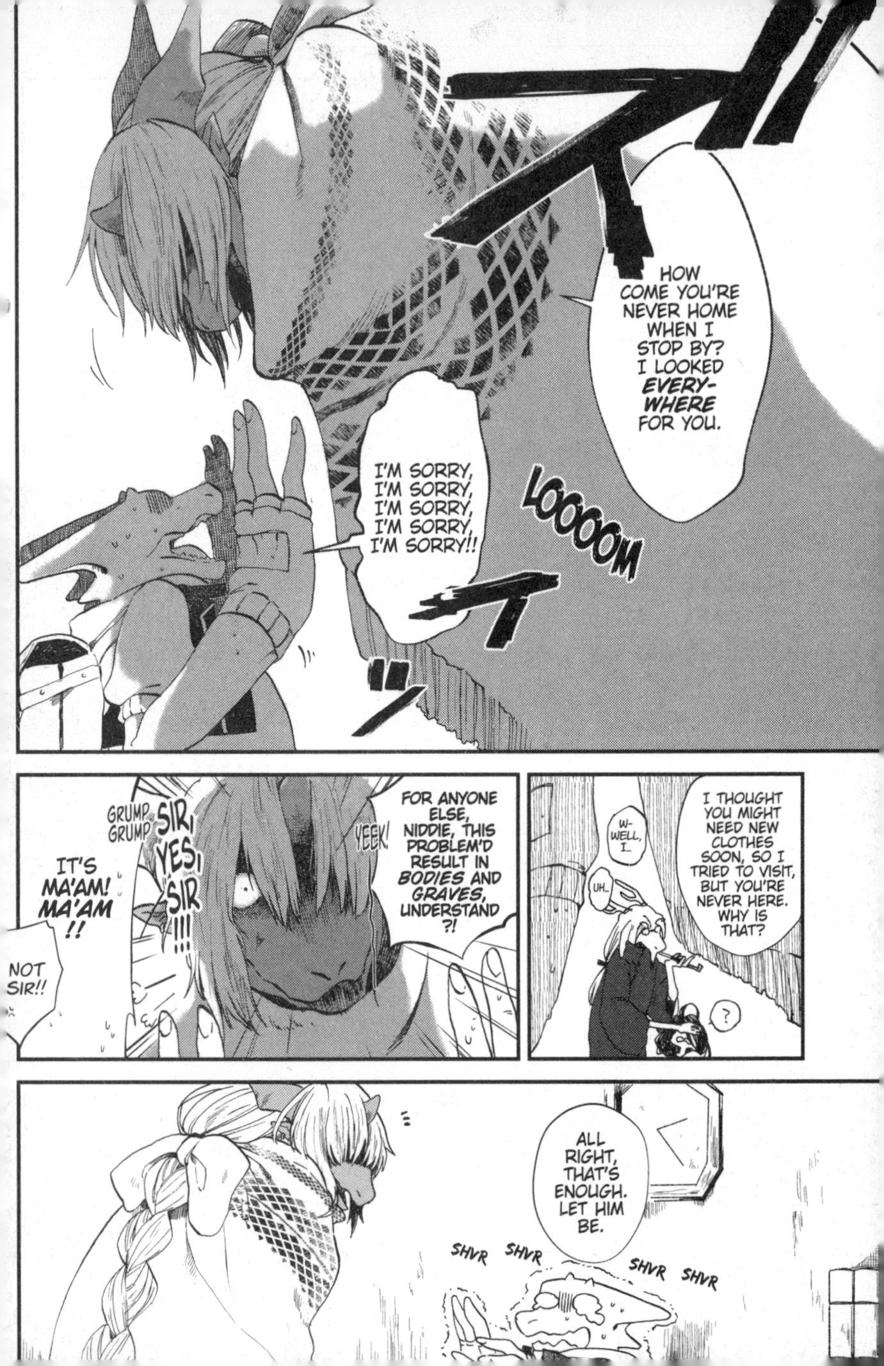
HOW COME YOU'RE NEVER HOME WHEN I STOP BY? I LOOKED EVERY-WHERE FOR YOU.
LOOOOOM
I'M SORRY, I'M SORRY, I'M SORRY, I'M SORRY, I'M SORRY!!
I THOUGHT YOU MIGHT NEED NEW CLOTHES SOON, SO I TRIED TO VISIT, BUT YOU'RE NEVER HERE. WHY IS THAT?
W-WELL, I...
UH...
?
FOR ANYONE ELSE, NIDDIE, THIS PROBLEM'D RESULT IN BODIES AND GRAVES, UNDERSTAND?!
YEEK!
SIR, YES, SIR!!!
GRUMP GRUMP
IT'S MA'AM! MA'AM!!
NOT SIR!!
ALL RIGHT, THAT'S ENOUGH. LET HIM BE.
SHVR SHVR
SHVR SHVR

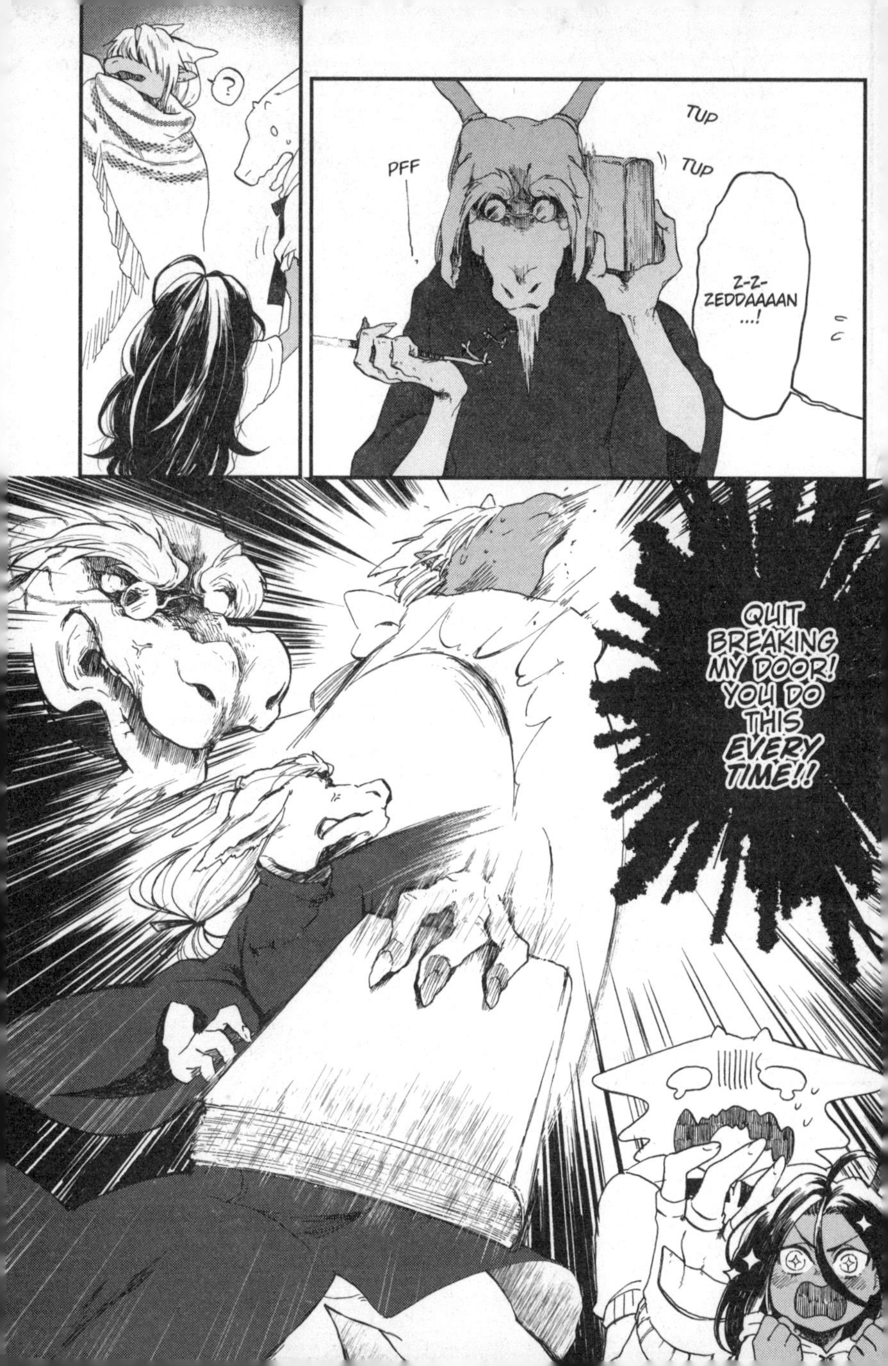
TUP
TUP
Z-Z-ZEDDAAAAN ...!
PFF
?
QUIT BREAKING MY DOOR! YOU DO THIS *EVERY TIME!!*

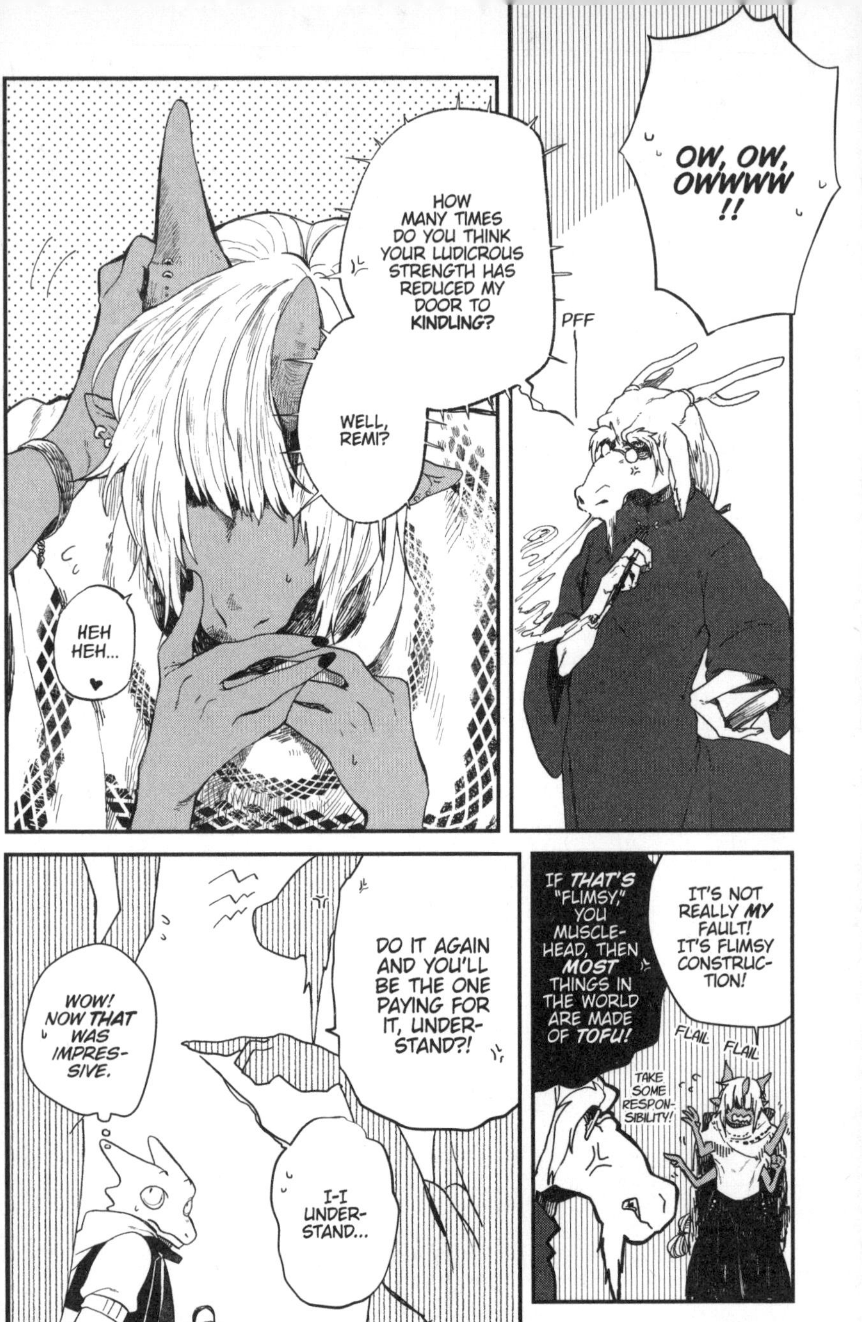
OW, OW, OWWWW!!
PFF
HOW MANY TIMES DO YOU THINK YOUR LUDICROUS STRENGTH HAS REDUCED MY DOOR TO KINDLING?
WELL, REMI?
HEH HEH... ♥
IT'S NOT REALLY MY FAULT! IT'S FLIMSY CONSTRUC-TION!
IF THAT'S "FLIMSY," YOU MUSCLE-HEAD, THEN MOST THINGS IN THE WORLD ARE MADE OF TOFU!
FLAIL FLAIL
TAKE SOME RESPON-SIBILITY!
DO IT AGAIN AND YOU'LL BE THE ONE PAYING FOR IT, UNDER-STAND?!
WOW! NOW THAT WAS IMPRES-SIVE.
I-I UNDER-STAND...

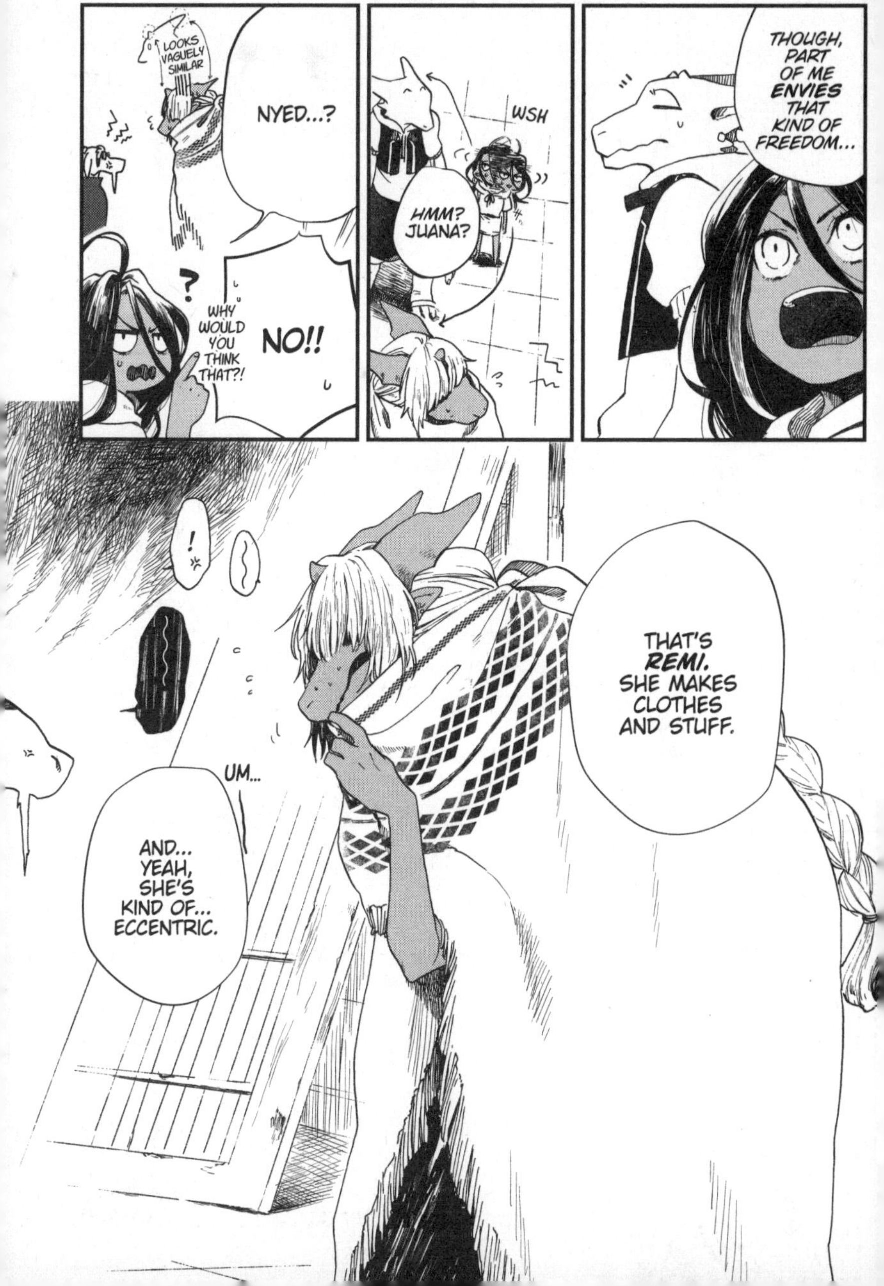
THOUGH, PART OF ME ENVIES THAT KIND OF FREEDOM...
WSH
HMM? JUANA?
NYED...?
LOOKS VAGUELY SIMILAR
NO!!
WHY WOULD YOU THINK THAT?!
!
THAT'S REMI. SHE MAKES CLOTHES AND STUFF.
UM...
AND... YEAH, SHE'S KIND OF... ECCENTRIC.

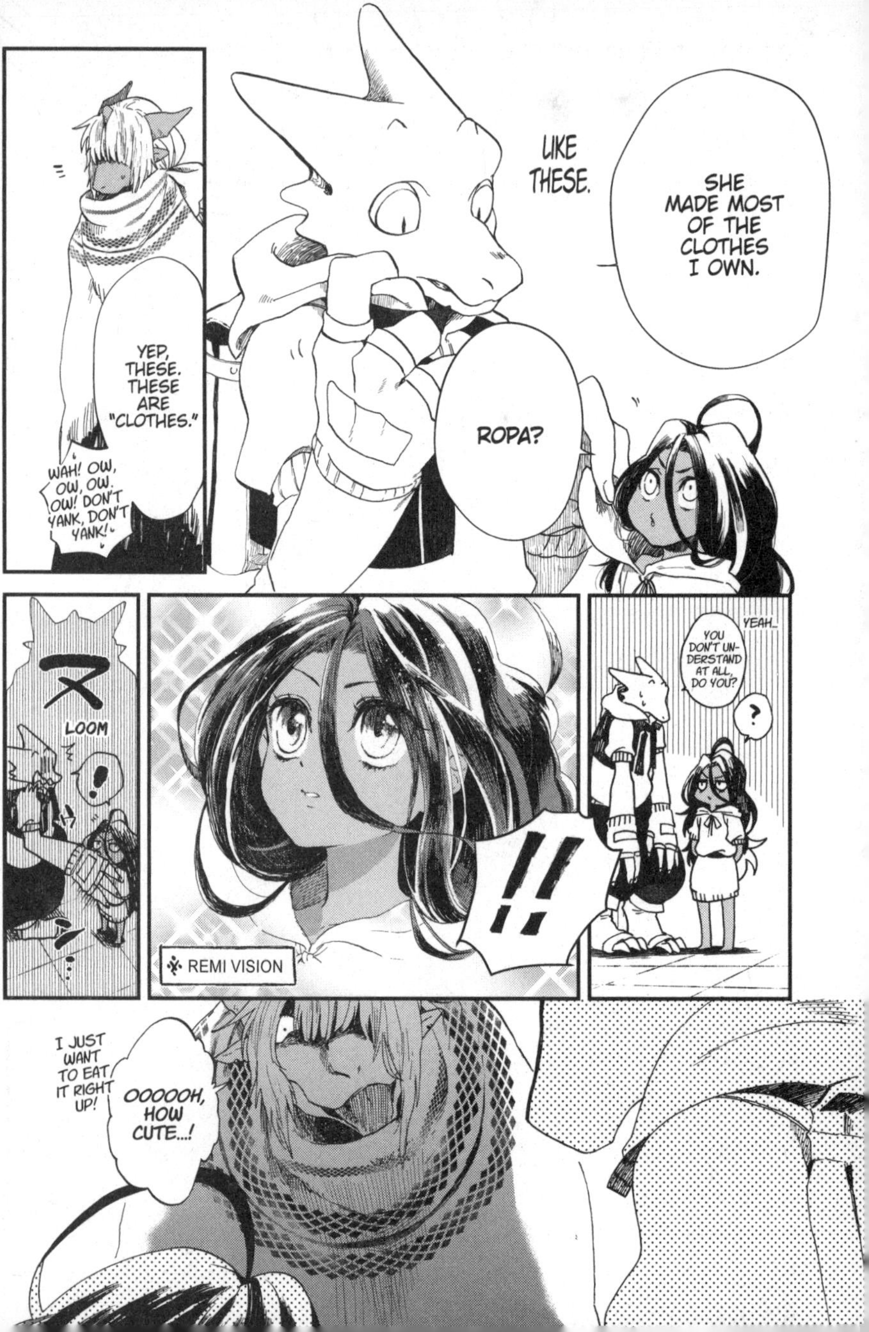
SHE MADE MOST OF THE CLOTHES I OWN.
LIKE THESE.
ROPA?
YEP, THESE. THESE ARE "CLOTHES."
WAH! OW, OW, OW. OW! DON'T YANK, DON'T YANK!
YEAH...
YOU DON'T UNDERSTAND AT ALL, DO YOU?
?
!!
REMI VISION
ヌ
LOOM
!
OOOOOH, HOW CUTE...!
I JUST WANT TO EAT IT RIGHT UP!

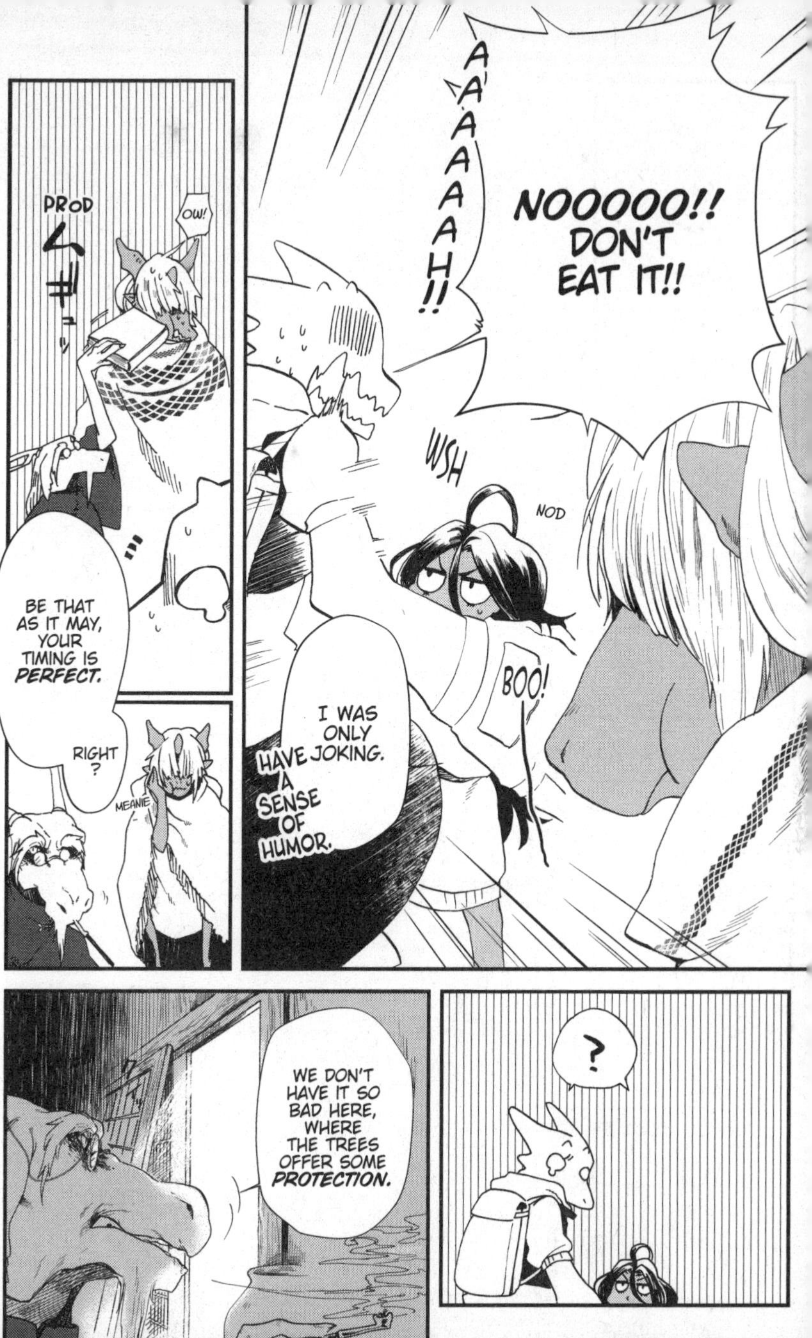
AAAAAAH!!
NOOOOO!! DON'T EAT IT!!
WSH
NOD
I WAS ONLY JOKING. HAVE A SENSE OF HUMOR.
BOO!
PROD
OW!
BE THAT AS IT MAY, YOUR TIMING IS PERFECT.
RIGHT?
MEANIE
?
WE DON'T HAVE IT SO BAD HERE, WHERE THE TREES OFFER SOME PROTECTION.

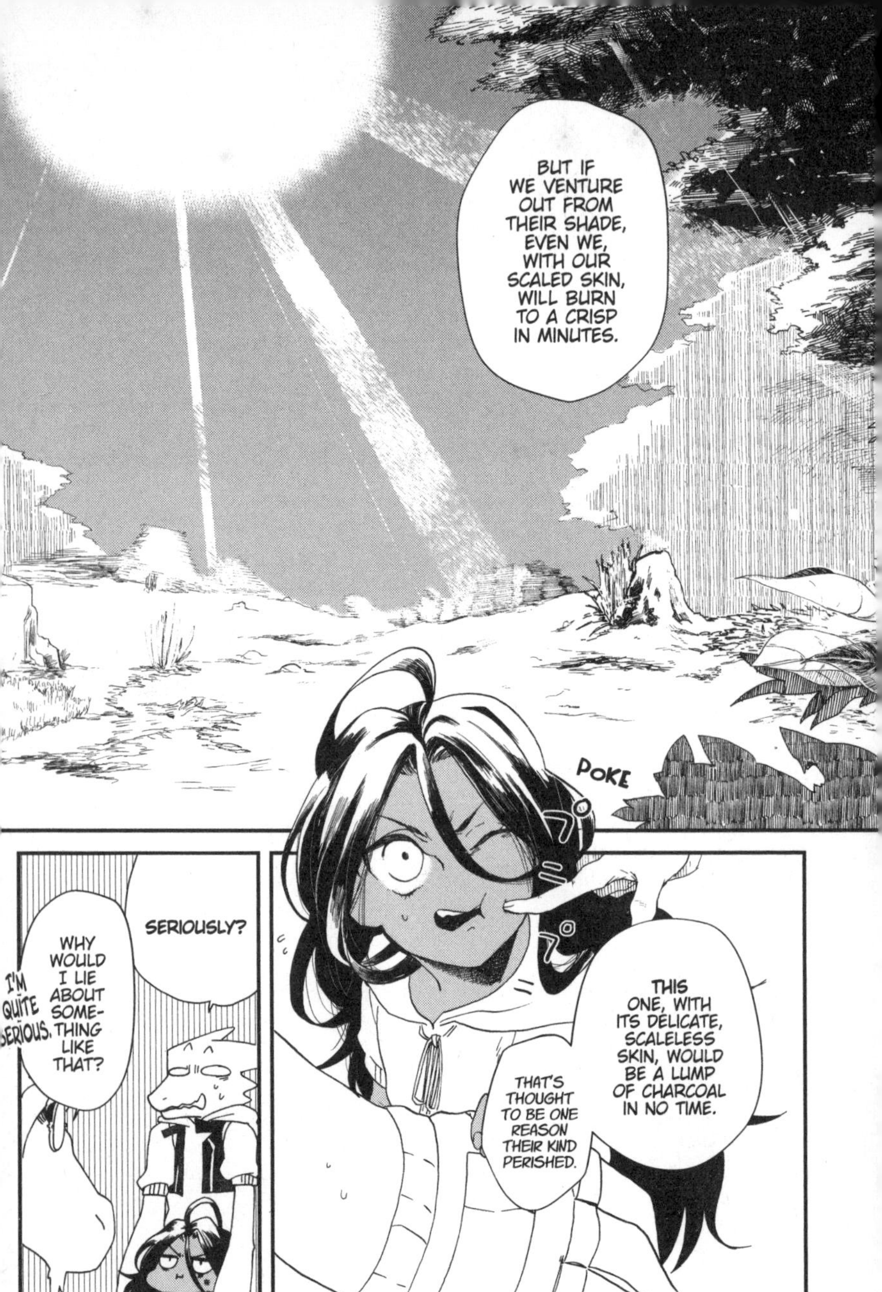
BUT IF WE VENTURE OUT FROM THEIR SHADE, EVEN WE, WITH OUR SCALED SKIN, WILL BURN TO A CRISP IN MINUTES.
POKE
THIS ONE, WITH ITS DELICATE, SCALELESS SKIN, WOULD BE A LUMP OF CHARCOAL IN NO TIME.
THAT'S THOUGHT TO BE ONE REASON THEIR KIND PERISHED.
SERIOUSLY?
WHY WOULD I LIE ABOUT SOME-THING LIKE THAT?
I'M QUITE SERIOUS.

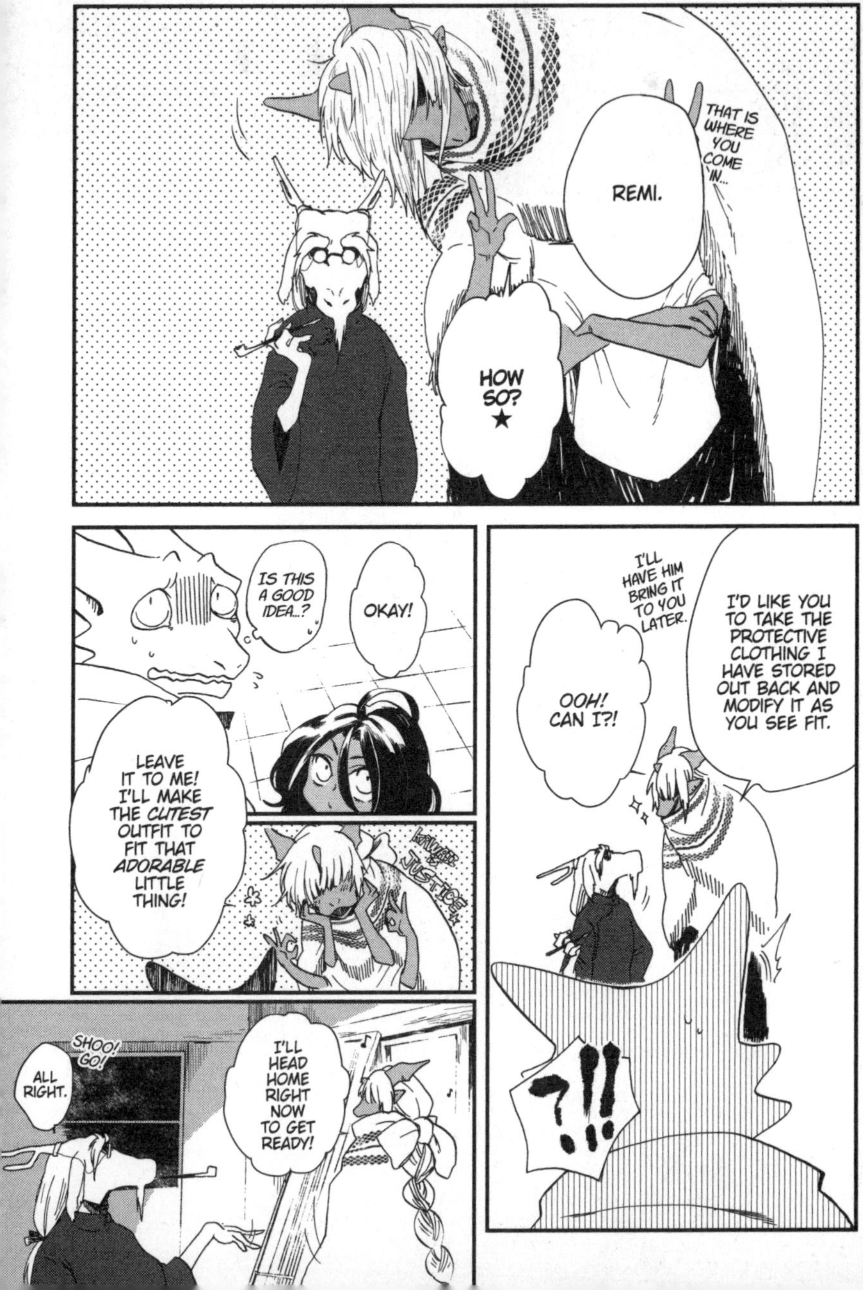
THAT IS WHERE YOU COME IN...
REMI.
HOW SO? ★
I'D LIKE YOU TO TAKE THE PROTECTIVE CLOTHING I HAVE STORED OUT BACK AND MODIFY IT AS YOU SEE FIT.
I'LL HAVE HIM BRING IT TO YOU LATER.
OOH! CAN I?!
?!!
OKAY!
IS THIS A GOOD IDEA...?
LEAVE IT TO ME! I'LL MAKE THE *CUTEST* OUTFIT TO FIT THAT *ADORABLE* LITTLE THING!
JUSTICE
I'LL HEAD HOME RIGHT NOW TO GET READY!
SHOO! GO!
ALL RIGHT.

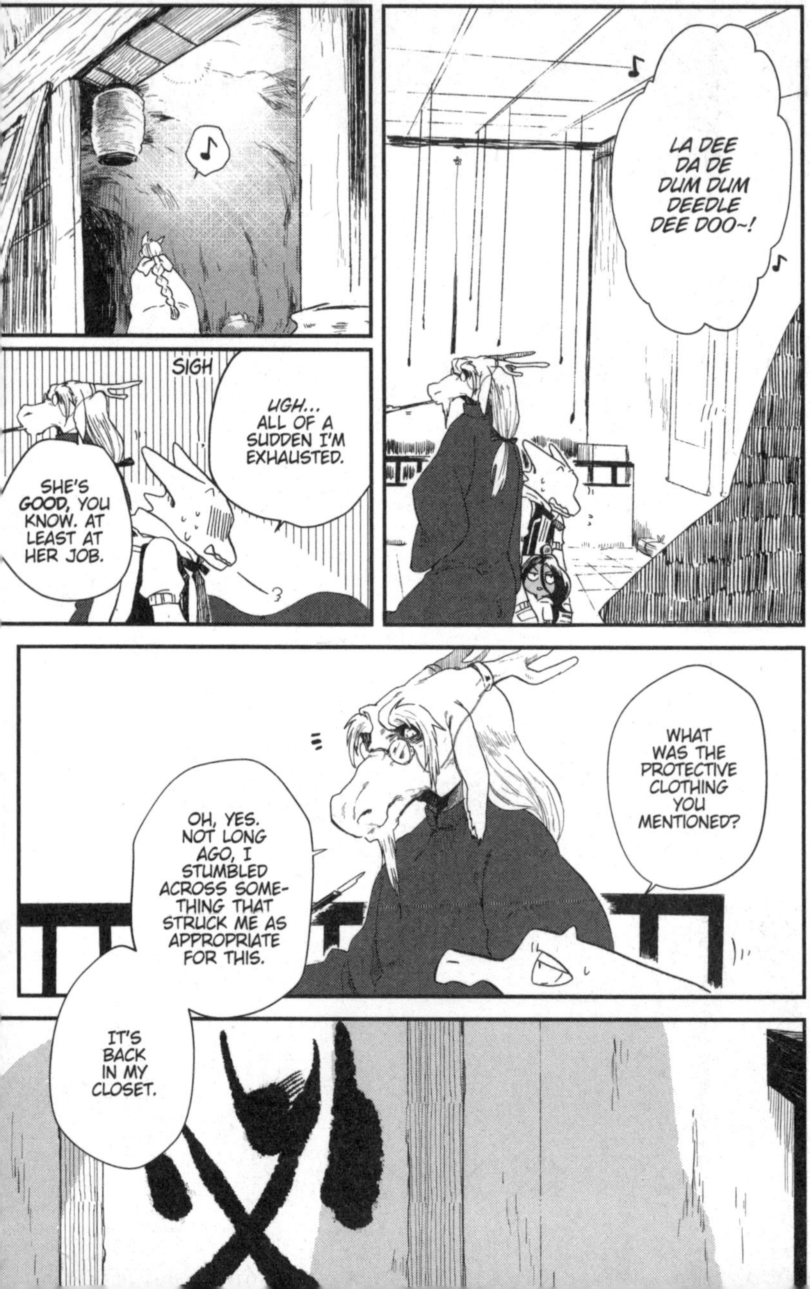
LA DEE DA DE DUM DUM DEEDLE DEE DOO~!
SIGH
UGH... ALL OF A SUDDEN I'M EXHAUSTED.
SHE'S GOOD, YOU KNOW. AT LEAST AT HER JOB.
WHAT WAS THE PROTECTIVE CLOTHING YOU MENTIONED?
OH, YES. NOT LONG AGO, I STUMBLED ACROSS SOME-THING THAT STRUCK ME AS APPROPRIATE FOR THIS.
IT'S BACK IN MY CLOSET.

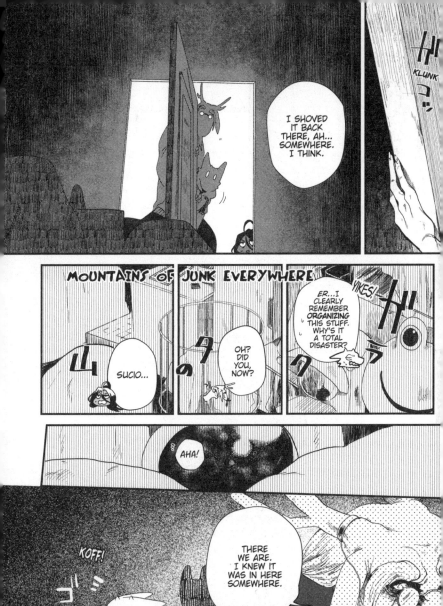

KLUNK

I SHOVED IT BACK THERE, AH... SOMEWHERE. I THINK.

MOUNTAINS OF JUNK EVERYWHERE

YIKES!

SUCIO...

OH? DID YOU, NOW?

ER...I CLEARLY REMEMBER ORGANIZING THIS STUFF. WHY'S IT A TOTAL DISASTER?

AHA!

KOFF!

THERE WE ARE. I KNEW IT WAS IN HERE SOMEWHERE.

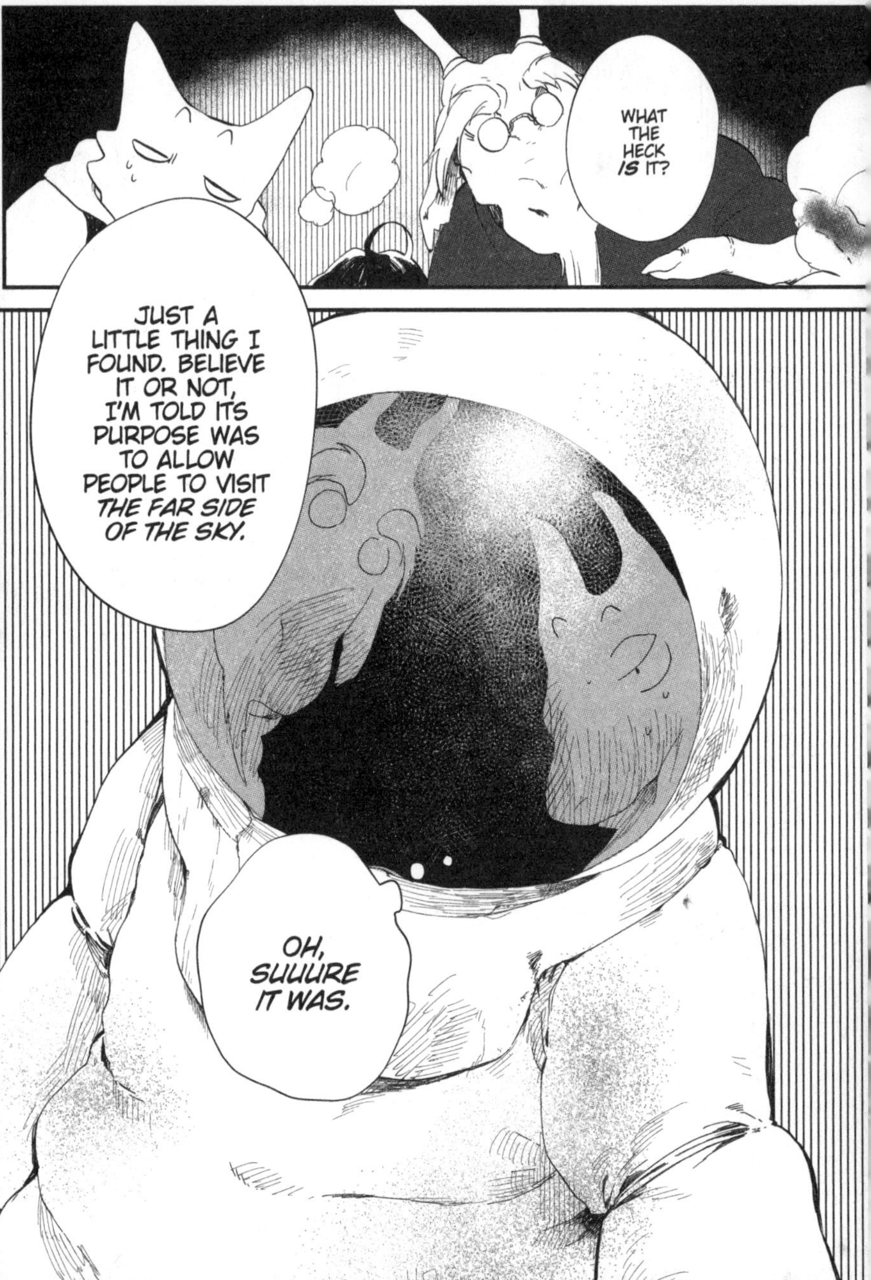
WHAT THE HECK *IS* IT?
JUST A LITTLE THING I FOUND. BELIEVE IT OR NOT, I'M TOLD ITS PURPOSE WAS TO ALLOW PEOPLE TO VISIT *THE FAR SIDE OF THE SKY.*
OH, SUUURE IT WAS.

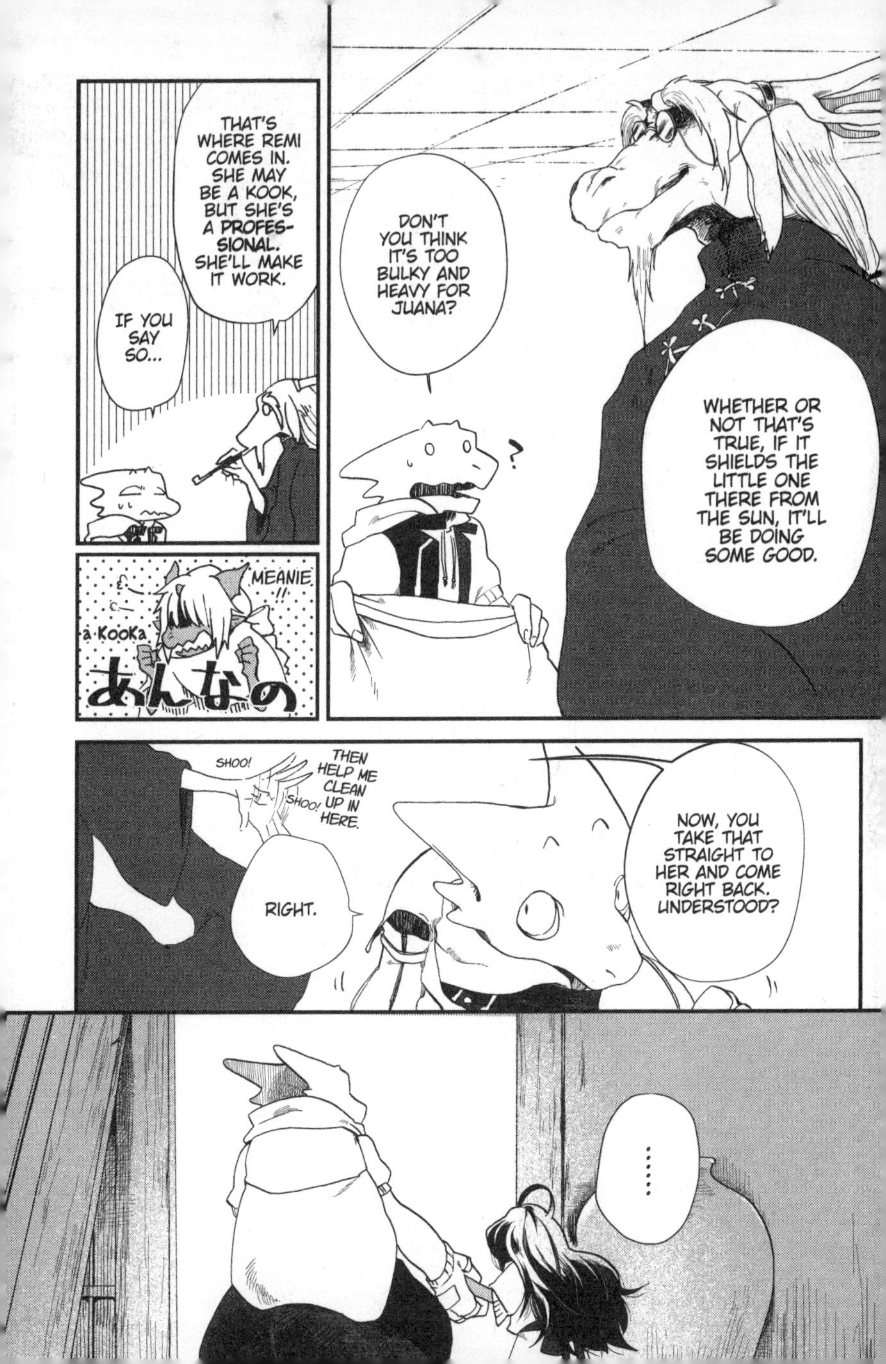
DON'T YOU THINK IT'S TOO BULKY AND HEAVY FOR JUANA?
?
WHETHER OR NOT THAT'S TRUE, IF IT SHIELDS THE LITTLE ONE THERE FROM THE SUN, IT'LL BE DOING SOME GOOD.
THAT'S WHERE REMI COMES IN. SHE MAY BE A KOOK, BUT SHE'S A PROFES-SIONAL. SHE'LL MAKE IT WORK.
IF YOU SAY SO...
MEANIE!!
a KooKa
あんなの
NOW, YOU TAKE THAT STRAIGHT TO HER AND COME RIGHT BACK. UNDERSTOOD?
RIGHT.
THEN HELP ME CLEAN UP IN HERE.
SHOO!
SHOO!
......

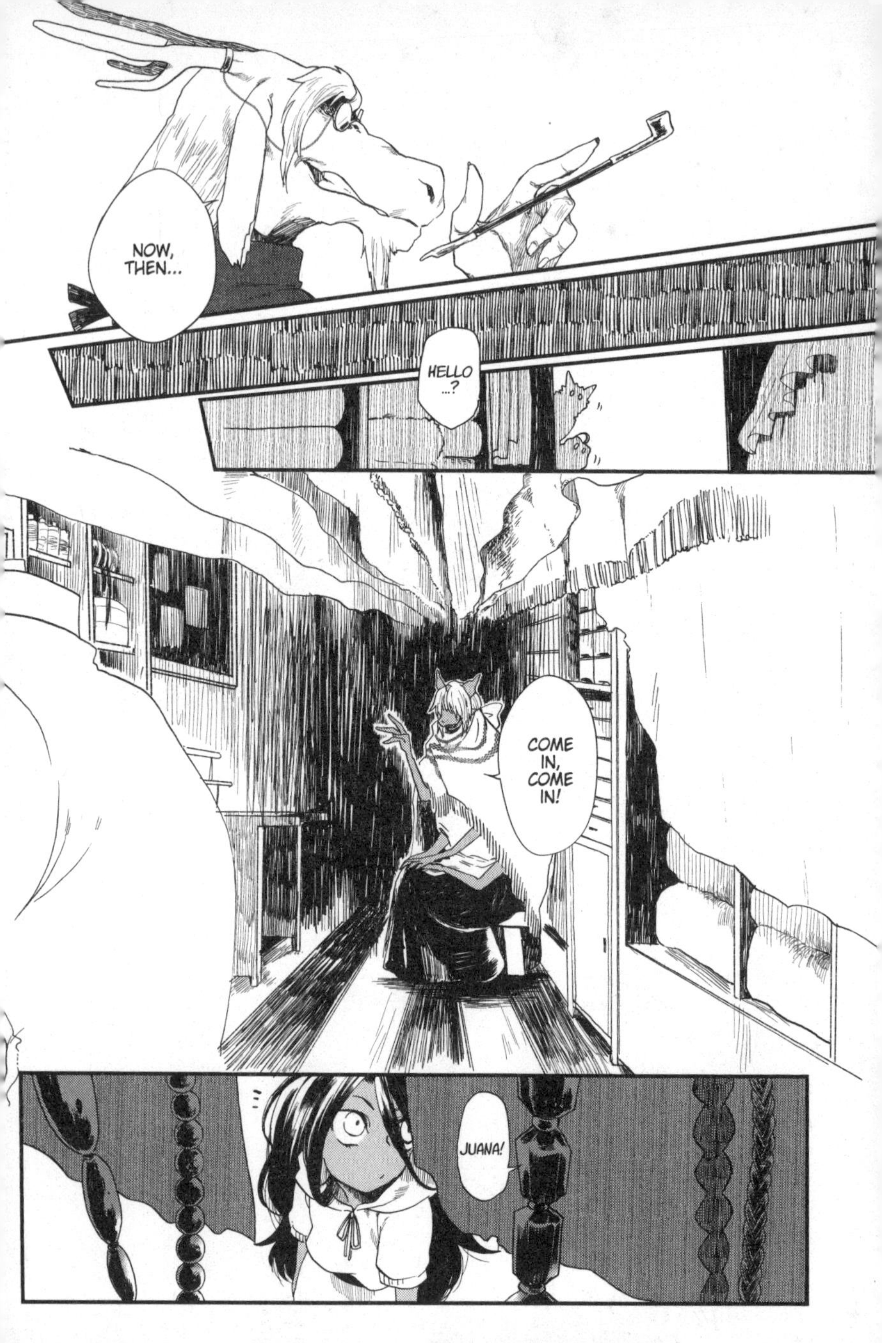
NOW, THEN...
HELLO...?
COME IN, COME IN!
JUANA!

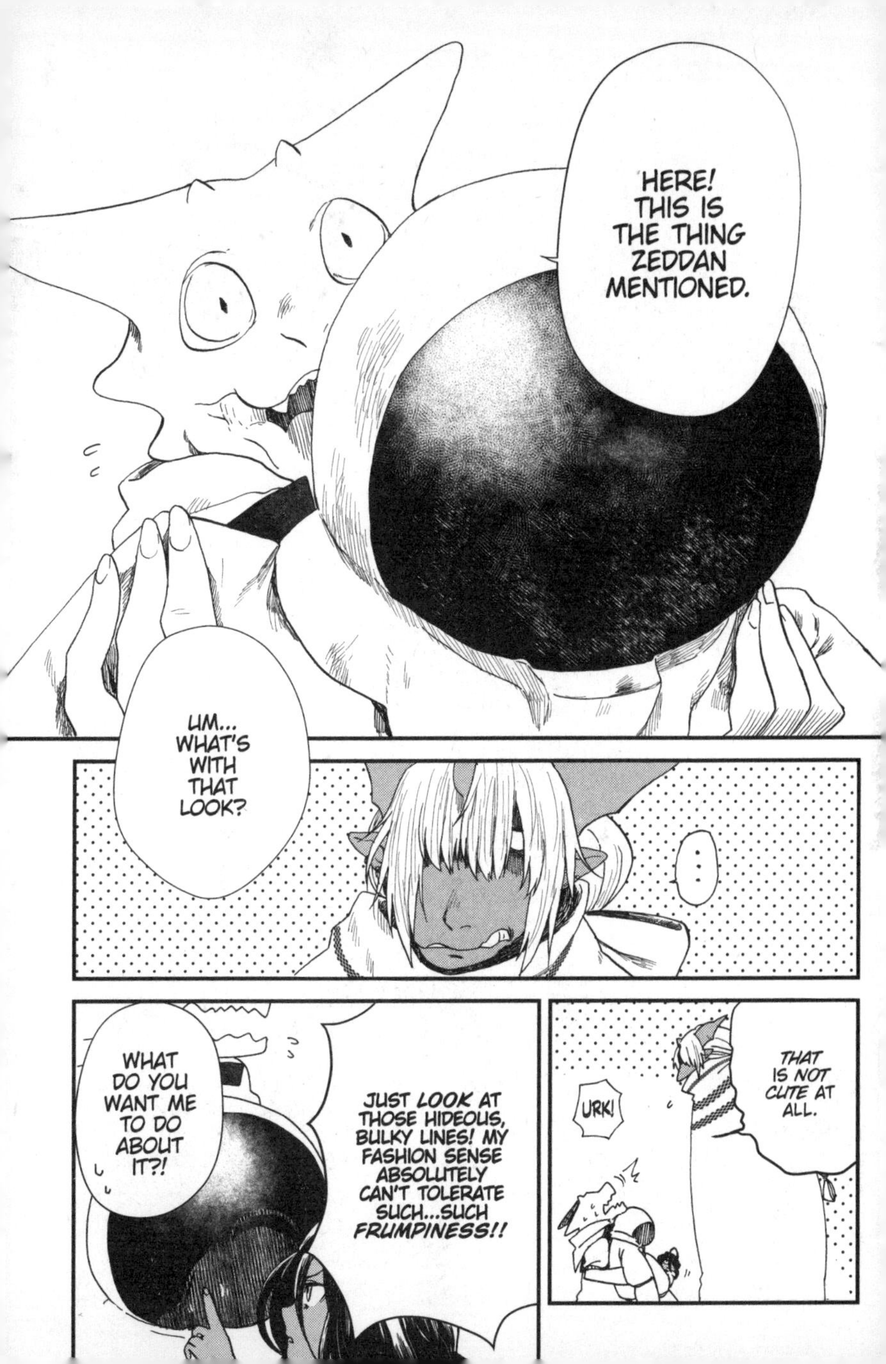
HERE! THIS IS THE THING ZEDDAN MENTIONED.
UM... WHAT'S WITH THAT LOOK?
...
THAT IS NOT CUTE AT ALL.
URK!
JUST *LOOK* AT THOSE HIDEOUS, BULKY LINES! MY FASHION SENSE ABSOLUTELY CAN'T TOLERATE SUCH...SUCH *FRUMPINESS!!*
WHAT DO YOU WANT ME TO DO ABOUT IT?!

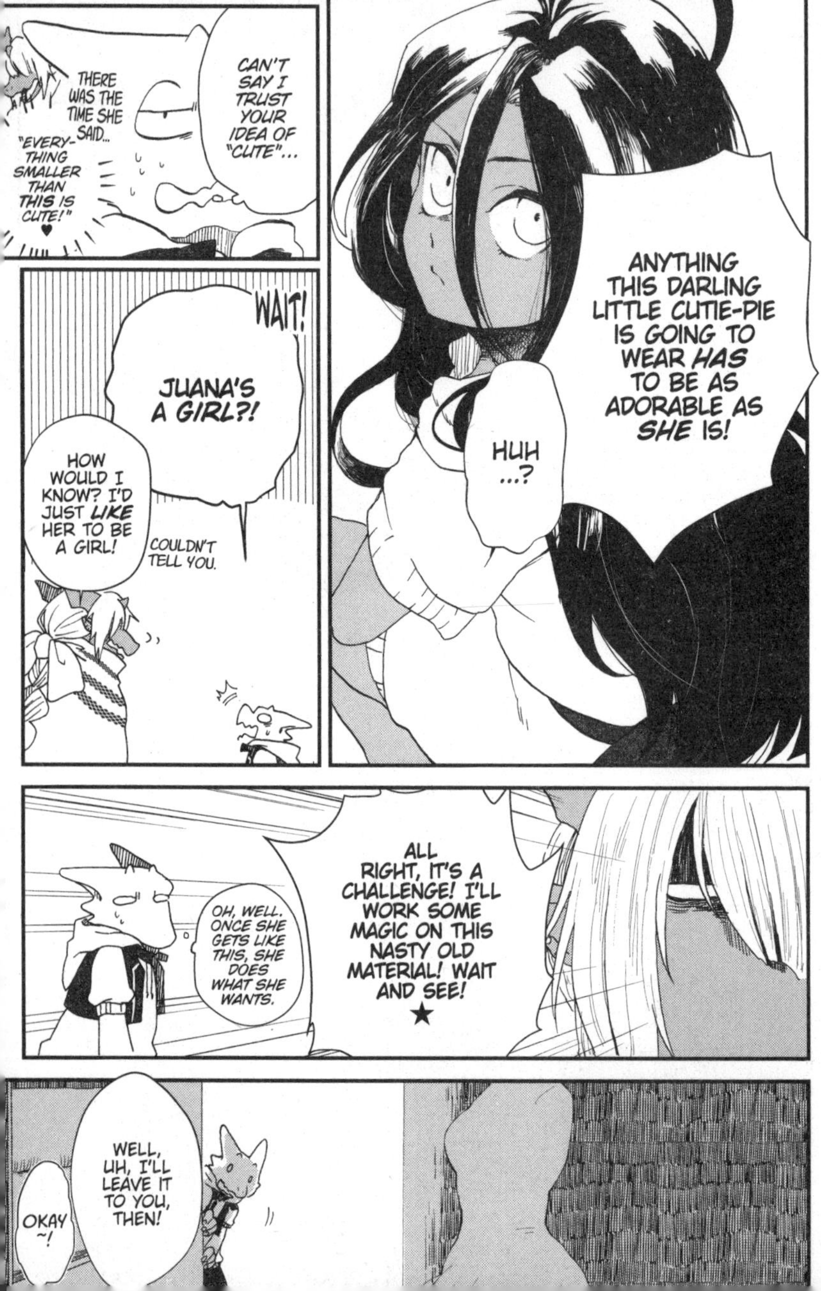
ANYTHING THIS DARLING LITTLE CUTIE-PIE IS GOING TO WEAR HAS TO BE AS ADORABLE AS SHE IS!
HUH ...?
CAN'T SAY I TRUST YOUR IDEA OF "CUTE"...
THERE WAS THE TIME SHE SAID... "EVERY-THING SMALLER THAN THIS IS CUTE!" ♥
WAIT!
JUANA'S A GIRL?!
COULDN'T TELL YOU.
HOW WOULD I KNOW? I'D JUST LIKE HER TO BE A GIRL!
ALL RIGHT, IT'S A CHALLENGE! I'LL WORK SOME MAGIC ON THIS NASTY OLD MATERIAL! WAIT AND SEE! ★
OH, WELL. ONCE SHE GETS LIKE THIS, SHE DOES WHAT SHE WANTS.
WELL, UH, I'LL LEAVE IT TO YOU, THEN!
OKAY ~!

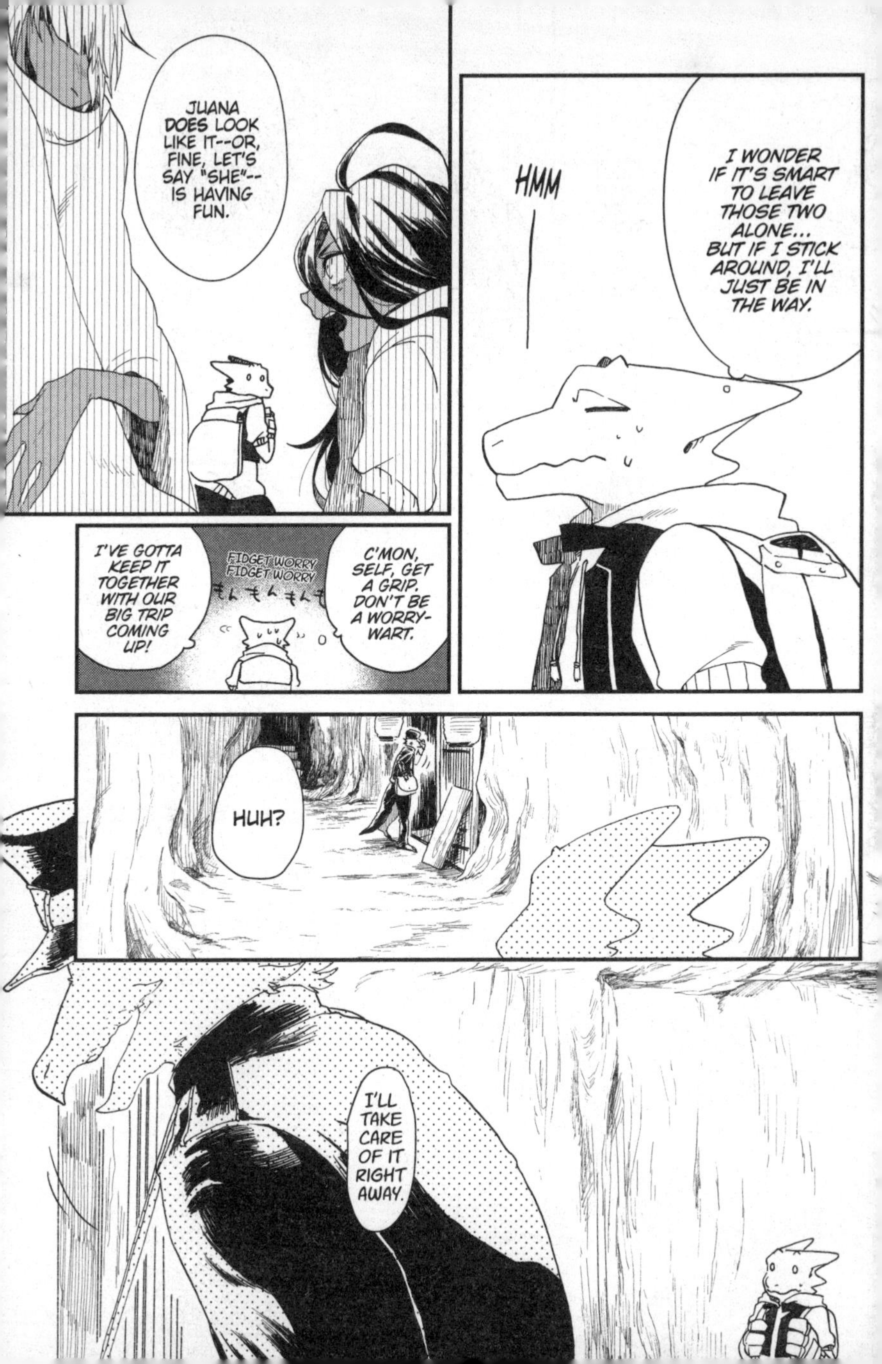
I WONDER IF IT'S SMART TO LEAVE THOSE TWO ALONE... BUT IF I STICK AROUND, I'LL JUST BE IN THE WAY.
HMM
JUANA DOES LOOK LIKE IT--OR, FINE, LET'S SAY "SHE"--IS HAVING FUN.
C'MON, SELF, GET A GRIP. DON'T BE A WORRY-WART.
FIDGET WORRY FIDGET WORRY
もんもんもんも
I'VE GOTTA KEEP IT TOGETHER WITH OUR BIG TRIP COMING UP!
HUH?
I'LL TAKE CARE OF IT RIGHT AWAY.

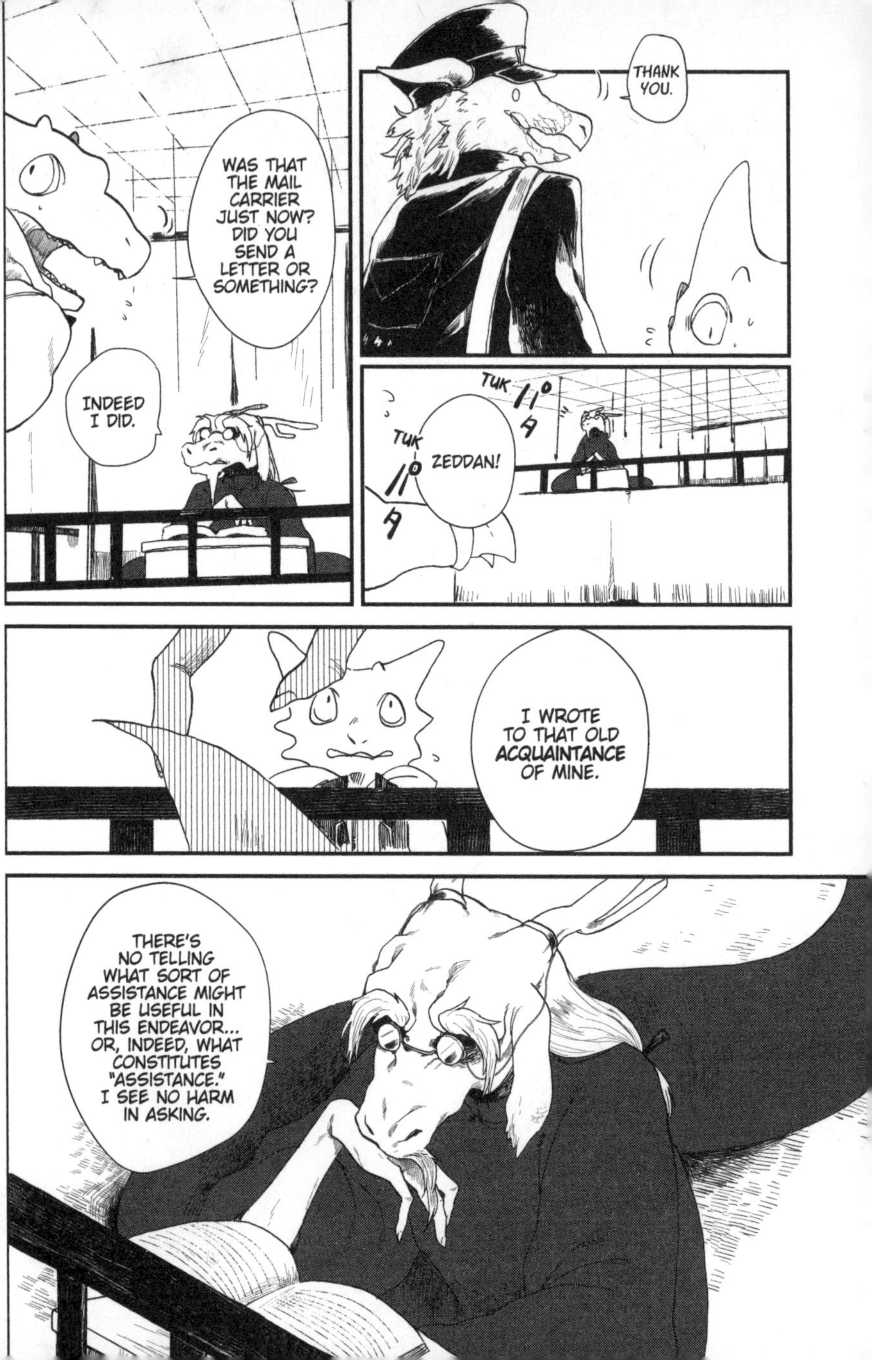
THANK YOU.
TUK
TUK
ZEDDAN!
WAS THAT THE MAIL CARRIER JUST NOW? DID YOU SEND A LETTER OR SOMETHING?
INDEED I DID.
I WROTE TO THAT OLD ACQUAINTANCE OF MINE.
THERE'S NO TELLING WHAT SORT OF ASSISTANCE MIGHT BE USEFUL IN THIS ENDEAVOR... OR, INDEED, WHAT CONSTITUTES "ASSISTANCE." I SEE NO HARM IN ASKING.

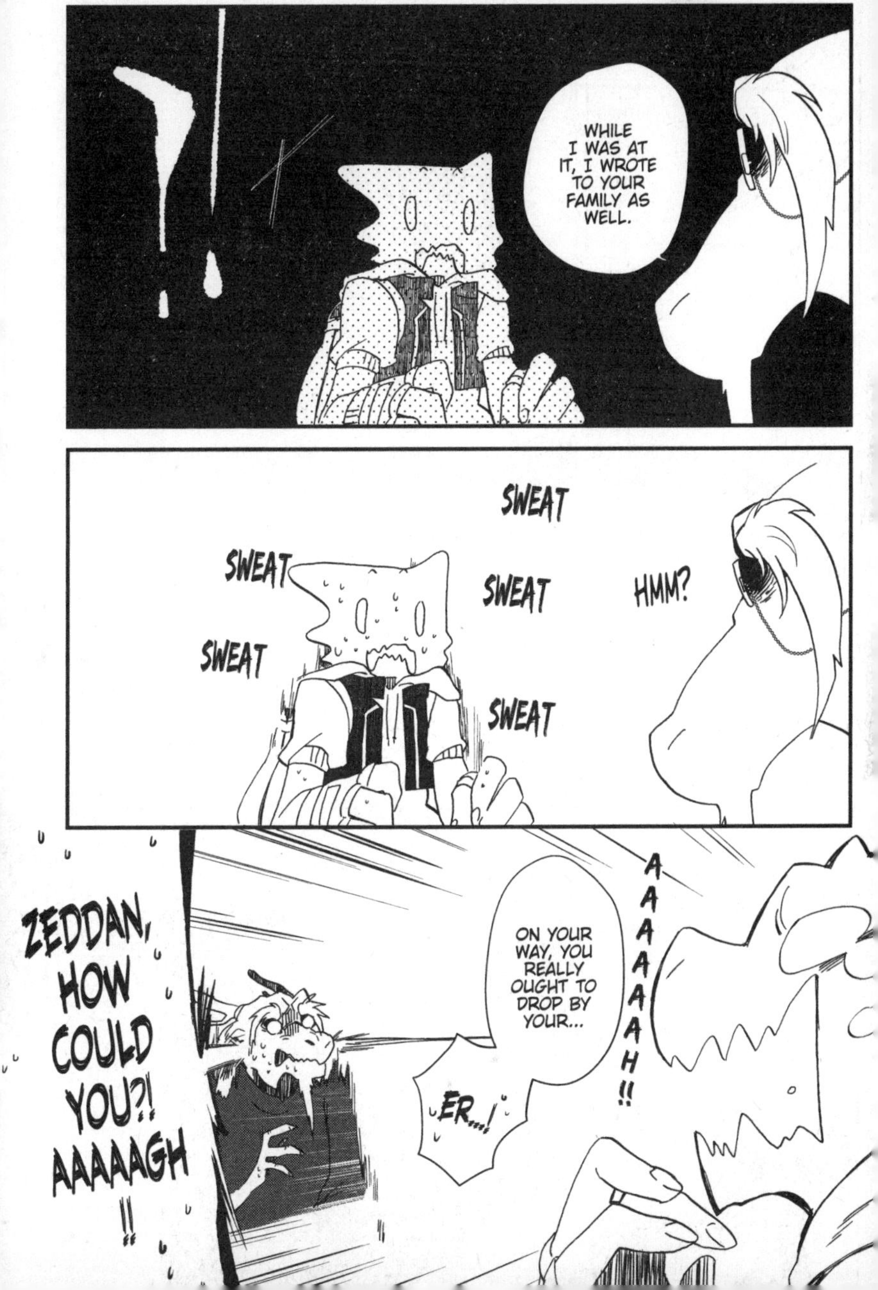

WHILE I WAS AT IT, I WROTE TO YOUR FAMILY AS WELL.
HMM?
SWEAT
SWEAT
SWEAT
SWEAT
SWEAT
AAAAAAAH!!
ON YOUR WAY, YOU REALLY OUGHT TO DROP BY YOUR...
ER...!
ZEDDAN, HOW COULD YOU?! AAAAAGH!!

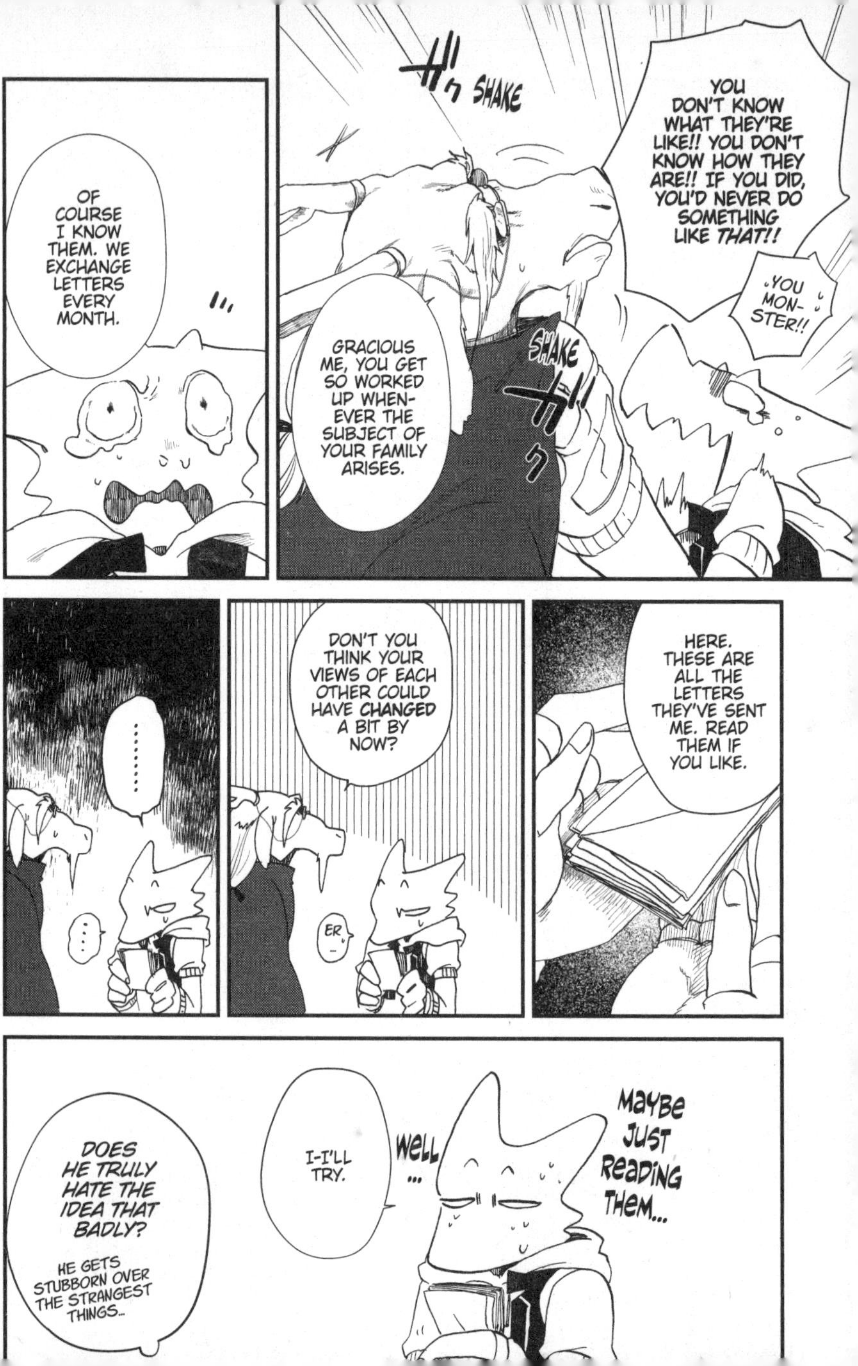
YOU DON'T KNOW WHAT THEY'RE LIKE!! YOU DON'T KNOW HOW THEY ARE!! IF YOU DID, YOU'D NEVER DO SOMETHING LIKE *THAT!!*
YOU MON-STER!!
SHAKE
GRACIOUS ME, YOU GET SO WORKED UP WHEN-EVER THE SUBJECT OF YOUR FAMILY ARISES.
SHAKE
OF COURSE I KNOW THEM. WE EXCHANGE LETTERS EVERY MONTH.
HERE. THESE ARE ALL THE LETTERS THEY'VE SENT ME. READ THEM IF YOU LIKE.
DON'T YOU THINK YOUR VIEWS OF EACH OTHER COULD HAVE CHANGED A BIT BY NOW?
ER...
......
...
MAYBE JUST READING THEM...
WELL...
I-I'LL TRY.
DOES HE TRULY HATE THE IDEA THAT BADLY?
HE GETS STUBBORN OVER THE STRANGEST THINGS..

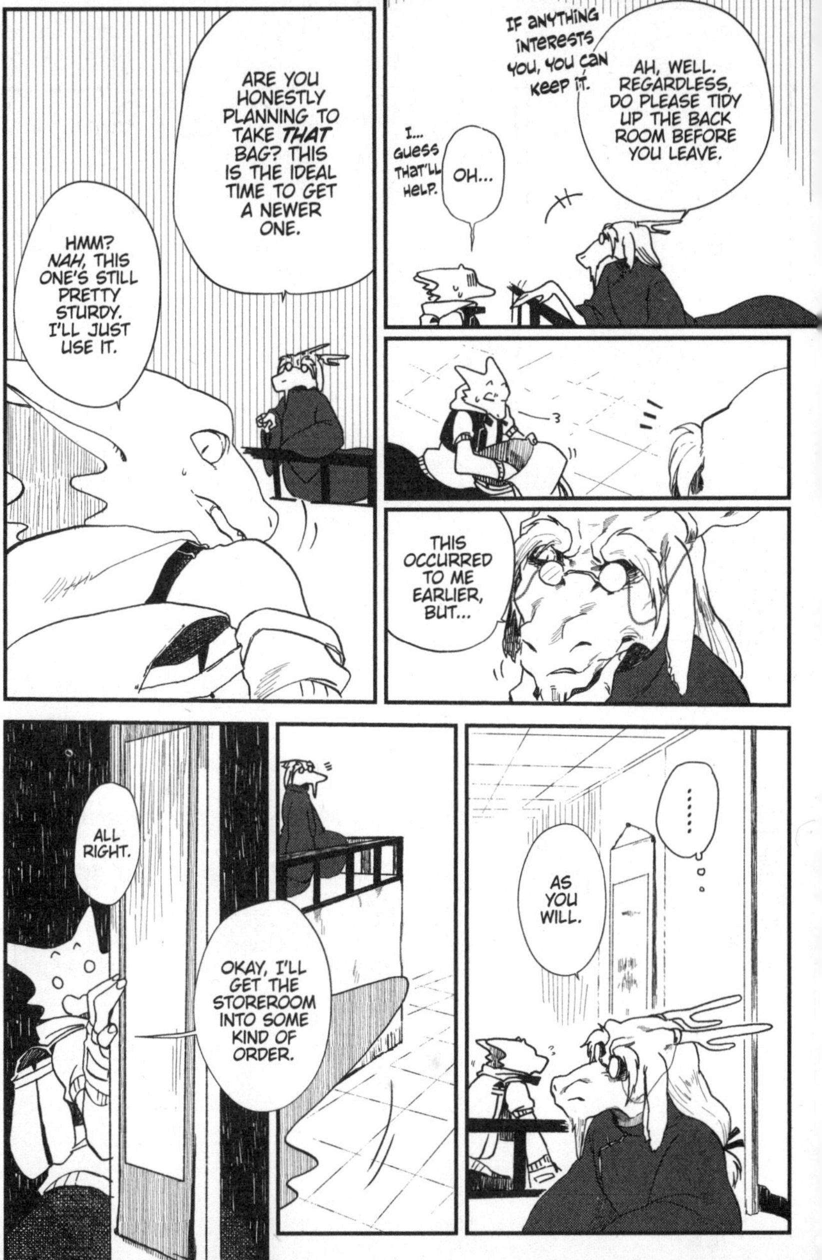
AH, WELL. REGARDLESS, DO PLEASE TIDY UP THE BACK ROOM BEFORE YOU LEAVE.
IF ANYTHING INTERESTS YOU, YOU CAN KEEP IT.
OH...
I... GUESS THAT'LL HELP.
THIS OCCURRED TO ME EARLIER, BUT...
ARE YOU HONESTLY PLANNING TO TAKE THAT BAG? THIS IS THE IDEAL TIME TO GET A NEWER ONE.
HMM? NAH, THIS ONE'S STILL PRETTY STURDY. I'LL JUST USE IT.
......
AS YOU WILL.
OKAY, I'LL GET THE STOREROOM INTO SOME KIND OF ORDER.
ALL RIGHT.

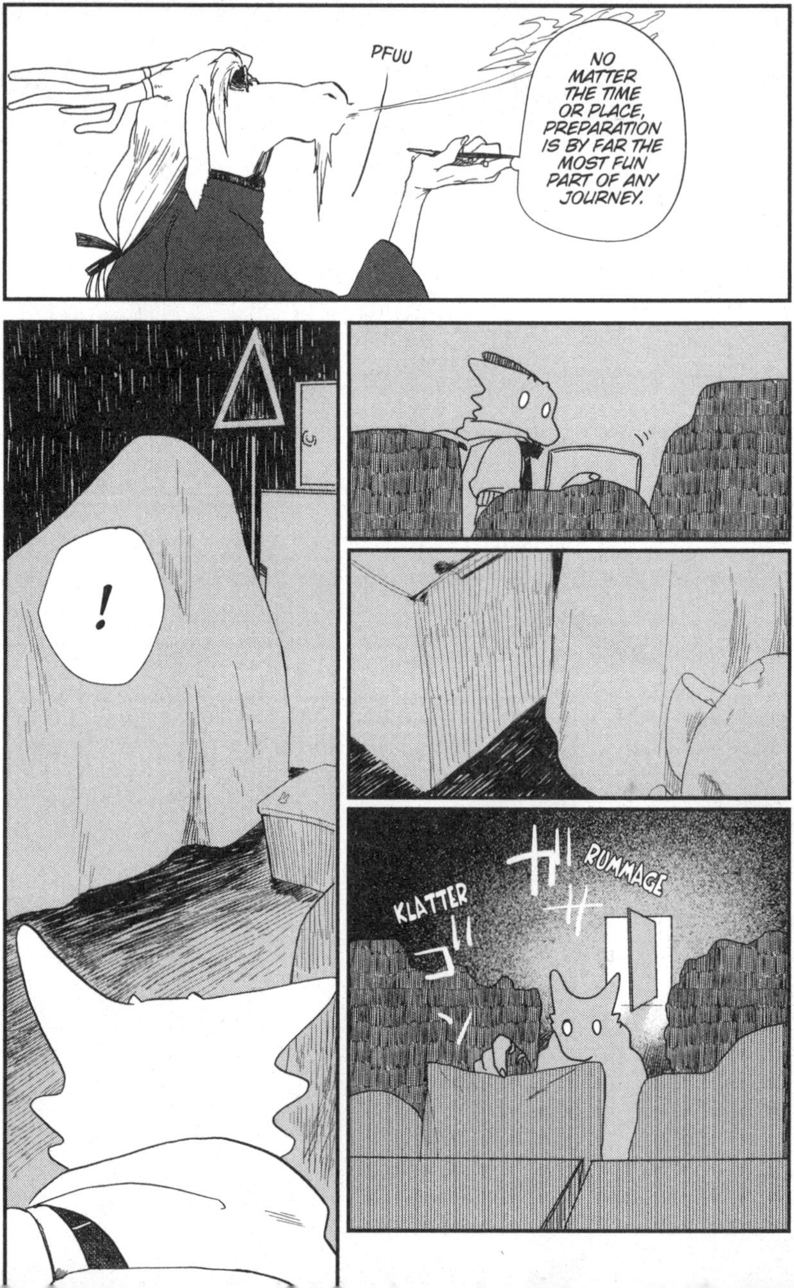
NO MATTER THE TIME OR PLACE, PREPARATION IS BY FAR THE MOST FUN PART OF ANY JOURNEY.
PFUU
RUMMAGE
KLATTER
!

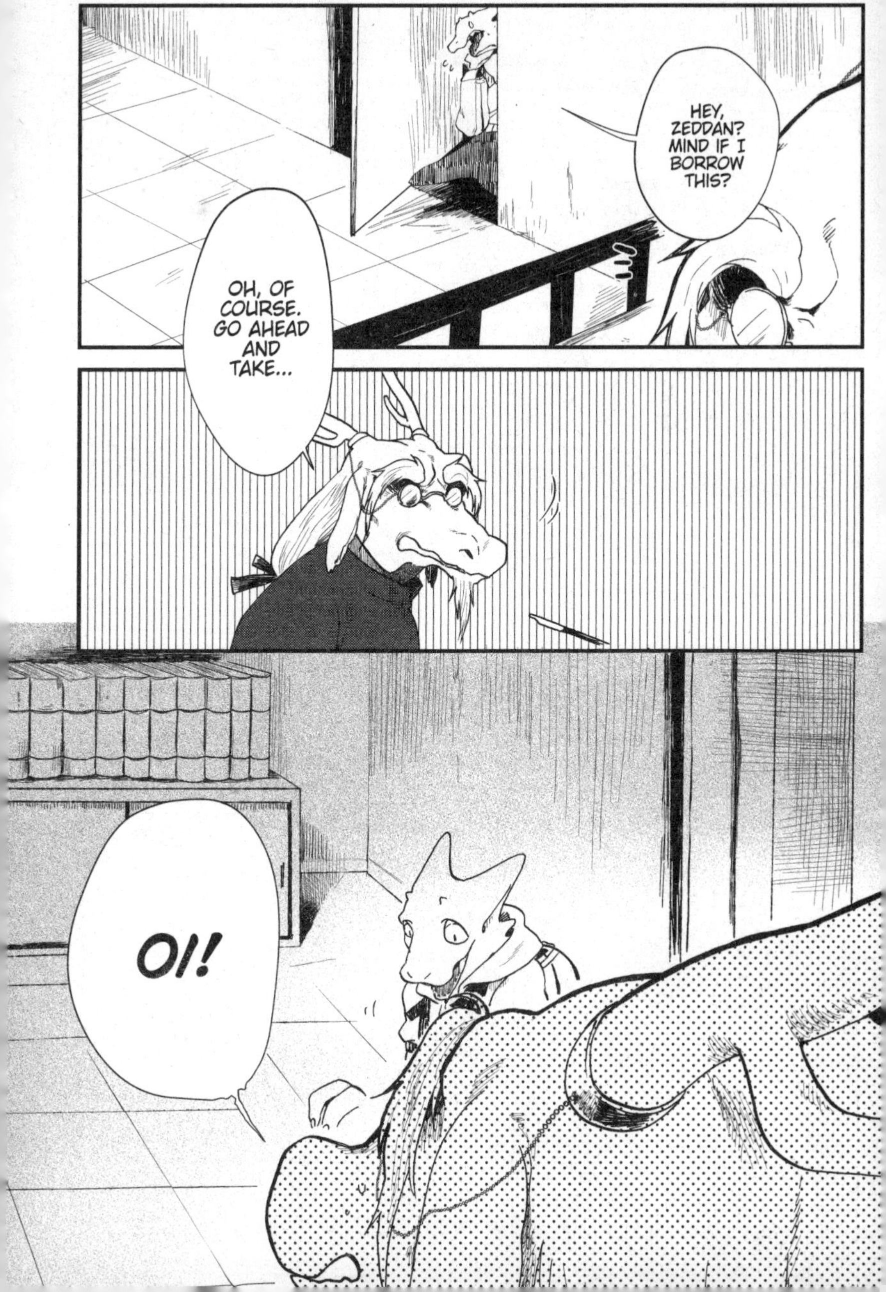
HEY, ZEDDAN? MIND IF I BORROW THIS?
OH, OF COURSE. GO AHEAD AND TAKE...
OI!

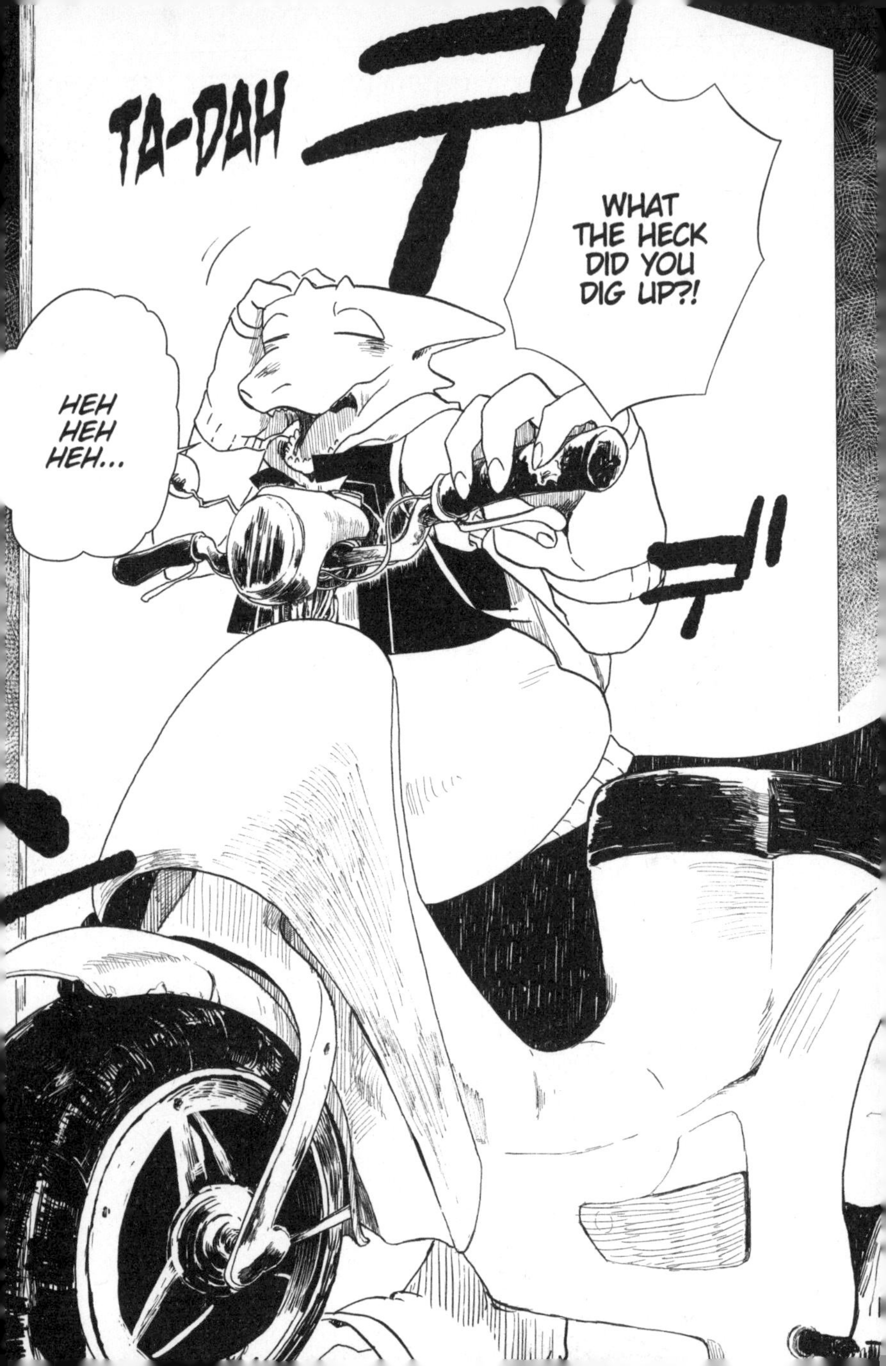
TA-DAH
WHAT THE HECK DID YOU DIG UP?!
HEH HEH HEH...

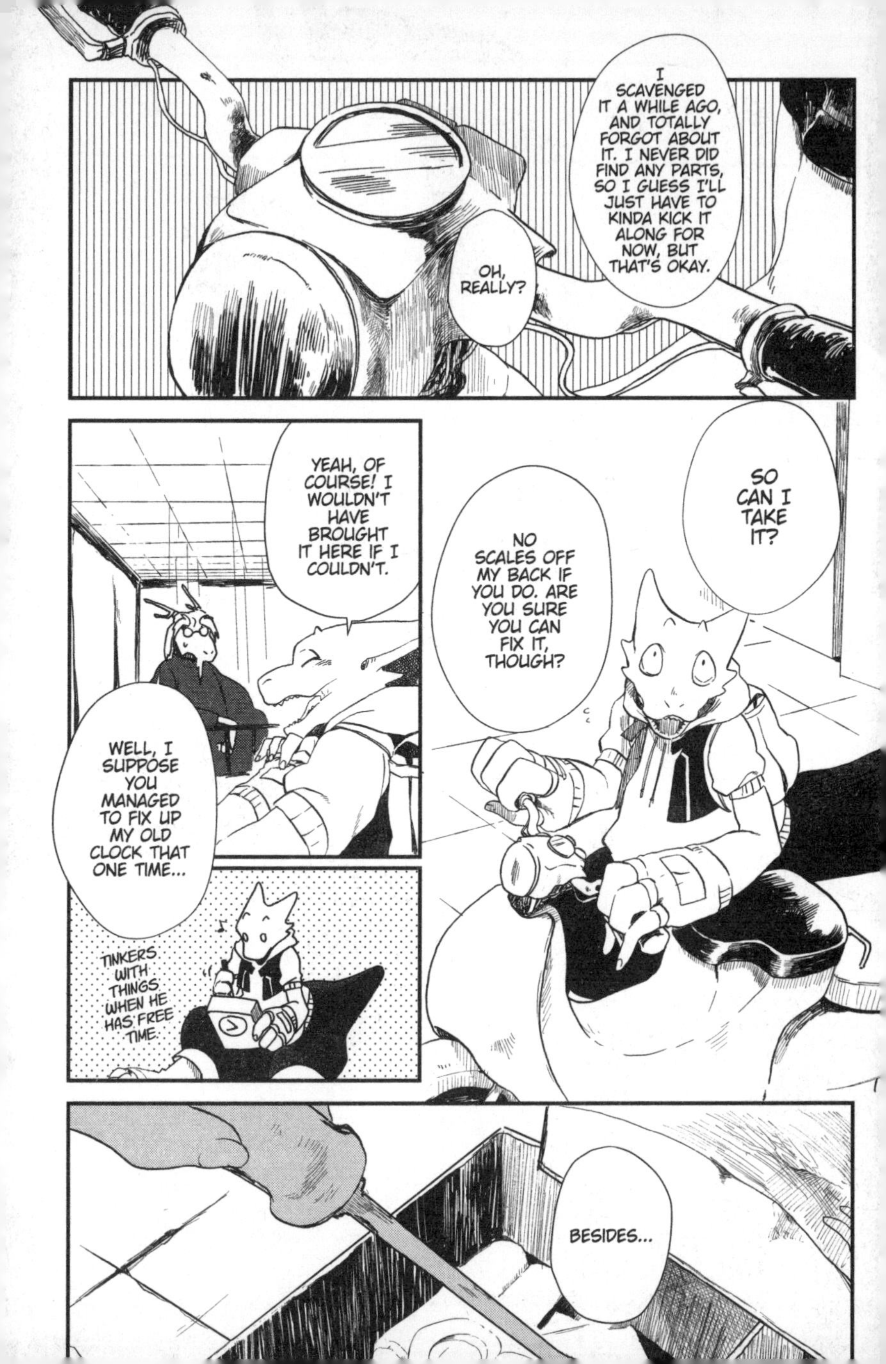
I SCAVENGED IT A WHILE AGO, AND TOTALLY FORGOT ABOUT IT. I NEVER DID FIND ANY PARTS, SO I GUESS I'LL JUST HAVE TO KINDA KICK IT ALONG FOR NOW, BUT THAT'S OKAY.
OH, REALLY?
SO CAN I TAKE IT?
NO SCALES OFF MY BACK IF YOU DO. ARE YOU SURE YOU CAN FIX IT, THOUGH?
YEAH, OF COURSE! I WOULDN'T HAVE BROUGHT IT HERE IF I COULDN'T.
WELL, I SUPPOSE YOU MANAGED TO FIX UP MY OLD CLOCK THAT ONE TIME...
TINKERS WITH THINGS WHEN HE HAS FREE TIME.
BESIDES...

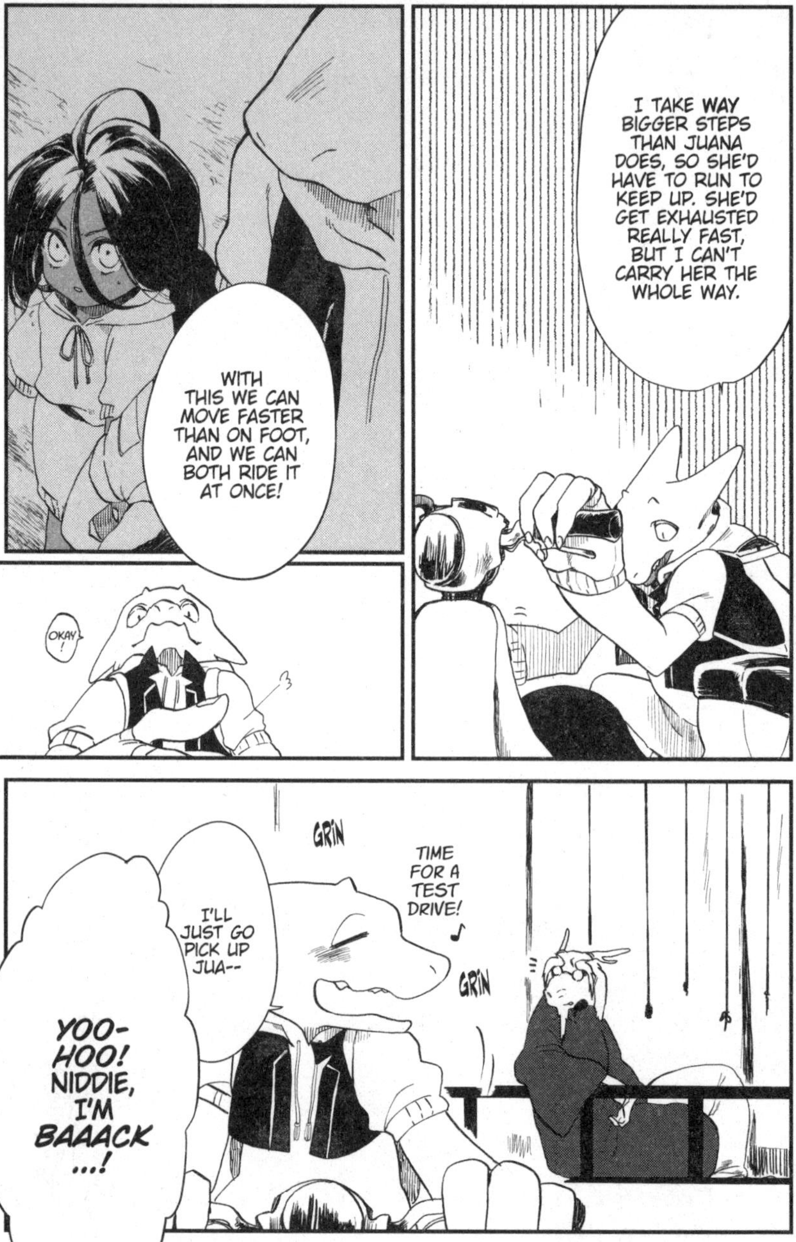
I TAKE WAY BIGGER STEPS THAN JUANA DOES, SO SHE'D HAVE TO RUN TO KEEP UP. SHE'D GET EXHAUSTED REALLY FAST, BUT I CAN'T CARRY HER THE WHOLE WAY.
WITH THIS WE CAN MOVE FASTER THAN ON FOOT, AND WE CAN BOTH RIDE IT AT ONCE!
OKAY!
GRIN
TIME FOR A TEST DRIVE!
GRIN
I'LL JUST GO PICK UP JUA--
YOO-HOO! NIDDIE, I'M BAAACK ...!

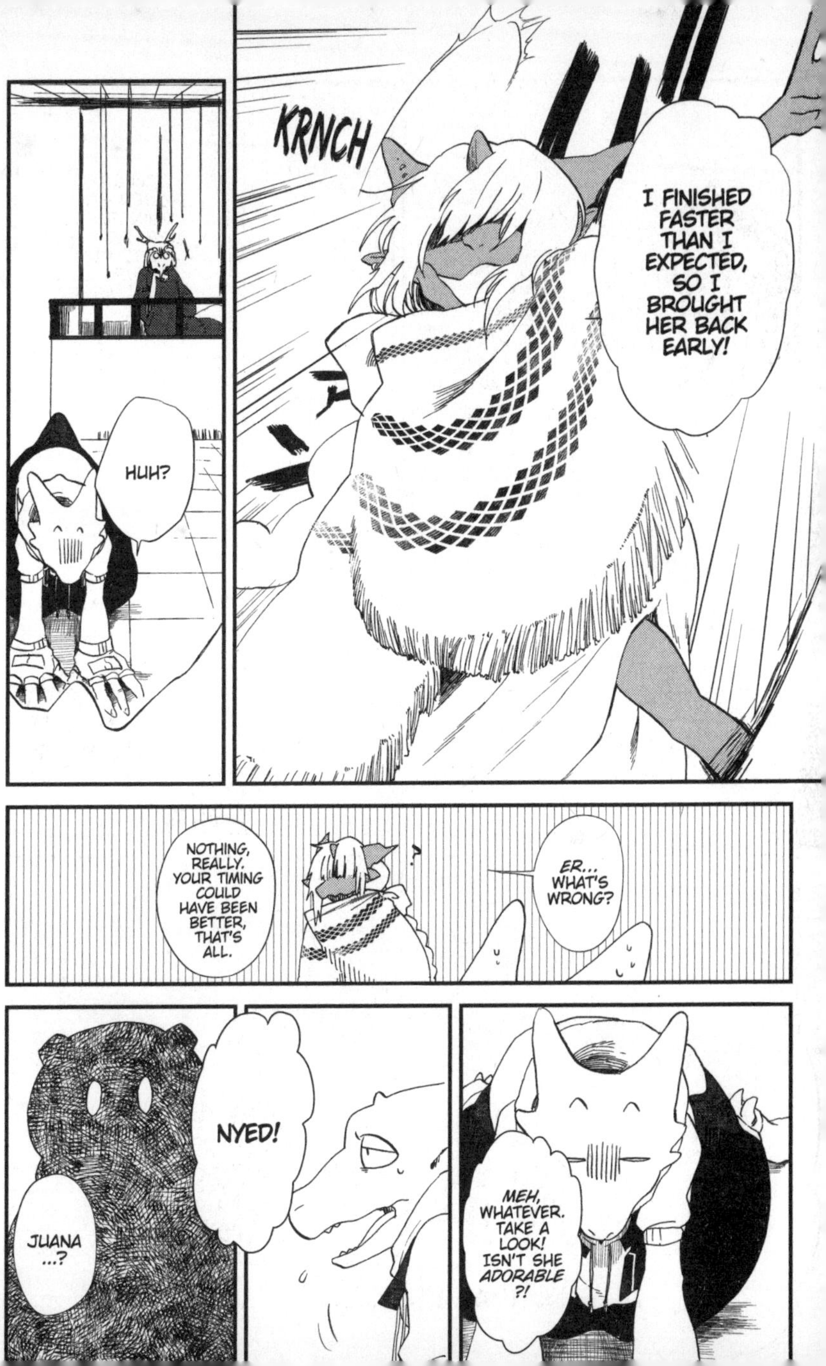
KRNCH
I FINISHED FASTER THAN I EXPECTED, SO I BROUGHT HER BACK EARLY!
HUH?
ER... WHAT'S WRONG?
?
NOTHING, REALLY. YOUR TIMING COULD HAVE BEEN BETTER, THAT'S ALL.
MEH, WHATEVER. TAKE A LOOK! ISN'T SHE *ADORABLE* ?!
NYED!
JUANA ...?

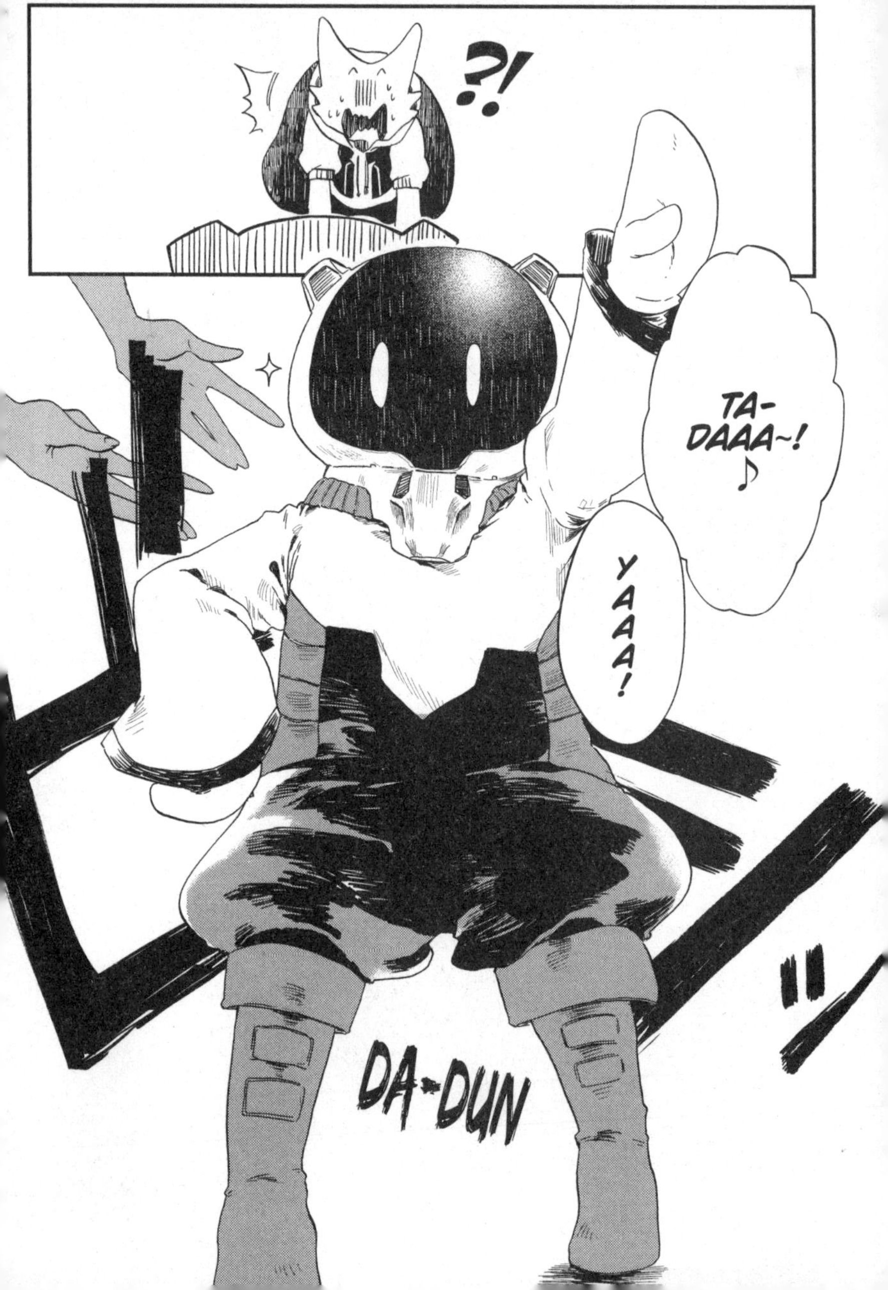
?!
TA-DAAA~! ♪
YAAAA!
DA-DUN

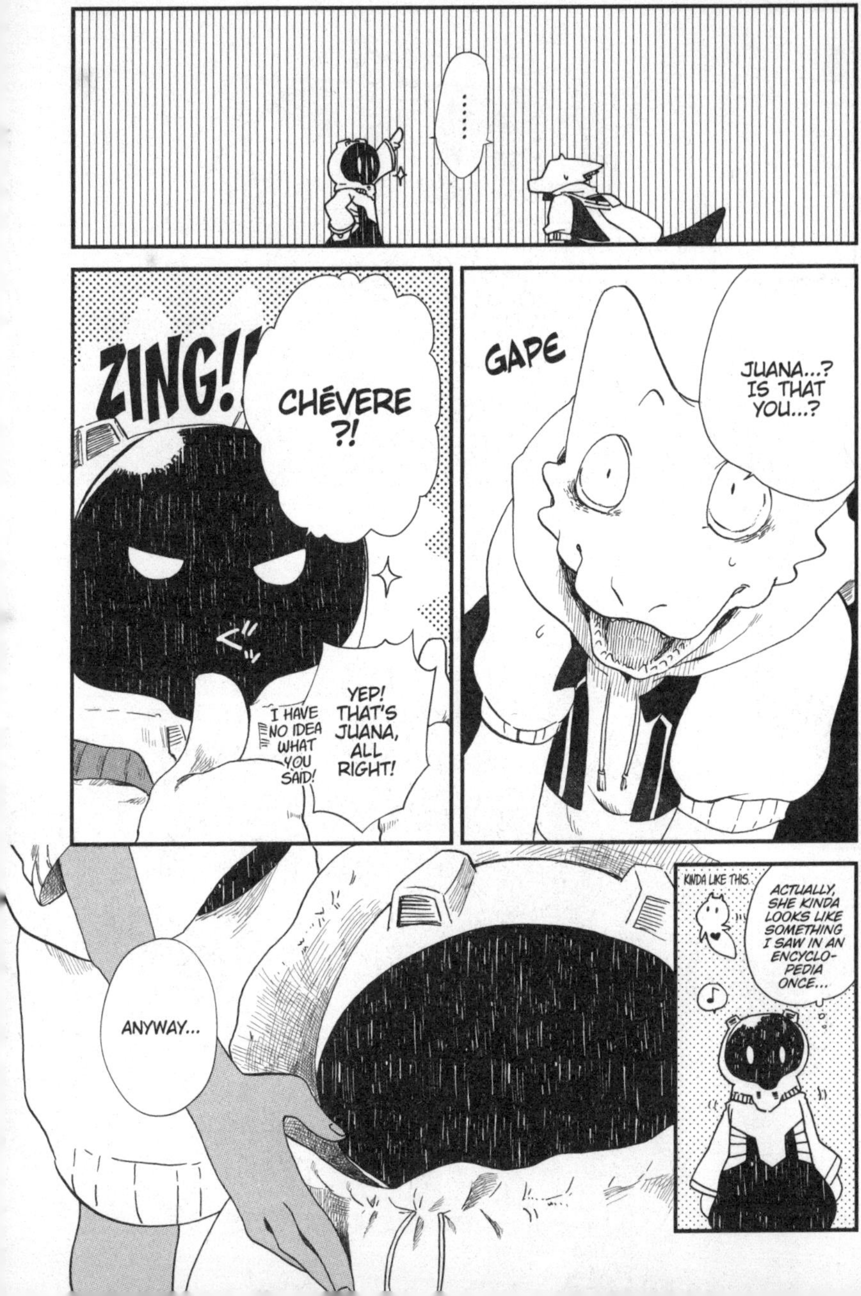
......
GAPE
JUANA...? IS THAT YOU...?
ZING!!
CHÉVERE ?!
YEP! THAT'S JUANA, ALL RIGHT!
I HAVE NO IDEA WHAT YOU SAID!
KINDA LIKE THIS.
ACTUALLY, SHE KINDA LOOKS LIKE SOMETHING I SAW IN AN ENCYCLOPEDIA ONCE...
ANYWAY...

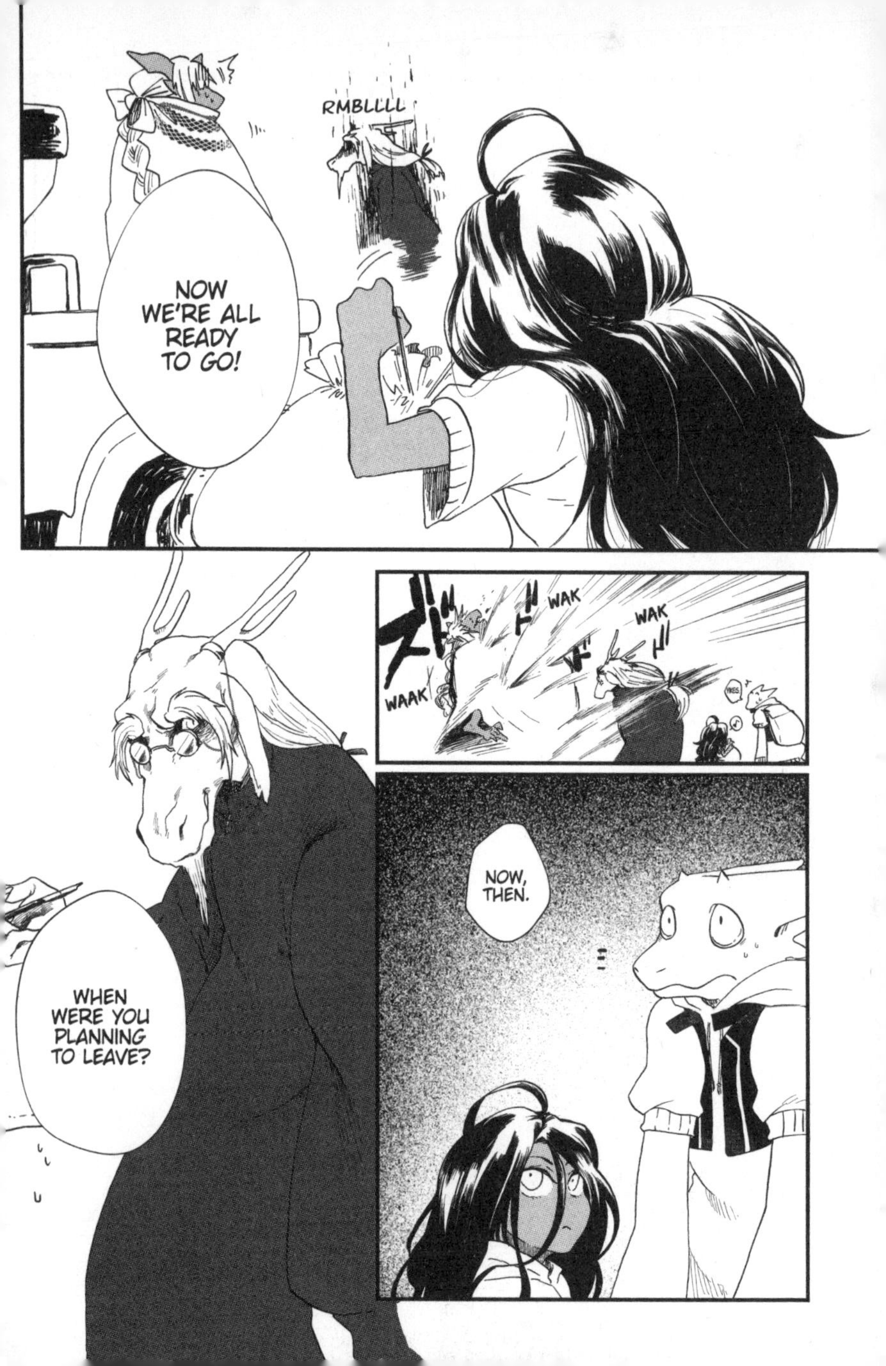
RMBLLLL
NOW WE'RE ALL READY TO GO!
WAK
WAK
WAAK
NOW, THEN.
WHEN WERE YOU PLANNING TO LEAVE?

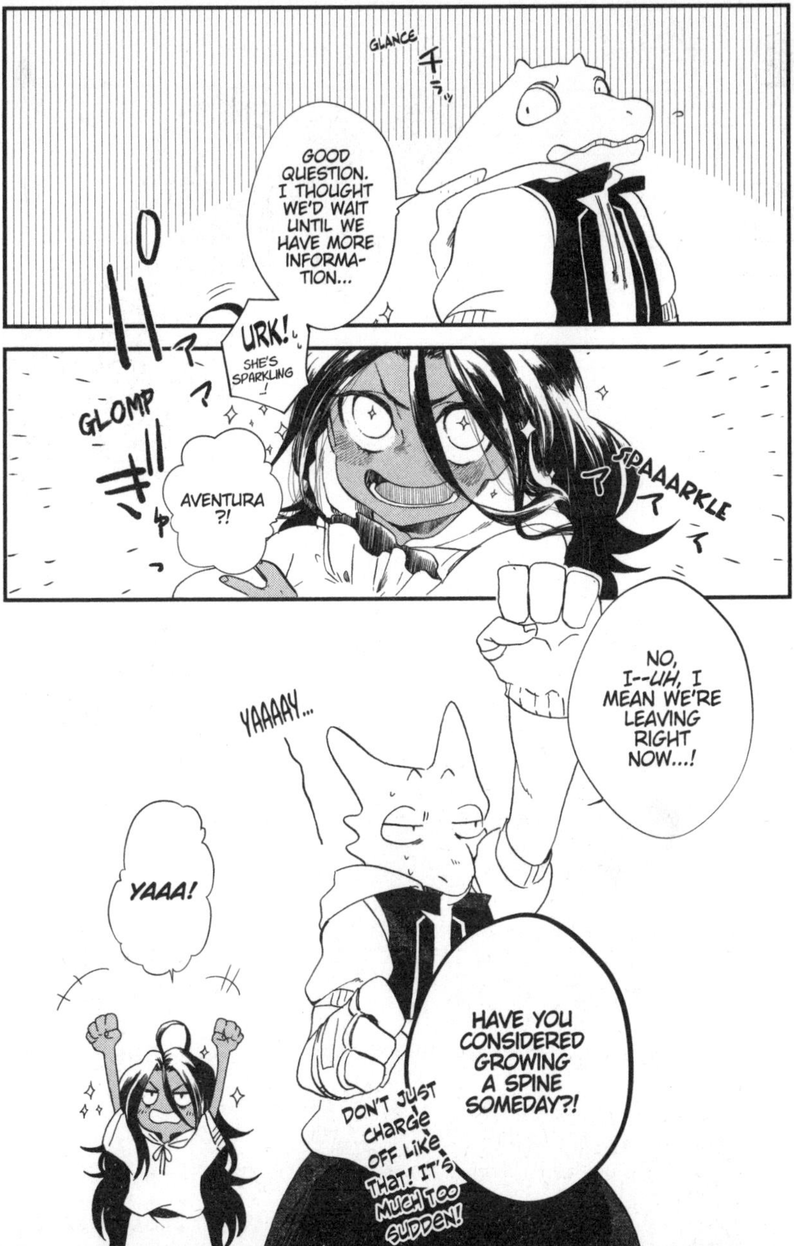
GLANCE
チラッ
GOOD QUESTION. I THOUGHT WE'D WAIT UNTIL WE HAVE MORE INFORMA-TION...
URK!
SHE'S SPARKLING!
SPAAAARKLE
AVENTURA?!
GLOMP
ぎゅっ
NO, I--UH, I MEAN WE'RE LEAVING RIGHT NOW...!
YAAAAY...
HAVE YOU CONSIDERED GROWING A SPINE SOMEDAY?!
DON'T JUST CHARGE OFF LIKE THAT! IT'S MUCH TOO SUDDEN!
YAAA!

Juana and the
Dragonewts'
Seven Kingdoms

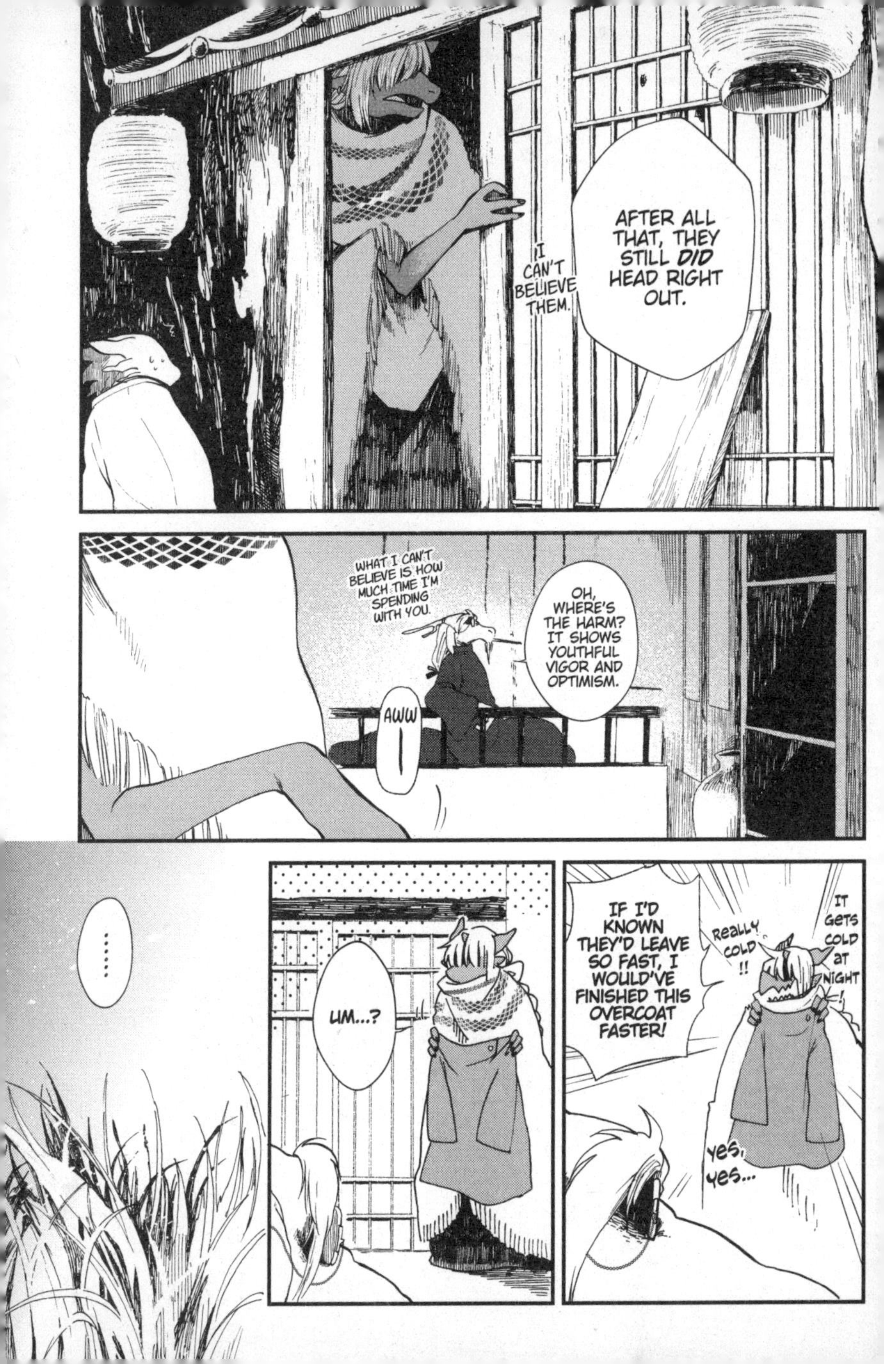
AFTER ALL THAT, THEY STILL *DID* HEAD RIGHT OUT.
I CAN'T BELIEVE THEM.
OH, WHERE'S THE HARM? IT SHOWS YOUTHFUL VIGOR AND OPTIMISM.
WHAT I CAN'T BELIEVE IS HOW MUCH TIME I'M SPENDING WITH YOU.
AWW
IF I'D KNOWN THEY'D LEAVE SO FAST, I WOULD'VE FINISHED THIS OVERCOAT FASTER!
IT GETS COLD at NIGHT!
Really COLD!!
Yes, yes...
UM...?
......

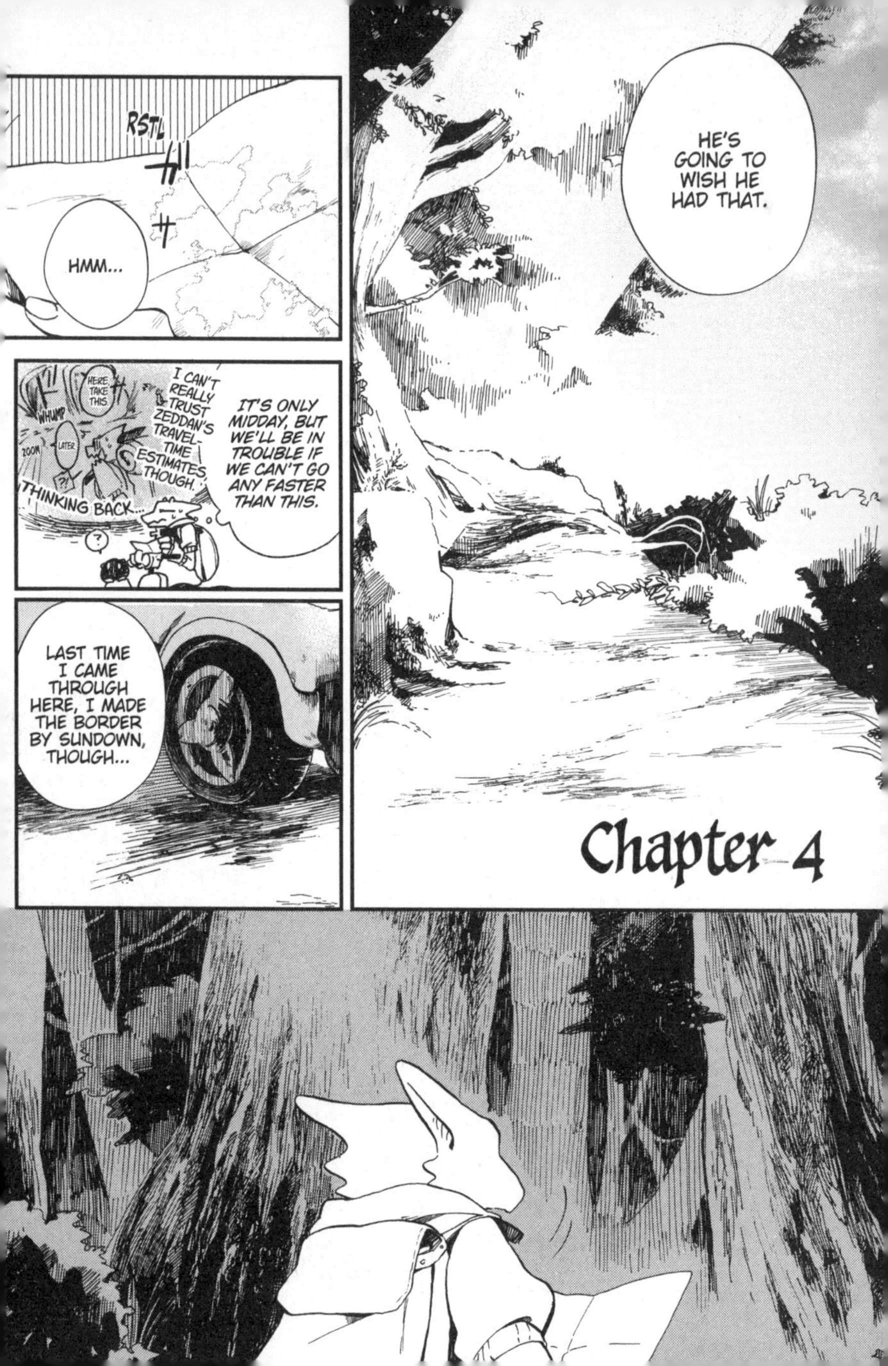
HE'S GOING TO WISH HE HAD THAT.
Chapter 4
RSTL
HMM...
IT'S ONLY MIDDAY, BUT WE'LL BE IN TROUBLE IF WE CAN'T GO ANY FASTER THAN THIS.
I CAN'T REALLY TRUST ZEDDAN'S TRAVEL-TIME ESTIMATES, THOUGH.
HERE, TAKE THIS.
WHUMP
LATER
ZOOM
?!
THINKING BACK...
?
LAST TIME I CAME THROUGH HERE, I MADE THE BORDER BY SUNDOWN, THOUGH...

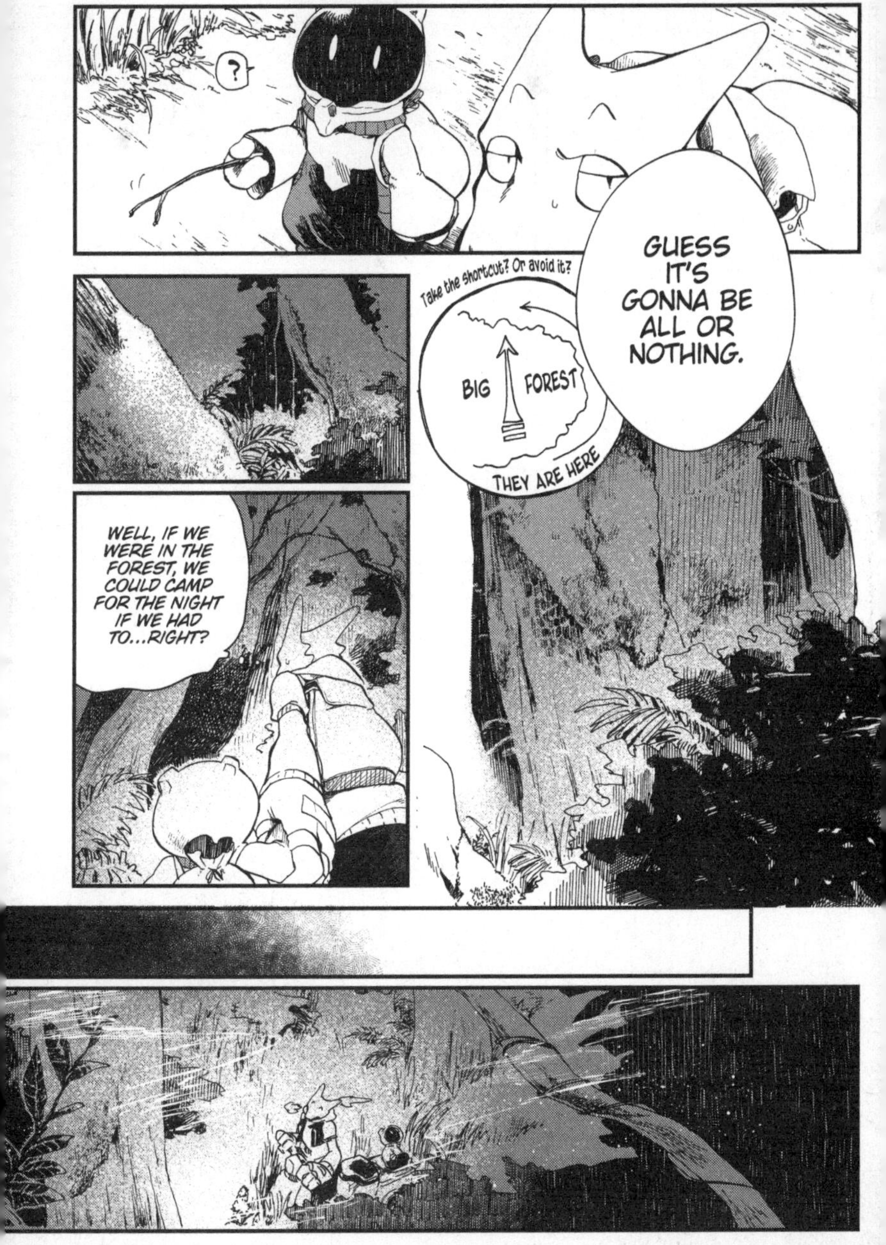
?
GUESS IT'S GONNA BE ALL OR NOTHING.
Take the shortcut? Or avoid it?
BIG FOREST
THEY ARE HERE
WELL, IF WE WERE IN THE FOREST, WE COULD CAMP FOR THE NIGHT IF WE HAD TO...RIGHT?

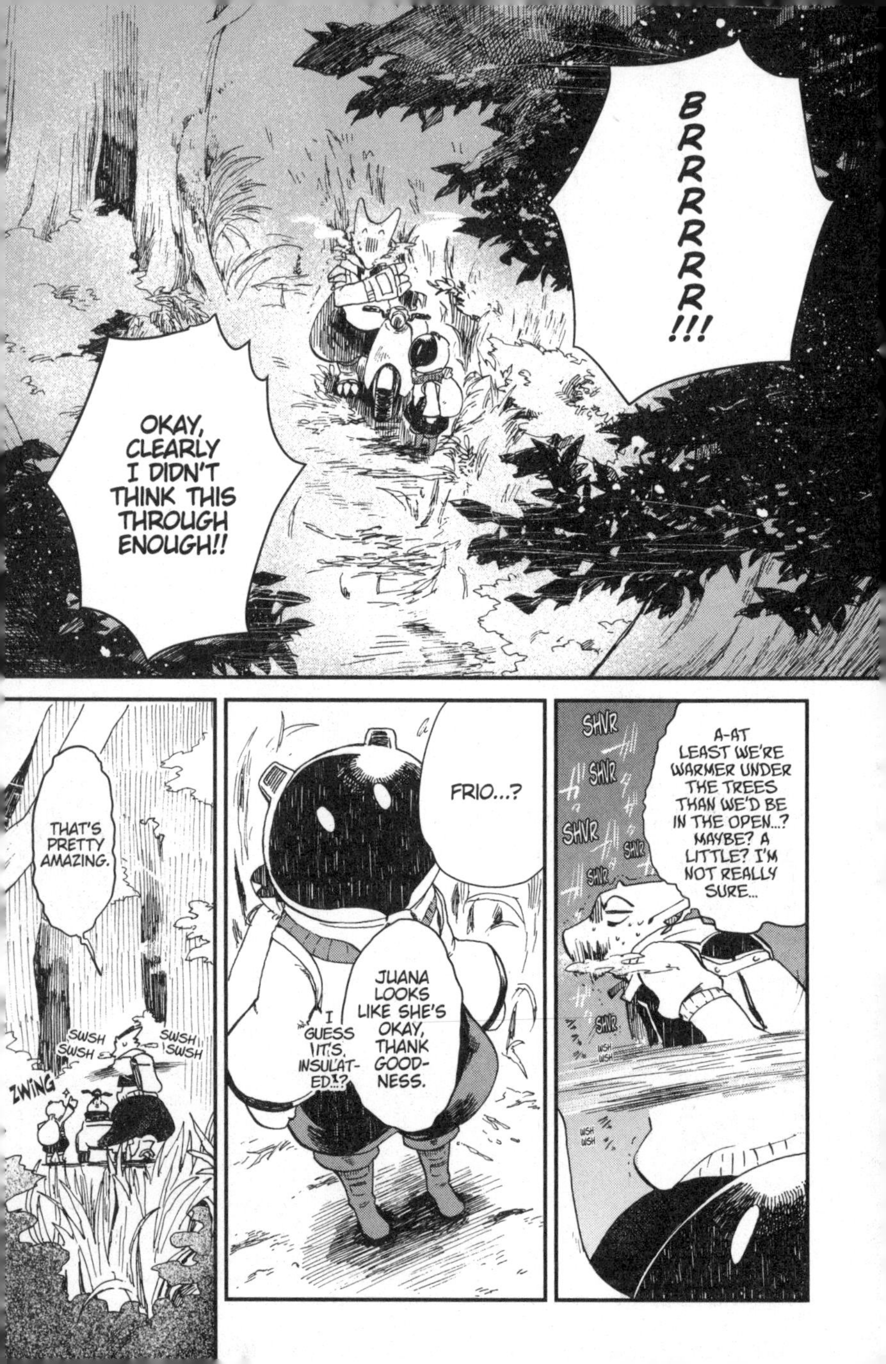
BRRRRRR!!!
OKAY, CLEARLY I DIDN'T THINK THIS THROUGH ENOUGH!!
A-AT LEAST WE'RE WARMER UNDER THE TREES THAN WE'D BE IN THE OPEN...? MAYBE? A LITTLE? I'M NOT REALLY SURE...
SHVR SHVR SHVR SHVR SHVR
SHVR
WSH WSH
WSH WSH
FRIO...?
JUANA LOOKS LIKE SHE'S OKAY, THANK GOOD-NESS.
I GUESS IT'S INSULAT-ED...!?
THAT'S PRETTY AMAZING.
SWSH SWSH
SWSH SWSH
ZWING

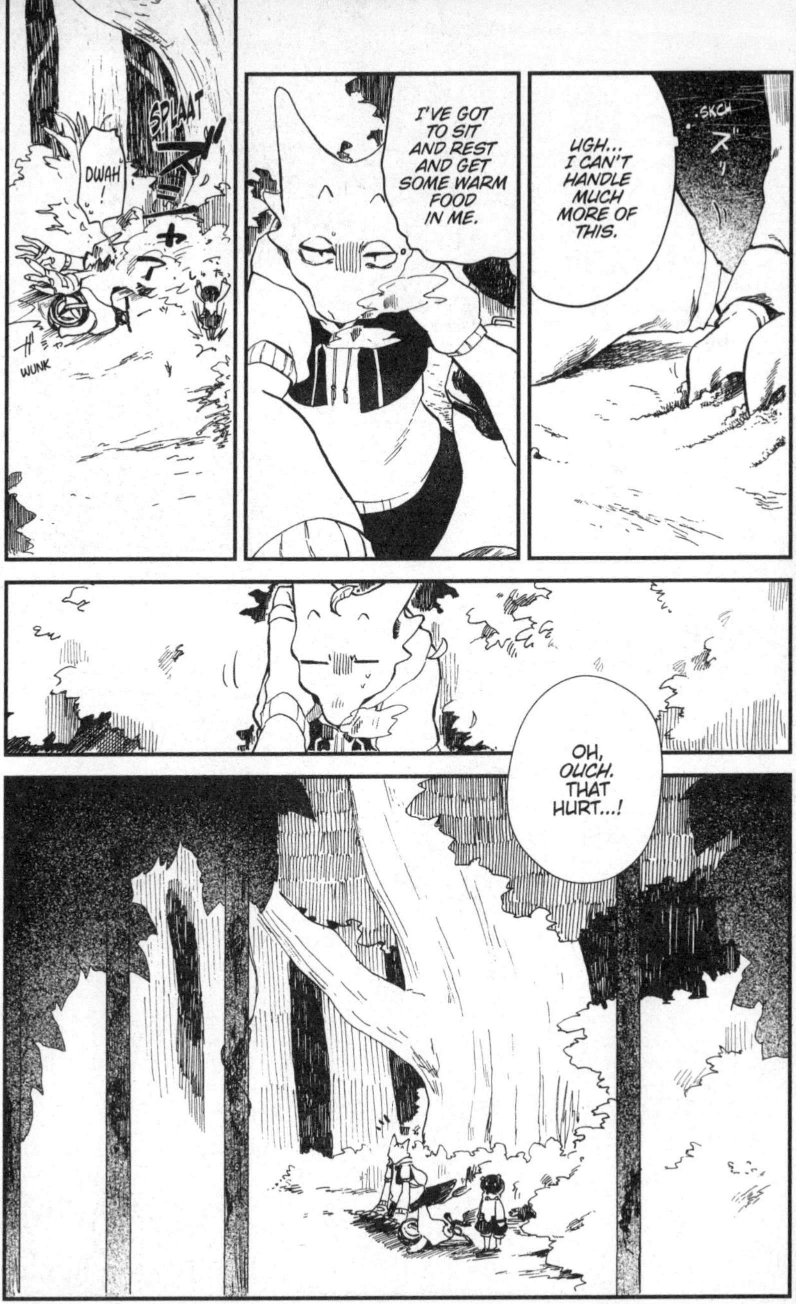
SKCH
UGH... I CAN'T HANDLE MUCH MORE OF THIS.
I'VE GOT TO SIT AND REST AND GET SOME WARM FOOD IN ME.
SPLAAT
DWAH!
WUNK
OH, OUCH. THAT HURT...!

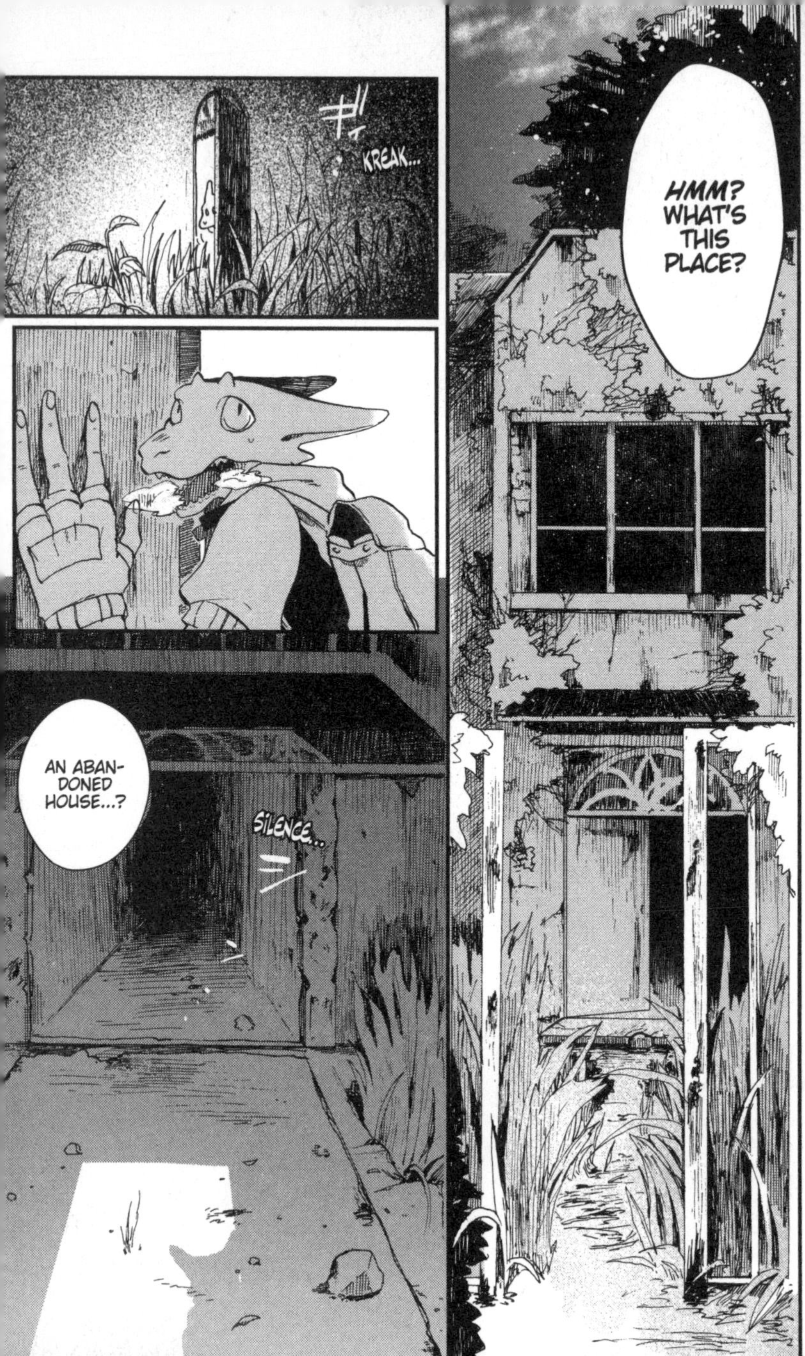
HMM? WHAT'S THIS PLACE?
KREAK...
AN ABAN-DONED HOUSE...?
SILENCE...

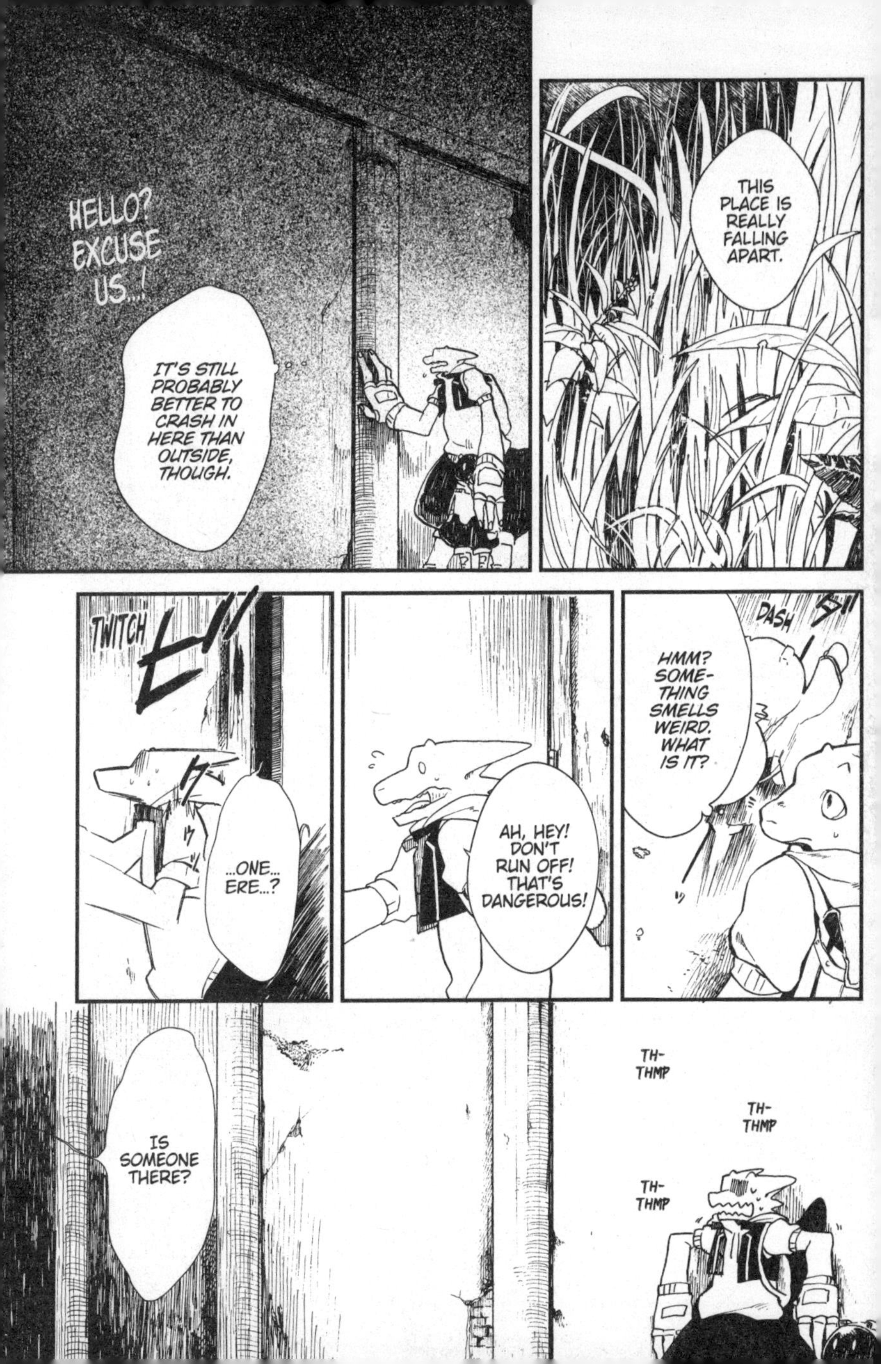
THIS PLACE IS REALLY FALLING APART.
HELLO? EXCUSE US...!
IT'S STILL PROBABLY BETTER TO CRASH IN HERE THAN OUTSIDE, THOUGH.
DASH
HMM? SOMETHING SMELLS WEIRD. WHAT IS IT?
AH, HEY! DON'T RUN OFF! THAT'S DANGEROUS!
TWITCH
...ONE... ERE...?
TH-THMP
TH-THMP
TH-THMP
IS SOMEONE THERE?

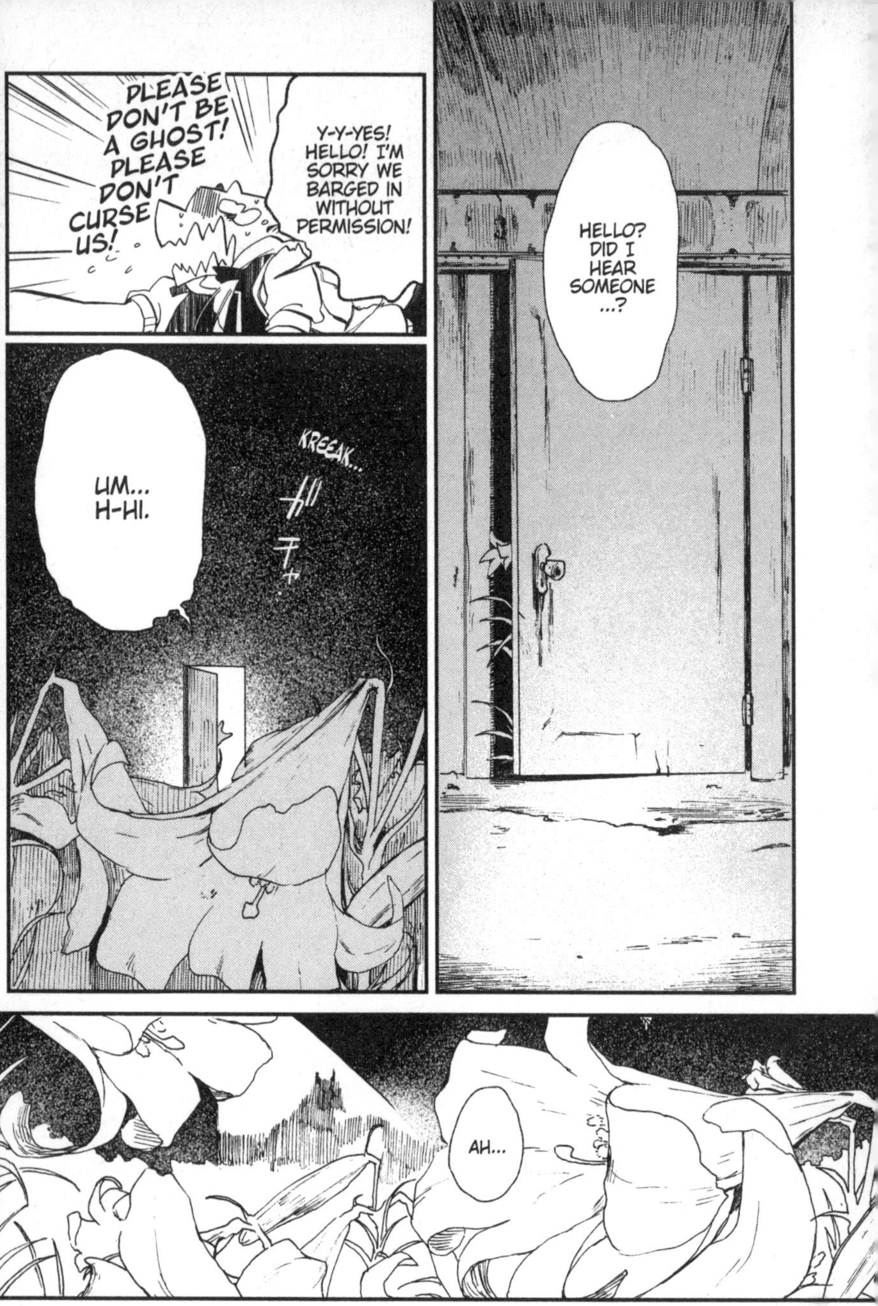
HELLO? DID I HEAR SOMEONE ...?
Y-Y-YES! HELLO! I'M SORRY WE BARGED IN WITHOUT PERMISSION!
PLEASE DON'T BE A GHOST! PLEASE DON'T CURSE US!
KREEAK...
UM... H-HI.
AH...

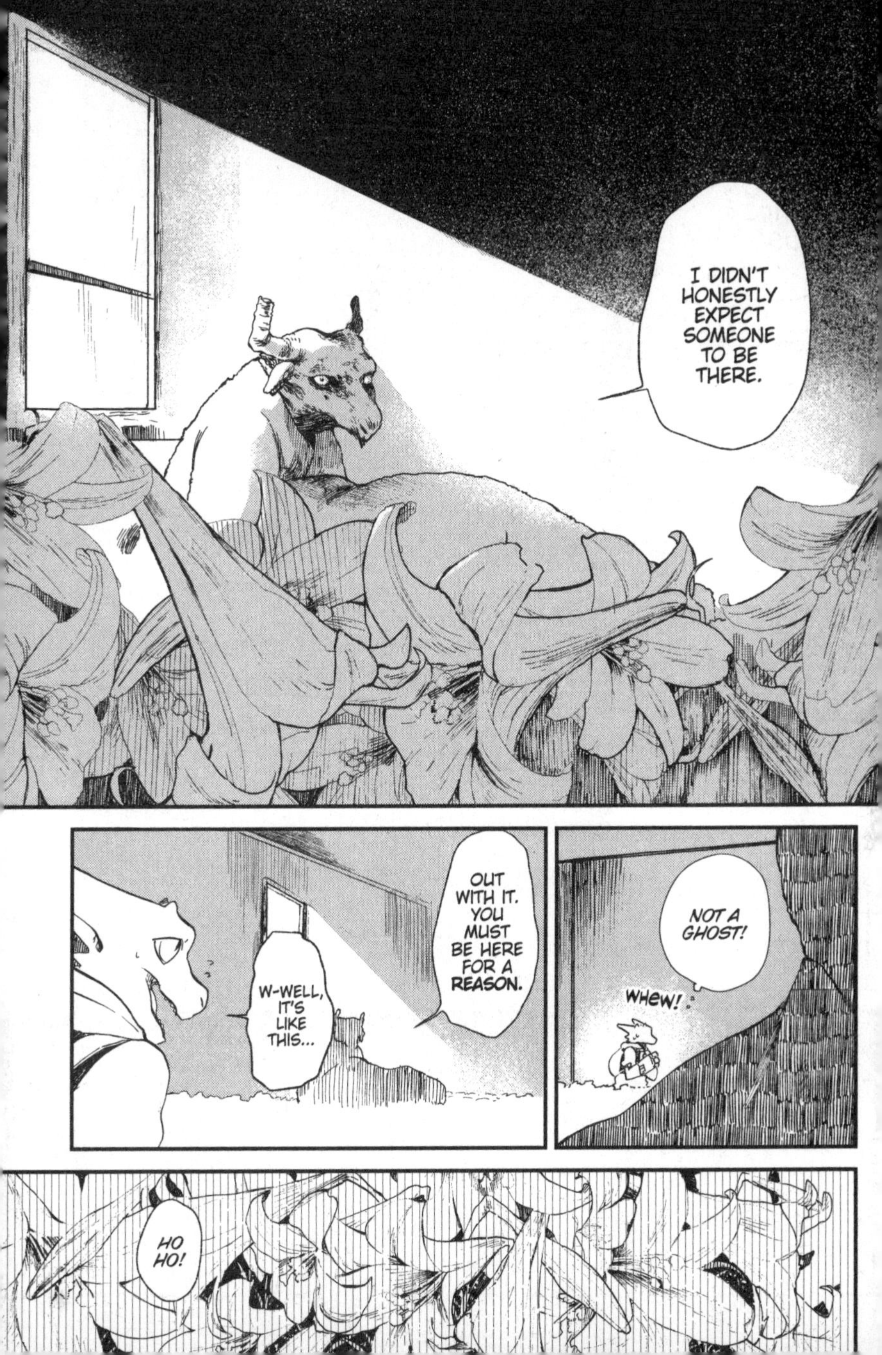
I DIDN'T HONESTLY EXPECT SOMEONE TO BE THERE.
NOT A GHOST!
WHEW!
OUT WITH IT. YOU MUST BE HERE FOR A REASON.
W-WELL, IT'S LIKE THIS...
HO HO!

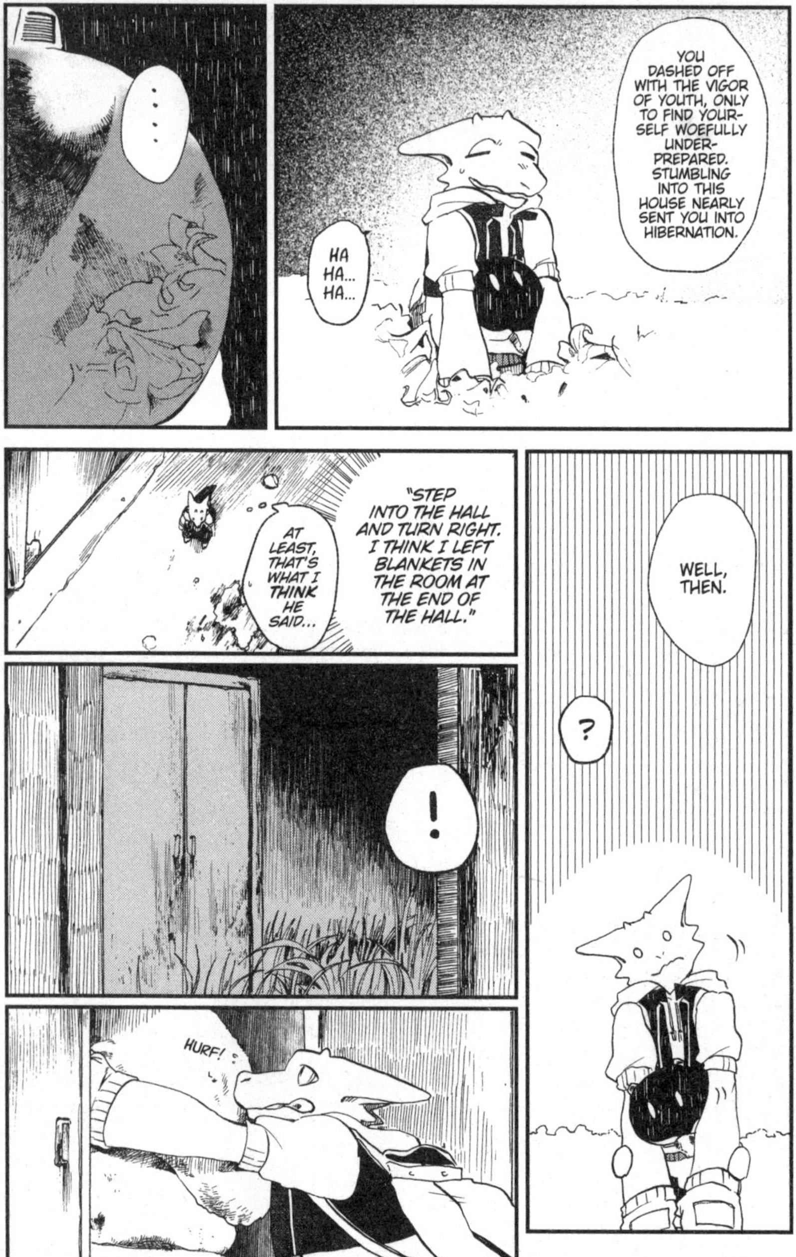
YOU DASHED OFF WITH THE VIGOR OF YOUTH, ONLY TO FIND YOURSELF WOEFULLY UNDER-PREPARED. STUMBLING INTO THIS HOUSE NEARLY SENT YOU INTO HIBERNATION.
HA HA... HA...
....
WELL, THEN.
?
"STEP INTO THE HALL AND TURN RIGHT. I THINK I LEFT BLANKETS IN THE ROOM AT THE END OF THE HALL."
AT LEAST, THAT'S WHAT I THINK HE SAID...
!
HURF!

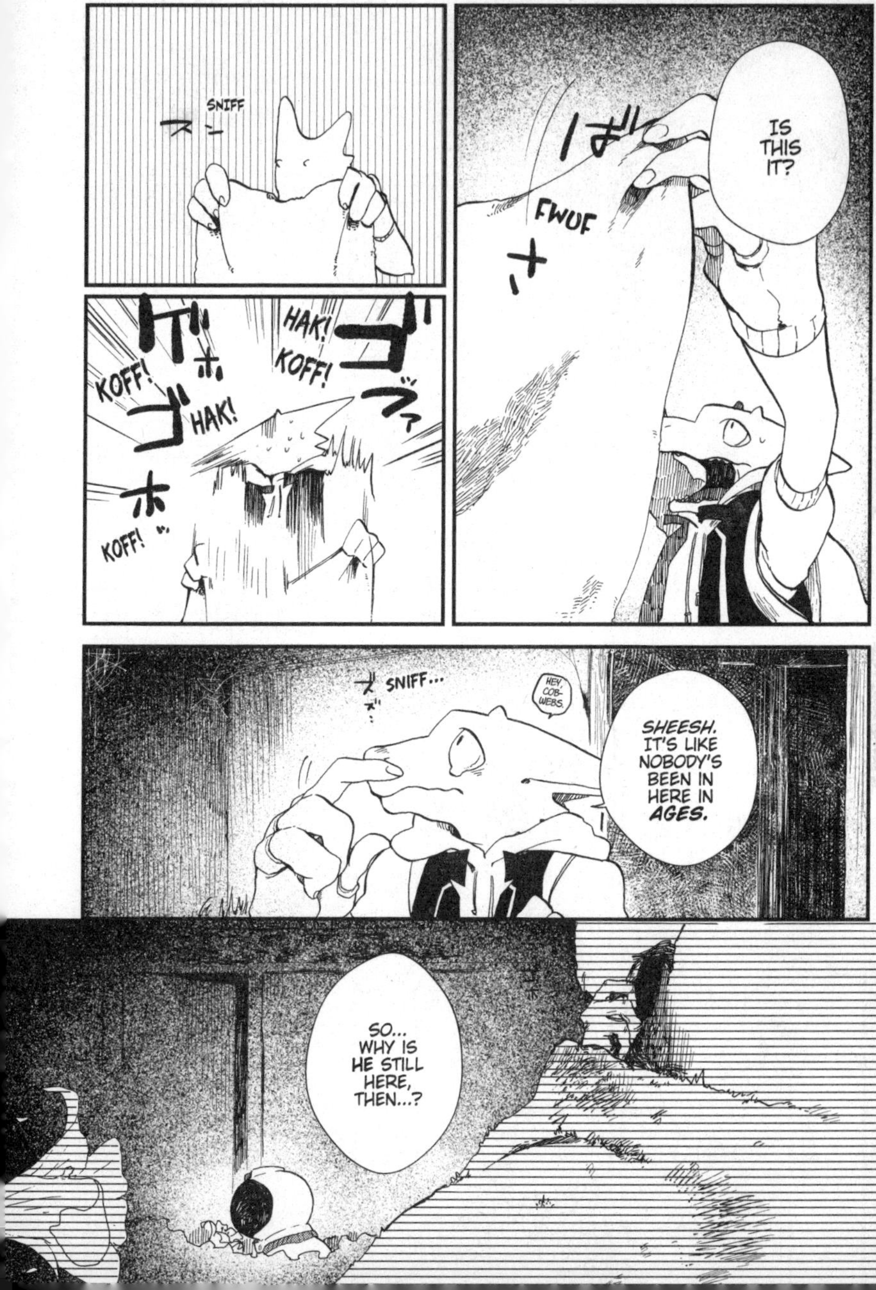
IS THIS IT?
FWUF
SNIFF
HAK! KOFF!
KOFF!
HAK!
KOFF!
SHEESH. IT'S LIKE NOBODY'S BEEN IN HERE IN AGES.
HEY, COB-WEBS.
SNIFF...
SO... WHY IS HE STILL HERE, THEN...?

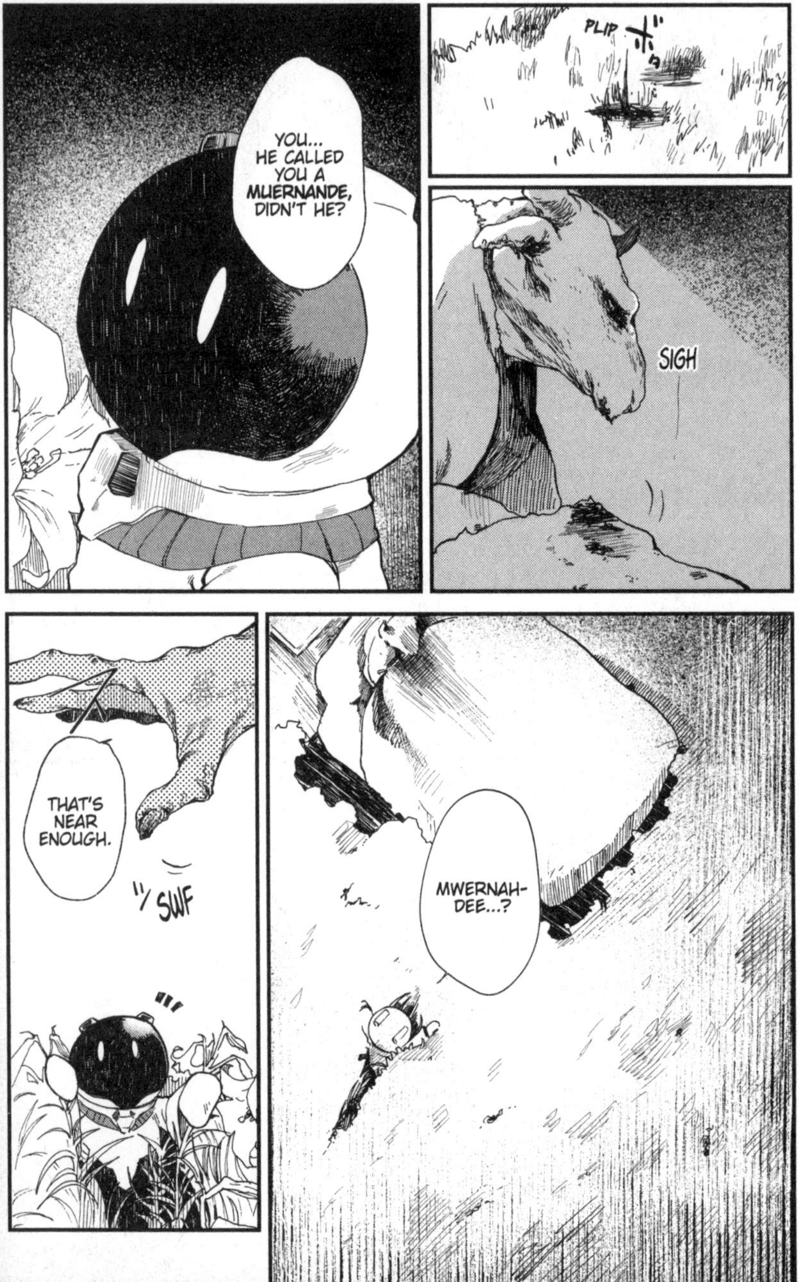
PLIP
SIGH
YOU... HE CALLED YOU A MUERNANDE, DIDN'T HE?
MWERNAH-DEE...?
THAT'S NEAR ENOUGH.
SWF

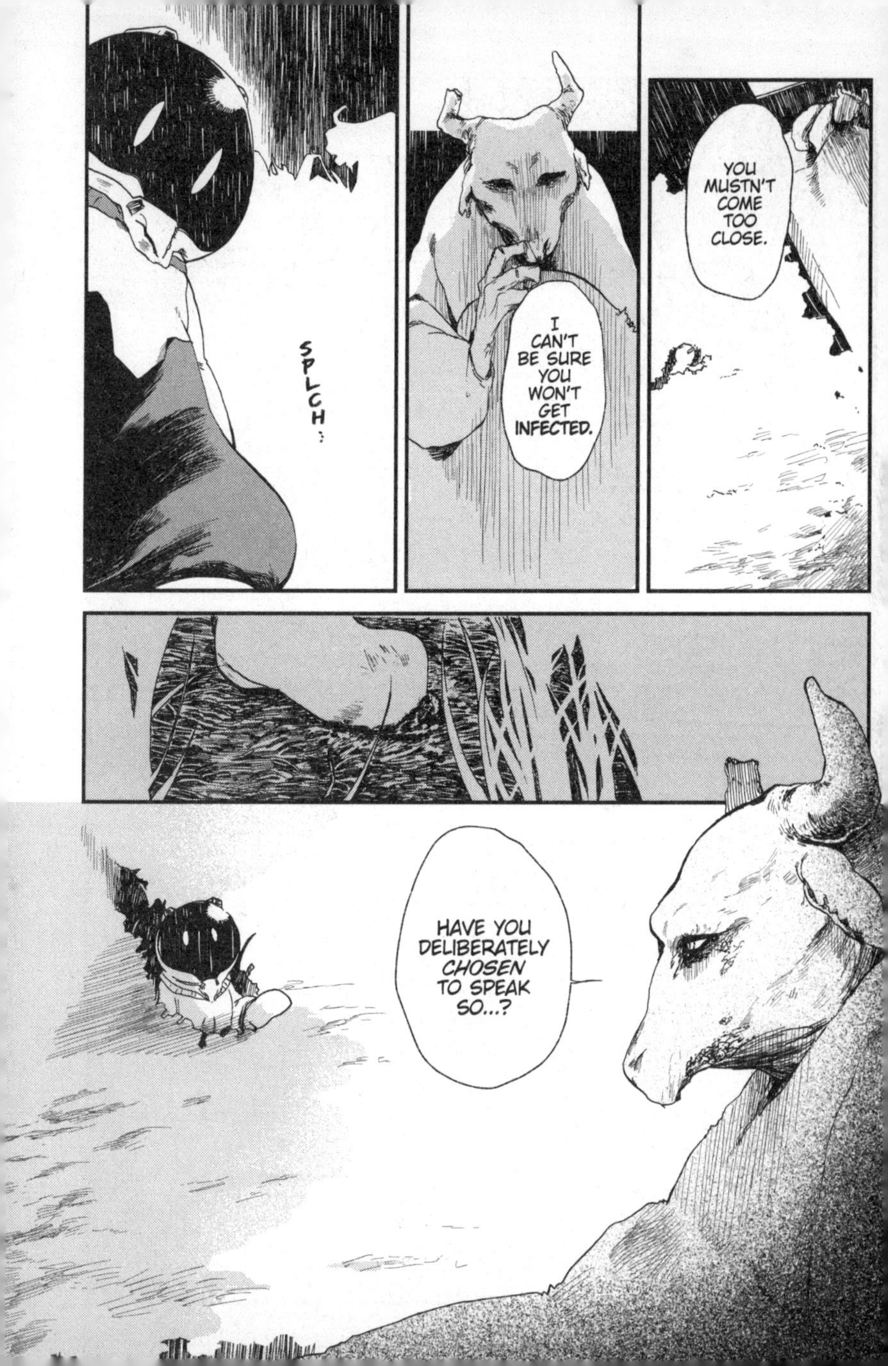
YOU MUSTN'T COME TOO CLOSE.
I CAN'T BE SURE YOU WON'T GET INFECTED.
SPLCH :
HAVE YOU DELIBERATELY *CHOSEN* TO SPEAK SO...?

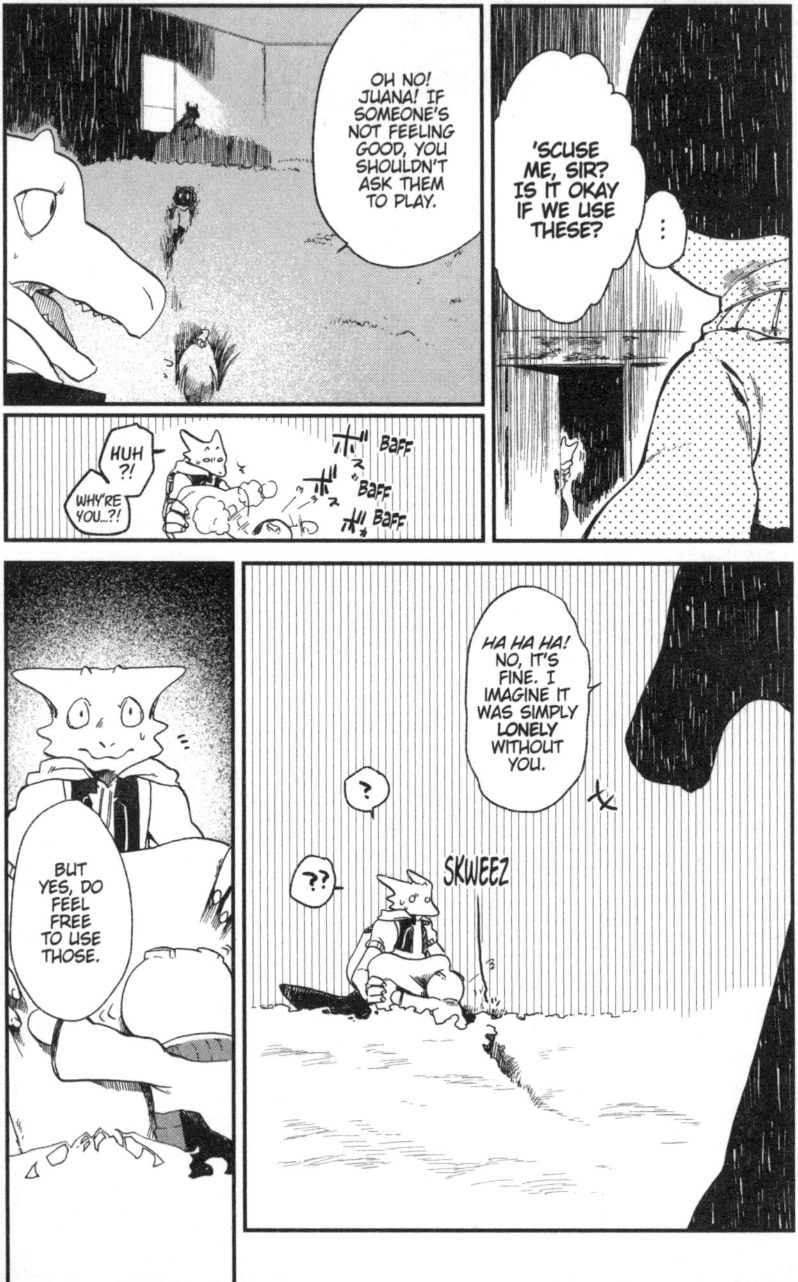
'SCUSE ME, SIR? IS IT OKAY IF WE USE THESE?
...
OH NO! JUANA! IF SOMEONE'S NOT FEELING GOOD, YOU SHOULDN'T ASK THEM TO PLAY.
BAFF
BAFF
BAFF
HUH?!
WHY'RE YOU...?!
HA HA HA! NO, IT'S FINE. I IMAGINE IT WAS SIMPLY LONELY WITHOUT YOU.
?
??
SKWEEZ
BUT YES, DO FEEL FREE TO USE THOSE.

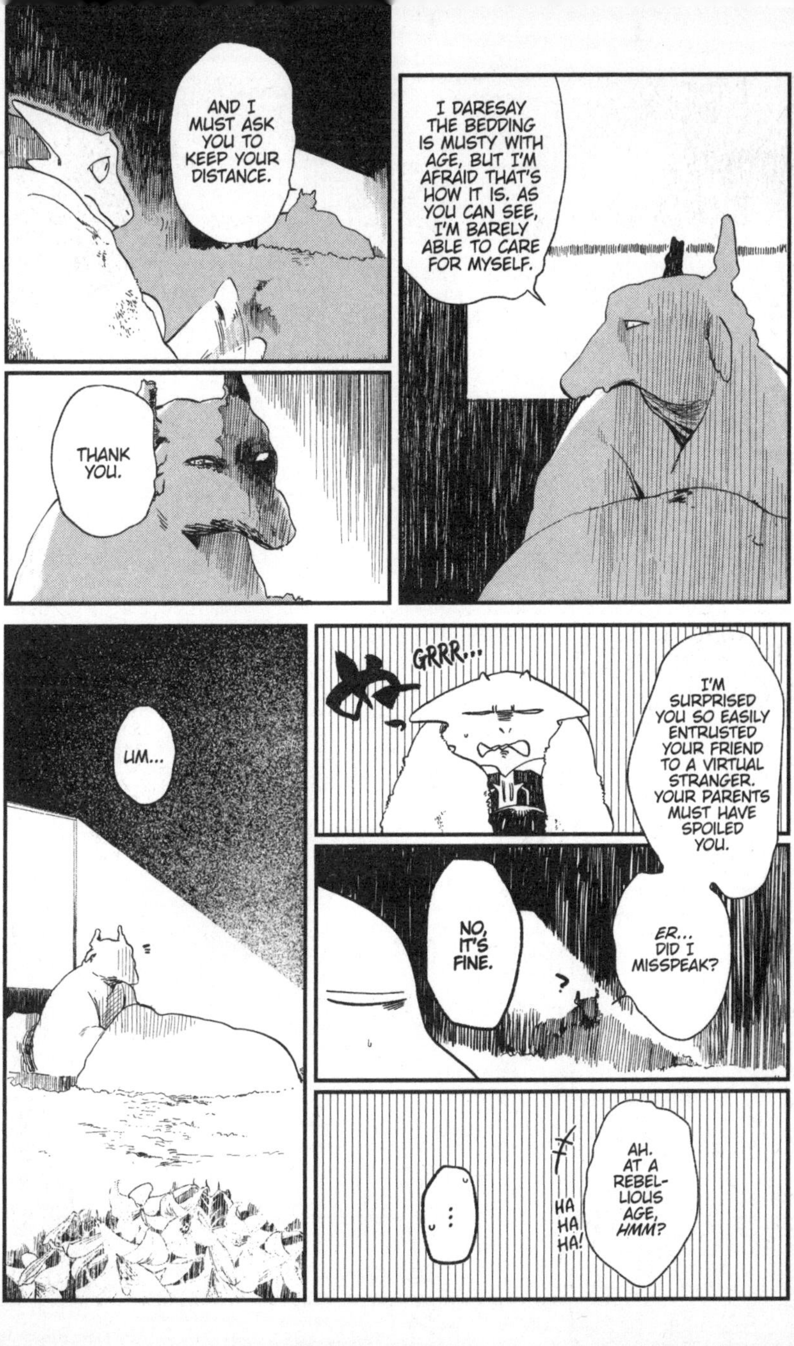
I DARESAY THE BEDDING IS MUSTY WITH AGE, BUT I'M AFRAID THAT'S HOW IT IS. AS YOU CAN SEE, I'M BARELY ABLE TO CARE FOR MYSELF.
AND I MUST ASK YOU TO KEEP YOUR DISTANCE.
THANK YOU.
GRRR...
I'M SURPRISED YOU SO EASILY ENTRUSTED YOUR FRIEND TO A VIRTUAL STRANGER. YOUR PARENTS MUST HAVE SPOILED YOU.
ER... DID I MISSPEAK?
NO, IT'S FINE.
AH. AT A REBEL-LIOUS AGE, HMM?
HA HA HA!
...
UM...

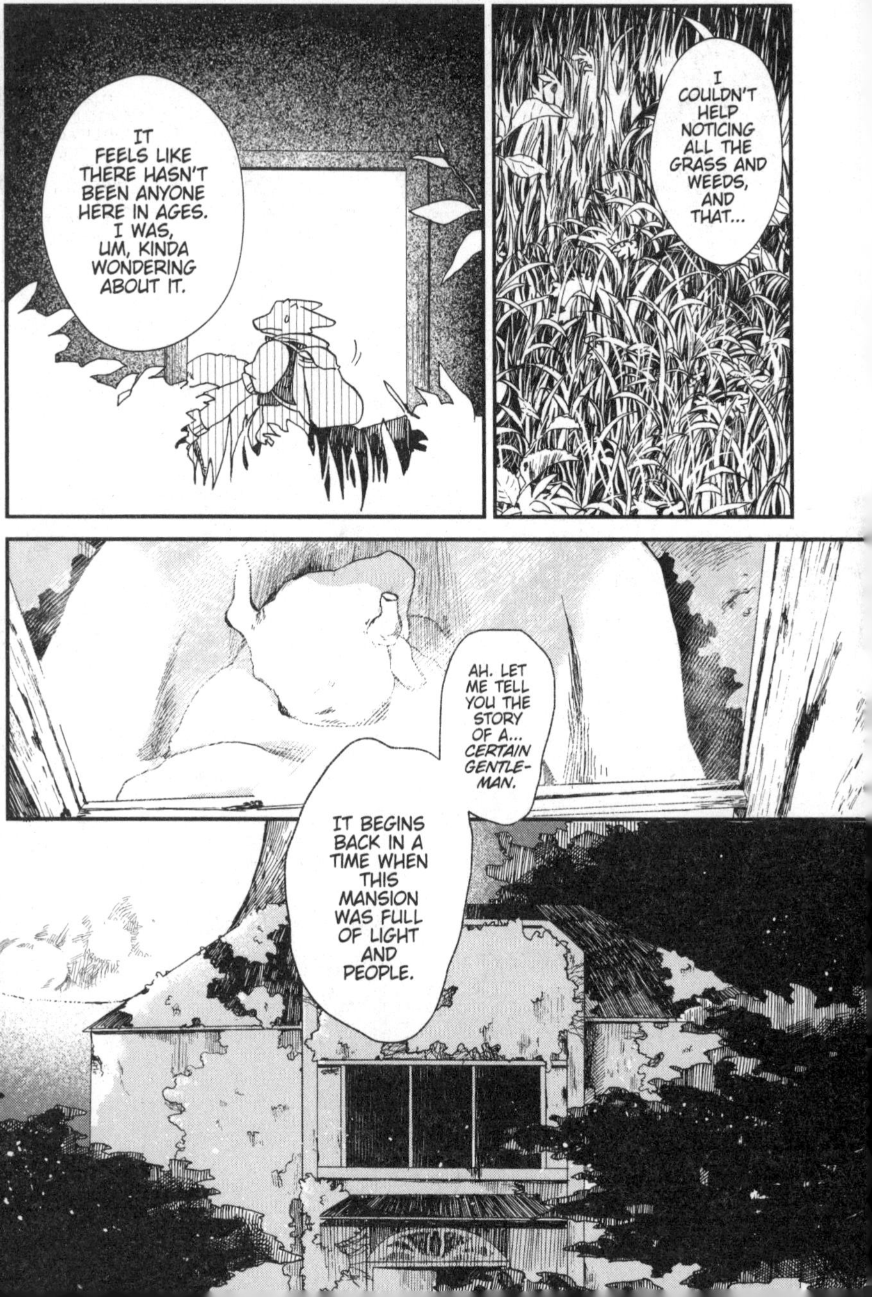
I COULDN'T HELP NOTICING ALL THE GRASS AND WEEDS, AND THAT...
IT FEELS LIKE THERE HASN'T BEEN ANYONE HERE IN AGES. I WAS, UM, KINDA WONDERING ABOUT IT.
AH. LET ME TELL YOU THE STORY OF A... *CERTAIN GENTLEMAN.*
IT BEGINS BACK IN A TIME WHEN THIS MANSION WAS FULL OF LIGHT AND PEOPLE.

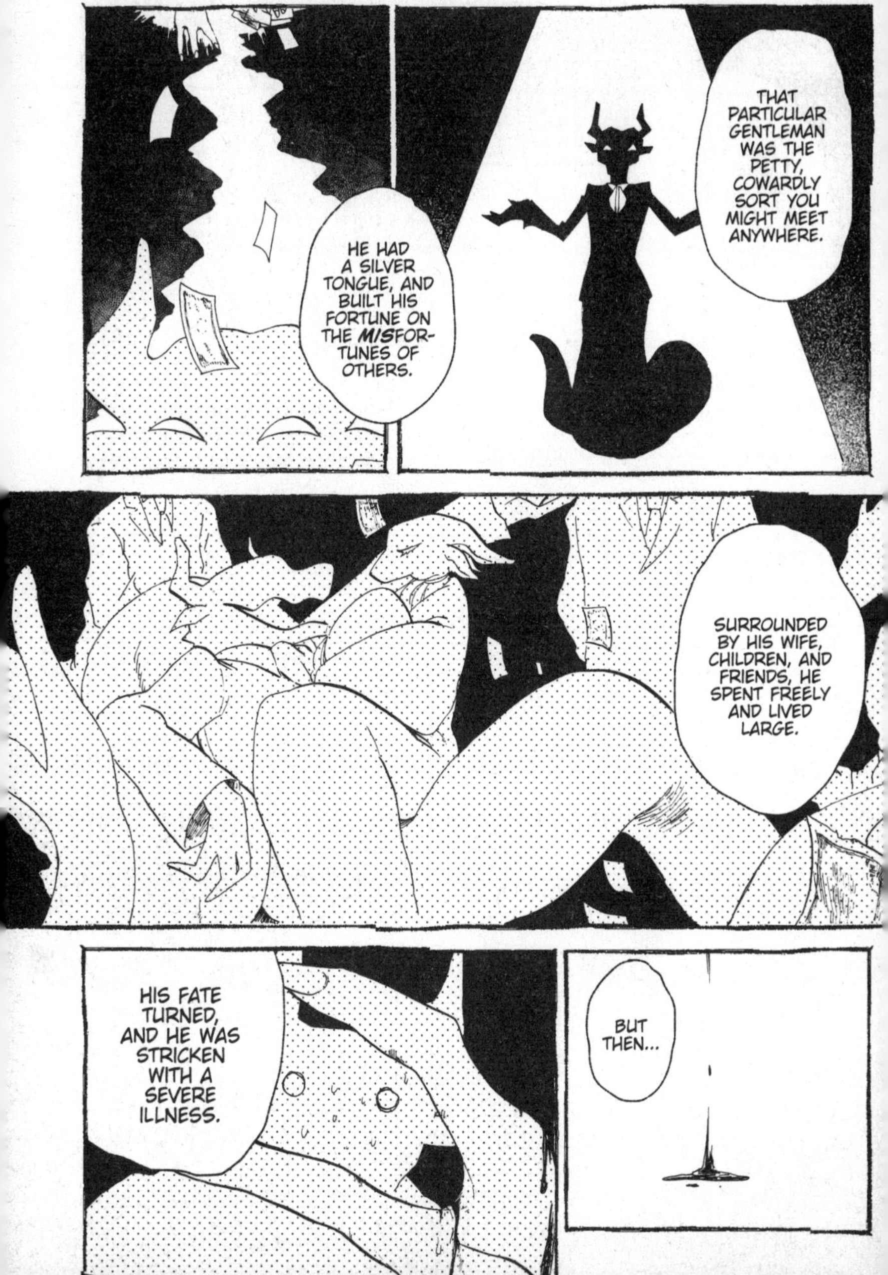
THAT PARTICULAR GENTLEMAN WAS THE PETTY, COWARDLY SORT YOU MIGHT MEET ANYWHERE.
HE HAD A SILVER TONGUE, AND BUILT HIS FORTUNE ON THE *MIS*FORTUNES OF OTHERS.
SURROUNDED BY HIS WIFE, CHILDREN, AND FRIENDS, HE SPENT FREELY AND LIVED LARGE.
BUT THEN...
HIS FATE TURNED, AND HE WAS STRICKEN WITH A SEVERE ILLNESS.

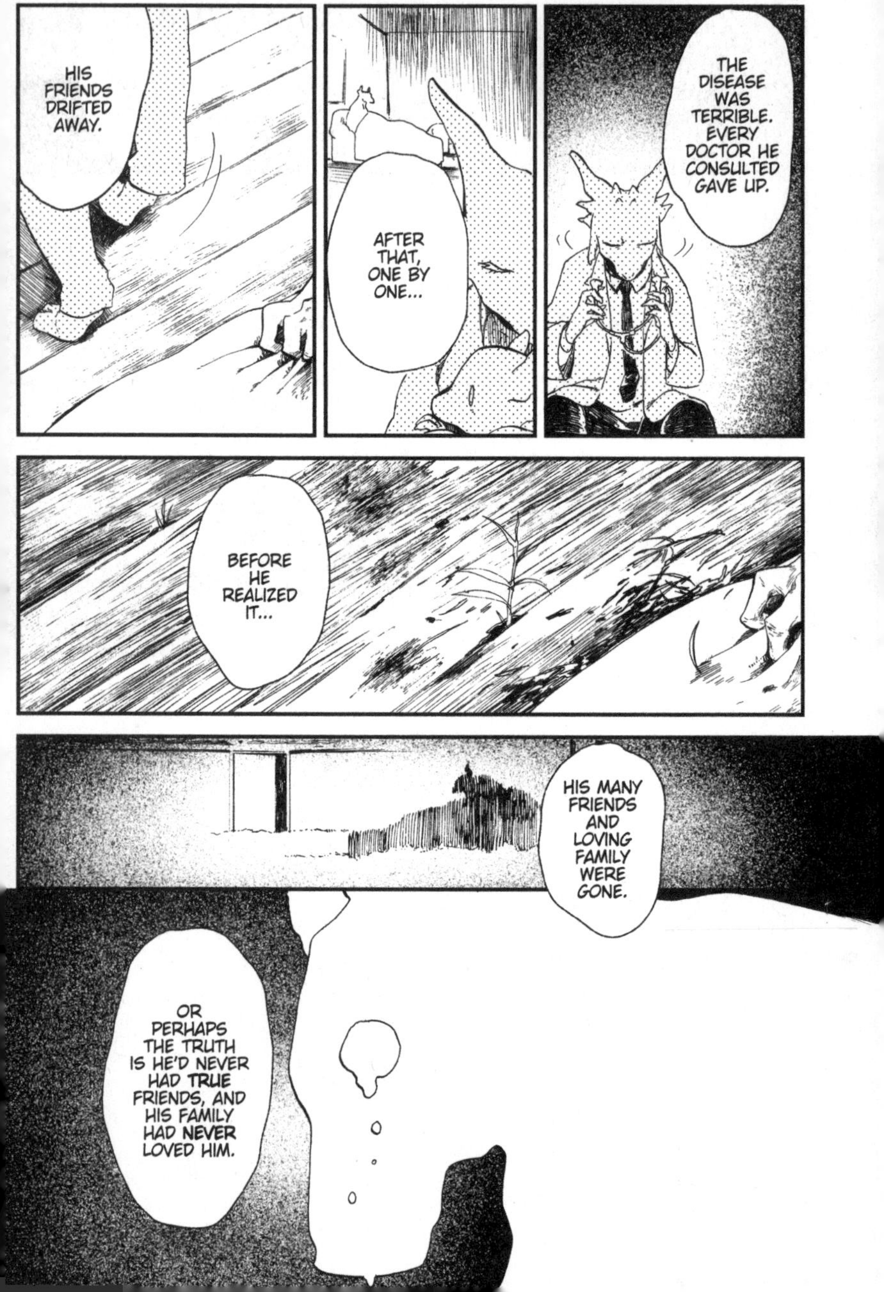
THE DISEASE WAS TERRIBLE. EVERY DOCTOR HE CONSULTED GAVE UP.
AFTER THAT, ONE BY ONE...
HIS FRIENDS DRIFTED AWAY.
BEFORE HE REALIZED IT...
HIS MANY FRIENDS AND LOVING FAMILY WERE GONE.
OR PERHAPS THE TRUTH IS HE'D NEVER HAD TRUE FRIENDS, AND HIS FAMILY HAD NEVER LOVED HIM.

JUST AS HE THOUGHT IT WAS HIS FATE TO BE FORGOTTEN ENTIRELY, TO FADE FROM THE WORLD...

GRIN

YOU ARRIVED.

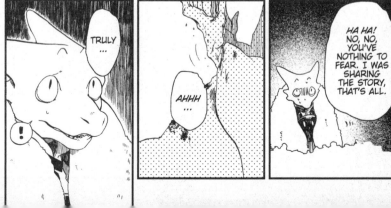

TRULY ...

AHHH ...

HA HA! NO, NO, YOU'VE NOTHING TO FEAR. I WAS SHARING THE STORY, THAT'S ALL.

IT IS
A GREAT
BLESSING
TO HAVE
SOMEONE
WITH ME IN
MY FINAL
HOURS.

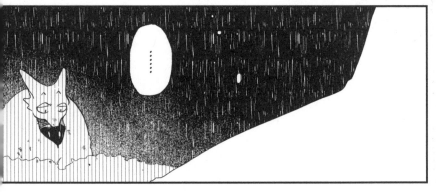

IT'S OKAY.

NYED?

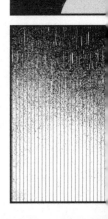

MY APOLOGIES. I FEAR I LET MY EMOTIONS CARRY ME AWAY FOR A MOMENT.

N-NO, IT'S ALL RIGHT! PLEASE DON'T MIND US!

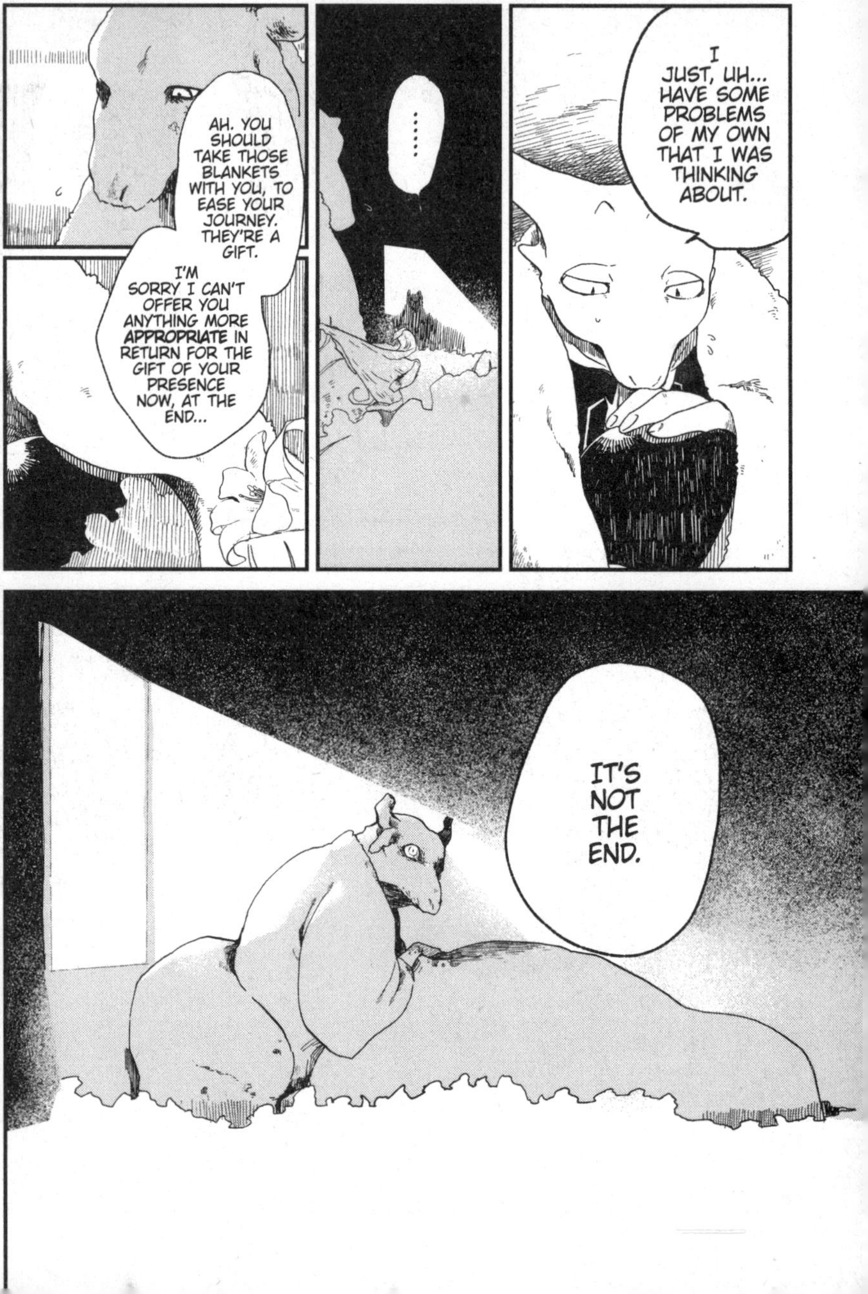
I JUST, UH... HAVE SOME PROBLEMS OF MY OWN THAT I WAS THINKING ABOUT.
......
AH. YOU SHOULD TAKE THOSE BLANKETS WITH YOU, TO EASE YOUR JOURNEY. THEY'RE A GIFT.
I'M SORRY I CAN'T OFFER YOU ANYTHING MORE **APPROPRIATE** IN RETURN FOR THE GIFT OF YOUR PRESENCE NOW, AT THE END...
IT'S NOT THE END.

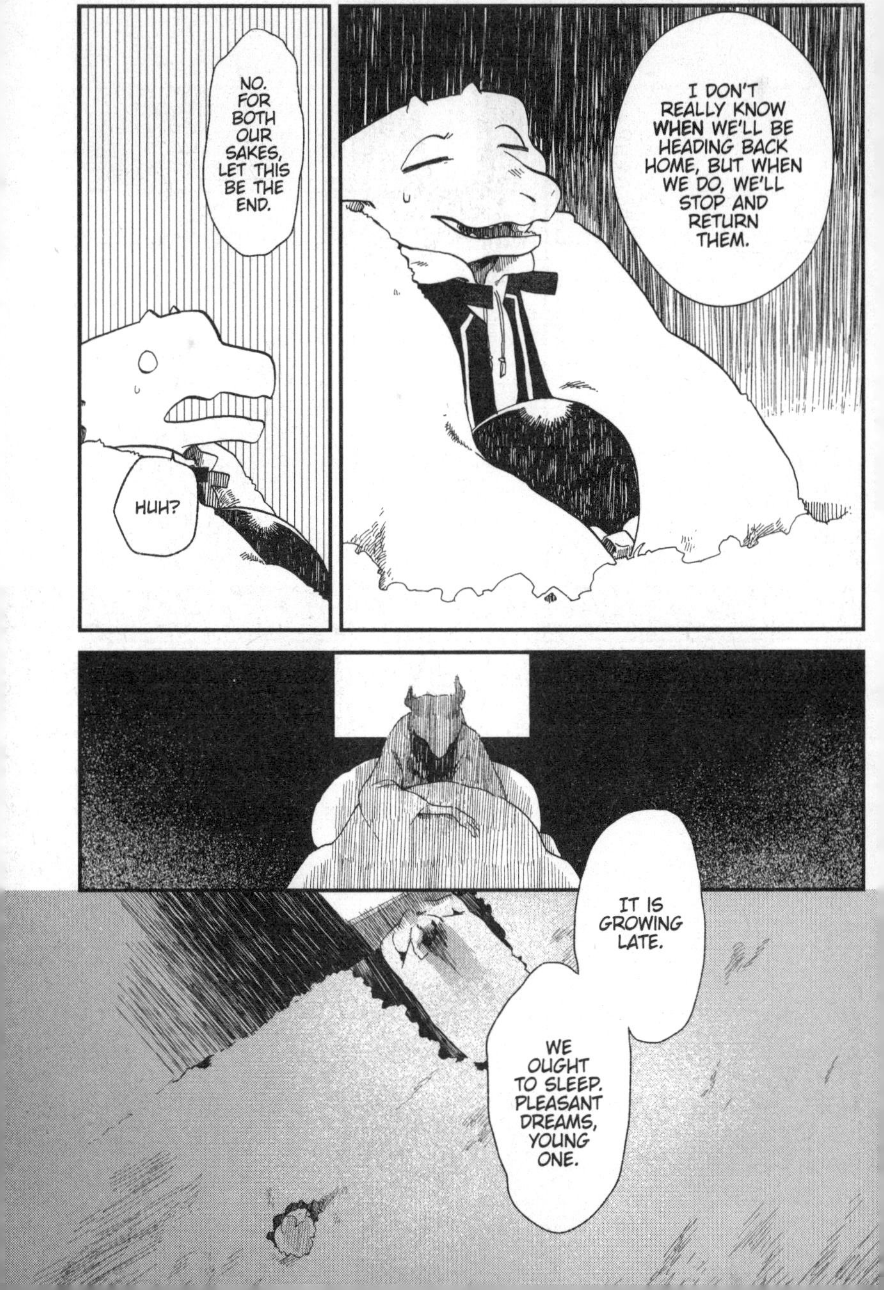
I DON'T REALLY KNOW WHEN WE'LL BE HEADING BACK HOME, BUT WHEN WE DO, WE'LL STOP AND RETURN THEM.
NO. FOR BOTH OUR SAKES, LET THIS BE THE END.
HUH?
IT IS GROWING LATE.
WE OUGHT TO SLEEP. PLEASANT DREAMS, YOUNG ONE.

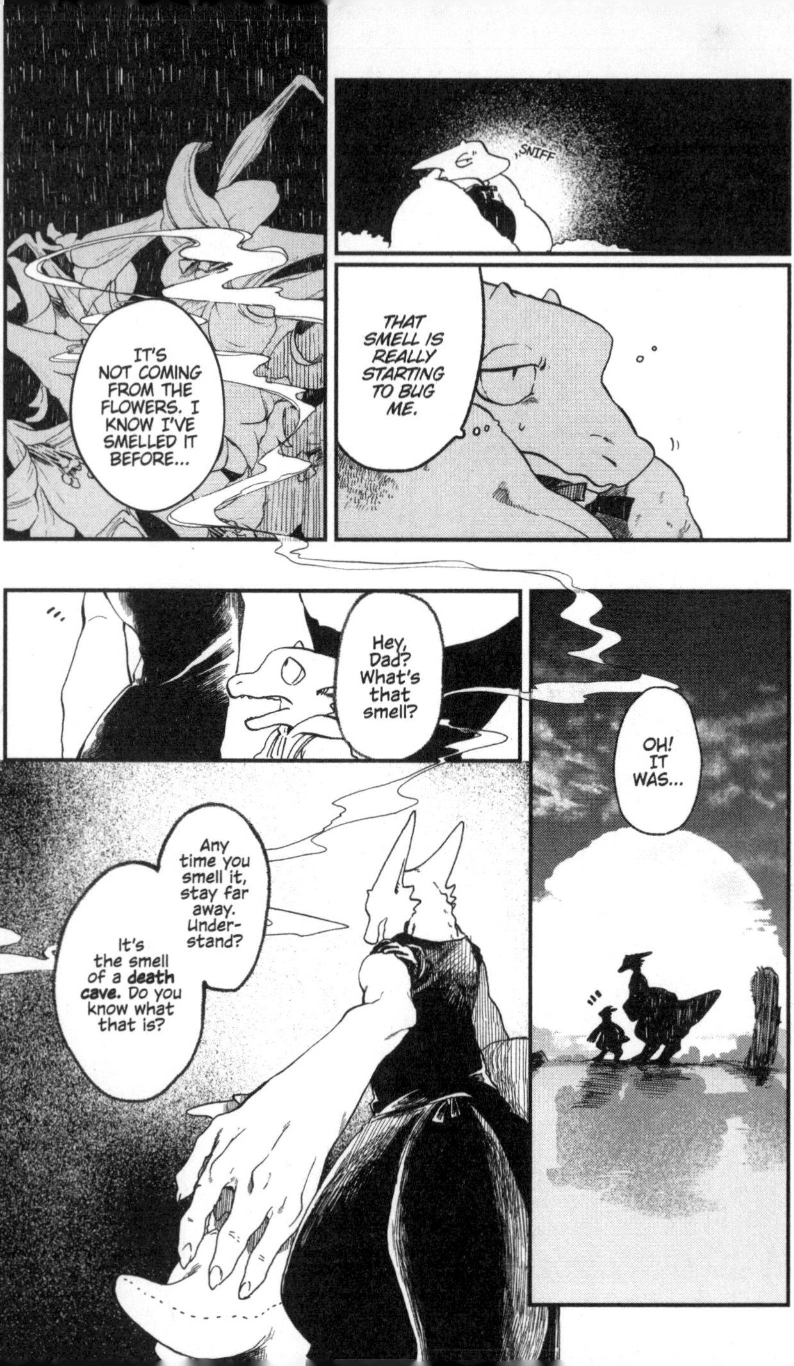
SNIFF
THAT SMELL IS REALLY STARTING TO BUG ME.
IT'S NOT COMING FROM THE FLOWERS. I KNOW I'VE SMELLED IT BEFORE...
OH! IT WAS...
Hey, Dad? What's that smell?
Any time you smell it, stay far away. Under-stand?
It's the smell of a **death cave.** Do you know what that is?

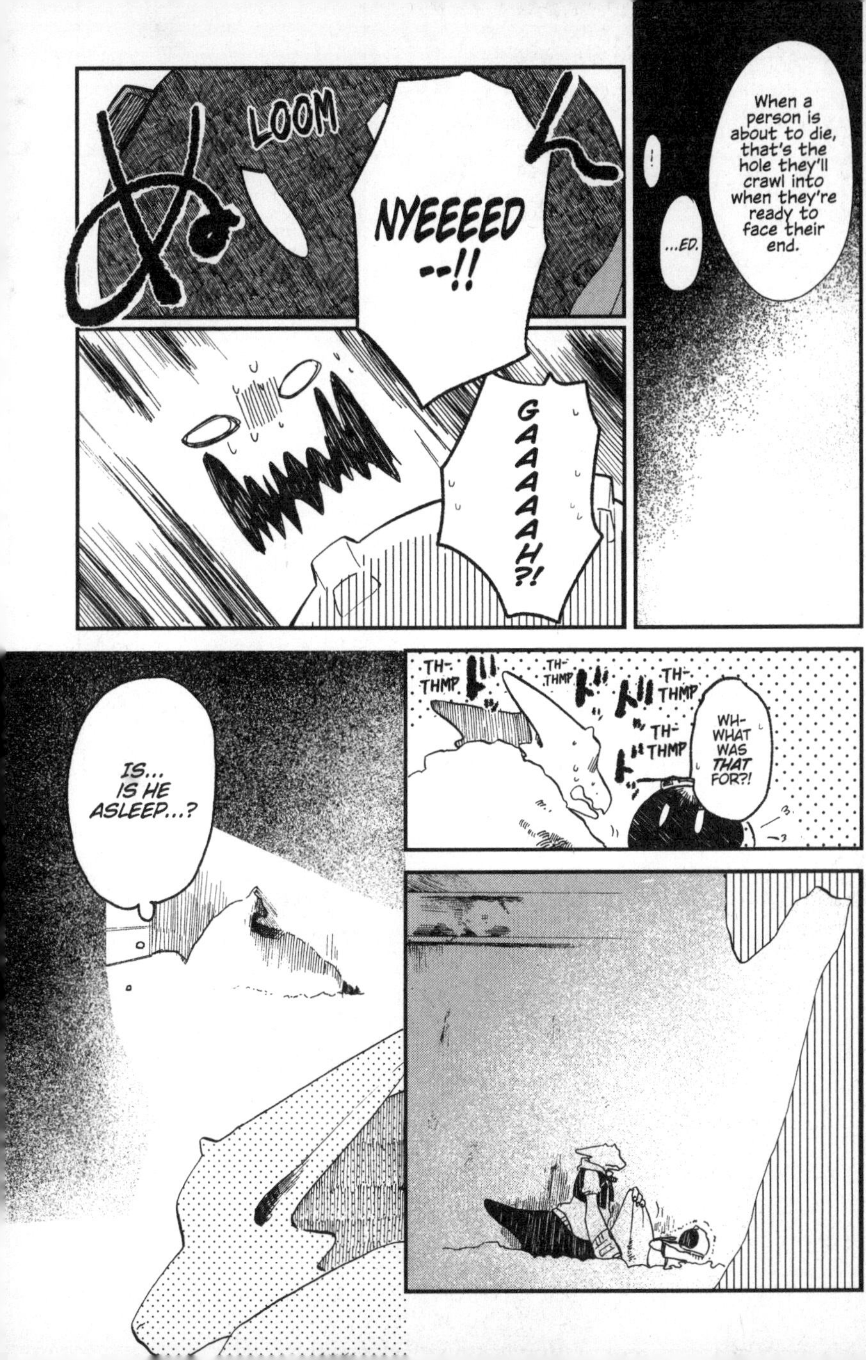
When a person is about to die, that's the hole they'll crawl into when they're ready to face their end.
!
...ED.
LOOM
NYEEEED--!!
GAAAAAAH?!
TH-THMP
TH-THMP
TH-THMP
TH-THMP
WH-WHAT WAS *THAT* FOR?!
IS... IS HE ASLEEP...?

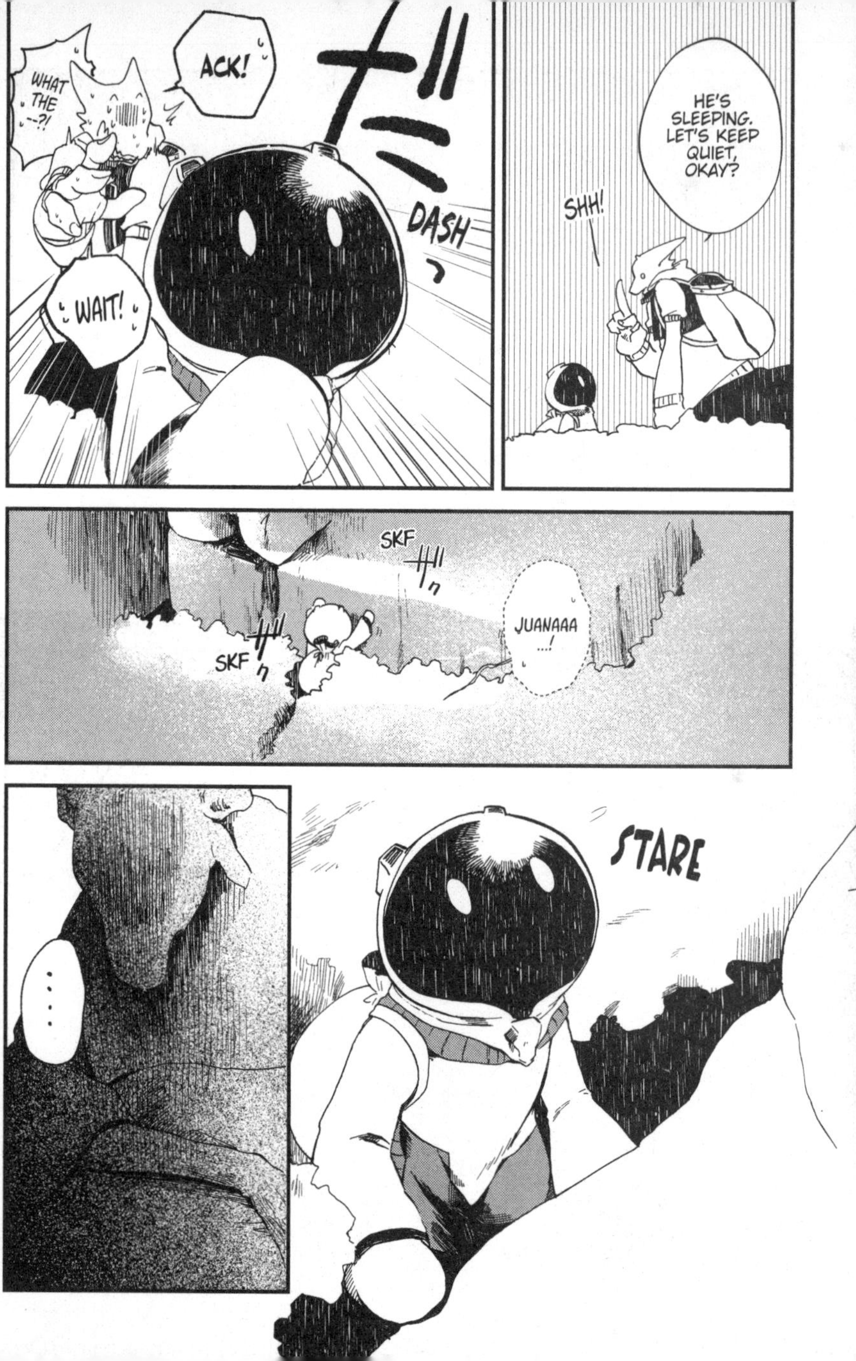
HE'S SLEEPING. LET'S KEEP QUIET, OKAY?
SHH!
ACK!
WHAT THE --?!
DASH
WAIT!
JUANAAA ...!
SKF
SKF
STARE
.....

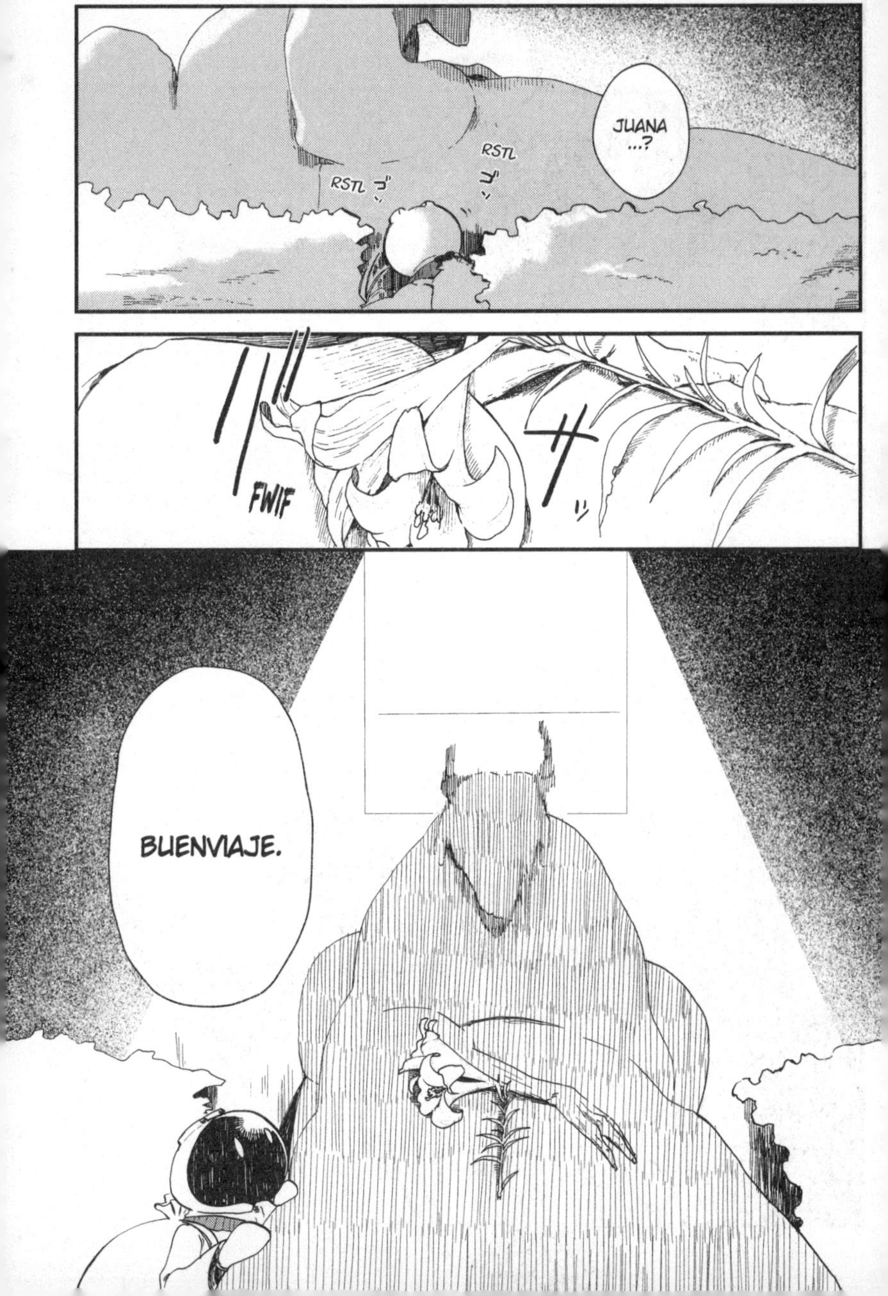
JUANA ...?
RSTL
RSTL
FWIF
BUENVIAJE.

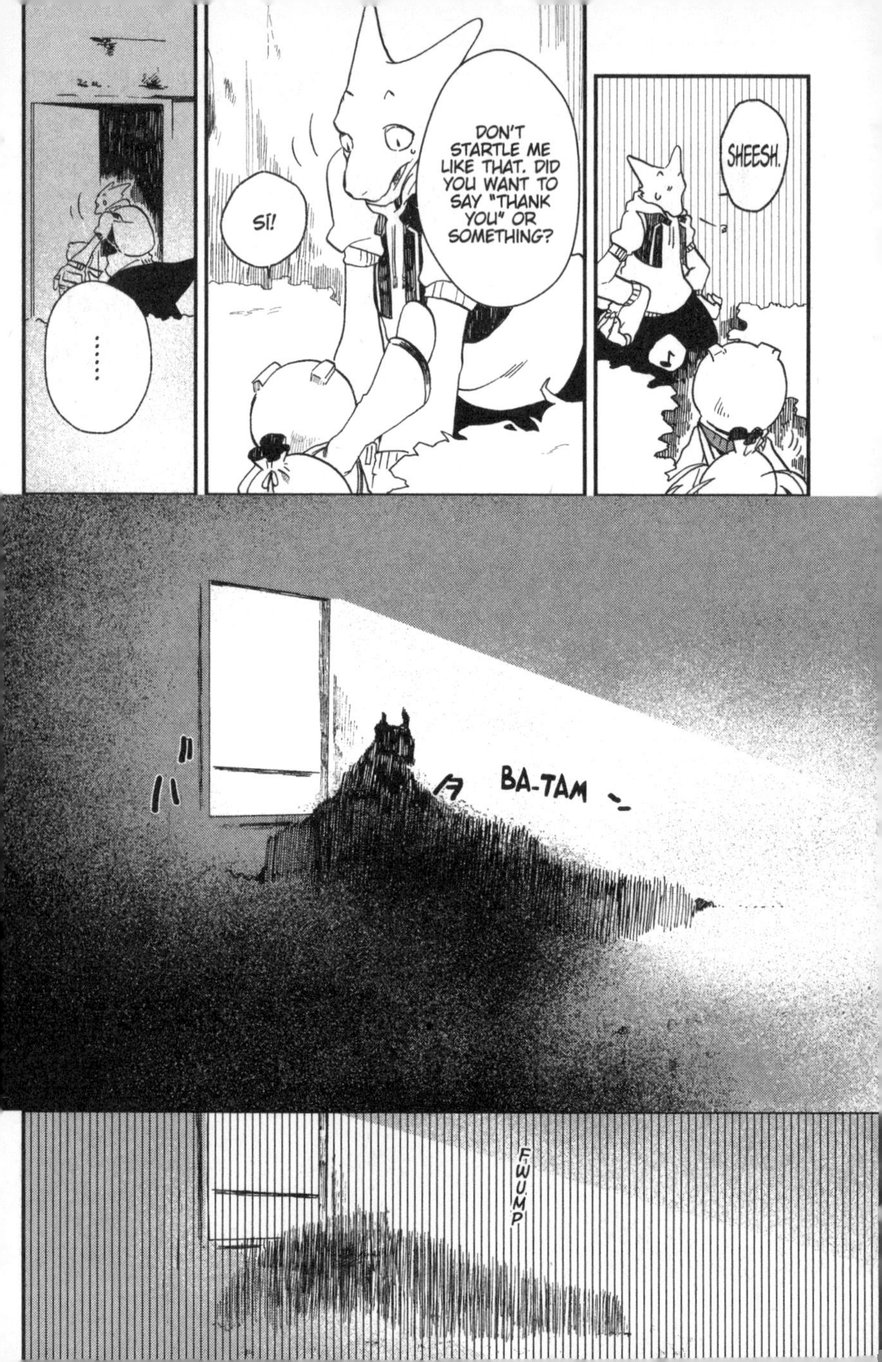
SHEESH.
DON'T STARTLE ME LIKE THAT. DID YOU WANT TO SAY "THANK YOU" OR SOMETHING?
SÍ!
......
BA-TAM
FWUMP

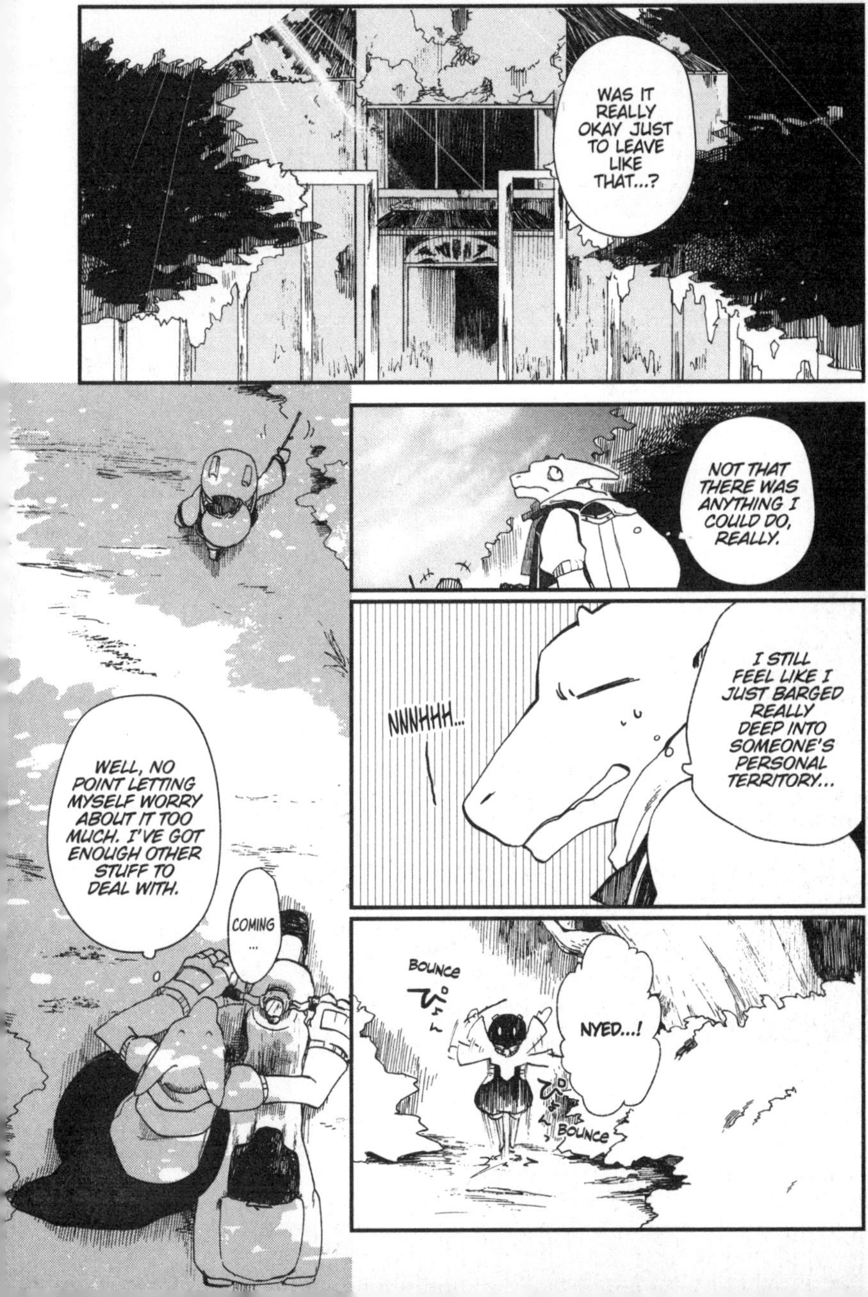
WAS IT REALLY OKAY JUST TO LEAVE LIKE THAT...?
NOT THAT THERE WAS ANYTHING I COULD DO, REALLY.
I STILL FEEL LIKE I JUST BARGED REALLY DEEP INTO SOMEONE'S PERSONAL TERRITORY...
NNNHHH...
NYED...!
BOUNCE
BOUNCE
WELL, NO POINT LETTING MYSELF WORRY ABOUT IT TOO MUCH. I'VE GOT ENOUGH OTHER STUFF TO DEAL WITH.
COMING ...

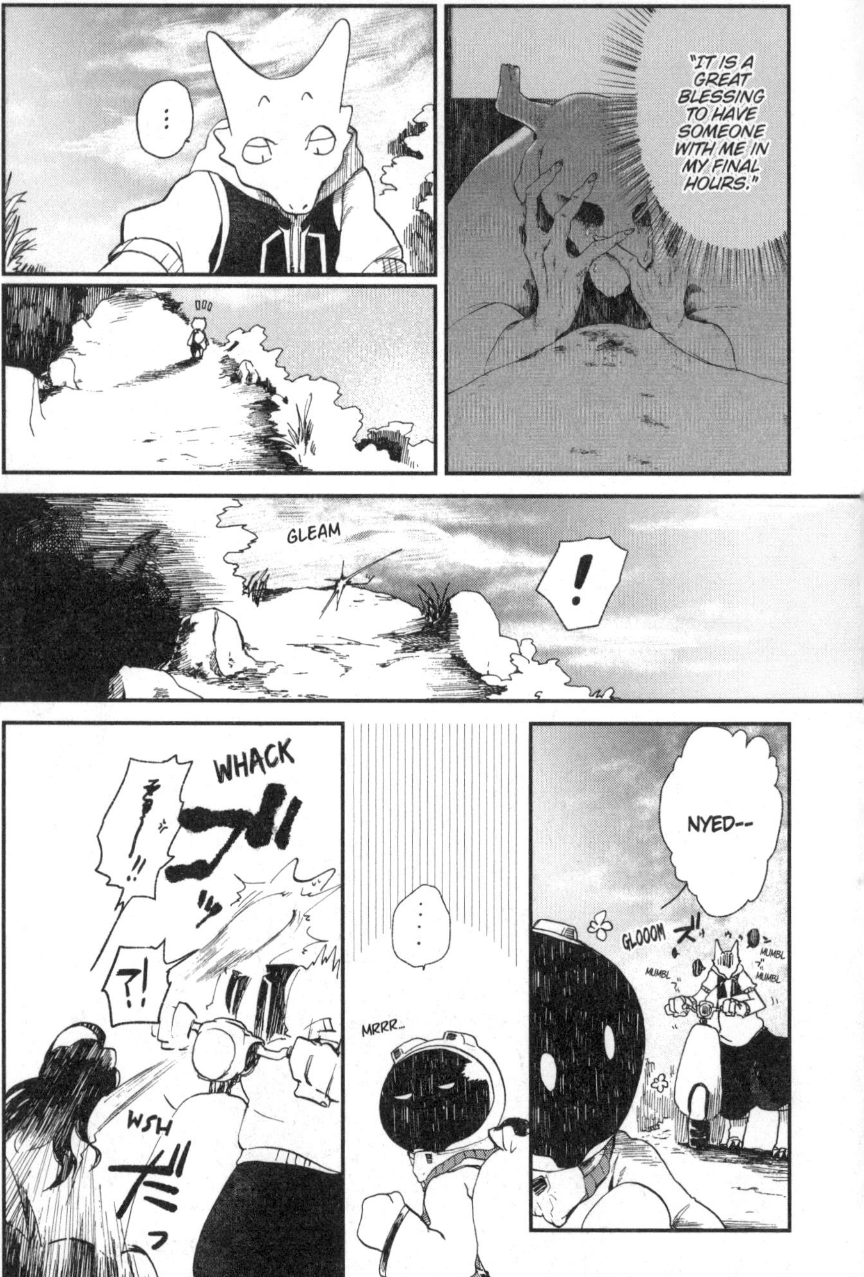
"IT IS A GREAT BLESSING TO HAVE SOMEONE WITH ME IN MY FINAL HOURS."
...
GLEAM
!
NYED--
GLOOOM
MUMBL
MUMBL
MUMBL
....
MRRR...
WHACK
?!
WSH

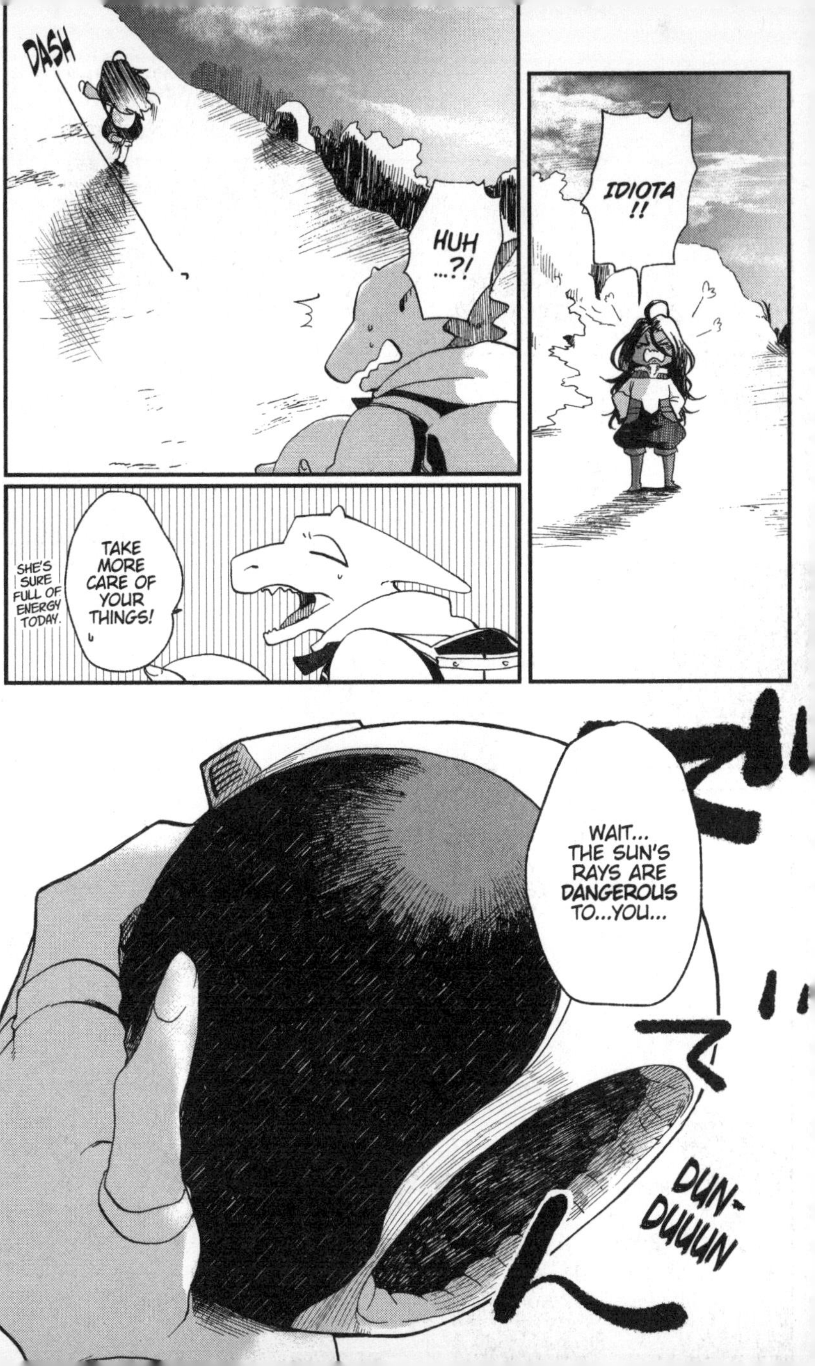
IDIOTA!!
DASH
HUH...?!
TAKE MORE CARE OF YOUR THINGS!
SHE'S SURE FULL OF ENERGY TODAY.
WAIT... THE SUN'S RAYS ARE DANGEROUS TO...YOU...
DUN-DUUUN

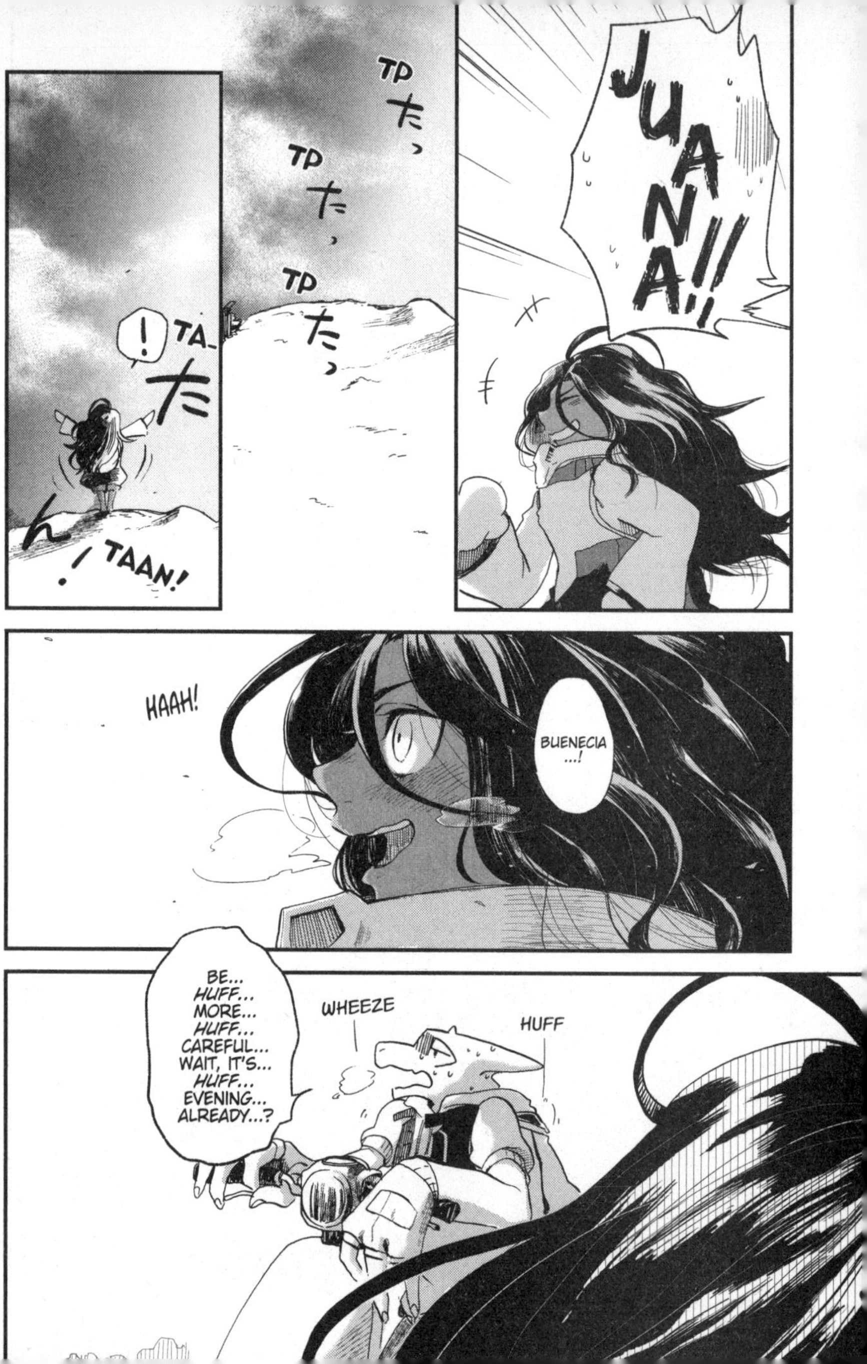
JUANA!!
TP たっ
TP たっ
TP たっ
!
TA- たん! TAAN!
HAAH!
BUENECIA ...!
BE... HUFF... MORE... HUFF... CAREFUL... WAIT, IT'S... HUFF... EVENING... ALREADY...?
WHEEZE
HUFF

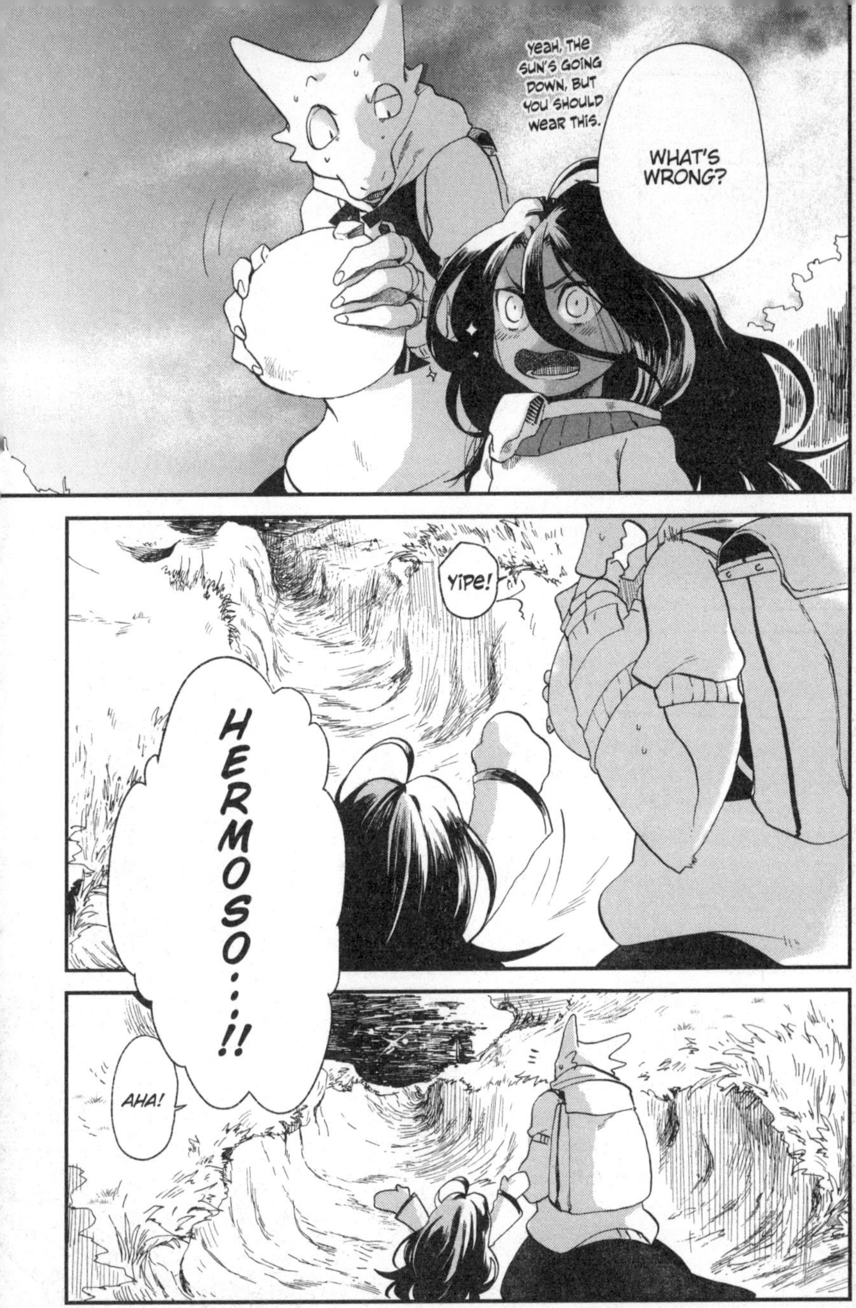
WHAT'S WRONG?
Yeah, the sun's going down, but you should wear this.
Yipe!
HERMOSO...!!
AHA!

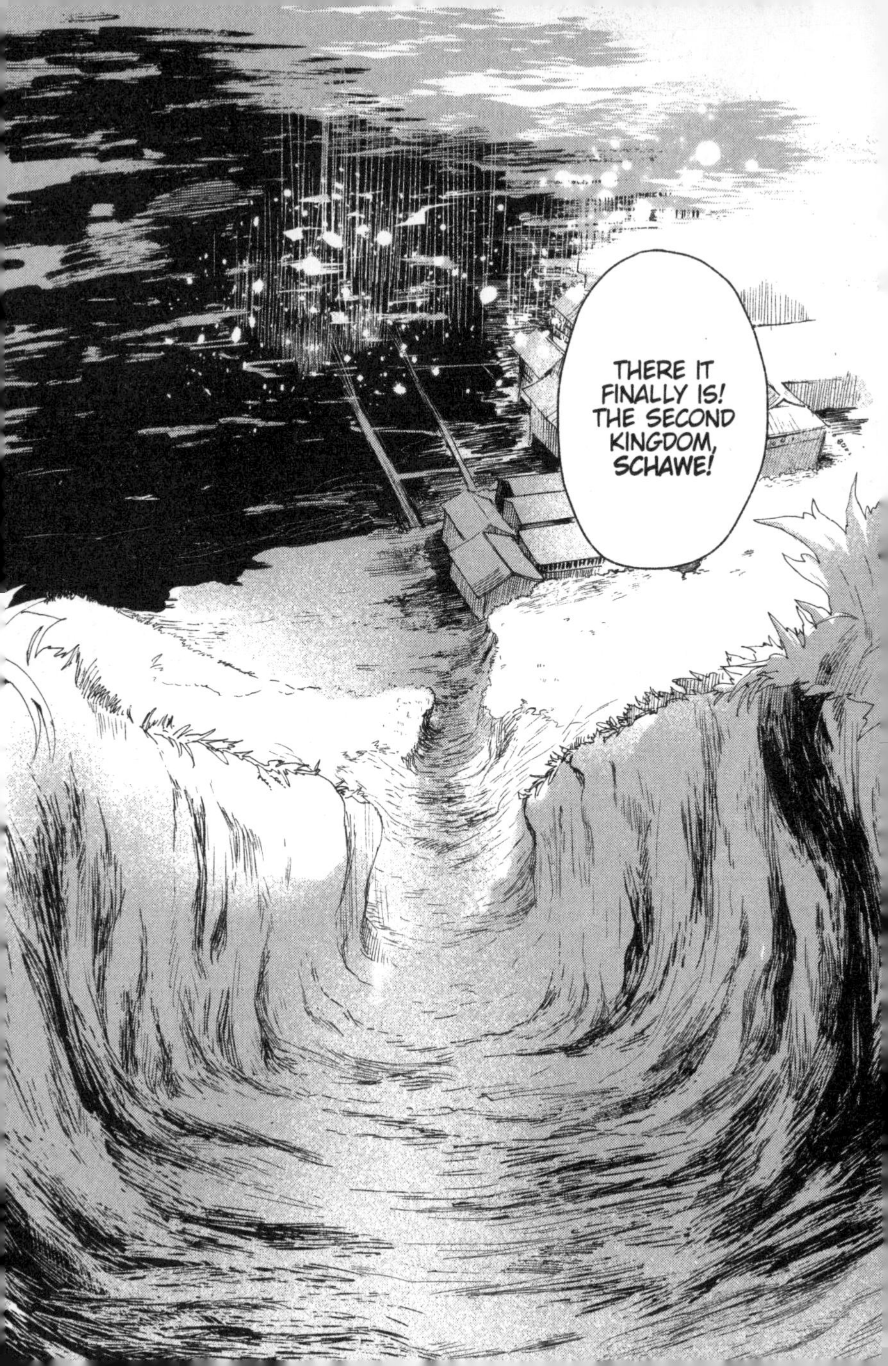
THERE IT FINALLY IS! THE SECOND KINGDOM, SCHAWE!

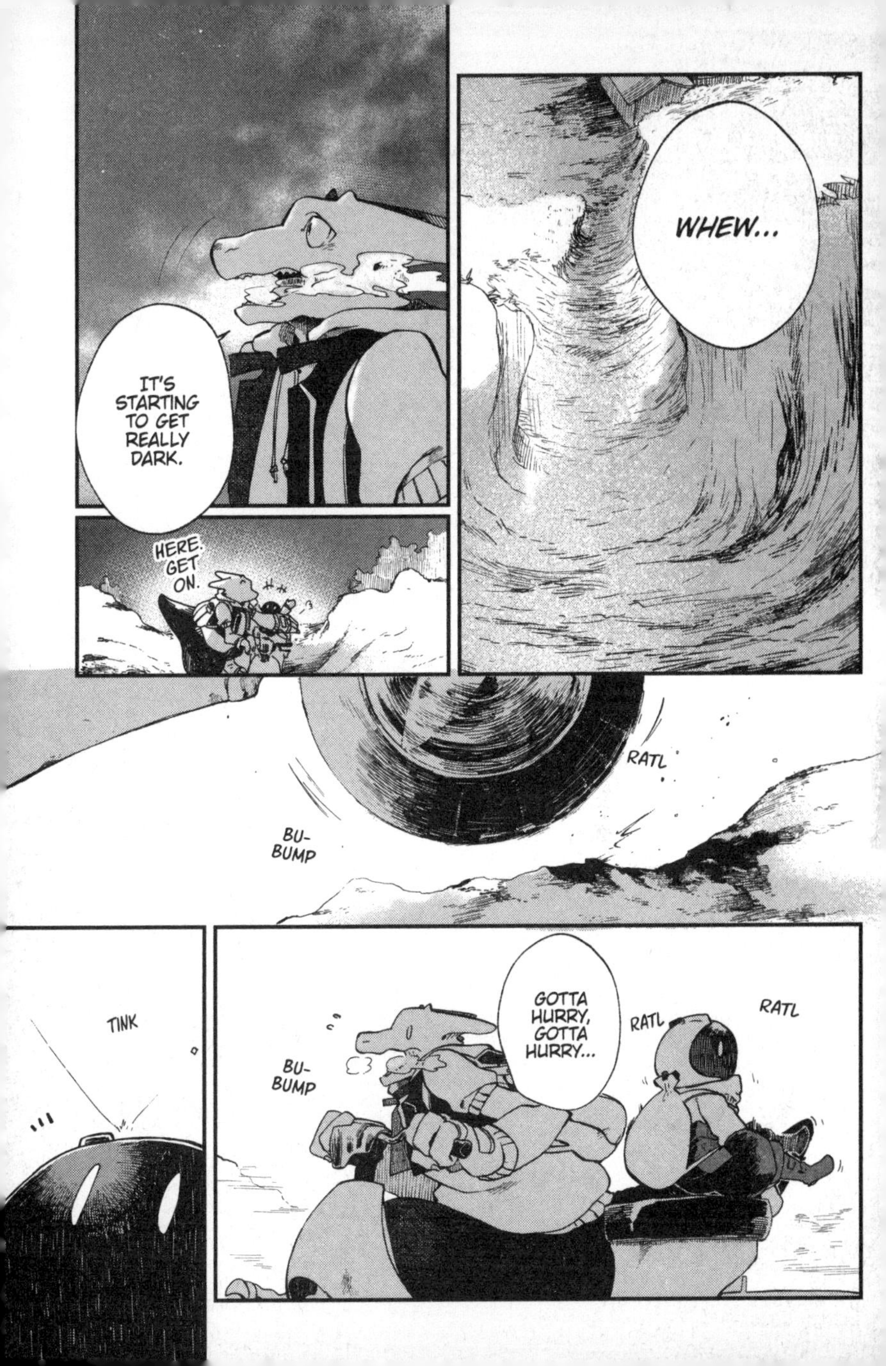
WHEW...
IT'S STARTING TO GET REALLY DARK.
HERE. GET ON.
RATL
BU-BUMP
RATL
RATL
GOTTA HURRY, GOTTA HURRY...
BU-BUMP
TINK

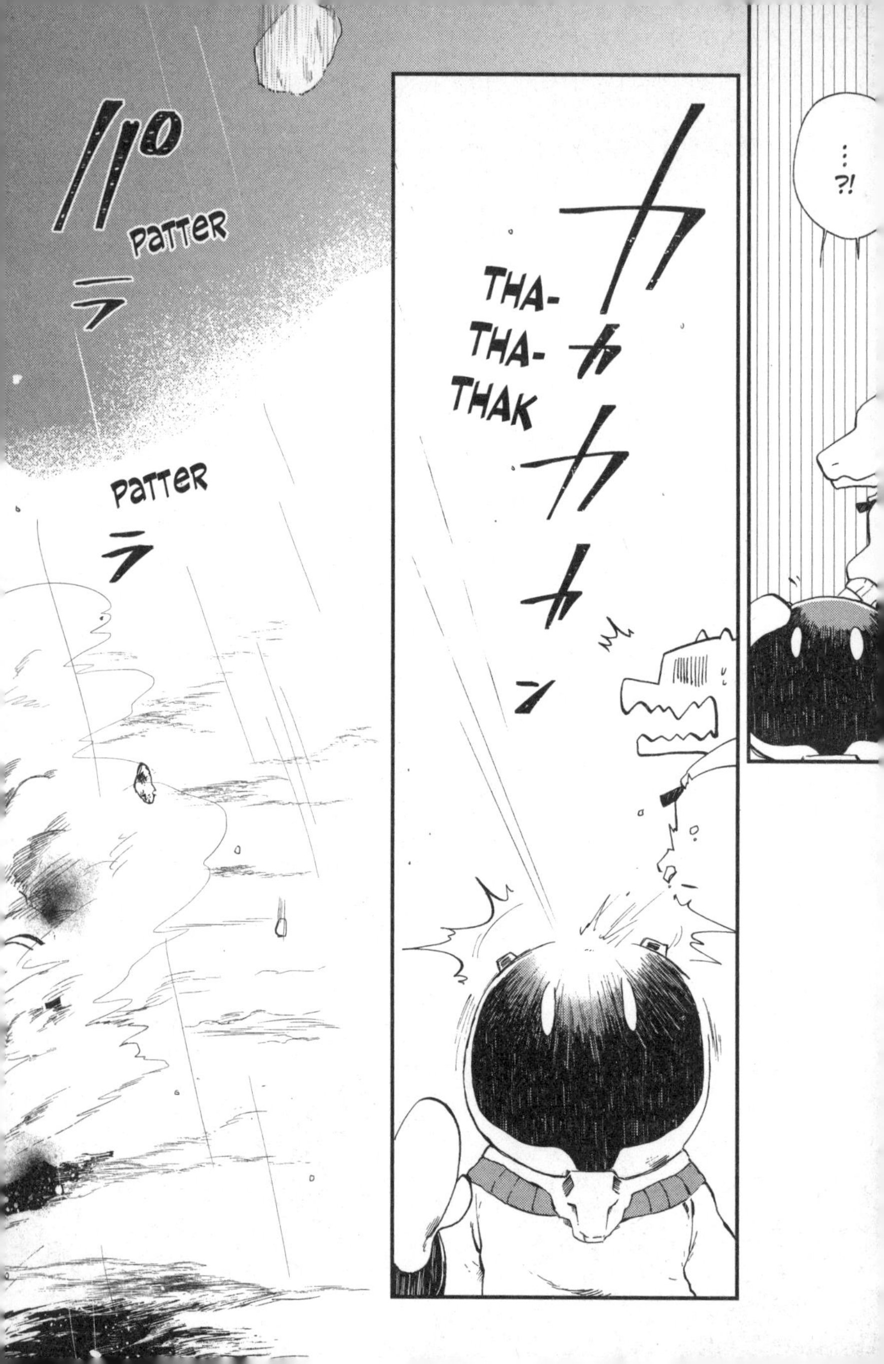
...?!
THA-THA-THAK
PATTER
PATTER

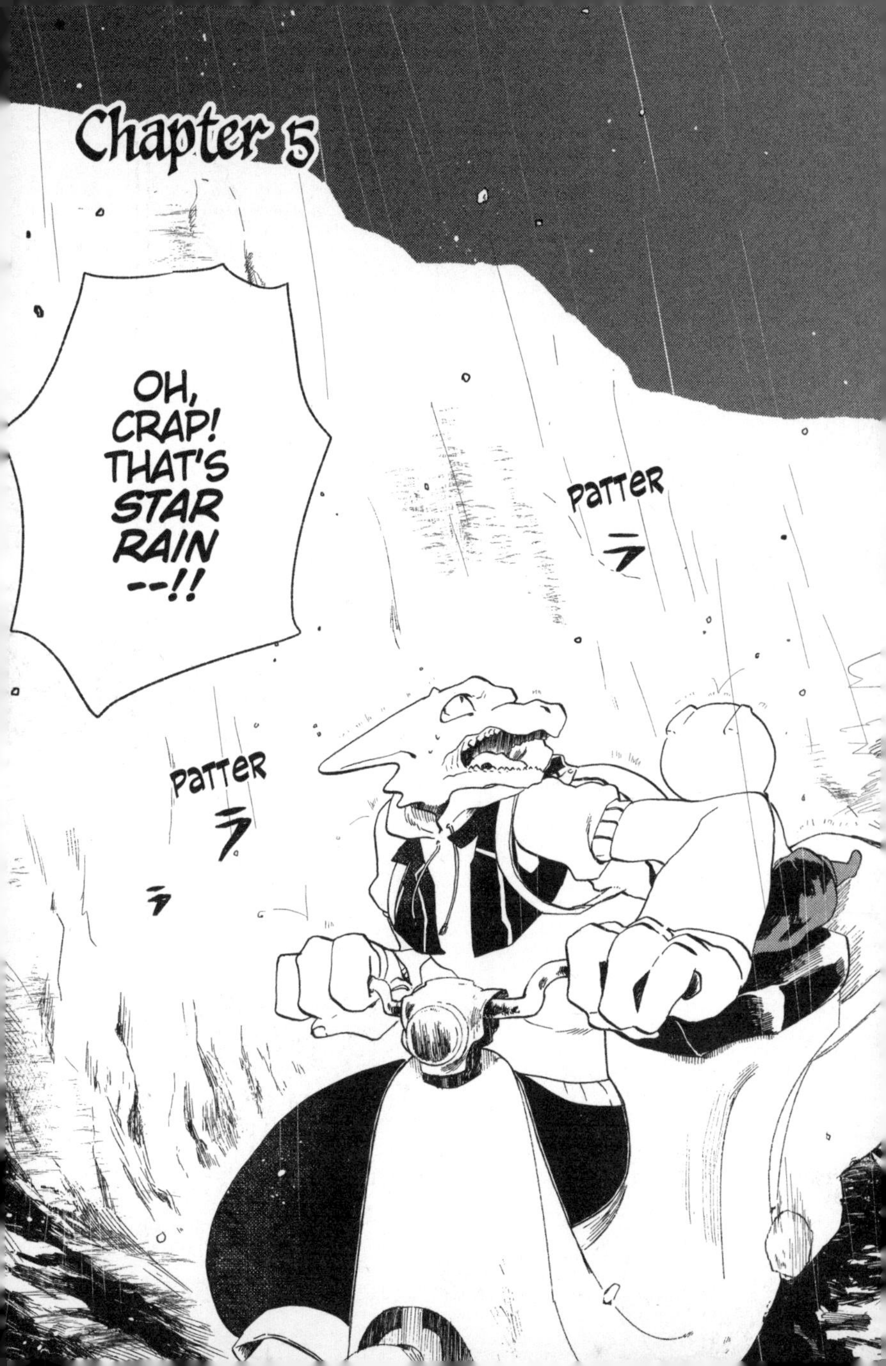
Chapter 5
OH, CRAP! THAT'S STAR RAIN --!!
PATTER
ラ
PATTER
ラ
ラ

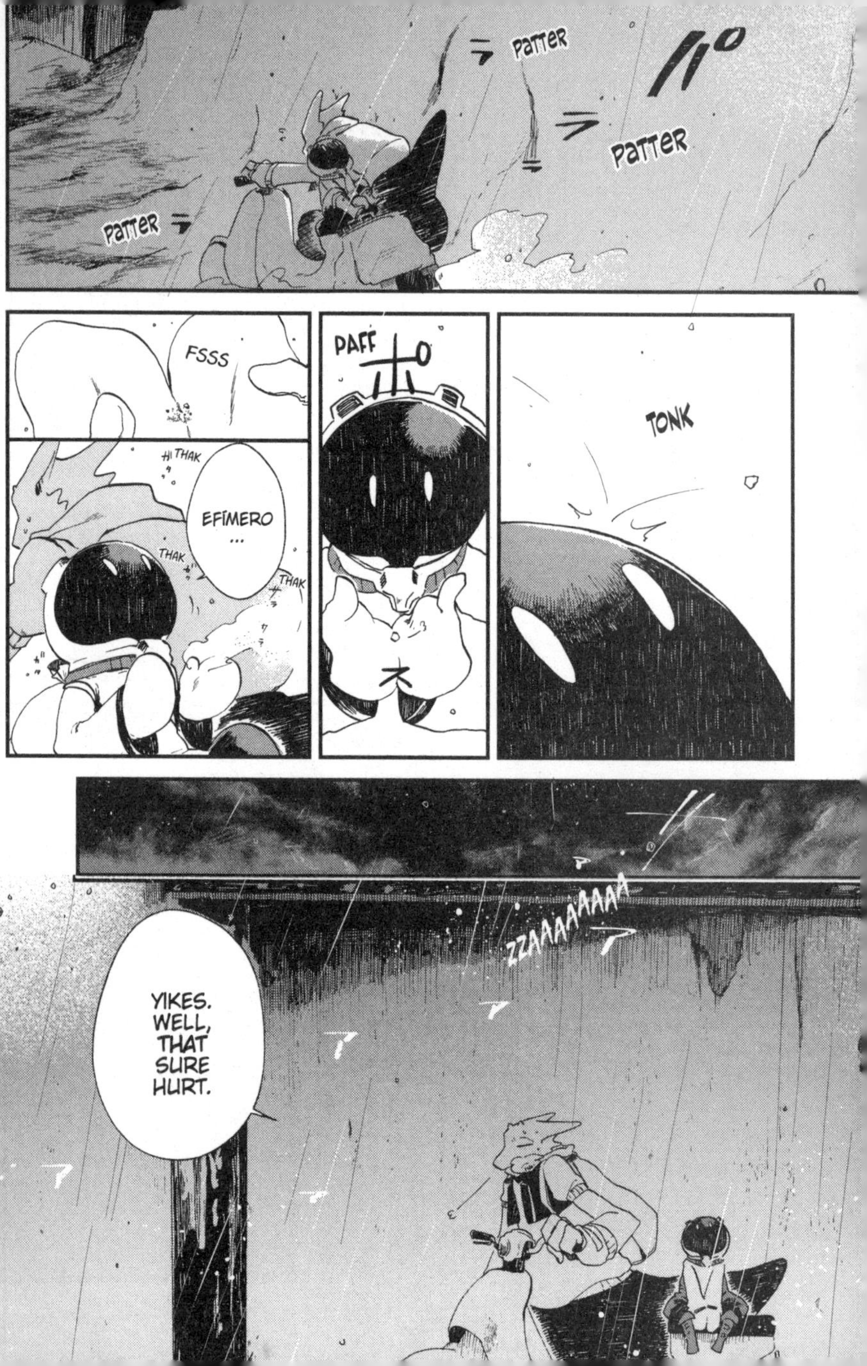
PATTER
PATTER
PATTER
TONK
PAFF
FSSS
THAK
EFÍMERO ...
THAK
THAK
ZZAAAAAAAA
YIKES. WELL, THAT SURE HURT.

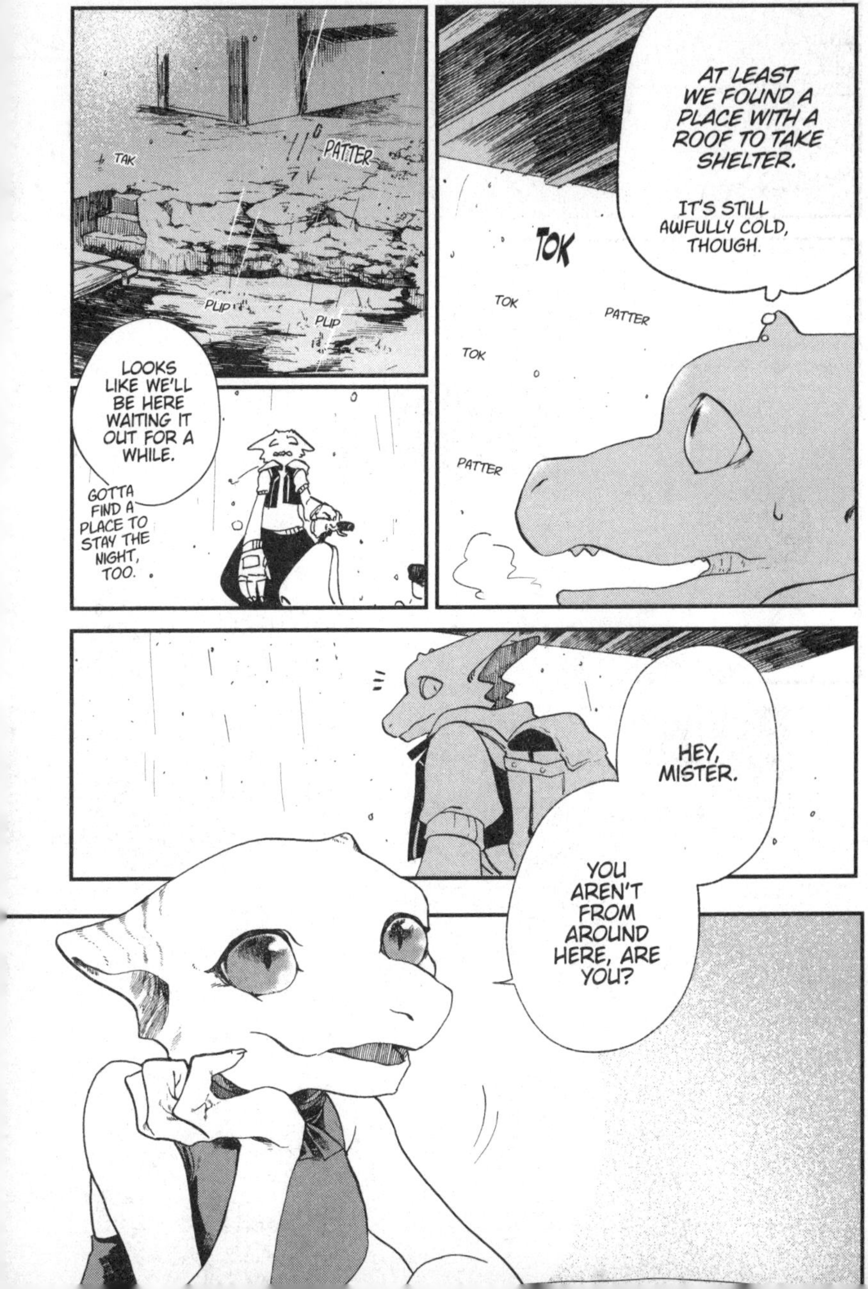
AT LEAST WE FOUND A PLACE WITH A ROOF TO TAKE SHELTER.
IT'S STILL AWFULLY COLD, THOUGH.
TOK
TOK
PATTER
TOK
PATTER
TAK
PATTER
PLIP
PLIP
LOOKS LIKE WE'LL BE HERE WAITING IT OUT FOR A WHILE.
GOTTA FIND A PLACE TO STAY THE NIGHT, TOO.
HEY, MISTER.
YOU AREN'T FROM AROUND HERE, ARE YOU?

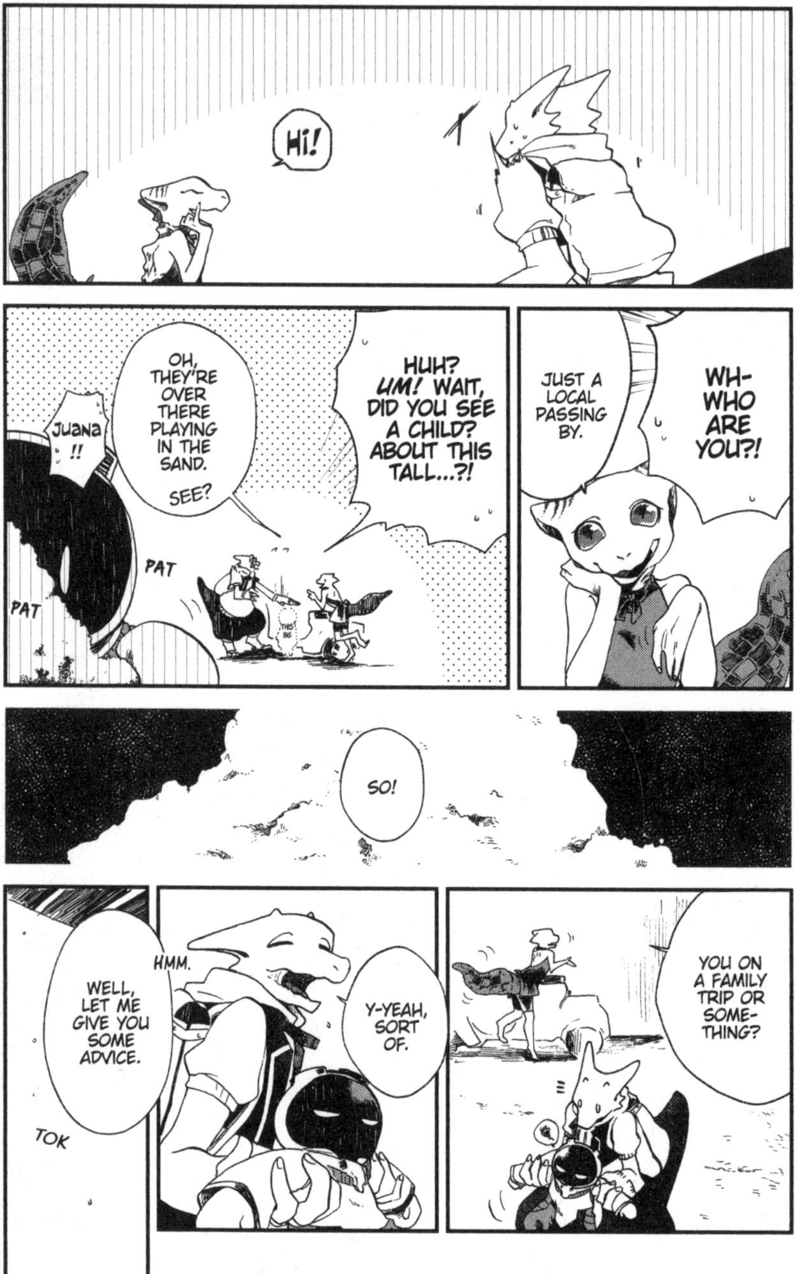
Hi!
WH- WHO ARE YOU?!
JUST A LOCAL PASSING BY.
HUH? UM! WAIT, DID YOU SEE A CHILD? ABOUT THIS TALL...?!
THIS BIG
OH, THEY'RE OVER THERE PLAYING IN THE SAND. SEE?
Juana !!
PAT
PAT
SO!
YOU ON A FAMILY TRIP OR SOME-THING?
Y-YEAH, SORT OF.
HMM.
WELL, LET ME GIVE YOU SOME ADVICE.
TOK

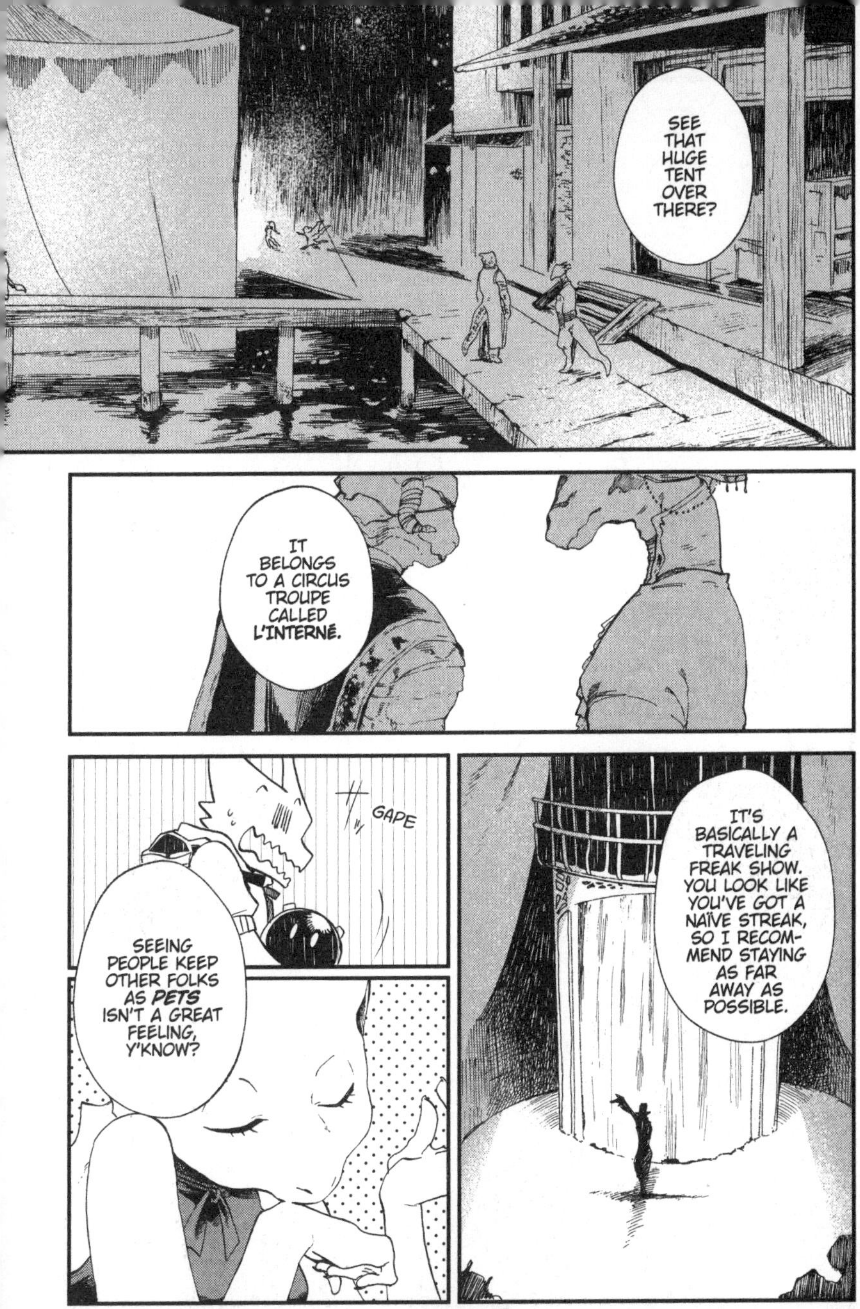
SEE THAT HUGE TENT OVER THERE?
IT BELONGS TO A CIRCUS TROUPE CALLED **L'INTERNÉ.**
IT'S BASICALLY A TRAVELING FREAK SHOW. YOU LOOK LIKE YOU'VE GOT A NAÏVE STREAK, SO I RECOM-MEND STAYING AS FAR AWAY AS POSSIBLE.
GAPE
SEEING PEOPLE KEEP OTHER FOLKS AS ***PETS*** ISN'T A GREAT FEELING, Y'KNOW?

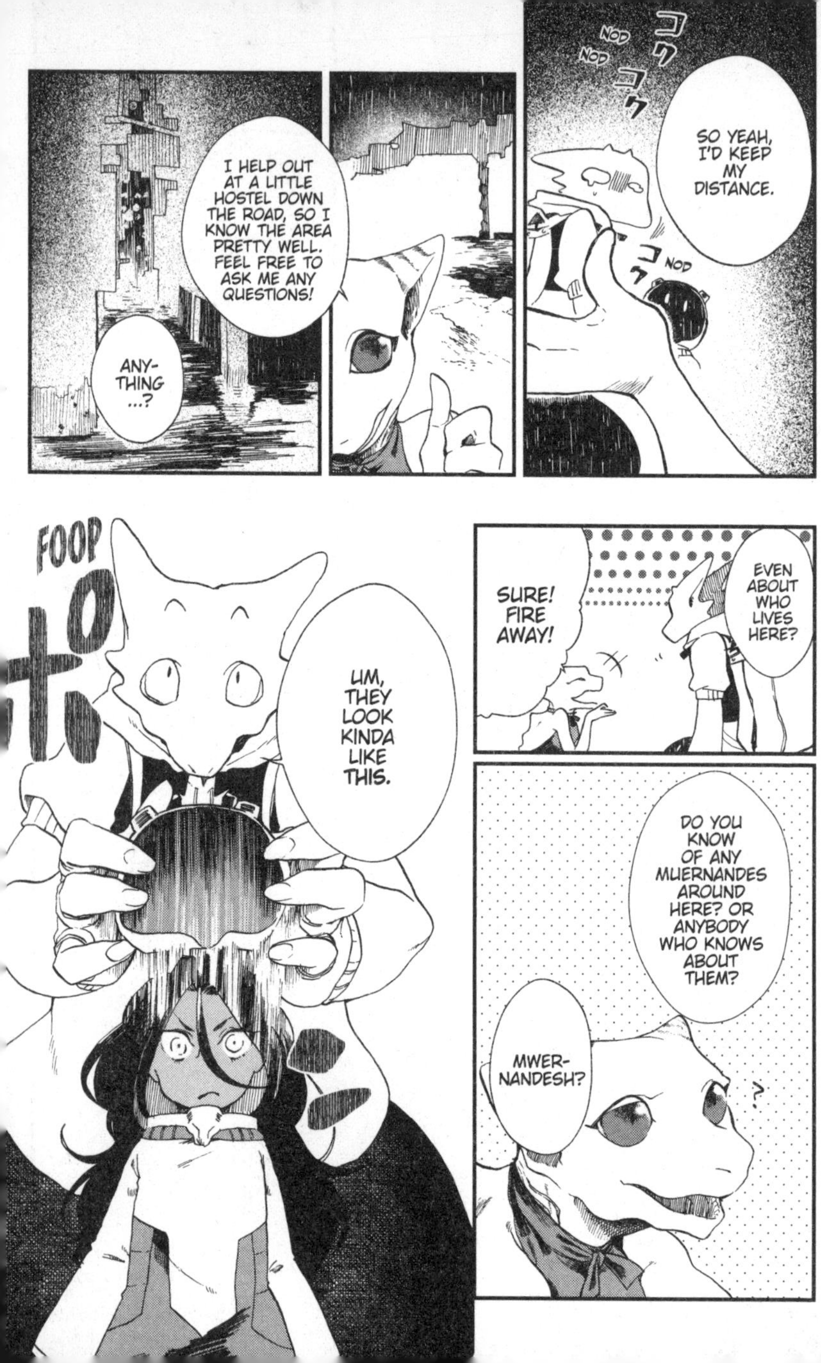
NOD NOD
SO YEAH, I'D KEEP MY DISTANCE.
NOD
I HELP OUT AT A LITTLE HOSTEL DOWN THE ROAD, SO I KNOW THE AREA PRETTY WELL. FEEL FREE TO ASK ME ANY QUESTIONS!
ANY-THING ...?
EVEN ABOUT WHO LIVES HERE?
SURE! FIRE AWAY!
DO YOU KNOW OF ANY MUERNANDES AROUND HERE? OR ANYBODY WHO KNOWS ABOUT THEM?
MWER-NANDESH?
FOOP
UM, THEY LOOK KINDA LIKE THIS.

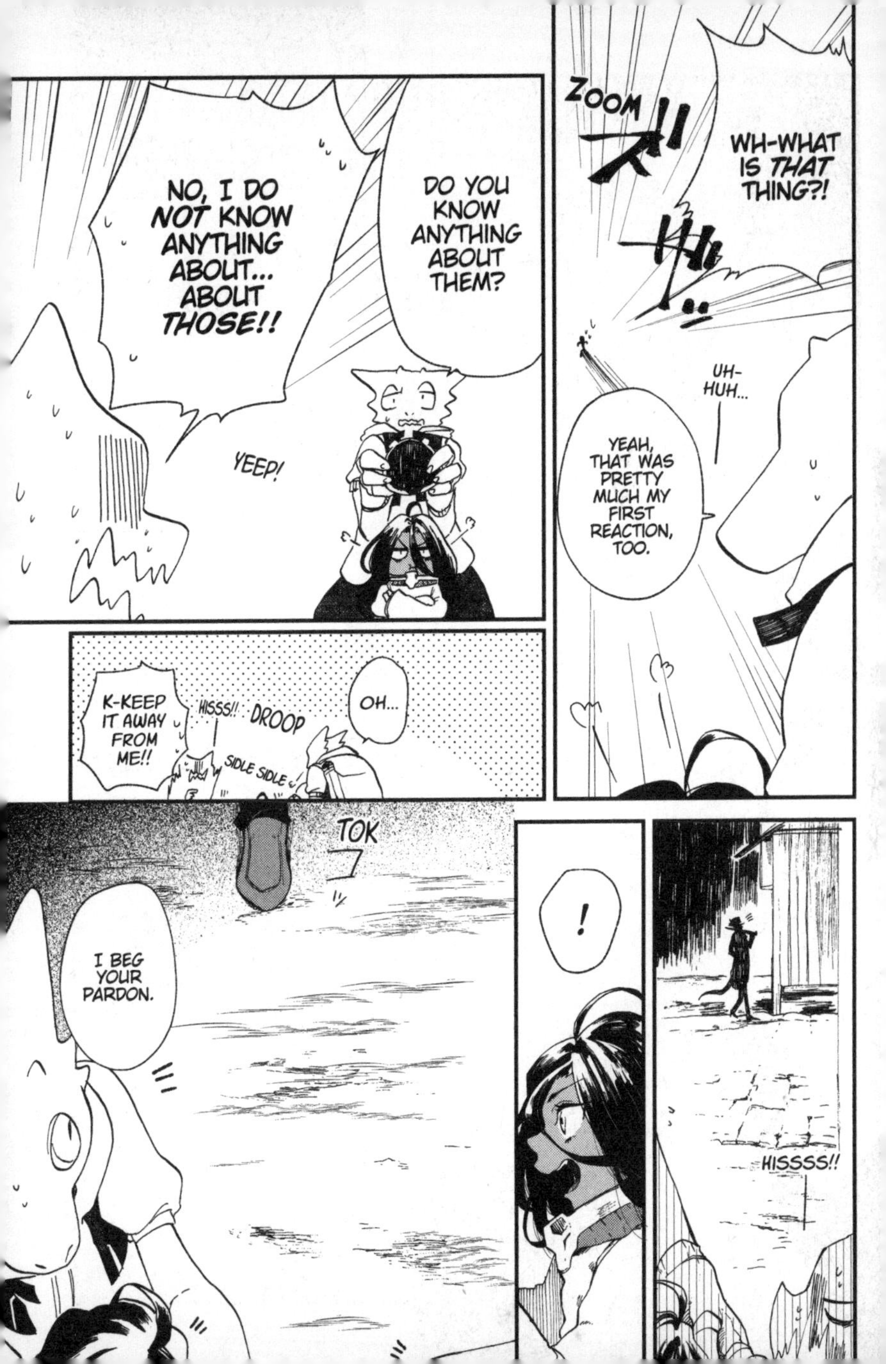
ZOOM
WH-WHAT IS *THAT* THING?!
UH-HUH...
YEAH, THAT WAS PRETTY MUCH MY FIRST REACTION, TOO.
DO YOU KNOW ANYTHING ABOUT THEM?
NO, I DO *NOT* KNOW ANYTHING ABOUT... ABOUT *THOSE!!*
YEEP!
OH...
DROOP
SIDLE SIDLE
HISSS!!
K-KEEP IT AWAY FROM ME!!
HISSSS!!
!
TOK
I BEG YOUR PARDON.

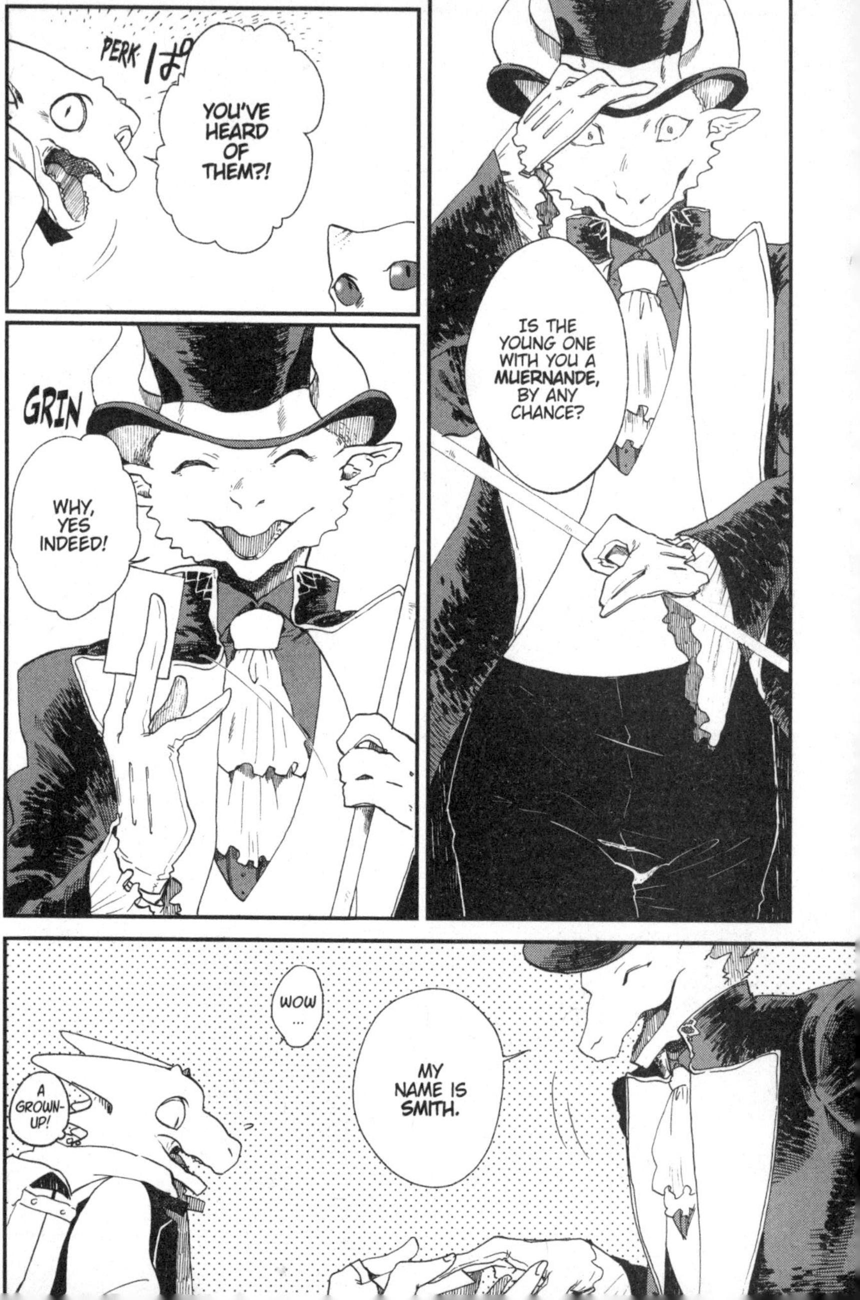

IS THE YOUNG ONE WITH YOU A MUERNANDE, BY ANY CHANCE?
PERK ぱ
YOU'VE HEARD OF THEM?!
GRIN
WHY, YES INDEED!
MY NAME IS SMITH.
WOW ...
A GROWN-UP!

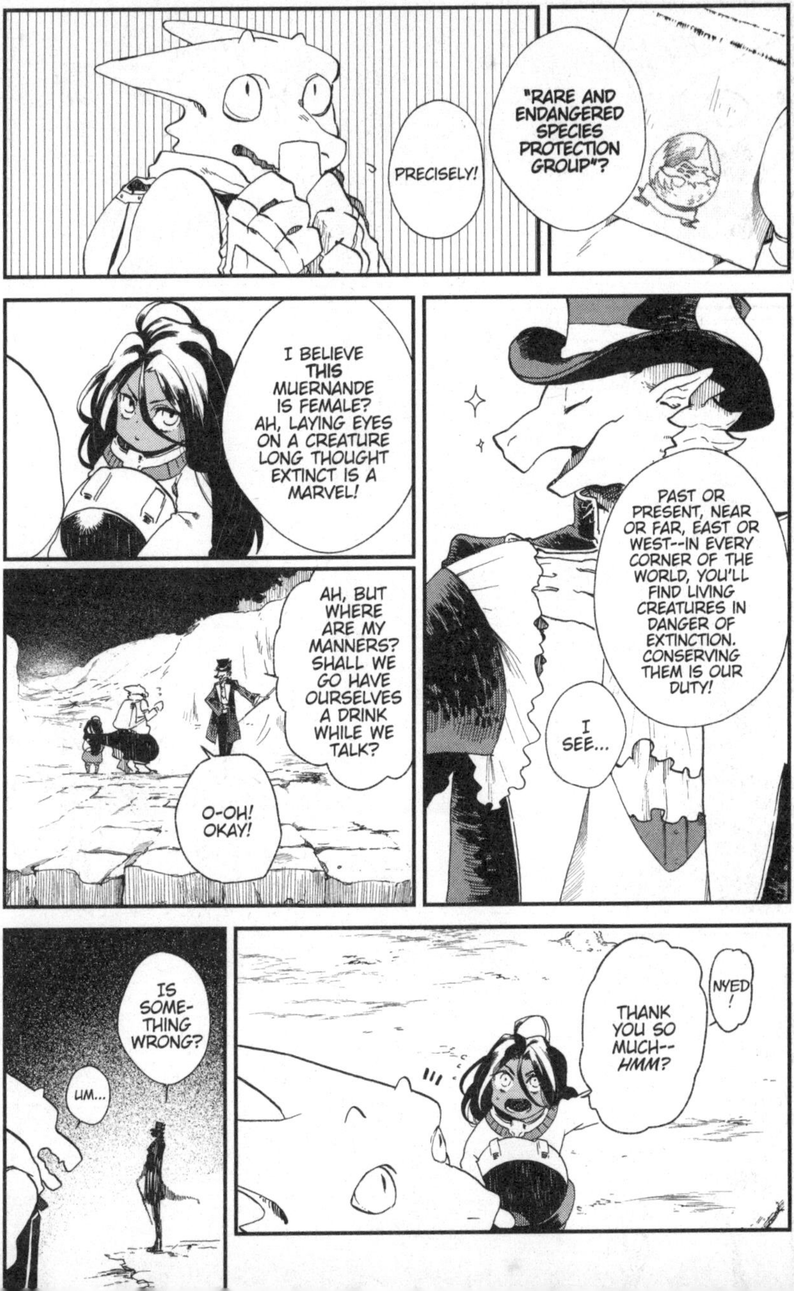
"RARE AND ENDANGERED SPECIES PROTECTION GROUP"?
PRECISELY!
PAST OR PRESENT, NEAR OR FAR, EAST OR WEST--IN EVERY CORNER OF THE WORLD, YOU'LL FIND LIVING CREATURES IN DANGER OF EXTINCTION. CONSERVING THEM IS OUR DUTY!
I SEE...
I BELIEVE THIS MUERNANDE IS FEMALE? AH, LAYING EYES ON A CREATURE LONG THOUGHT EXTINCT IS A MARVEL!
AH, BUT WHERE ARE MY MANNERS? SHALL WE GO HAVE OURSELVES A DRINK WHILE WE TALK?
O-OH! OKAY!
NYED!
THANK YOU SO MUCH-- *HMM?*
IS SOMETHING WRONG?
UM...

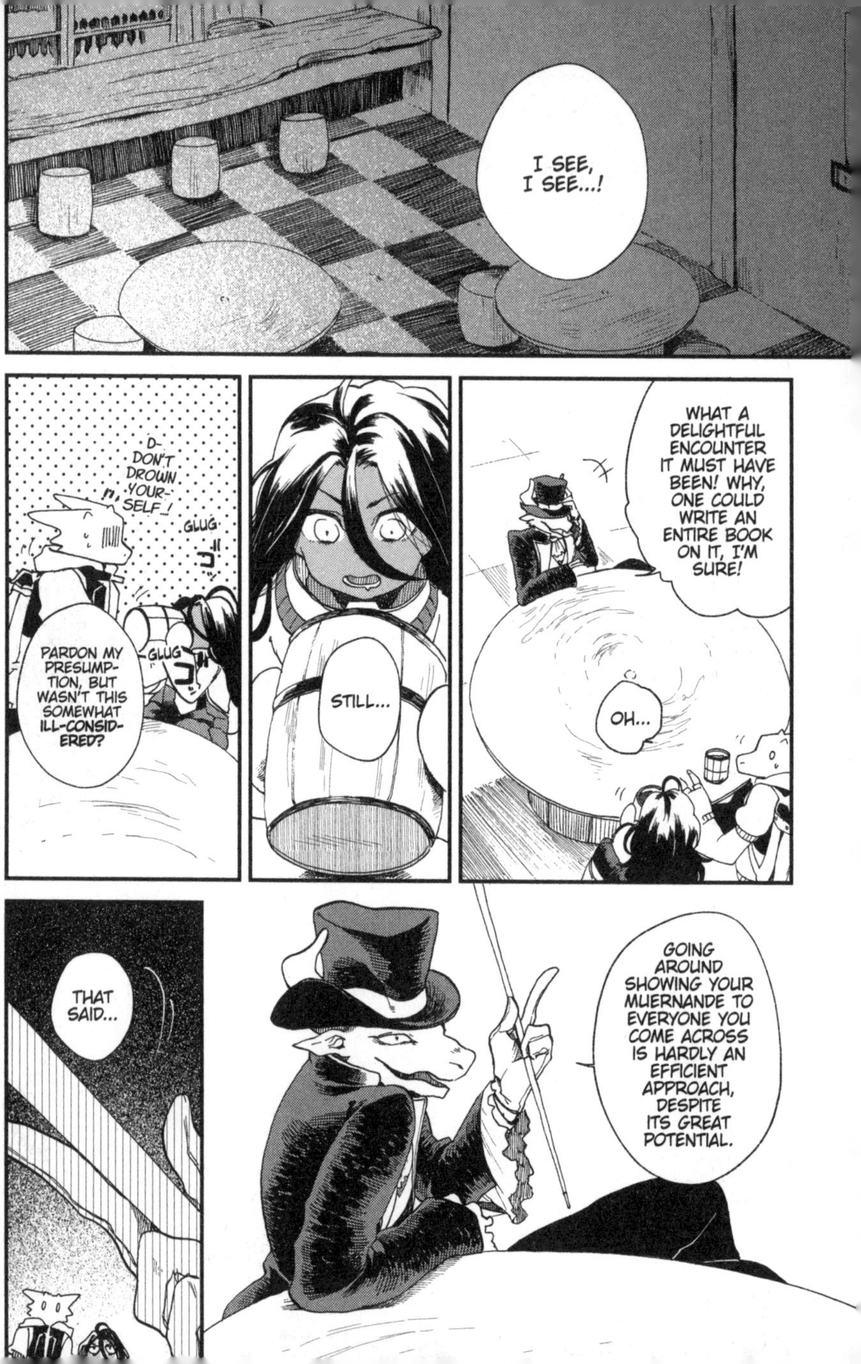

I SEE, I SEE...!
WHAT A DELIGHTFUL ENCOUNTER IT MUST HAVE BEEN! WHY, ONE COULD WRITE AN ENTIRE BOOK ON IT, I'M SURE!
OH...
STILL...
D-DON'T DROWN YOURSELF..!
GLUG
GLUG
PARDON MY PRESUMPTION, BUT WASN'T THIS SOMEWHAT ILL-CONSIDERED?
GOING AROUND SHOWING YOUR MUERNANDE TO EVERYONE YOU COME ACROSS IS HARDLY AN EFFICIENT APPROACH, DESPITE ITS GREAT POTENTIAL.
THAT SAID...

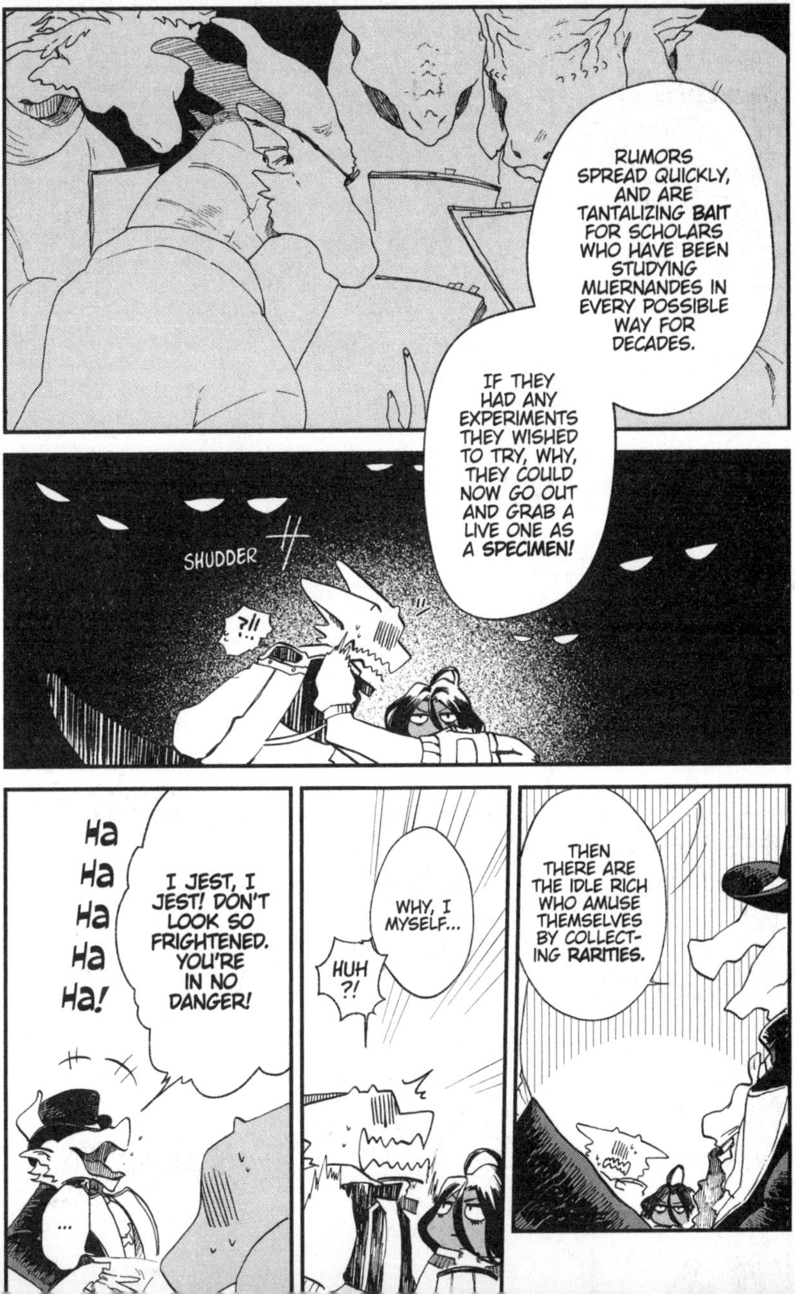
RUMORS SPREAD QUICKLY, AND ARE TANTALIZING BAIT FOR SCHOLARS WHO HAVE BEEN STUDYING MUERNANDES IN EVERY POSSIBLE WAY FOR DECADES.
IF THEY HAD ANY EXPERIMENTS THEY WISHED TO TRY, WHY, THEY COULD NOW GO OUT AND GRAB A LIVE ONE AS A SPECIMEN!
SHUDDER
?!!
THEN THERE ARE THE IDLE RICH WHO AMUSE THEMSELVES BY COLLECT-ING RARITIES.
WHY, I MYSELF...
HUH ?!
I JEST, I JEST! DON'T LOOK SO FRIGHTENED. YOU'RE IN NO DANGER!
HA HA HA HA HA!
...

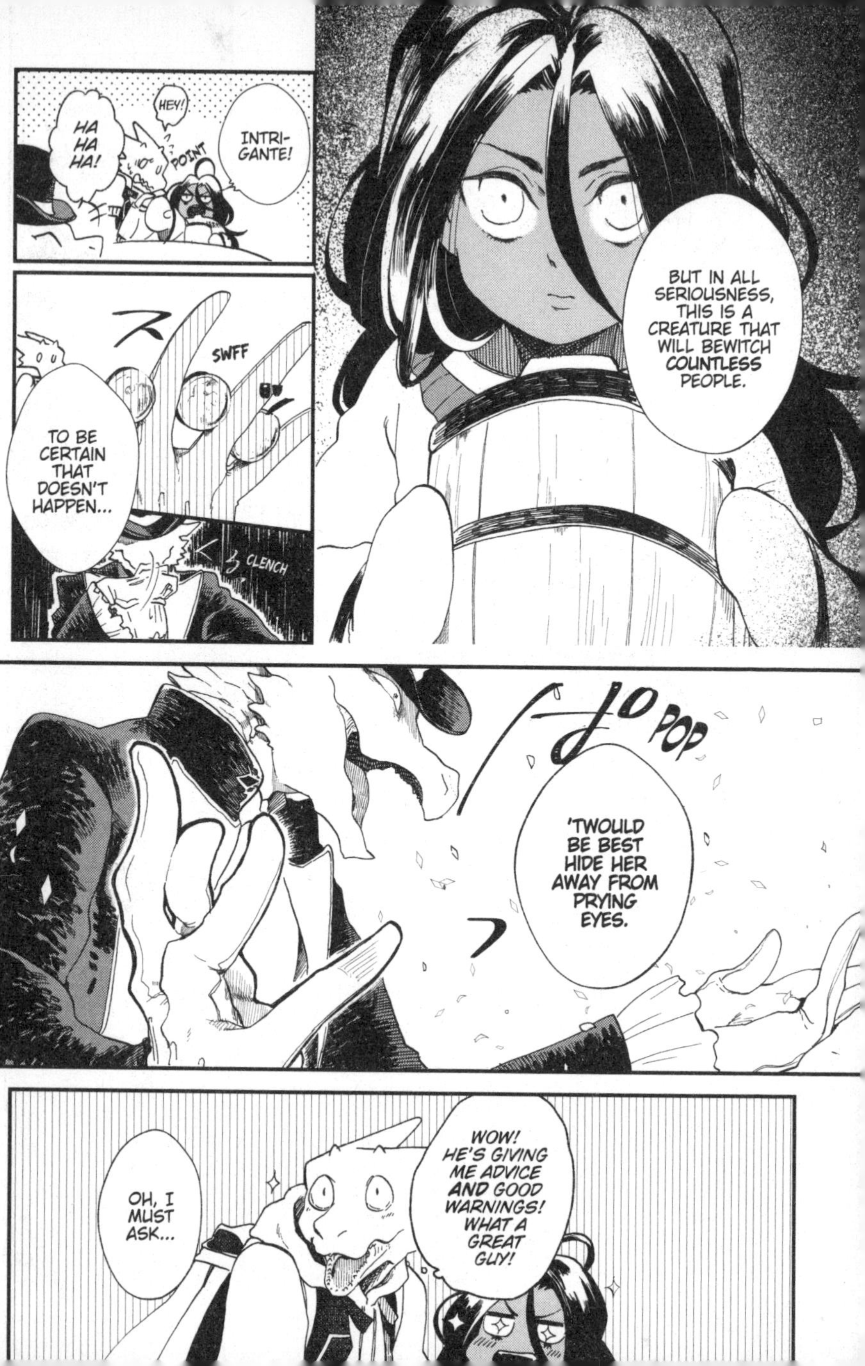
BUT IN ALL SERIOUSNESS, THIS IS A CREATURE THAT WILL BEWITCH COUNTLESS PEOPLE.
INTRI-GANTE!
HEY!
POINT
HA HA HA!
SWFF
TO BE CERTAIN THAT DOESN'T HAPPEN...
CLENCH
POP
'TWOULD BE BEST HIDE HER AWAY FROM PRYING EYES.
WOW! HE'S GIVING ME ADVICE AND GOOD WARNINGS! WHAT A GREAT GUY!
OH, I MUST ASK...

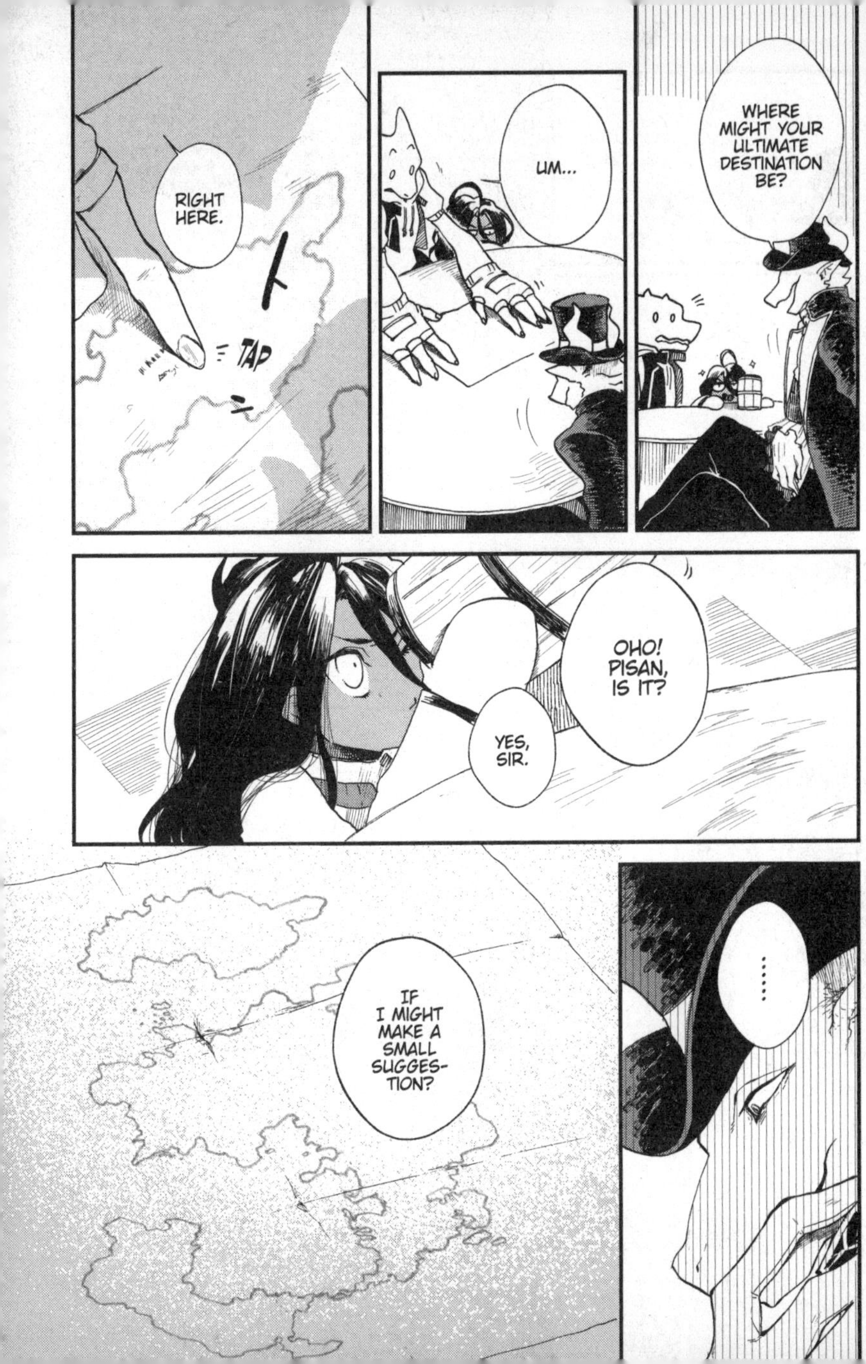
WHERE MIGHT YOUR ULTIMATE DESTINATION BE?
UM...
RIGHT HERE.
TAP
OHO! PISAN, IS IT?
YES, SIR.
......
IF I MIGHT MAKE A SMALL SUGGES-TION?

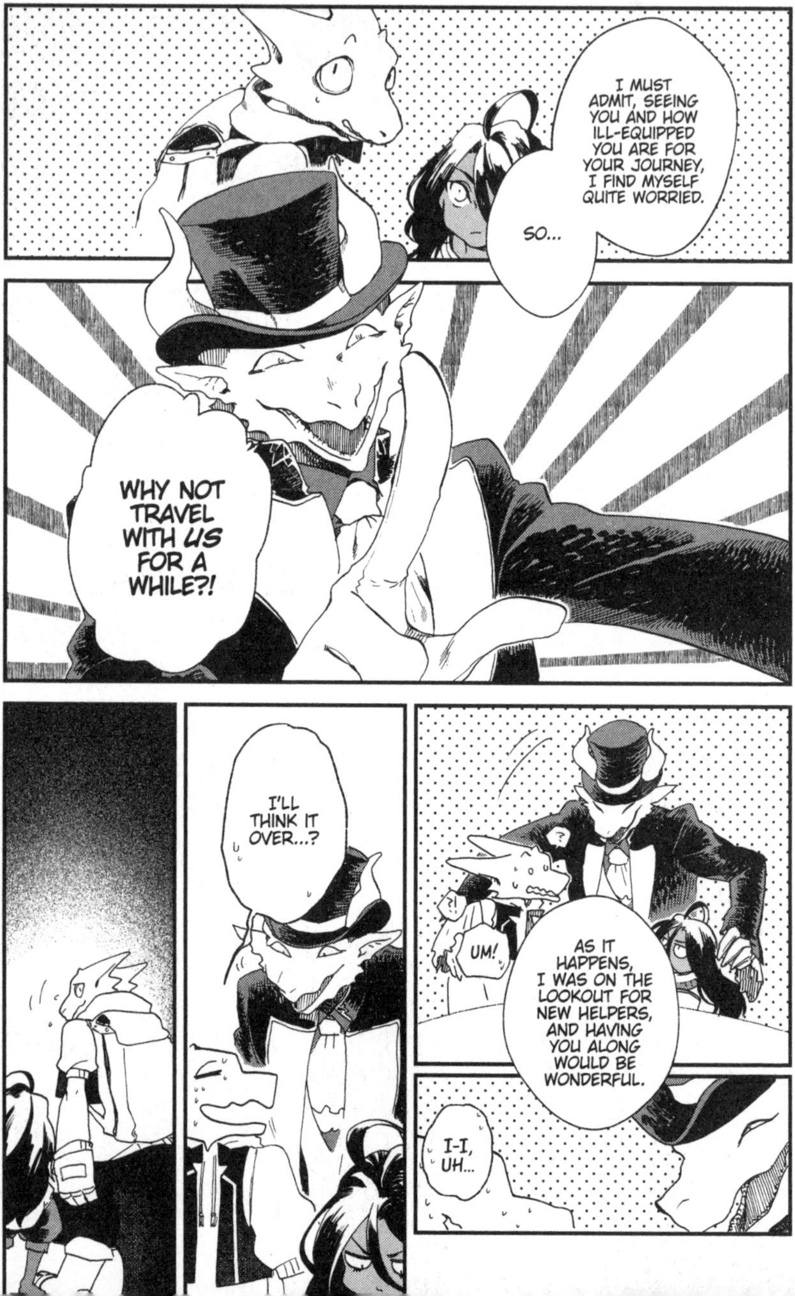
I MUST ADMIT, SEEING YOU AND HOW ILL-EQUIPPED YOU ARE FOR YOUR JOURNEY, I FIND MYSELF QUITE WORRIED.
SO...
WHY NOT TRAVEL WITH US FOR A WHILE?!
AS IT HAPPENS, I WAS ON THE LOOKOUT FOR NEW HELPERS, AND HAVING YOU ALONG WOULD BE WONDERFUL.
UM!
I-I, UH...
I'LL THINK IT OVER...?

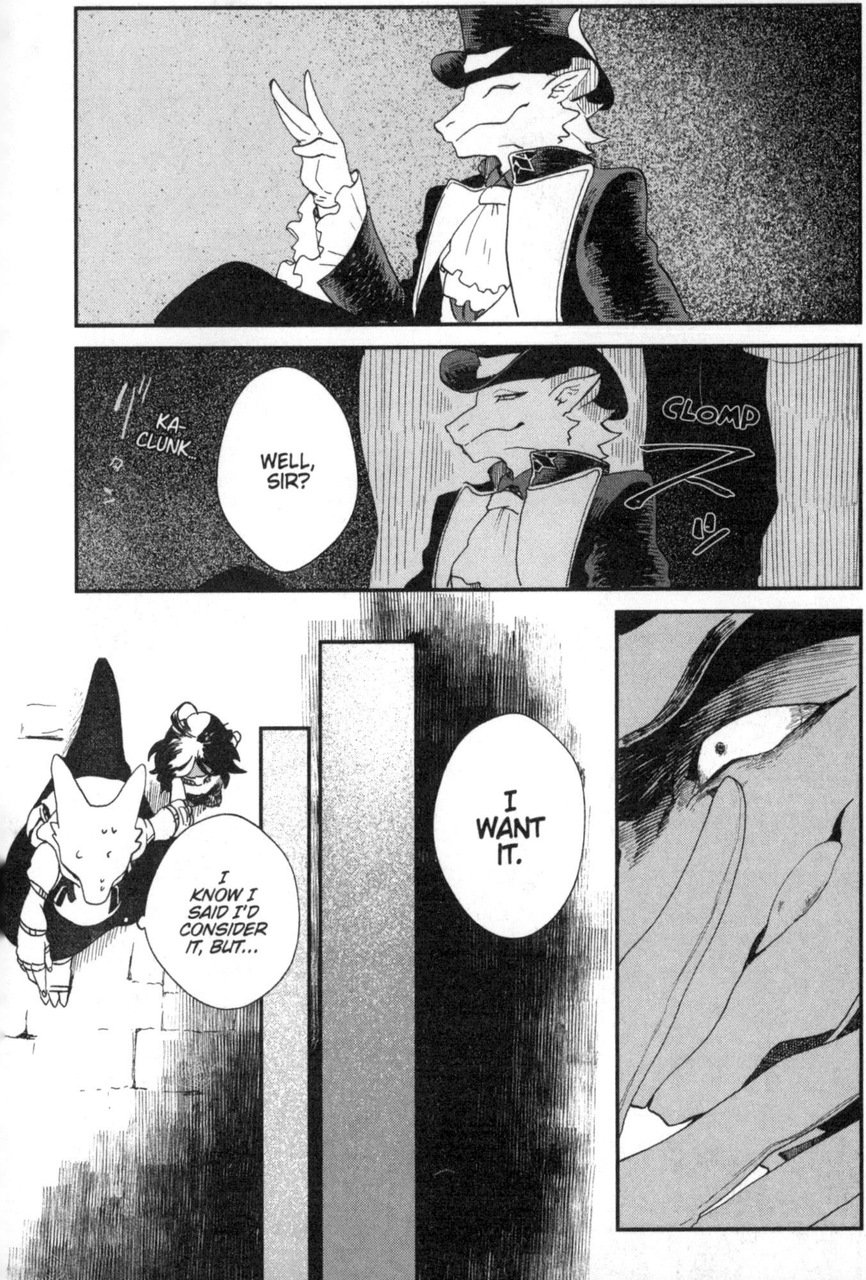
CLOMP
WELL, SIR?
KA-CLUNK...
I WANT IT.
I KNOW I SAID I'D CONSIDER IT, BUT...

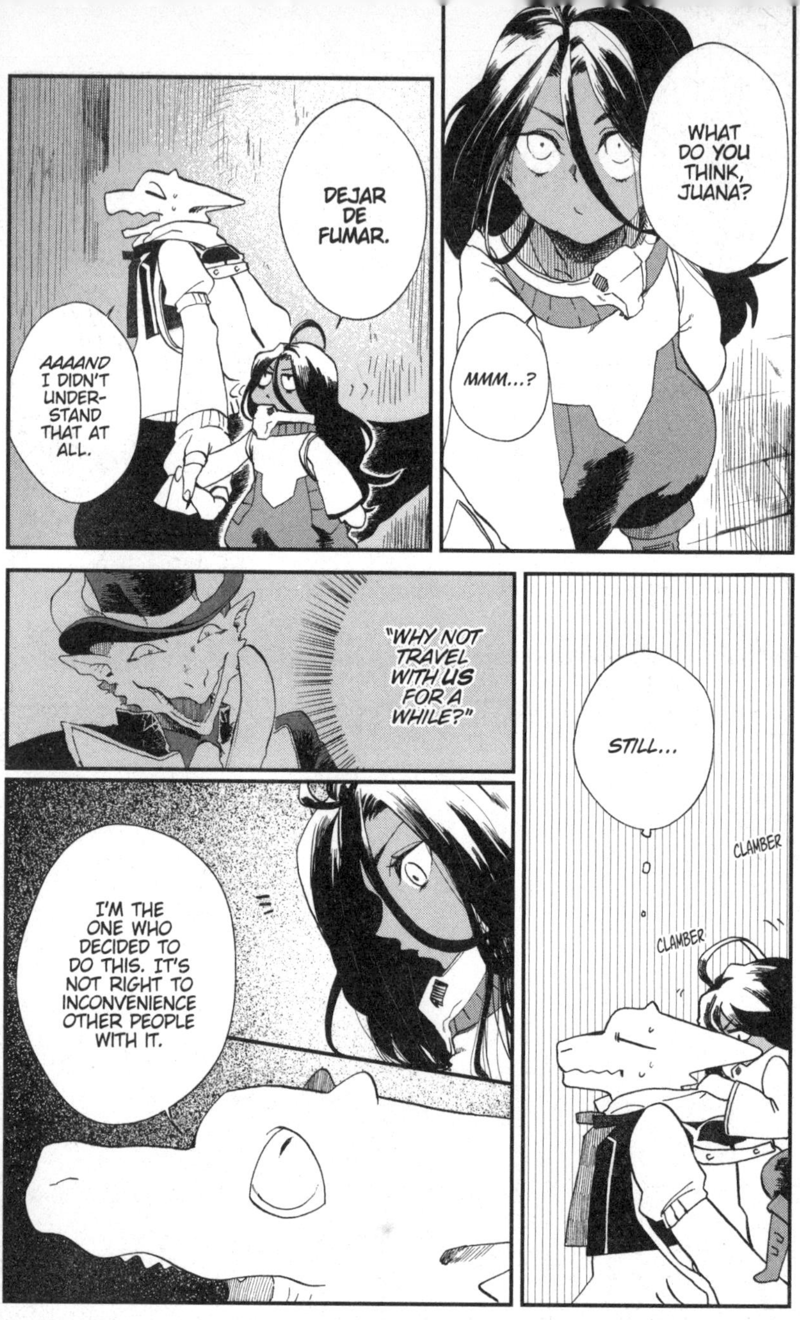
WHAT DO YOU THINK, JUANA?
MMM...?
DEJAR DE FUMAR.
AAAAND I DIDN'T UNDER-STAND THAT AT ALL.
STILL...
CLAMBER
CLAMBER
"WHY NOT TRAVEL WITH US FOR A WHILE?"
I'M THE ONE WHO DECIDED TO DO THIS. IT'S NOT RIGHT TO INCONVENIENCE OTHER PEOPLE WITH IT.

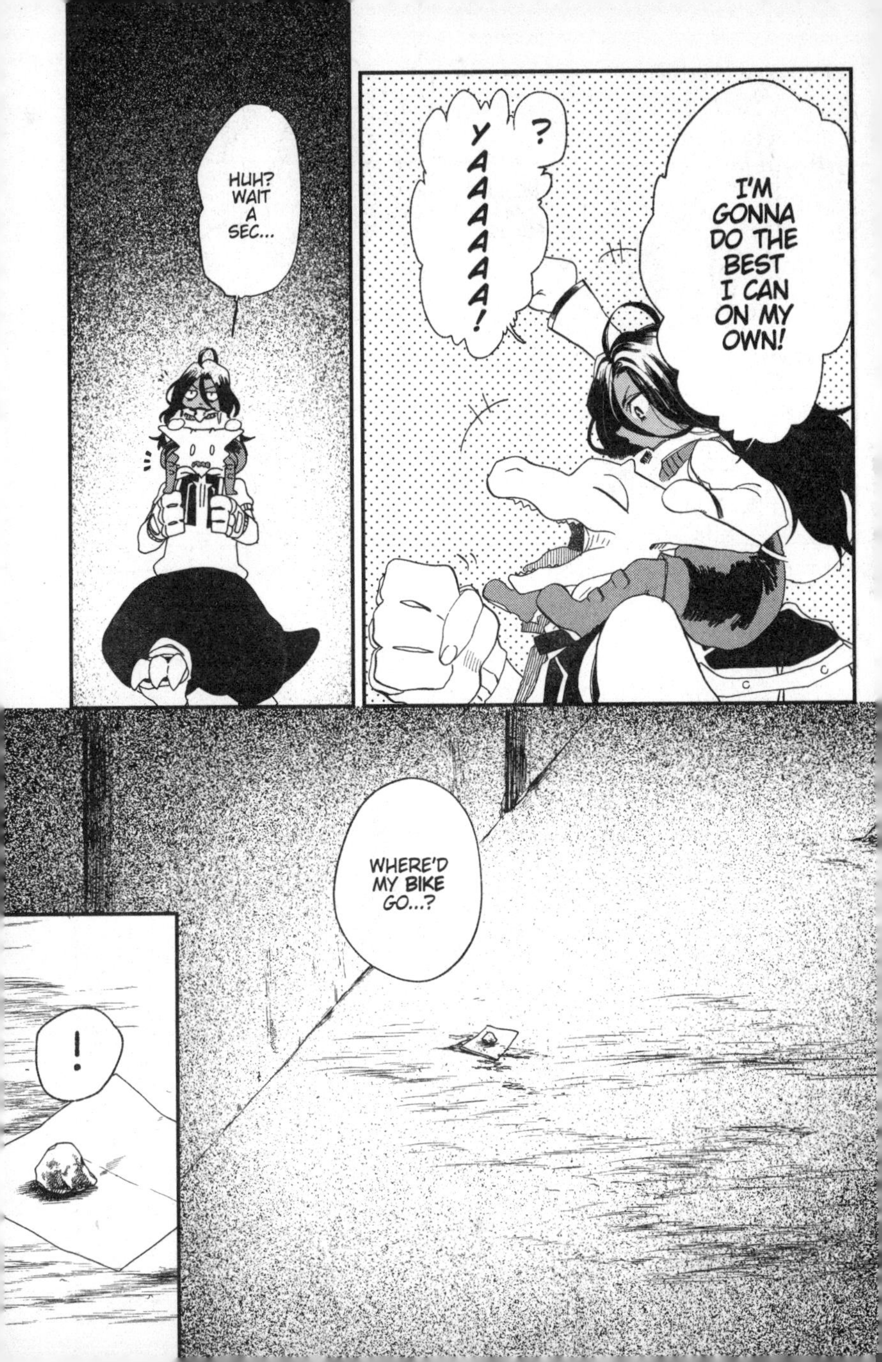
I'M GONNA DO THE BEST I CAN ON MY OWN!
?
YAAAAAA!
HUH? WAIT A SEC...
WHERE'D MY BIKE GO...?
!

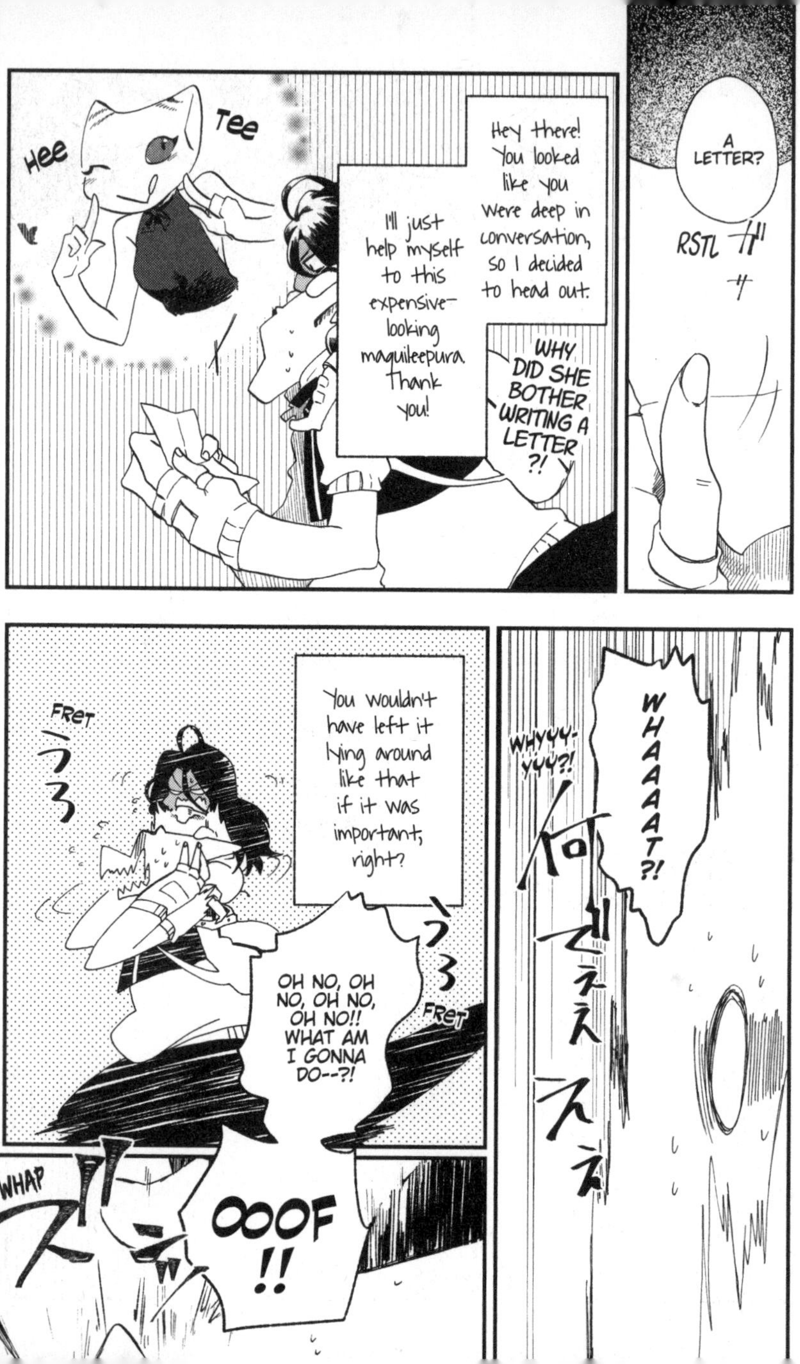
A LETTER?
RSTL
Hey there! You looked like you were deep in conversation, so I decided to head out.
I'll just help myself to this expensive-looking maquileepura. Thank you!
Tee
Hee
WHY DID SHE BOTHER WRITING A LETTER?!
WHAAAAAT?!
WHYYY-YYY?!
You wouldn't have left it lying around like that if it was important, right?
FRET
FRET
OH NO, OH NO, OH NO, OH NO!! WHAT AM I GONNA DO--?!
WHAP
OOOF!!

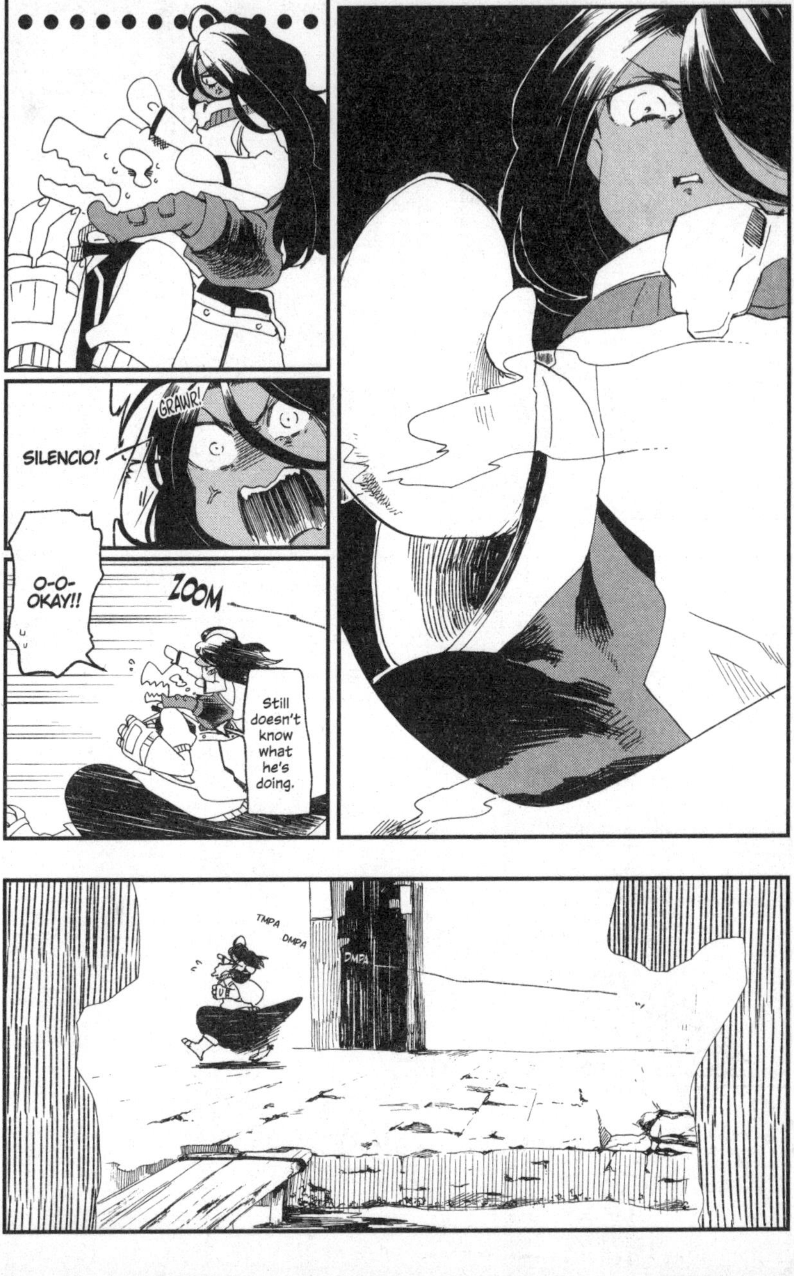
....
GRAWR!
SILENCIO!
O-O-OKAY!!
ZOOM
Still doesn't know what he's doing.
TMPA
DMPA
DMPA

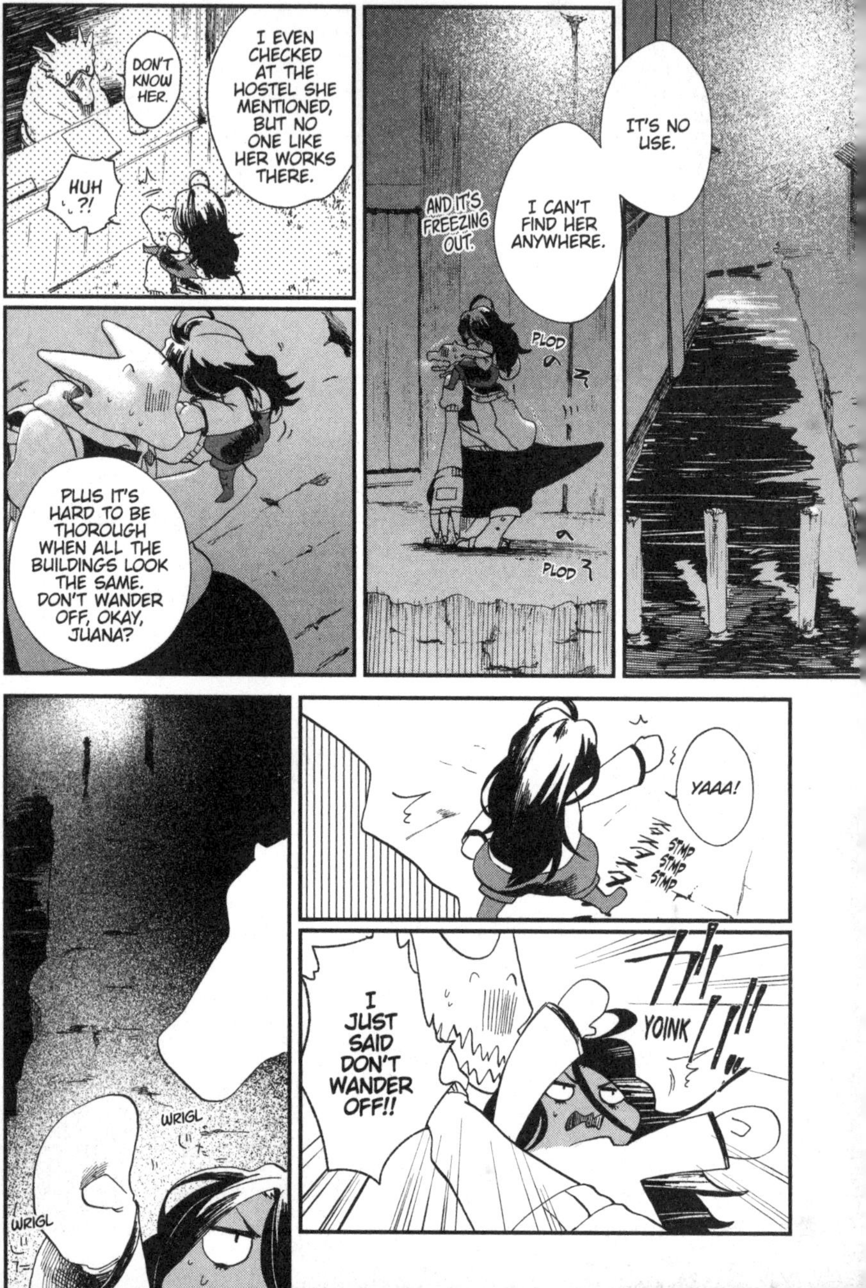
IT'S NO USE.
I CAN'T FIND HER ANYWHERE.
AND IT'S FREEZING OUT.
PLOD
PLOD
I EVEN CHECKED AT THE HOSTEL SHE MENTIONED, BUT NO ONE LIKE HER WORKS THERE.
DON'T KNOW HER.
HUH?!
PLUS IT'S HARD TO BE THOROUGH WHEN ALL THE BUILDINGS LOOK THE SAME. DON'T WANDER OFF, OKAY, JUANA?
YAAA!
STMP STMP STMP
YOINK
I JUST SAID DON'T WANDER OFF!!
WRIGL
WRIGL

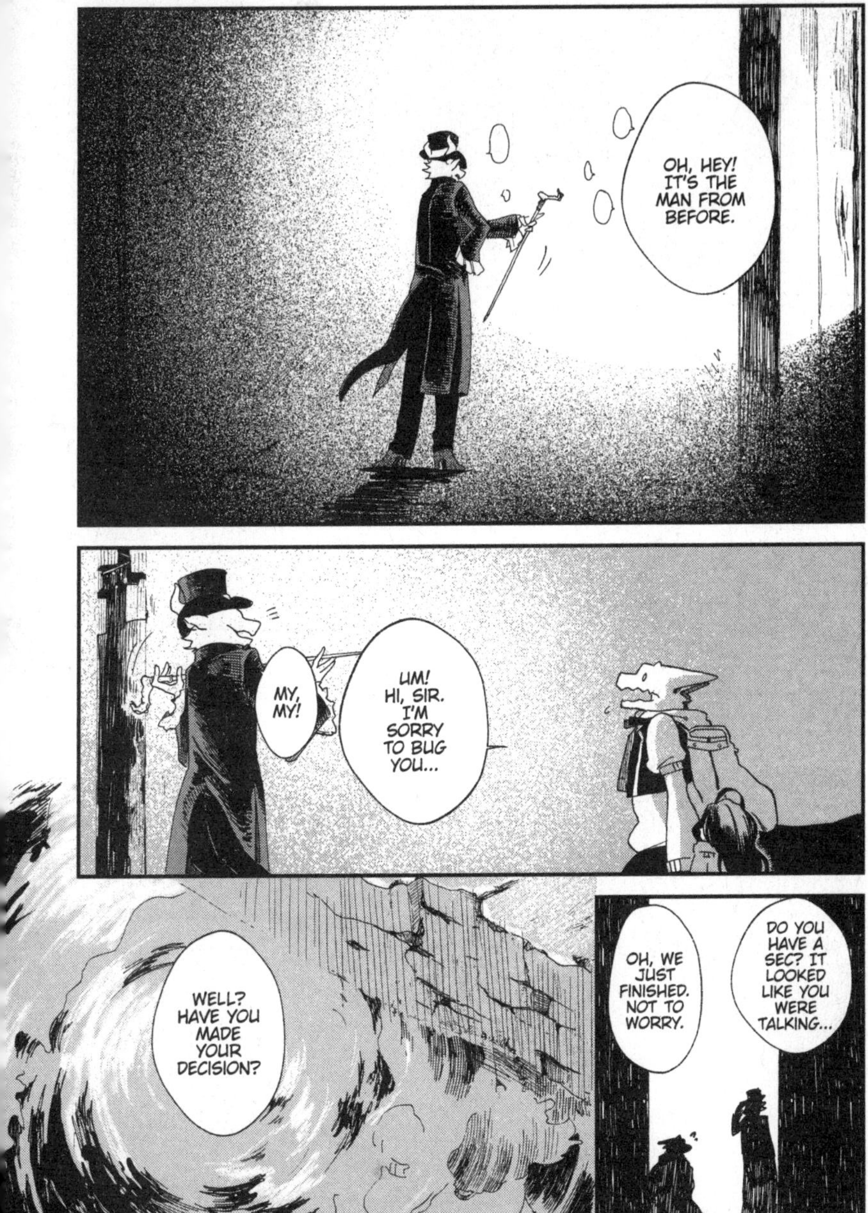
OH, HEY! IT'S THE MAN FROM BEFORE.
UM! HI, SIR. I'M SORRY TO BUG YOU...
MY, MY!
DO YOU HAVE A SEC? IT LOOKED LIKE YOU WERE TALKING...
OH, WE JUST FINISHED. NOT TO WORRY.
WELL? HAVE YOU MADE YOUR DECISION?

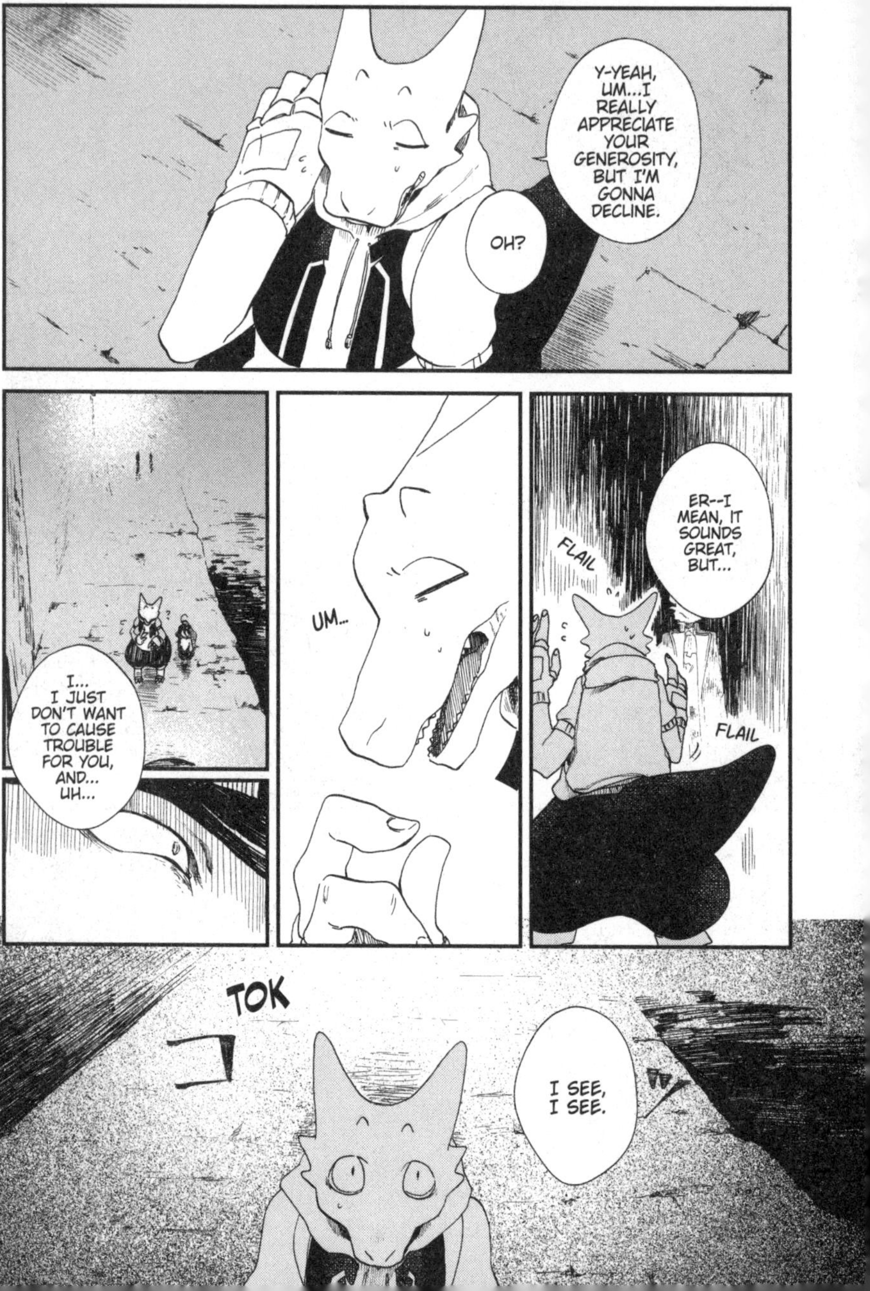
Y-YEAH, UM...I REALLY APPRECIATE YOUR GENEROSITY, BUT I'M GONNA DECLINE.
OH?
FLAIL
ER--I MEAN, IT SOUNDS GREAT, BUT...
FLAIL
UM...
I... I JUST DON'T WANT TO CAUSE TROUBLE FOR YOU, AND... UH...
TOK
I SEE, I SEE.

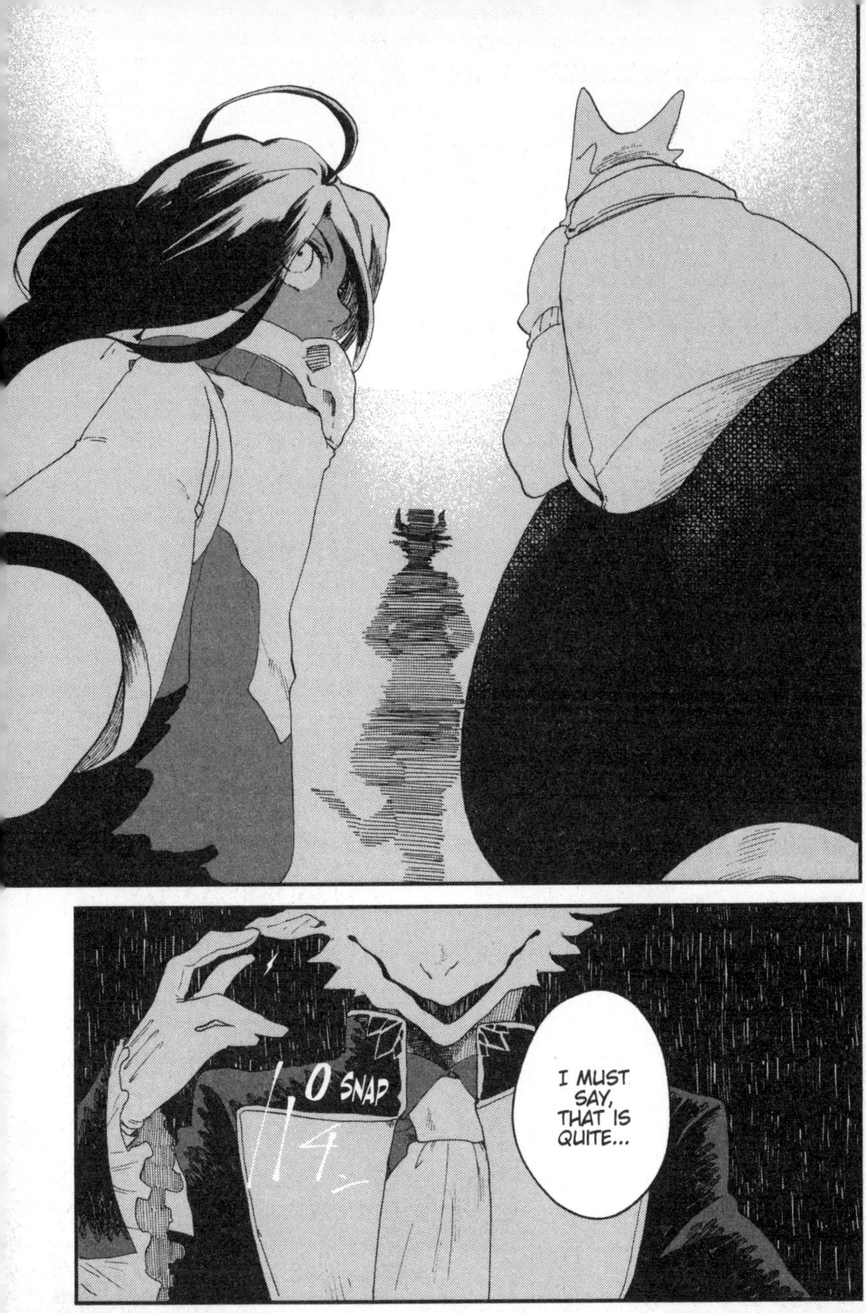
SNAP
I MUST SAY, THAT IS QUITE...

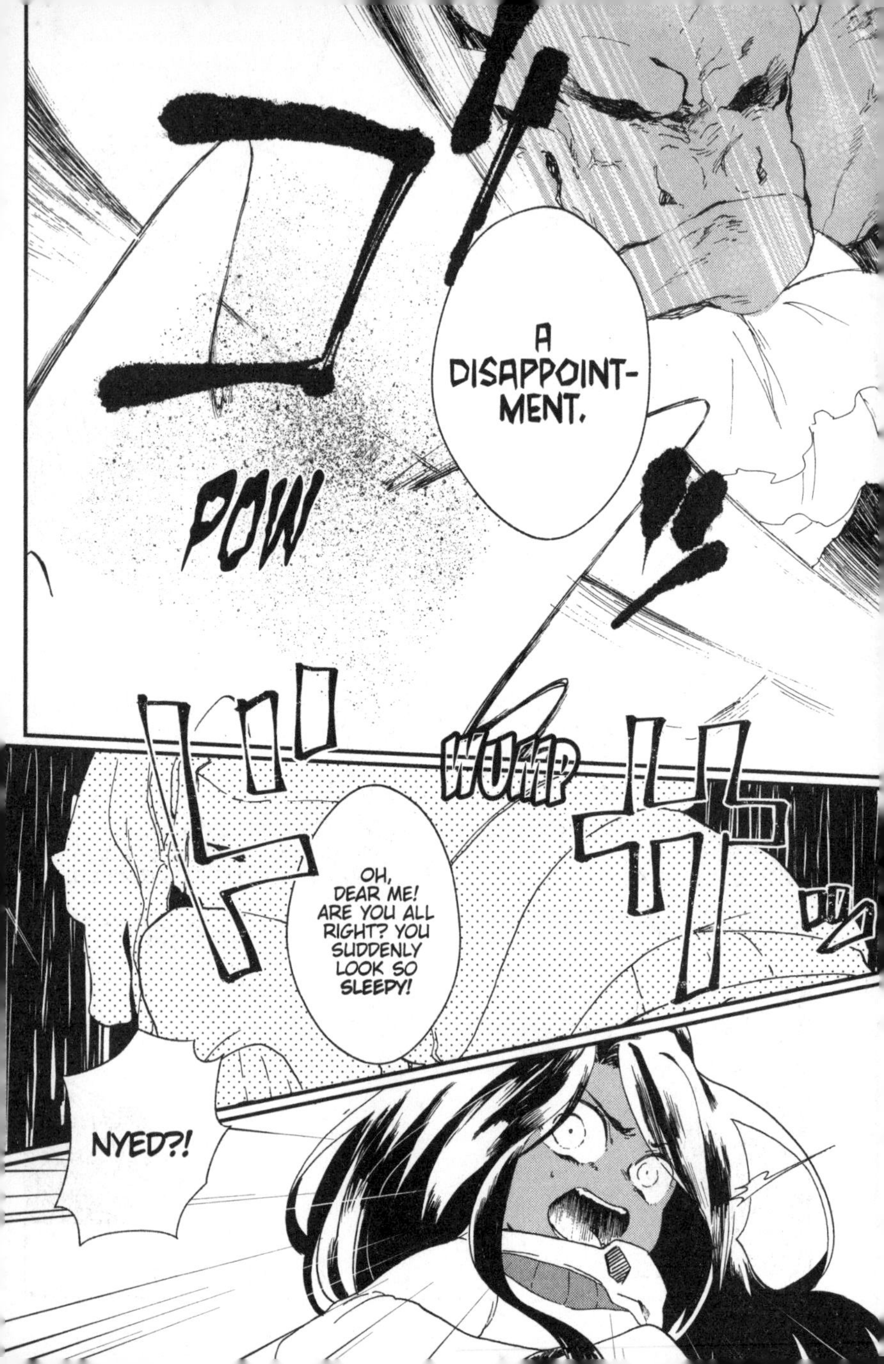
A DISAPPOINT-MENT.
POW
WUMP
OH, DEAR ME! ARE YOU ALL RIGHT? YOU SUDDENLY LOOK SO SLEEPY!
NYED?!

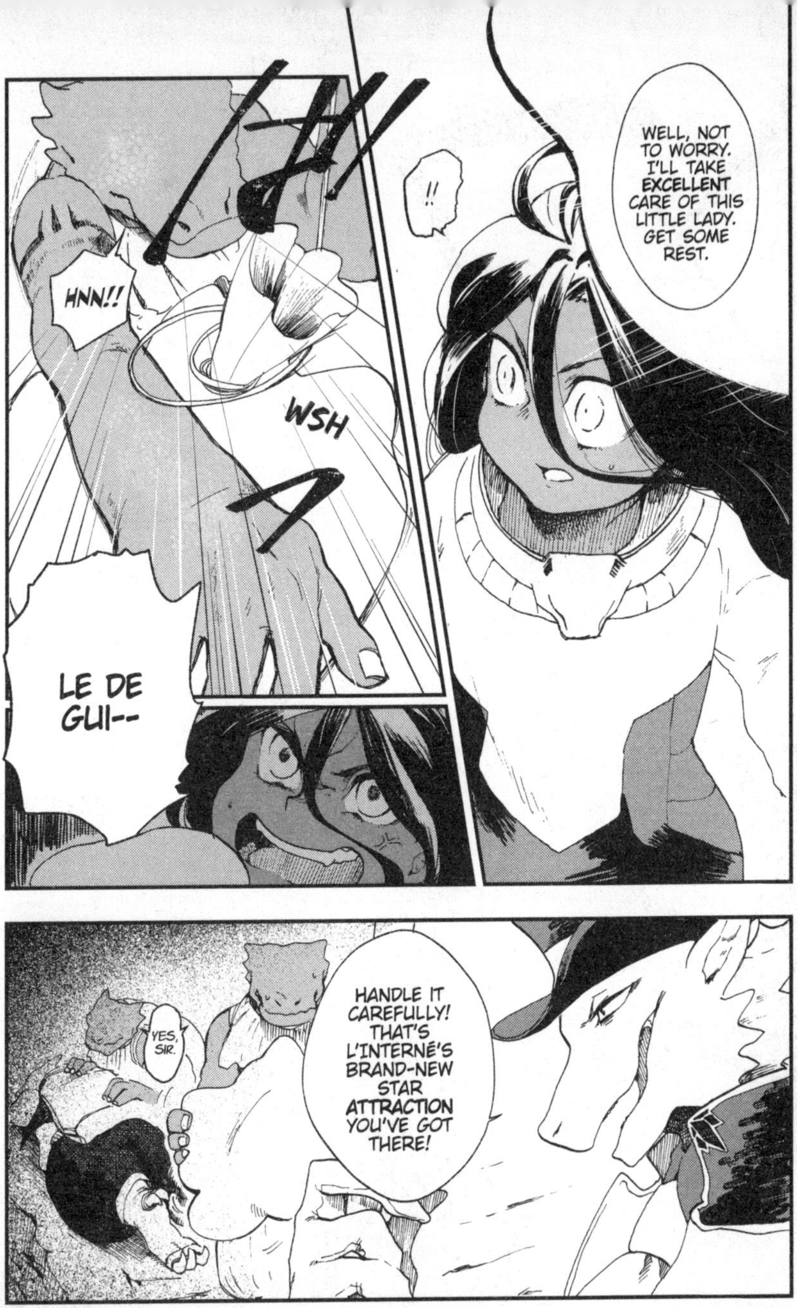
WELL, NOT TO WORRY. I'LL TAKE EXCELLENT CARE OF THIS LITTLE LADY. GET SOME REST.
!!
HNN!!
WSH
LE DE GUI--
HANDLE IT CAREFULLY! THAT'S L'INTERNÉ'S BRAND-NEW STAR ATTRACTION YOU'VE GOT THERE!
YES, SIR.

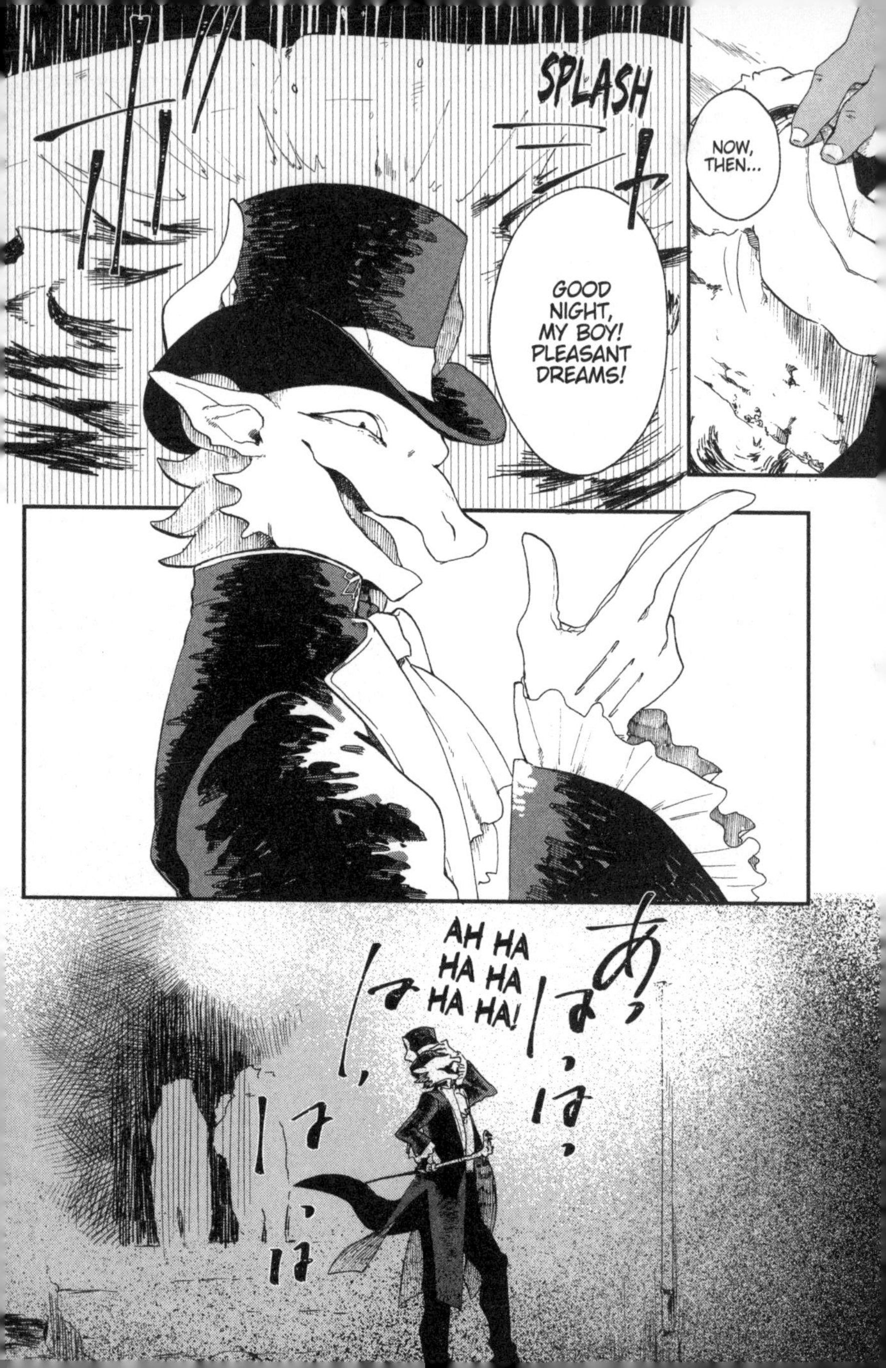
NOW, THEN...
SPLASH
GOOD NIGHT, MY BOY! PLEASANT DREAMS!
AH HA HA HA HA HA!

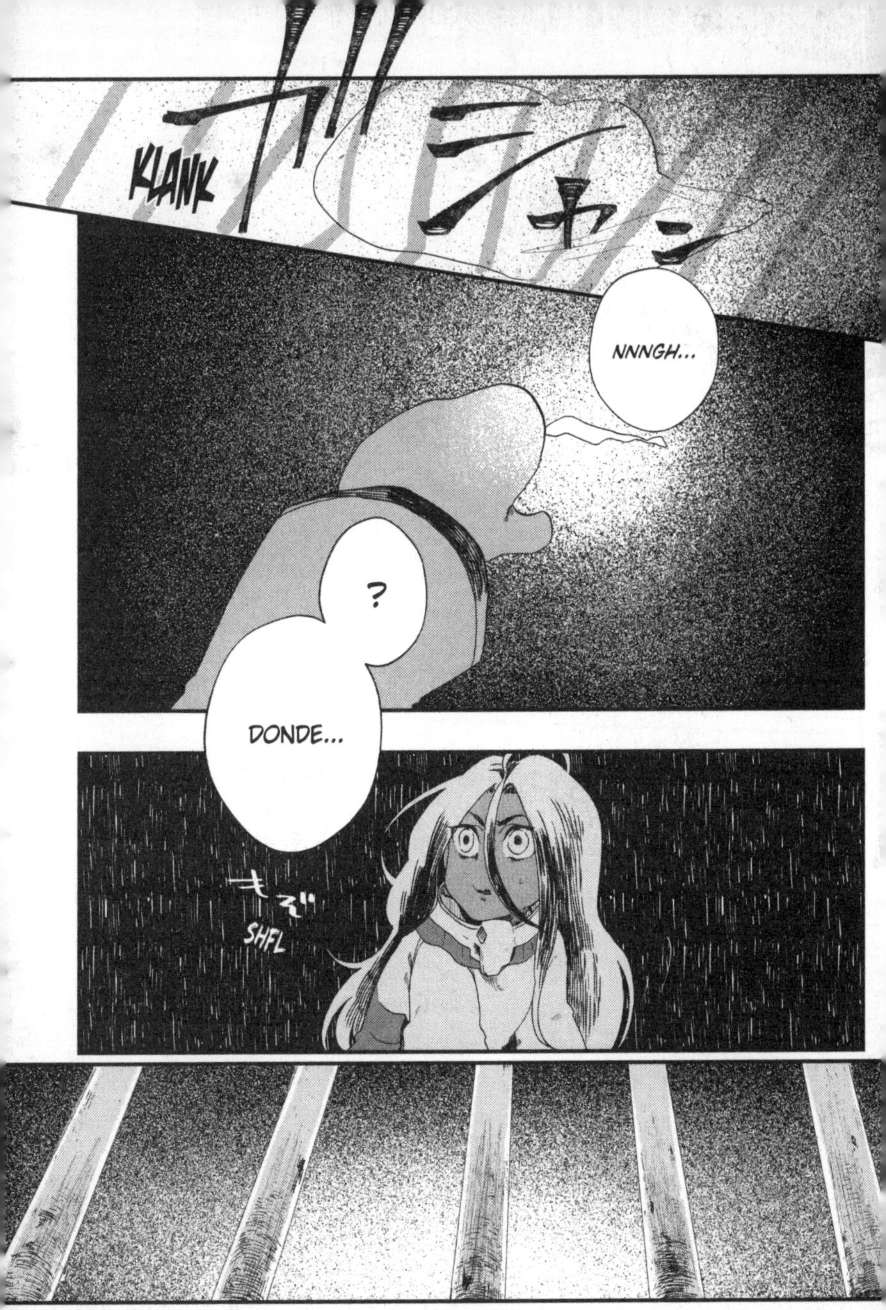
ガシャン
KLANK
NNNGH...
?
DONDE...
SHFL

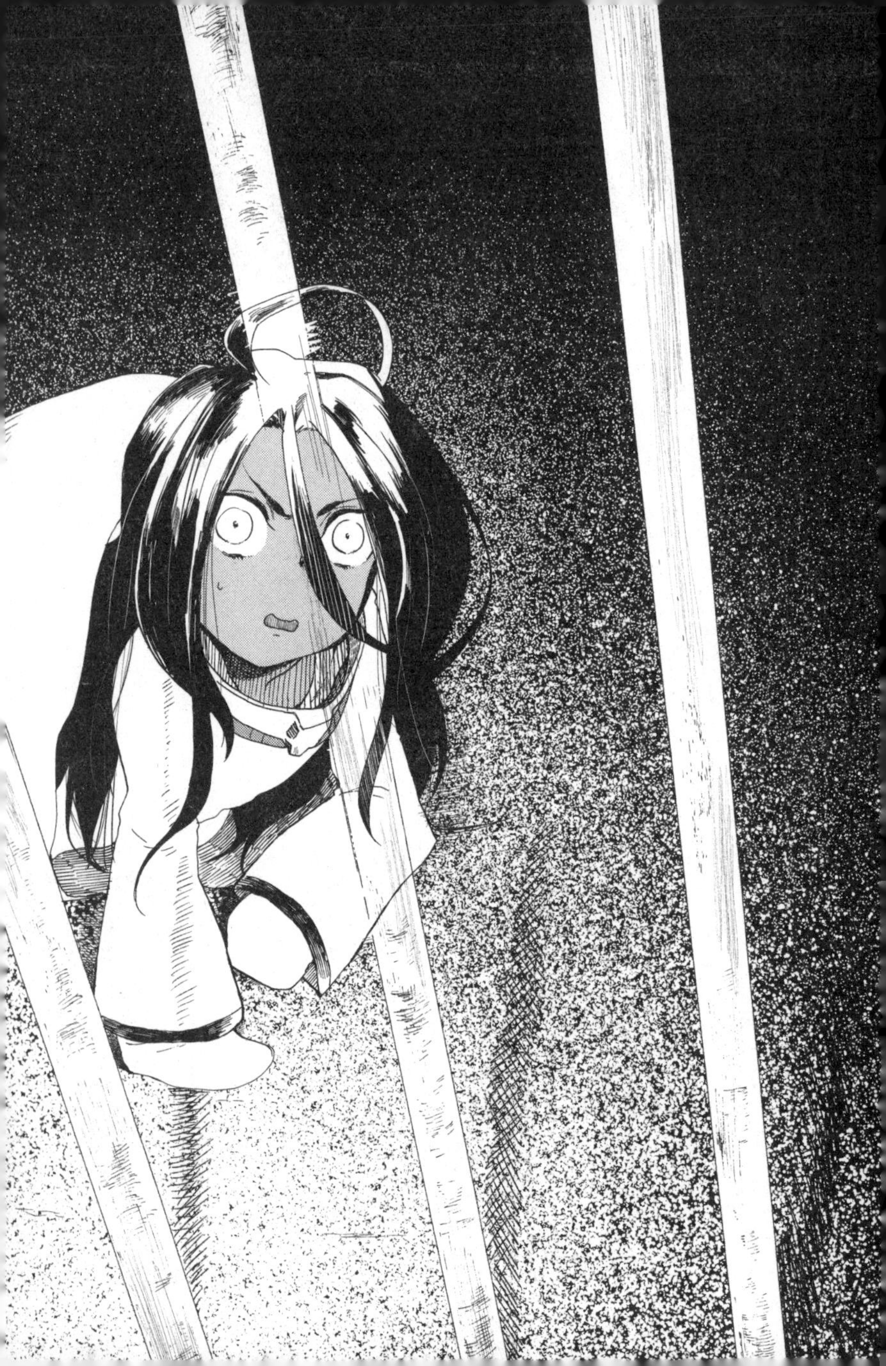

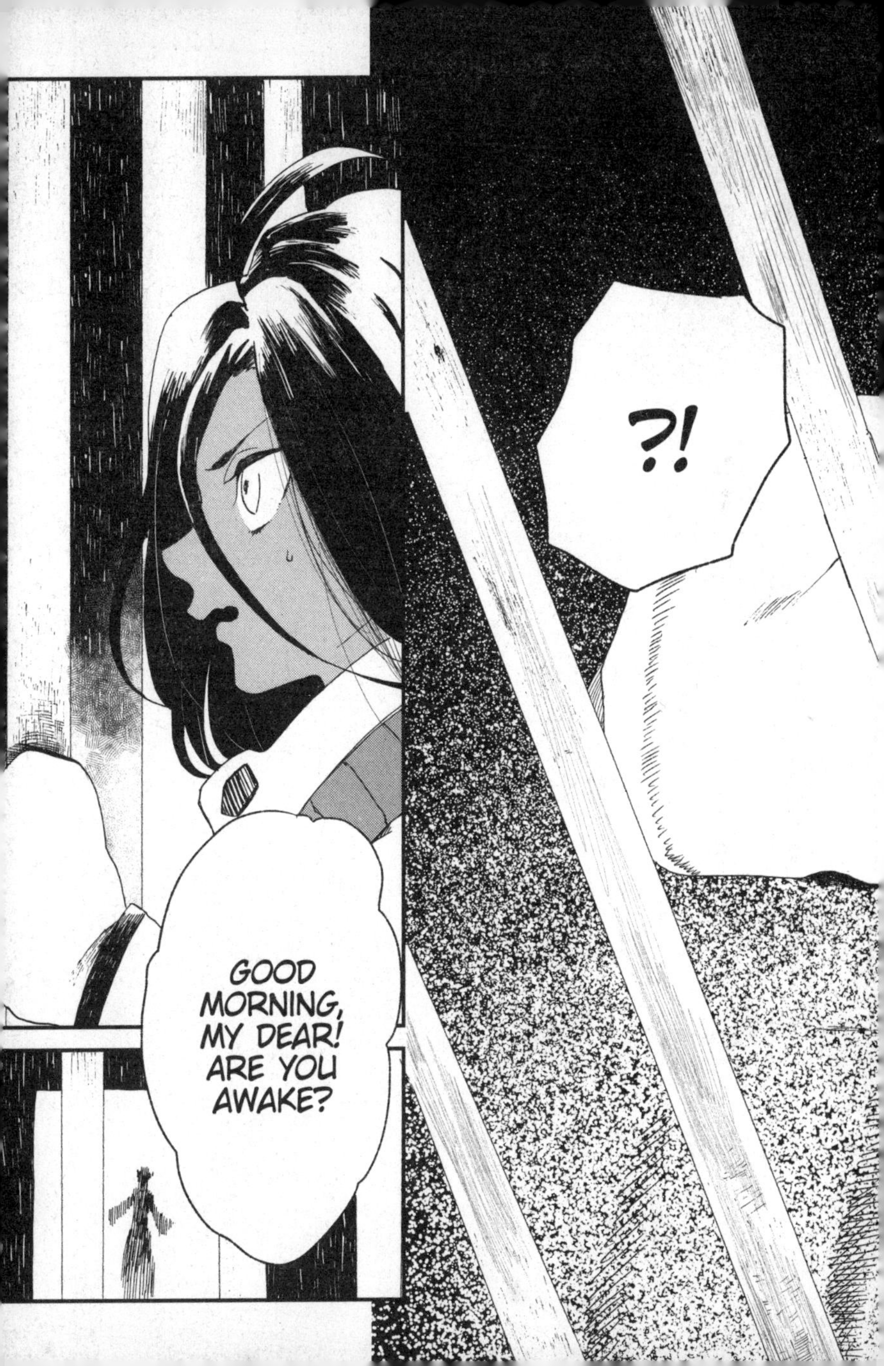
?!
GOOD MORNING, MY DEAR! ARE YOU AWAKE?

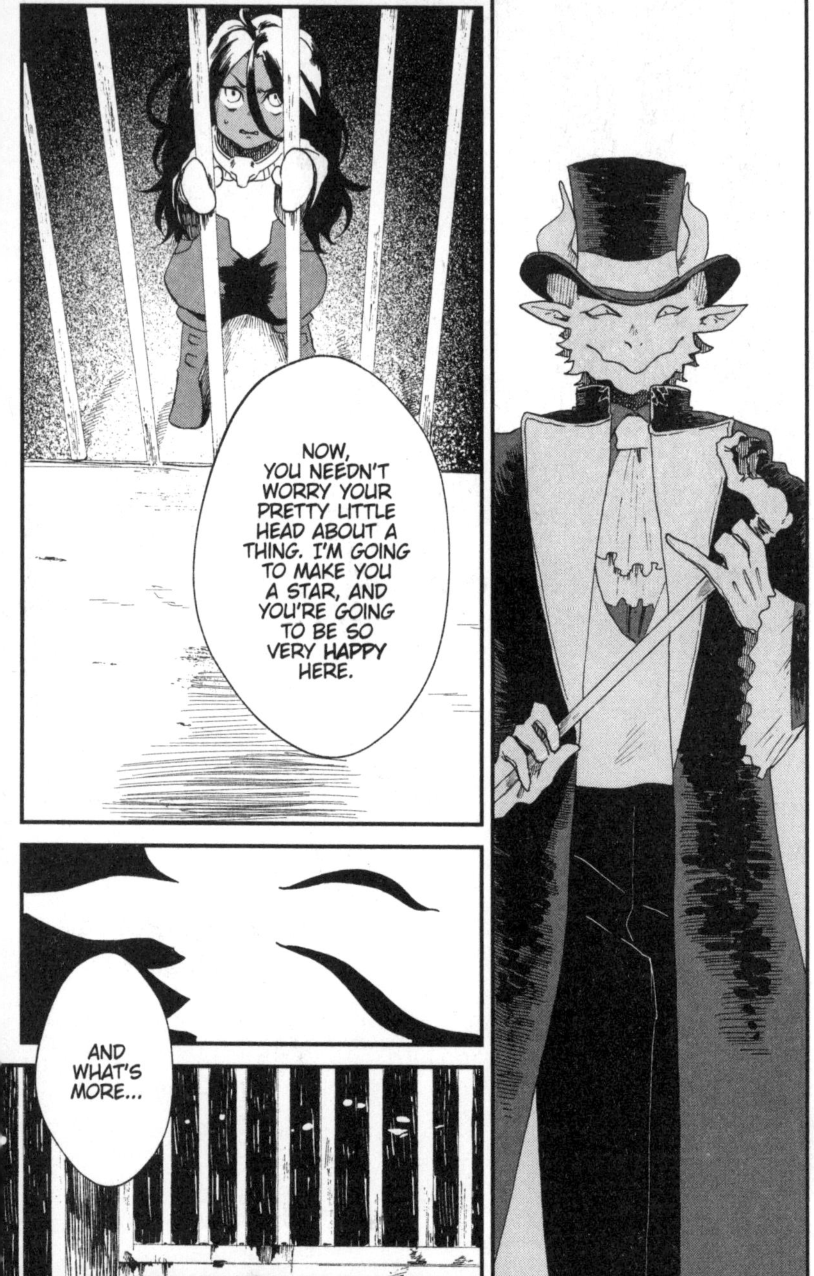
NOW, YOU NEEDN'T WORRY YOUR PRETTY LITTLE HEAD ABOUT A THING. I'M GOING TO MAKE YOU A STAR, AND YOU'RE GOING TO BE SO VERY HAPPY HERE.
AND WHAT'S MORE...

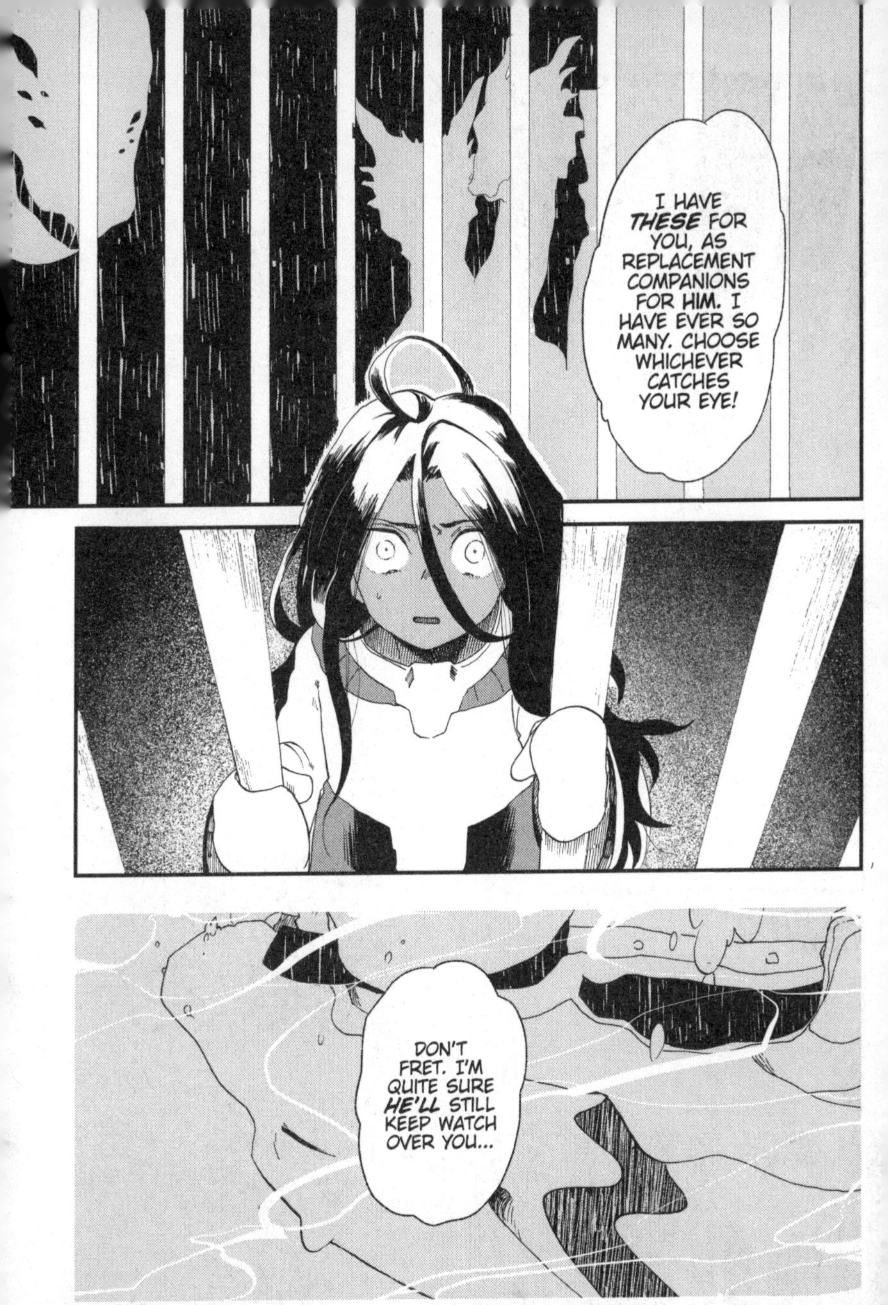
I HAVE *THESE* FOR YOU, AS REPLACEMENT COMPANIONS FOR HIM. I HAVE EVER SO MANY. CHOOSE WHICHEVER CATCHES YOUR EYE!
DON'T FRET. I'M QUITE SURE *HE'LL* STILL KEEP WATCH OVER YOU...

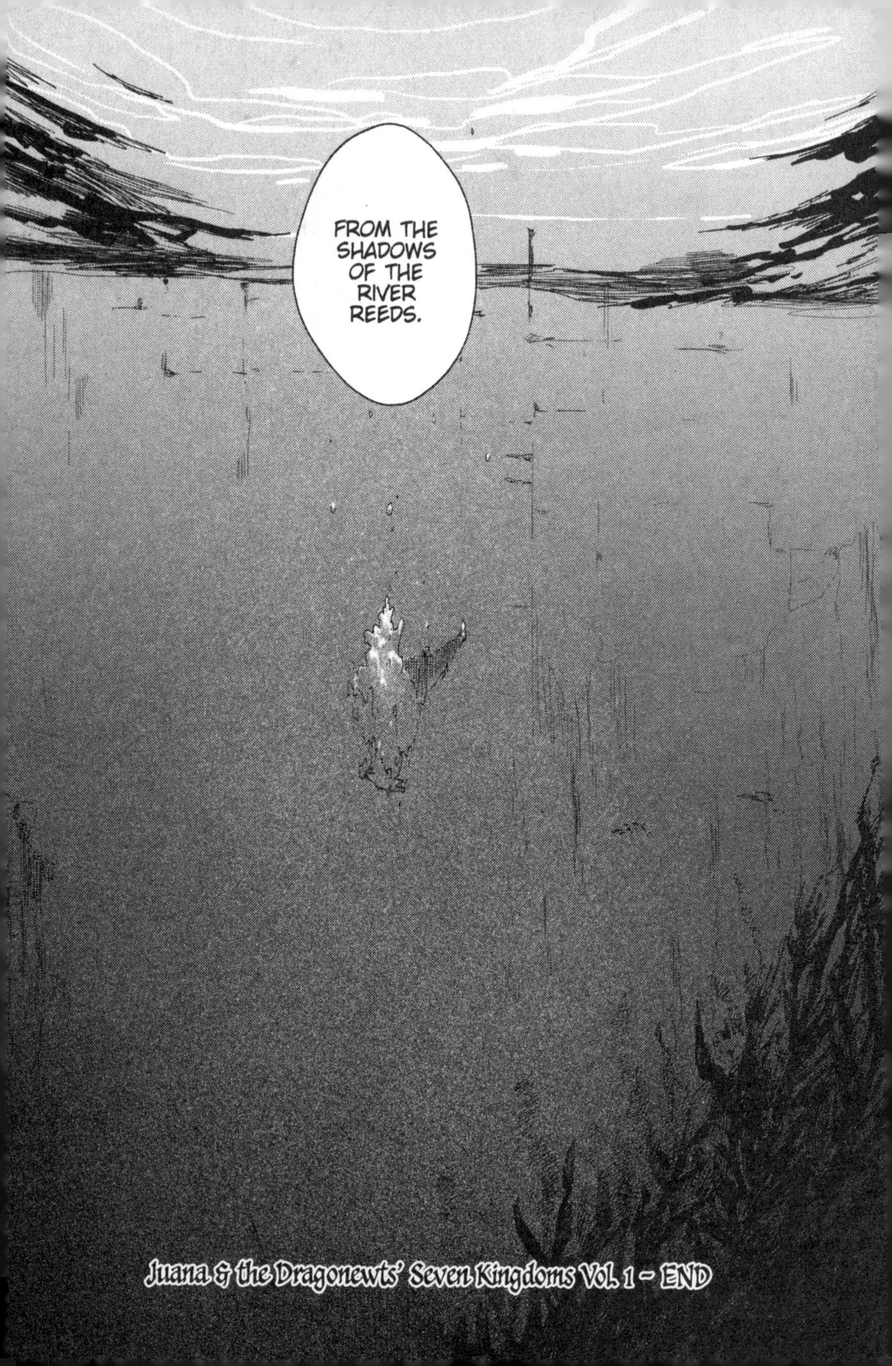
FROM THE SHADOWS OF THE RIVER REEDS.
Juana & the Dragonewts' Seven Kingdoms Vol. 1 - END

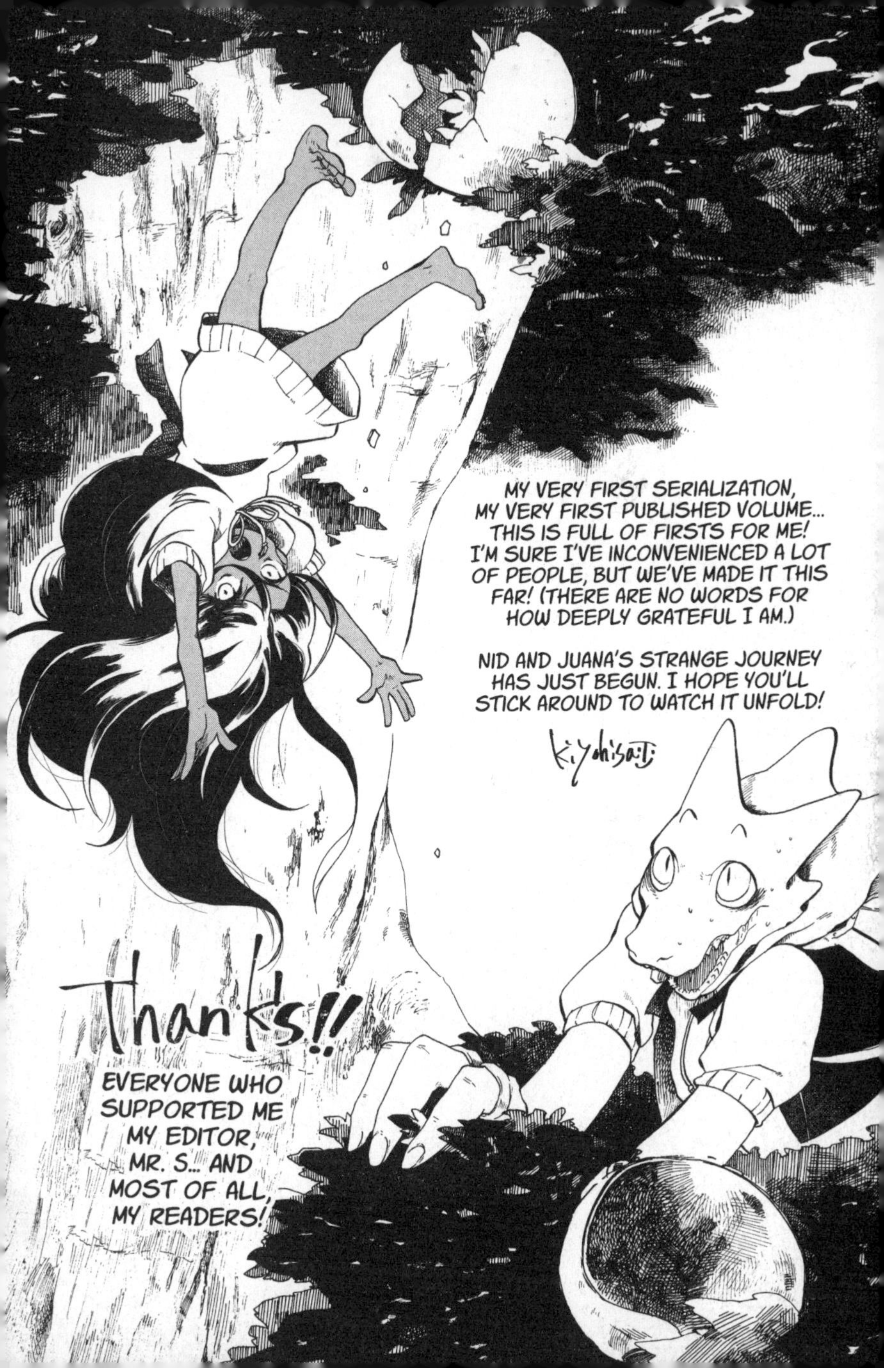
MY VERY FIRST SERIALIZATION, MY VERY FIRST PUBLISHED VOLUME... THIS IS FULL OF FIRSTS FOR ME! I'M SURE I'VE INCONVENIENCED A LOT OF PEOPLE, BUT WE'VE MADE IT THIS FAR! (THERE ARE NO WORDS FOR HOW DEEPLY GRATEFUL I AM.)
NID AND JUANA'S STRANGE JOURNEY HAS JUST BEGUN. I HOPE YOU'LL STICK AROUND TO WATCH IT UNFOLD!
Kiyohisa Tj
Thanks!!
EVERYONE WHO SUPPORTED ME MY EDITOR, MR. S... AND MOST OF ALL, MY READERS!

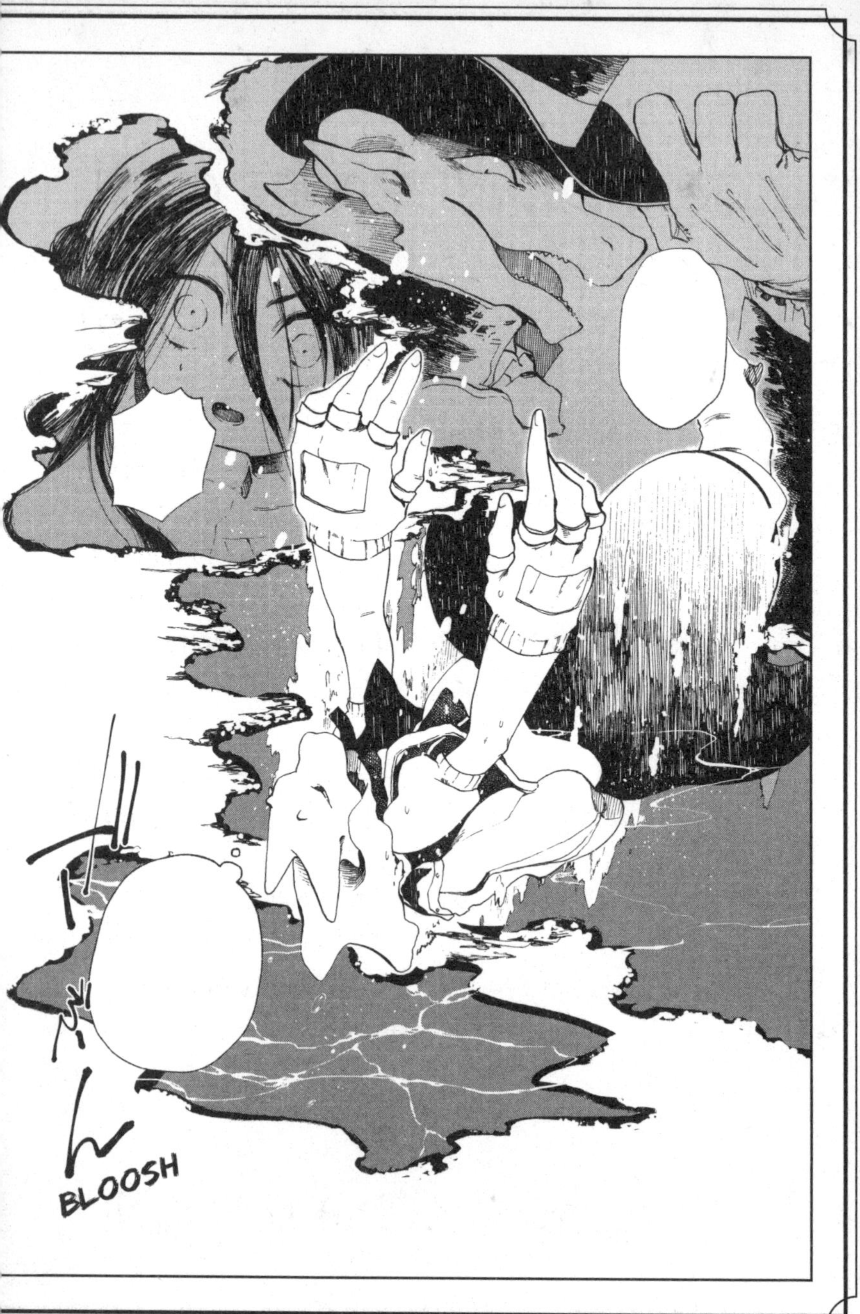
BLOOSH

When other people's greed threatens them, what will become of Nid and Juana?!

Juana was all alone in the world, without friends or even any others of her own kind. Nid, despite being unable to communicate with her, chose to help her as best he could. But Juana was a rare creature, and there are people in the world who long to own rare things...

With Juana taken prisoner and Nid sinking in frigid water, will the two ever see each other alive again...?

The tale of a journey and of two different races learning to come together-- and for once, it's *homo sapiens* that is the creature out of myth.

VOLUME 2 COMING SOON!

SEVEN SEAS ENTERTAINMENT PRESENTS

Juana
and the
Dragonewts'
Seven Kingdoms

story and art by KIYOHISA TANAKA

...WT'S SEVEN KINGDOMS VOL. 1

...2017 by MAG Garden Corporation, Tokyo.
...ged through TOHAN CORPORATION, Tokyo.

...reproduced or transmitted in any form without
...yright holders. This is a work of fiction. Names,
...ts are the products of the author's imagination
...emblance to actual events, locales, or persons,
living or dead, is entirely coincidental.

Seven Seas books may be purchased in bulk for promotional, educational, or
business use. Please contact your local bookseller or the Macmillan Corporate
and Premium Sales Department at 1-800-221-7945, extension 5442, or by
e-mail at MacmillanSpecialMarkets@macmillan.com.

Seven Seas and the Seven Seas logo are trademarks of
Seven Seas Entertainment, LLC. All rights reserved.

ISBN: 978-1-626927-49-0

Printed in Canada

First Printing: January 2018

10 9 8 7 6 5 4 3 2 1

PROOFREADER
Danielle King

ASSISTANT EDITOR
Jenn Grunigen

PRODUCTION ASSISTANT
CK Russell

PRODUCTION MANAGER
Lissa Pattillo

EDITOR-IN-CHIEF
Adam Arnold

PUBLISHER
Jason DeAngelis

FOLLOW US ONLINE: *www.gomanga.com*

READING DIRECTIONS

This book reads from *right to left*, Japanese style.
If this is your first time reading manga, you start
reading from the top right panel on each page and
take it from there. If you get lost, just follow the
numbered diagram here. It may seem backwards at
first, but you'll get the hang of it! Have fun!!

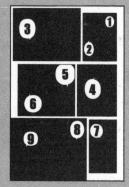